MODES OF DISCOURSE

In studying discourse, the problem for the linguist is to find a fruitful level of analysis. Carlota Smith offers a new approach with this study of discourse passages, units of several sentences or more. She introduces the key idea of the "Discourse Mode," identifying five modes: Narrative, Description, Report, Information, Argument. These are realized at the level of the passage, and cut across genre lines. Smith shows that the modes, intuitively recognizable as distinct, have linguistic correlates that differentiate them. She analyzes the properties that distinguish each mode, focusing on grammatical rather than lexical information. The book also examines linguistically based features that appear in passages of all five modes: topic and focus, variation in syntactic structure, and subjectivity, or point of view. Operating at the interface of syntax, semantics, and pragmatics, the book will appeal to researchers and graduate students in linguistics, stylistics, and rhetoric.

CARLOTA S. SMITH is Centennial Professor of Linguistics at the University of Texas. She is the author of *The Parameter of Aspect* (second edition, 1997). Her current research is at the interface of syntax, semantics, and pragmatics, especially in texts.

In this series

Earlier titles not listed are also available

CAMBRIDGE STUDIES IN LINGUISTICS

General editors: P. AUSTIN, J. BRESNAN, B. COMRIE,
W. DRESSLER, C. J. EWEN, R. LASS, D. LIGHTFOOT,
I. ROBERTS, S. ROMAINE, N. V. SMITH

Modes of Discourse

MODES OF DISCOURSE

THE LOCAL STRUCTURE OF TEXTS

CARLOTA S. SMITH

University of Texas

CAMBRIDGE
UNIVERSITY PRESS

PUBLISHED BY THE PRESS SYNDICATE OF THE UNIVERSITY OF CAMBRIDGE
The Pitt Building, Trumpington Street, Cambridge CB2 1RP, United Kingdom

CAMBRIDGE UNIVERSITY PRESS
The Edinburgh Building, Cambridge, CB2 2RU, UK
40 West 20th Street, New York, NY 10011-4211, USA
477 Williamstown Road, Port Melbourne, VIC 3207, Australia
Ruiz de Alarcón 13, 28014 Madrid, Spain
Dock House, The Waterfront, Cape Town 8001, South Africa

http://www.cambridge.org

First published 2003

Printed in the United Kingdom at the University Press, Cambridge

Typeface Times 10/13 pt   *System* LATEX 2$_\varepsilon$ [TB]

A catalogue record for this book is available from the British Library

ISBN 0 521 78169 8 hardback

To John

Contents

ix

Preface

This work would not have been possible without many kinds of support that I have received from individuals and institutions. I am grateful to them all. The New York Community Trust has supported much of my research on discourse. It also funded three small conferences on discourse at the University of Texas which advanced the work. I received a Faculty Research Award from the University of Texas Research Institute in 1994, which enabled me to pursue this project. During that period I spent some time as a Visiting Scholar at the Maison Suger of the CNRS in Paris. I was the beneficiary of a Dean's Fellow award from the College of Liberal Arts in 1998.

Parts of this work have been presented at conferences and colloquia. I benefited greatly from the discussions that followed, as well as the presentations themselves. They include three conferences on discourse structure at the University of Texas; an International Round Table on The Syntax of Tense and Aspect at Université de Paris, 2000; a symposium on Information Structure in a Cross-Linguistic Perspective at the University of Oslo, 2000; a conference on Linguistics in the Next Decade at the Academia Sinica, Taipei, Taiwan, 2000; a Linguistics Colloquium at the University of Siena in 1998; an invited lecture series at the City University of Hong Kong in 1998.

I would like to thank the members of a seminar on text structure that I taught at the University of Texas in the Fall of 2001: Behrad Aghei, Robert M. Brown, Pascal Denis, Q Wan Kim, Christian Rathmann, Brian Reese, Dong-Rhin Shin, Cholthicha Sudmuk, and Jiun-Shiung Wu. Their questions and comments on an earlier version of this manuscript were extremely helpful. I owe a special debt to Keith Walters, who read the entire manuscript and gave me many valuable suggestions on content, presentation, and relevant material. I also thank Pascal Denis, my research assistant during the critical stages of manuscript preparation; he asked penetrating questions and provided very useful technical advice. Finally, I thank the people with whom I have worked at the Cambridge

University Press in the publication of this book, especially Neil Smith for shocking, useful comments on an earlier version of the manuscript; I thank Leigh Mueller, who did the copy-editing, for her careful work and good humor; and I thank Jackie Warren for shepherding the book through the publication process.

Introduction

This book is a partial answer to the question: what can close linguistic analysis bring to the understanding of discourse? Discourse studies have focused on pragmatic factors such as genre expectations, discourse coherence relations, and inference. In part this has been a natural reaction to earlier, rather unsuccessful attempts to apply the techniques of linguistic analysis beyond the sentence. The current emphasis also follows from increased understanding of the area of pragmatics, and of the role of context in language use and interpretation.

It has sometimes seemed, though, that nothing at all is conveyed by linguistic forms, while everything is due to pragmatics or lexical content. I attempt to right the balance here, at least in part. I propose a local level of discourse, the Discourse Mode, which has linguistic properties and discourse meaning. I posit five modes: Narrative, Report, Descriptive, Information, and Argument.

The Discourse Modes are classes of discourse passages, defined by the entities they introduce into the universe of discourse and their principle of progression. The discourse entities are essentially aspectual. They include the familiar Events and States, and some less-familiar categories. The Discourse Modes grew out of my work on aspect and tense. In studies of situation types in discourse, I noticed interesting differences between passages of different types. Investigating further, I arrived at the Discourse Modes. If I am right about their contribution to discourse, they make it clear that temporality is one of the key sub-systems in language.

I characterize the modes by their linguistic features, that is, grammatical forms with consistent interpretations. The linguistic features of the modes are covert categories in the sense of Whorf (1956). They are not overtly marked but they have characteristic patterns of distribution, and of interpretation. These properties are subtle, but they are demonstrably part of a person's knowledge of language. The emphasis throughout this book is on grammatical rather than lexical features of discourse.

The modes are, therefore, linguistic categories. I was curious to know whether they would be related to anything in the field of rhetoric. When I looked at the literature, I found to my surprise that the Discourse Modes have counterparts in rhetorical tradition. The Modes correspond to "text types" which have been recognized as important in discourse but not analyzed before, I believe, in terms of their linguistic properties. This correspondence is independent validation of the idea of Discourse Modes, I think.

One major goal of this book, then, is to present and explore the notion of Discourse Modes as a significant category in discourse.

Another goal is to use grammatical forms as a tool for exploring the complexity of discourse. I wanted to understand and make precise the different kinds of information that a discourse conveys. It has always intrigued me that one recognizes immediately whether an example is constructed or "real." Constructed examples seem thin, simplistic. I conjecture that one reason is density of information, or lack of it. We construct examples to investigate or demonstrate a particular point – say, anaphoric or tense patterns – and our examples convey information about that point. The constructed examples have little other information, however. Natural texts, in contrast, convey information of several kinds.

Using passages of Discourse Modes as a basis, I study two other kinds of information conveyed by the sentences of a text: subjectivity and surface structure presentation.

I argue that we can distinguish "subjective" sentences from others on the basis of a set of linguistic forms that convey a particular voice. By subjectivity I include such notions as point of view, perspective, and content of mind. When we encounter such forms, we ascribe responsibility for them to the author or another source. I present a "composite" account, stating rules that look at subjective forms in a sentence and in context. The rules assign the role of Responsible Source to a participant in the text situation or to the author.

Surface structure presentation concerns how syntactic structures give cues to the organization of a sentence, and how it affects continuity in the sentences of a text. I take the notion of sentence topic as the main organizing factor. The area is a thorny one but I hope to have found a useful synthesis. I use the notions of topic and strong focus to examine the presentational features of non-canonical syntactic structures. I bring together facts and theories about the discourse effects of syntax, although the account is not exhaustive. There are many studies of single structures, or closely related structures. After looking at such studies I analyze the syntactic structures in a group of texts, with special attention to the combinations that appear.

The study is at the interface of syntax, semantics, and pragmatics. It is informed by some of the insights of Cognitive Science, especially the analytic stance. I attempt to understand and explain some of the complexity of discourse. I also attempt to formalize the analysis, using the dynamic framework of Discourse Representation Theory, due originally to Kamp (1981) and Heim (1982). One of the questions that I deal with in the book is what kinds of information can and cannot be analyzed within this framework.

What is new here is the distinction between grammatical and lexical information for texts; the information-based, composite feature approach to presentation and point of view; the Discourse Modes themselves.

The inquiry was carried out with a group of natural texts that I read, analyzed, and used for examples. They range in length from books of several hundred pages to short newspaper articles. I worked with what seemed intuitively to be good examples of different genres. The core set consists of twenty texts, which I consulted often. The core was supplemented by other texts that I remembered or encountered by chance in the course of doing the work. I am aware that this is a small sample and can only be taken as suggestive, perhaps representative. Larger-scale studies are needed to supplement this exploratory work.

Most of the texts offer examples of more than one mode, as expected. One of the arguments that I make in favor of the Discourse Modes is that texts are quite varied, usually having passages of more than one mode. Some of the texts that I used are presented in an appendix.

This work is intended for linguists of different stripes, and others interested in discourse. Since the book includes formalization, some sections are quite technical, but they are, I hope, made reasonably accessible by the explanations.

I   Discourse structure

1   *The study of discourse*

This book studies discourse passages from a linguistic point of view. Discourse is made up of sentences, and through linguistic analysis we have learned a good deal about them. The perspective of linguistics, however, can't be used directly to study an entire discourse. Novels, histories, arguments, and other types of discourse are activities with their own character and conventional structure. Receivers draw on discourse knowledge to construct interpretations.

The first problem for the linguist interested in close study of discourse, then, is to find a fruitful level for analysis. Larger units are organized primarily by convention and expectation. I will work more locally, at the level of the passage. There are intuitive differences between the passages of a discourse. People recognize passages of several kinds, namely Narrative, Description, Report, Information, and Argument. The intuitions are linguistically based: the passages have a particular force and make different contributions to a text. They can be identified by characteristic clusters of linguistic features. I shall say that a passage of text with certain features realizes a particular "Discourse Mode." The Discourse Mode is appropriate for close linguistic analysis, because at this level linguistic forms make a difference. Discourse Modes appear in texts of all types of activity, or genres. I use the terms "discourse" for spoken and written material, "text" for written material.

The Discourse Modes constitute an interesting level of text structure. I analyze them in two ways. I first discuss the differences between text passages of each mode. I then look at passages in terms of subjectivity and surface structure presentation, features that the modes have in common. Much of the analysis is formalized in the framework of Discourse Representation Theory.

Part I of this book discusses the Discourse Modes and lays out the context for the inquiry. Part II presents the linguistic characterization of the modes, emphasizing the differences between them. Part III discusses subjectivity and surface structure presentation across modes. Text passages are thus considered from complementary points of view in the second and third parts of the book. The different analyses are brought together in Part IV.

Section 1.1 of this chapter introduces the Discourse Modes; 1.2 outlines the approach to texts and analysis that I take in this book; 1.3 presents the main ideas to be developed later, with examples of passages analyzed for different kinds of information that they convey; 1.4 concludes with summary characterization of the modes and brief comments on the importance of temporality for human beings.

1.1   Discourse Modes

I recognize five modes: Narrative, Description, Report, Information, and Argument. This list is not exhaustive, but I think it covers the major modes that appear in texts. I do not deal with conversation, nor procedural discourse.[1] The modes can be characterized with two features. Each mode introduces certain types of situation – Event, State, generalization, abstraction – into the universe of discourse. The modes also have characteristic principles of progression, temporal and atemporal. There are linguistic correlates to these features. Knowledge of one's language includes knowledge of these forms and meanings, some of them quite subtle.

The notion of Discourse Mode accounts for the variety that one finds in texts. Actual texts are usually not monolithic. In narratives, for instance, the significant unit is the episode: a group of Events and States in sequence that are bound together by a unifying theme. Narrative episodes, however, rarely consist only of sequence. There are also descriptive passages, and perhaps argument as well. Similarly the expository genres often have narrative sequences which support the main line of argument. Narrative, description, and argument make different contributions to a text, and have different linguistic features and interpretations. Each constitutes a distinct Discourse Mode.

The short passages below exemplify the five modes; they are taken from a group of texts that will be discussed repeatedly throughout this book.[2] Sources for the natural examples are listed at the end of each chapter; some of the texts are reproduced in Appendix A.

(1)   She put on her apron, took a lump of clay from the bin and weighed off enough
        for a small vase. The clay was wet. Frowning, she cut the lump in half with a

---

1. Persuasive discourse is not listed separately. All genres and modes of discourse may have a persuasive component.
2. The texts were chosen to provide a variety of examples. They include short stories, novels, books, articles from journals and newspapers. They were analyzed intensively by the author. Appendix A provides a list of the texts and significant fragments from the ones most often used.

(2)

cheese-wire to check for air bubbles, then slammed the pieces together much harder than usual. A fleck of clay spun off and hit her forehead, just above her right eye.

(2) In the passenger car every window was propped open with a stick of kindling wood. A breeze blew through, hot and then cool, fragrant of the woods and yellow flowers and of the train. The yellow butterflies flew in at any window, out at any other.

(3) Near a heavily fortified Jewish settlement in the Gaza Strip, an Israeli soldier and a Palestinian policeman were wounded as Palestinian protests for the release of 1,650 prisoners degenerated into confrontations. Israeli military officials say they are investigating the source of fire that wounded the soldier.

(4) Thanks to advanced new imaging techniques, the internal world of the mind is becoming more and more visible. Just as X-ray scans reveal our bones, the latest brain scans reveal the origin of our thoughts, moods, and memories. Scientists can observe how the brain registers a joke or experiences a painful memory.

(5) The press has trumpeted the news that crude oil prices are three times higher than they were a year ago. But it was the $10 or $11 price of February 1999, not the one today, that really deserved the headlines.

In order, these fragments exemplify the modes of Narrative, Description, Report, Information, and Argument. Passages of the Discourse Modes are linguistic units, since they have recognizable linguistic features. They also have rhetorical significance. In fact the Discourse Modes are text units both linguistically and notionally. They function as a bridge between the sentences of a text and the more abstract structures that it evokes. The relations between Discourse Modes and such abstract structures are discussed in Chapter 11.

In close analysis of a text one considers the linguistic forms, asking what information is conveyed by the sentences and sentence sequences of a discourse. Since this study is limited to written texts I do not discuss such matters as stress and intonation, audience, or specific setting.

The inquiry shows that the information in a text is varied at the local level, providing multiple meanings. Thus the analysis in this book is a partial explication of text complexity.

1.2 *Approaches to the study of texts*

1.2.1 *Linguistic features and discourse structure*

Discourse is a human activity with language at the center. Types of discourse are usefully grouped into genres, each genre with its own purpose, structure, and conventions. Knowing the genre of a discourse provides indispensable cues to its structure.

The idea of discourse as a type of activity helps us to discard our customary expectations and to analyze it afresh (Levinson 1979/1992). The idea harks back at least to Wittgenstein's "language games." The term was coined to draw attention to language as part of action. This passage from Wittgenstein's *Brown Book* outlines a simple language game:

> Its function is the communication between a builder A and his man B. B has to bring A building stones. There are cubes, bricks, slabs, beams, columns. The language consists of the words "cube," "brick," "slab," "beam," and "column." A calls out one of these words, upon which B brings a stone of a certain shape.

In a different game, calling out the same word would have different force. A and B might be archaeologists investigating a site, for instance, and A might call out a word – *column, brick* – to convey to B what he has found. To interpret A's utterances, we have to understand the language game being played: the activity and the role that language plays in it. Wittgenstein glosses the term "language game" as referring to "the whole, consisting of language and the actions into which it is woven."[3]

Knowing the language game, or genre, requires knowledge of an activity as a whole. This knowledge is not conveyed by linguistic forms. The global structure of a discourse is rarely if ever stated explicitly. People understand discourse with different kinds of information, including what is conveyed by linguistic forms. They use general information about genre and principles of communication, and specific information about a particular case. There are some differences among genres. Scientific articles and textbooks often lay out the specific relations between their parts, whereas literary genres tend to be less explicit.

1.2.2   The linguistic approach

At the level of the passage, close linguistic analysis of discourse can be fruitfully pursued. I am interested in working out information that is conveyed by linguistic forms, directly and indirectly. To interpret text passages, people draw on syntactic, semantic, and pragmatic knowledge; see Chapter 3 for some discussion.

I rely on two insights in the analysis. The first is that linguistic meaning is often due to a group of forms – a composite – rather than to a single form.

---

3. R. Rhees, in a Preface to *The Blue and Brown Books*, says that Wittgenstein introduced the notion of language games "in order to shake off the idea of a necessary form of language . . . He is insisting that . . . understanding is not one thing: it is as various as the language games themselves." *The Blue and Brown Books* were dictated in 1934–35 and published in 1958.

Whether a sentence expresses an Event or a State, for instance, depends on the composite of the verb and its arguments, as well as adverbials in the sentence. Together, these forms express a State or an Event. The composite approach is used throughout the book.

The second insight is that grammatical terms such as tense and pronouns often have two different functions in discourse. Besides the direct information that they code in a sentence, they give cues to local text structure. Maintenance or change of pronouns, for instance, often indicates continuity or change of direction. In this way grammatical forms contribute to the pattern of a text.

I work with surface syntactic structures. I assume a generative syntax with movement rules. The surface syntax makes available the constituent structure of a sentence, grammatical relations such as subject and object, and the semantic features associated with particular morphemes and constituents. For specificity, I use structures roughly following generative theory of the 1990s, somewhat simplified.[4] I use only surface structures in this book: no syntactic rules are stated.

I take the stance of the receiver of a text. I assume that receivers assemble and interpret the different cues that a text contains. They include lexical and semantic choices, syntactic and information structure, patterns within and across sentences, cue words, typography. The preferred interpretation is the one most compatible with all the information available. I do not attempt to model the actual processes involved nor the shifts in attention as readers make their way through a text. The analysis is not a psycholinguistic one but an idealization, in the tradition of modern linguistics. The interpretation is given in the form of an ongoing semantic-pragmatic structure, in the framework of Discourse Representation Theory. This theory is explicitly formulated to deal with discourse.

Sentences in discourse have a dual nature that has been difficult to understand. The difficulty is that sentences are self-contained units from a certain point of view; but for interpretation they depend on linguistic and extra-linguistic context. This dependence cannot be captured simply by making connections between sentences. The meaning of a sentence often requires information from the context. The realization that sentence meaning can be elucidated only in context is the leading idea of Discourse Representation Theory (Kamp 1981; Heim

---

4. The syntactic surface structures that I use are based on such works as Culicover (1997) which are in the Principles and Parameters generative framework. I do not take a position on types of movement rules or the mechanisms that trigger movement.

  There is no level of Logical Form in this approach: the semantic interpretation is developed in the Discourse Representation Theory framework.

1982). As discourse is dynamic, so representations must be: new information is added, familiar entities are referred to, situations change. The representation is updated as a discourse develops.

Rules of the theory construct a representation from information in the surface structure of sentences. The representation gives the conceptual information that a receiver grasps in understanding discourse. Text representation consists of "discourse entities" for individuals, situations, and times; and conditions that characterize the entities. In some cases a discourse entity is embedded in a sub-structure and is not available as antecedent for anaphoric reference. Embeddings represent the scopal effects of operators such as negation, quantifiers, and modality. There is a second, truth-conditional level, at which the structure is interpreted within a formal model.

Information about Discourse Mode and some aspects of presentational structure will be encoded in Discourse Representation Structures. I introduce the theory and its representations in Chapter 3; later chapters formalize the analysis in the structures of the theory. Given the richness of the information that is conveyed in sentences, an interesting question arises: how much of the information conveyed by a sentence should survive in representations of text meaning? This question is particularly difficult for those aspects of meaning that are clearly not truth-conditional. The question will be discussed from time to time throughout the book.

1.3   Overview of key ideas

I introduce four key ideas explored in later chapters of this book, and then present multiple analyses of text passages in which all of them are exhibited.

1.3.1   Situation type, text progression, subjectivity, surface structure presentation

Types of situation: the sentences of a text introduce situations into the universe of discourse. Events and States are the basic types in most studies of aspect and discourse. Adding to this tradition, I recognize General Statives and Abstract Entities as two other types. General Statives are expressed by generic and generalizing sentences. They invoke patterns of Events and States rather than particular situations. The complement clauses of certain predicates refer to facts and propositions, which are Abstract Entities. Situations of all types are entered in the structures of Discourse Representation Theory as entities, along with individuals and times. They are known as "situation entities," discussed in Chapters 2 and 4.

Text progression: there are several principles of text progression among the Discourse Modes. In Narrative, situations are related to each other and dynamic Events advance narrative time. In Reports, situations are related to Speech Time and time progresses forward and backward from that time. In Description, time is static and the text progresses in spatial terms through the scene described. The Information and Argument modes are atemporal and progress by a metaphoric path through the domain of the text. Text progression is discussed in Chapters 5 and 6.

Subjectivity: I distinguish "subjective" sentences from others on the basis of a set of grammatical forms. All forms of subjectivity convey access to mind – either the mind of the writer or a text participant – through communication, mental state, perception, and perspective. For each subjective expression a Responsible Source must be identified. The main predicate of a sentence may indicate communication, mental state, evaluation. The arguments of the predicate may indicate perspective with deictic pronouns and reflexives. Modals, adverbials, parentheticals indicate evaluation and evidentiality. Subjective forms appear in passages of all the Discourse Modes. Subjectivity is discussed in Chapter 7.

Surface structure presentation: presentational features organize the information in a sentence, usually into topic and comment, focus and background. These features appear in all text passages. I develop an integrative approach, drawing on current linguistic insights and traditional Prague School views. Presentational information depends on syntactic surface structure, the linear and grammatical position of phrases. I will be particularly interested in presentational progression, which tracks the shifts from one topic to another in the sentences of a discourse.[5] The topic phrase gives the referent that a sentence is about. The main criteria for identifying the topic phrase are salience, coreferentiality, and continuity.[6] See Chapters 8 and 9 for discussion.

Presentational structure is also known as "information structure"; I prefer the term "presentation" because texts convey other kinds of information besides that of topic, focus, and associated notions such as familiarity status.

---

5. The notion of presentational progression is unlike the shifting of attention in reading a text, studied in psycholinguistics and artificial intelligence. The processes involved in understanding are beyond the scope of this discussion.
6. Local continuity looks for a topic phrase that is coreferential with the topic phrase immediately preceding. Global continuity looks for a topic phrase that is coreferential with other phrases in the context. These factors are recognized in other approaches to local relations between sentences such as Centering Theory, which ranks local continuity above global continuity (Walker *et al.* 1998). See Chapter 6 for discussion.

1.3.2   Multiple analysis of text passages

Discourse Mode, subjectivity, and presentational progression are the main concerns of this book. They convey information that complements the lexical and rhetorical aspects of a text. This section offers passages of three Discourse Modes, analyzed for these features.

The Discourse Modes differ in the type of situation entities they introduce, and their principle of text progression. Forms of subjectivity and presentational progression are found in all the modes of discourse. I discuss these features of passages in the Narrative, Report, and Information modes. The passages are given more than once. The first version shows the situation entities and text progression. Information about subjectivity is added next, and then presentational progression. The final version displays together the different kinds of information conveyed by a passage.

The first passage I discuss is in the Narrative mode. Characteristically, a narrative introduces Events and States into the universe of discourse. The text progresses as narrative time advances. This advancement is based on sequence: we interpret the events of a narrative as occurring in sequence, one after another. Aspectual and temporal linguistic cues in a passage trigger the interpretation of advancement. Bounded events advance narrative time; temporal adverbials also advance it. Event clauses with the perfective viewpoint express bounded events; the progressive expresses ongoing events. The perfective is conveyed by the simple form of the verb, the progressive by the auxiliary *be+ing (called* vs. *was calling)*. These points are discussed in Chapters 2 and 4.

The narrative passage below introduces Events and States. They are marked with subscripts for each tensed clause; E = bounded event, S = State. Arrows preceding a clause indicate temporal advancement. Clauses that are not preceded by arrows do not advance narrative time. When a sentence has more than one tensed clause the clauses are distinguished by letter (1a, b, etc.).

(6)   Narrative a: situations and text progression
       $1_E \rightarrow$ A few days later I called on Dr P and his wife at home, with the score of the Dichterliebe in my briefcase and a variety of odd objects for the testing of perception. $2a_E \rightarrow$ Mrs. P showed me into a lofty apartment, b_S which recalled fin-de-siècle Berlin. $3a_S$ A magnificent old Bösendorfer stood in State in the centre of the room, b_S and all around it were music stands, instruments, scores. $4a_S$ There were books, b_S there were paintings, c_S but the music was central. $5a_E \rightarrow$ Dr. P came in, a little bowed, b_E and$\rightarrow$ advanced with outstretched hand to the grandfather clock, c_E but, hearing my voice,$\rightarrow$ corrected himself, d_E and$\rightarrow$ shook hands with me. $6a_E \rightarrow$ We exchanged greetings b_E and$\rightarrow$ chatted a little of current concerts and performances. 7 Diffidently, $a_E \rightarrow$ I asked him b_S if he would sing.

Each E in this passage advances the narrative: the clauses express bounded Events. State sentences such as 2a, 3a–b, and 4a–b do not advance narrative time.

Now I add forms of subjectivity. They indicate access to mind, of either the author or a participant. There is only one such form in this passage, a verb with an implicit experiencer argument, given in bold.

(7) Narrative b: situations, text progression, **subjectivity**
     $1_E \rightarrow$ A few days later I called on Dr P and his wife at home, with the score of the Dichterliebe in my briefcase and a variety of odd objects for the testing of perception. $2a_E \rightarrow$ Mrs. P showed me into a lofty apartment, b_S which **recalled** fin-de-siècle Berlin. $3a_S$ A magnificent old Bösendorfer stood in state in the centre of the room, b_S and all around it were music stands, instruments, scores. $4a_S$ There were books, b_S there were paintings, c_S but the music was central. $5a_E \rightarrow$ Dr. P came in, a little bowed, b_E and $\rightarrow$ ø advanced with outstretched hand to the grandfather clock, c_E but, ø hearing my voice, $\rightarrow$ corrected himself, d_E and $\rightarrow$ ø shook hands with me. $6a_E \rightarrow$ We exchanged greetings b_E and $\rightarrow$ ø chatted a little of current concerts and performances. 7 Diffidently, $a_E \rightarrow$ I asked him b_S if he would sing.

The verb *recall* implies an experiencer (recalled to someone). Since the passage is in the first person, participant and narrator are the same. We infer that the narrator perceives the room according to the description in sentences 3 and 4. The first person pronouns woven into the passage do not convey subjectivity in the intended sense of access to mind.

Finally, information about surface presentational progression is added. The topic phrases of each clause, in italics, provide the steps of progression through the passage.

(8) Narrative c: situations, text progression, **subjectivity**, *topic*
     $1_E \rightarrow$ A few days later *I* called on Dr P and his wife at home, with the score of the Dichterliebe in my briefcase and a variety of odd objects for the testing of perception. $2a_E \rightarrow$ Mrs. P showed *me* into a lofty apartment, b_S *which* **recalled** fin-de-siècle Berlin. $3a_S$ A *magnificent old Bösendorfer* stood in state in the centre of the room, b_S and all around it were music stands, instruments, scores. $4a_S$ There were books, b_S there were paintings, c_S but *the music* was central. $5a_E \rightarrow$ *Dr. P* came in, a little bowed, b_E and $\rightarrow$ ø advanced with outstretched hand to the grandfather clock, c_E but, ø hearing my voice, $\rightarrow$ corrected himself, d_E and $\rightarrow$ ø shook hands with me. $6a_E \rightarrow$ *We* exchanged greetings b_E and $\rightarrow$ ø chatted a little of current concerts and performances. 7 Diffidently, $a_E \rightarrow$ *I* asked him b_S if *he* would sing.

The topic phrases are subjects in S1, 2b, 3a, 4c, and the clauses of 5, 6, and 7. This is the most common position for topics. Topic phrases are discussed in Chapters 8 and 10. S3b and 4a–b are non-canonical structures without topic phrases; see Chapter 9.

The next example is in the Report mode. Reports are similar to Narrative in the situations they introduce: Events and States, and sometimes General Statives. They have a different principle of progression, however. In the Report mode, situations are related to the time of the report, Speech Time, rather than to each other. The text progresses as time changes. The linguistic cues to change are tensed verbs, modals, and adverbs that convey temporal information. In (9) the adverbials and tensed verbs are underlined.

(9)   Report a: situations and text progression
    $1a_{E1}$ A week after Ethiopia started an offensive b_{E2} that it says is aimed at ending the two-year-old war, c_{S1} it is now clear d_{S2} that the whole of Eritrea could become a battlefield. 2 With hundreds of civilians fleeing the region, a_{E3} Colonel Kidane said b_{E4} Ethiopian soldiers continue to skirmish with Eritrean soldiers on the run here in western Eritrea.
    $3a_{E5}$ Tonight, Ethiopian officials said b_{E6} planes bombed the main Eritrean military training center at Sawa, an American-built base 100 miles west of Asmara, the capital. $4a_{E7}$ The officials also said b_s they had taken a village, Maidema, 30 miles from Asmara, on the way from the western front to the central front along the disputed border. $5a_{S3}$That is where the next round of fighting, b_{S4} already heavy, is generally expected.

The time talked about moves back and forth from past to present, with one modal future ("could become") and one past perfect ("had taken"). Both modal and perfect clauses are stative.

Subjective and presentational features are added in (10). The topic phrases are italicized; subjective features are in bold.

(10)   Report b: situations, text progression, **subjectivity**, *topic*
    $1a_{E1}$ A week after *Ethiopia* started an offensive b_{E2} that *it* says is aimed at ending the two-year-old war, c_{S1} it is **now** clear d_{S2} that *the whole of Eritrea* **could** become a battlefield. 2 With hundreds of civilians fleeing the region, a_{E3} *Colonel Kidane* said b_{E4} *Ethiopian soldiers* continue to skirmish with Eritrean soldiers on the run **here** in western Eritrea.
    $3a_{E5}$ **Tonight,** *Ethiopian officials* said b_{E6} *planes* bombed the main Eritrean military training center at Sawa, an American-built base 100 miles west of Asmara, the capital. $4a_{E7}$ *The officials* also said b_{E8} *they* had taken a village, Maidema, 30 miles from Asmara, on the way from the western front to the central front along the disputed border. $5a_{S3}$That is where *the next round of fighting*, b_{S4} already heavy, is generally expected.

The passage has deictic and evaluative subjective features. The deictics indicate the time and place of the reporter ("now," "here," "tonight"), in addition to their locating function. The evaluative "clear" implies an evaluator (clear to someone) and the modal "could" suggests access to a mind. The Responsible Source is the author, since no plausible text participant is available. The topic phrase is the subject in all but two clauses of this passage.

The next example is Information, an atemporal mode. The situation entities introduced include a significant number of facts and propositions, and generalizing statives. They do not involve particular situations located at a time and place. Therefore text progression in this mode cannot be based on temporal or spatial location. Passages in the atemporal modes progress by metaphorical motion through the semantic domain of the text. Motion, or lack of it, depends on metaphorical changes of location. We track location in this sense by identifying a Primary Referent in each tensed clause in a passage, and considering the location of the primary referents.

The Primary Referent is semantically central in the situation expressed. In Events, the Primary Referent is what moves or changes. In States, the Primary Referent is located or characterized; or emergent, dependent on the State for existence. The Primary Referent of a clause usually coincides with the argument that has the thematic role of Theme/Patient. Criteria for determining Primary Referents are discussed in Chapter 6.

The fragment in (11) is an Information passage. It introduces Generalizing Statives, except for S2b which refers to a Fact. These situations are typical of the Informative mode. In addition, the Primary Referent phrases are shown with underlining for each tensed clause. In S2 the extraposed clause is Primary Referent for the main clause, indicated by the underlining of "S" which precedes the clause. Ge = Generalizing Stative. Within the extraposed clause the Primary Referent is also underlined.

(11)   Information a: situations and Primary Referents
1a_{Ge} When people try to get a message from one individual to another in the party game "telephone," b_{Ge} they usually garble the words beyond recognition. 2a_{Ge} It might seem surprising, then, b_{Fact} that mere molecules inside our cells constantly enact their own version of telephone without distorting the relayed information in the least.

3_{Ge} Actually, no one could survive without such precise signalling in cells. 4a_{Ge} The body functions properly only because b_{Ge} cells communicate with one another constantly. 5_{Ge} Pancreatic cells, for instance, release insulin to tell muscle cells to take up sugar from the blood for energy. 6a_{Ge} Cells of the immune system instruct their cousins to attack invaders, b_{Ge} and cells of the nervous system rapidly fire <u>messages</u> to and from the brain. 7a_{Ge} Those messages elicit <u>the right responses</u> only b_{Ge}because <u>they</u> are transmitted accurately far into a recipient cell and to the exact molecules able to carry out the directives. 8_{Ge} But how do circuits within cells achieve <u>this high-fidelity transmission</u>?

Metaphorical progression in the first paragraph moves from "a message" to the smaller unit "the words" to a particular type of message – "their own version of telephone." The Primary Referent in the second paragraph changes from people to "body," "cells" of several kinds, "insulin," then back to messages of a different nature.

I now add subjective forms to the fragment, which begins an article. Several appear in S2 and others are scattered throughout. All evoke the author as Responsible Source. The evaluative adjective implies an experiencer; in this context it refers to people in general, including the author. The direct question of S8 also indicates subjectivity: the author directly addresses the audience. Example (12) presents the fragment with all the types of information noted:

(12)   Information b: situations, <u>Primary Referents</u>, **subjectivity**
        1a_{Ge} When people try to get <u>a message</u> from one individual to another in the party game telephone, b_{Ge} they usually garble <u>the words</u> beyond recognition. 2a_{Ge} It **might seem surprising, then,** b_{Fact} that mere molecules inside **our** cells constantly enact <u>their own version of telephone</u> without distorting the relayed information in the least.
        3_{Ge} **Actually**, no <u>one</u> **could** survive without such precise signalling in cells. 4a_{Ge} <u>The body</u> functions properly only because b_{Ge} cells communicate with one another constantly. 5_{Ge} Pancreatic cells, **for instance**, release <u>insulin</u> to tell muscle cells to take up sugar from the blood for energy. 6a_{Ge} Cells of the immune system instruct <u>their cousins</u> to attack invaders, b_{Ge} and cells of the nervous system rapidly fire <u>messages</u> to and from the brain. 7a_{Ge} Those messages elicit <u>the right responses</u> only b_{Ge} because <u>they</u> are transmitted accurately far into a recipient cell and to the exact molecules able to carry out the directives. 8_{Ge} **But** how do circuits within cells achieve <u>this high-fidelity transmission</u>?

The subjective forms in S2 are predicative, deictic, modal, adverbial. They are part of the main sentence, though they do not involve either topic or Primary Referent phrases. The concentration of subjective forms in this sentence, the second of the article, conveys subjectivity which can be maintained with fewer subjective forms later. S8 is in question form, directly invoking author and reader. This pattern of subjectivity is fairly typical of informative prose. The author is not a participant but can be glimpsed from time to time.

Next, information about presentational progression is added, with the topic phrases in italics:

(13)   Informative c: situations, <u>Primary Referents</u>, **subjectivity**, *topic*

1a_{Ge} When *people* try to get <u>a message</u> from one individual to another in the party game telephone, b_{Ge} <u>they</u> usually garble <u>the words</u> beyond recognition. 2a_{Ge} It **might seem surprising, then,** b_{Fact} that <u>mere molecules</u> inside our cells constantly enact <u>their own version of telephone</u> without distorting the relayed information in the least.

    3_{Ge} **Actually,** *no* <u>one</u> **could** survive without such precise signalling in cells. 4a_{Ge} <u>The body</u> functions properly only because b_{Ge} *cells* communicate with one another constantly. 5_{Ge} *Pancreatic cells,* **for instance,** release <u>insulin</u> to tell muscle cells to take up sugar from the blood for energy. 6a_{Ge} *Cells of the immune system* instruct <u>their cousins</u> to attack invaders, b_{Ge} and *cells of the nervous system* rapidly fire <u>messages</u> to and from the brain. 7a_{Ge} *Those messages* elicit <u>the right responses</u> only b_{Ge} because <u>they</u> are transmitted accurately far into a recipient cell and to the exact molecules able to carry out the directives. 8_{Ge} **But** how do *circuits* within cells achieve <u>this high-fidelity transmission</u>?

The single instance of non-canonical syntax, the extraposed *that*-clause in S2, removes the possibility of a topic phrase in subject position.

    The two kinds of progression provide a dual patterning in texts. Topic and Primary Referent phrases appear in two patterns. Primary Referent phrase and topic phrase may coincide, or interact in counterpoint. In the latter case the topic phrase is subject and the Primary Referent phrase is in the predicate. While topic phrases tend to be subjects, Primary Referent phrases tend to appear in the predicate unless a clause is intransitive. The topic phrase performs its canonical function as the starting point of the sentence; it serves to introduce the Primary Referent.

    The multiple analyses above give a kind of thick description of text passages. This demonstration sets the stage for the detailed analysis to follow in the later parts of the book. In Chapter 10 I return to the multiple approach, this time with summary and discussion that in effect bring together the main points of the analyses.

1.4   Conclusion

Summarizing, I give below a brief characterization of the modes, listing the main properties of each

    The Narrative mode
      Situations: primarily specific Events and States
      Temporality: dynamic, located in time
      Progression: advancement in narrative time

The Report mode
  Situations: primarily Events, States, General Statives
  Temporality: dynamic, located in time
  Progression: advancement anchored to Speech Time
The Description mode
  Situations: primarily Events and States, and ongoing Events
  Temporality: static, located in time
  Progression: spatial advancement through the scene or object
The Information mode
  Situations: primarily General Statives
  Temporality: atemporal
  Progression: metaphorical motion through the text domain
The Argument mode
  Situations: primarily Facts and Propositions, General Statives
  Temporality: atemporal
  Progression: metaphorical motion through the text domain

The entities differ in abstractness and temporality. The most specific are situations which are located in the world at a particular time and place. General Statives – Generic and Generalizing sentences – are also located, but they express a pattern of situations rather than a specific situation. Facts and Propositions, the most abstract entities, are not located in the world. Because of these differences, information about the domains of time and space, or the absence of it, is a revealing feature in a text.

The notion of "predominant entity" is flexible. Entities predominate when there are relatively many of that type, or if they are highlighted in the text by syntax and/or position in a passage.

Discourse conveys several kinds of information. Underlying a story, historical account, or argument is information about situations and participants, time and place, continuity, text progression of two kinds, point of view. Part of the complexity of a text comes from its multiple linguistic cues to inter-related meanings, expressed simultaneously. This book explores how some of these meanings arise.

I have emphasized that temporal factors are important for the modes. The point is supported by empirical findings which show that people notice temporality in texts. Faigley & Meyer (1983) did an experimental study in which readers classified texts. In three experiments, subjects were presented with a varied group of texts and asked to sort them "according to type." The subjects were identified as high- and low-knowledge readers, graduate students and undergraduates respectively. They did not receive special training for the experimental tasks.

When genre and subject matter were controlled, temporality was the feature that explained the results. The temporal and aspectual information of a text correlated with the subjects' classifications. All subjects put texts into three classes, identified by Faigley & Meyer as (a) narrative, (b) process-description, (c) definition–classification. Temporality was recognized on a continuum, Faigley & Meyer suggest. Passages with many events (narration) are at one end and passages with many statives are at the other (description, classification). In the middle are passages with unspecified time, often with modals such as *should*, *would*, *could*, etc.

This work confirms the importance of temporality that we have arrived at on a linguistic basis. The conclusions of Faigley & Meyer go beyond temporality as such: they claim that there is a cognitive basis for text types if genre is controlled. Their notion of "text types" is that of traditional rhetoric. Although traditional text types are not defined in linguistic terms, they are remarkably close to the Discourse Modes arrived at independently here, as I show in 2.4 below.

Time is one of the key factors that affects behavior, memory, and thinking. We are only dimly aware of the "biological clocks" in the brain that synchronize body functions with day and night and track the passage of time. Recent work has led to understanding of how the body keeps time through circadian rhythms, or "body time" (Wright 2002). However, we do not yet understand very much about "mind time." Mind time deals with the brain mechanisms for organizing time, and the consciousness and perception of time (Damasio 2002). Time is currently under study in anthropology, biology, neuroscience, philosophy, physics. That time plays a role in so many aspects of human life may partly explain its importance in cognition and discourse.

Example sources in this chapter (page nos. are given only for examples from books):

(1) Peter Robinson, *A Necessary End*, New York: Avon Books, 1989, p. 182.
(2) Eudora Welty, *Delta Wedding*, New York: Harcourt, Brace, 1945, p. 1.
(3) Barak fights on many fronts. *New York Times*, May 20, 2000.
(4) Mapping thoughts and even feelings. *New York Times*, May 20, 1999.
(5) Robert Mosbacher, Cheap oil's tough bargains. *New York Times*, March 13, 2000.
(6–8) Oliver Sacks, *The Man who Mistook His Wife for a Hat*, New York: Harper & Row, 1970, p. 11.
(9–10) After a victory, Ethiopia looks toward other fronts. *New York Times*, May 20, 2000.
(11–13) John Scott & Tony Pawson, Cell communication. *Scientific American*, June 2000.

2   Introduction to the Discourse Modes

People intuitively recognize passages of the Discourse Modes, although they are probably unaware of the linguistic basis for the differences between them. Each mode – Narrative, Description, Report, Information, Argument – introduces certain entities into the universe of discourse, with a related principle of discourse progression. The features have linguistic correlates of a temporal nature. In fact temporality in the larger sense is the key to the discourse modes. Temporal factors are woven into the fabric of a language and are part of our tacit knowledge of language structure.

I use the term "passage" for text segments that realize a discourse mode. Passages must be long enough to establish the linguistic features that determine a mode. Two sentences suffice to do this. Intuitions are particularly strong when there is a shift of mode. As an example, consider (1), the beginning of an article from the *National Geographic*. The discourse mode shifts twice: from Information to Narrative and back to Information. The title and paragraphing follow the original.

(1)   Listening to Humpbacks
        1 When a big whale dives, currents set in motion by the passage of so many tons of flesh come eddying back up in a column that smooths the restless surface of the sea. 2 Naturalists call this lingering spool of glassy water the whale's footprint. 3 Out between the Hawaiian islands of Maui and Lanai, Jim Darling nosed his small boat into a fresh swirl. 4 The whale that had left it was visible 40 feet below, suspended head down in pure blueness with its 15-foot-long arms, or flippers, flared out to either side like wings. 5 "That's the posture humpbacks most often assume when they sing," Darling said. 6 A hydrophone dangling under the boat picked up the animal's voice and fed it into a tape recorder . . .
        7 With the notes building into phrases and the phrases into repeated themes, the song may be the longest – up to 30 minutes – and the most complex in the animal kingdom. 8 All the humpbacks in a given region sing the same song, which is constantly evolving.

The first two sentences express generalizations about humpback whales. At Sentence 3 there is a shift to Narrative: the sentences express specific Events, temporally ordered one after the other. The text returns to the Information mode at sentence 7.

In this chapter I give a general account of the Discourse Modes and the linguistic features that distinguish them. I then use these notions to discuss background and foreground in text passages. Finally, I put the notion of Discourse Modes in context, discussing related ideas in the field of rhetoric and in linguistic studies of discourse.

Section 2.1 discusses the types of entities introduced into the universe of discourse; 2.2 considers text progression in the temporal modes; 2.3 and 2.4 discuss the temporal and atemporal Discourse Modes; 2.5 considers relevant rhetorical and linguistic work.

2.1 The entities introduced in texts

One way of getting at what a text is about is to ask what sorts of things it brings into the universe of discourse. NounPhrases (NP) introduce individuals: people, places, objects, ideas, etc.; tenses and time adverbs introduce times; clauses introduce situations, e.g. events, and states. This discussion focuses on situations. The types of situations introduced in a text are the main determining factor of the Discourse Modes.

2.1.1 Classes of situation entities

People classify situations in the world into categories such as Event and State through their perceptual and cognitive abilities. Language classifies along the same lines. In every clause an event, state, or other situation is introduced by the main verb and its arguments, the "verb constellation."[1] Verb constellations indirectly classify situations into idealized "situation types," a group of semantic concepts. The situations are classified by clusters of their internal temporal properties.

This sense of the temporal involves internal features of a situation that are related to the passage of time. The features involve beginnings and endings, intervals, dynamic stages; they determine the way a situation unfolds in time. The features have linguistic correlates. Thus the situation types are covert linguistic categories, with distinct distributional and interpretive properties. The

---

1. The interpretation of a verb constellation may be affected by an adverbial, as in "John read a book for an hour." The durative adverbial changes the interpretation of "John read a book" from telic (conveying that he finished the book) to atelic: "he did some book reading."

situation types are aspectual in nature; they are discusssed in detail in Chapter 4. I recognize three classes of situation entity: situations, General Statives, and Abstract Entities. Situations consist of Events and States. Events differ from States in the feature of dynamism. Events are dynamic, with successive stages that take time, while States are static. Example (2) gives simple sentences that express situations:

(2)   Sentences expressing situations
         a We walked to school.   Event
         b Bill won the race.   Event
         c Lee is sick.   State
         d They believe in miracles.   State
         e We have already eaten dinner. State

Example (2e) is a construction known as the "perfect," which expresses the State that results from the occurrence of an Event or the existence of a State. Perfects are a type of State. Situations of all kinds take place or hold in the world, and have temporal and spatial coordinates; they are also known as eventualities, following Bach (1981). The term "situation" is used for both the general class and the sub-types of Event and State.

General Statives do not express particular events or states, so that they are relatively abstract and non-dynamic in nature. Generic sentences say something about a kind, or an abstract individual. Generalizing sentences express a pattern rather than a particular event or state. Examples of each are given in (3):

(3)   Sentences expressing General Statives
         a Dinosaurs are now extinct.   Generic
         b The lion has a bushy tail.   Generic
         c Mary speaks French.   Generalizing
         d John always fed the cats last year.   Generalizing

Generalizing sentences do not express specific episodes or isolated facts, but instead a pattern or regularity (Krifka *et al.* 1995). They concern objects and individuals that are located in the world; note the explicit references to time in (3a) and (3d).

Even more abstract are Facts and Propositions, the class of abstract entities. Facts are the objects of knowledge, while Propositions are the objects of belief. The complement clauses of certain predicates refer to Facts and Propositions and introduce those entities into the universe of discourse. The examples of (4) illustrate:

(4)   Sentences with complements referring to abstract entities
       a I know that Mary refused the offer.   Fact
       b Mary's refusal of the offer was significant. Fact
       c I believe that Mary refused the offer.   Proposition
       d Mary's refusing the offer was unlikely.   Proposition

The subject or object complement clauses refer to abstract entities. They are not spatially or temporally located in the world, although the situations they refer to may be located.

Complement clauses refer to Facts and Propositions. There are, of course, many sentences that express Facts and Propositions directly. They cannot be distinguished linguistically, and are therefore beyond the scope of this discussion. This sense of "proposition" should not be confused with the general use of the term, in which a Proposition is the sense of a sentence, the content that it expresses.

The class of non-dynamic entities is varied: it includes States, General Statives, and abstract entities. The Discourse Mode passages in which these entities predominate are not organized temporally. The feature of dynamism is essential to the temporal advancement of narrative passages, as I show below.

2.2   *Text progression in the temporal modes*

As the reader progresses through a text, one part paves the way for the next. On reaching the conclusion or dénouement one has traversed the full text and is in a position to structure and understand it fully. This kind of understanding holds beyond the first reading of a text. Literally, too, the reader progresses through a text. Since language is sequential, one processes a word, phrase, or sentence and then another that follows it. Shifts in focus of attention are discussed in psycholinguistics and artificial intelligence. I will be concerned here with text progression in the first sense.

The Discourse Modes have principles of progression that differ according to type of entity and text organization. Texts progress according to changes in location, temporal or spatial; or to changes in metaphorical location. The dynamic temporal modes, Report and Narrative, progress as time advances. Time is static in the temporal mode of Description. Receivers progress by traversing the space described, mimicking the experience of the narrator or reporter.

To understand the atemporal modes we need something other than spatial or temporal progression. I propose that we treat the semantic domain of an atemporal discourse as terrain to be traversed: a metaphorical space. With the spatial metaphor we have the possibility of metaphorical motion by a Primary Referent from one part of the domain to another. We identify a Primary Referent in each clause. We then look for the metaphorical location of that referent in the domain of the text, proceeding intuitively across domains. Space is not unidimensional, like time: it allows travel in many directions. The complexity of space is needed for metaphorical motion: motion in a text domain can be hierarchically up or down, lateral, diagonal, etc. The atemporal modes progress by metaphorical changes of location through the information space of the text.

In the following sections I discuss progression in each of the discourse modes. I use the term "advancement" for progression that depends on temporal or spatial location. The supporting linguistic analysis is presented in Part II of this book.

2.2.1   Narrative progression

Narrative presents a sequence of events and states that have the same participants and/or a causal or other consequential relation (Labov & Waletzky 1966, Moens 1987). They occur in a certain order, which is crucial for understanding. Narratives appear in many genres. They predominate in novels, short stories, histories; and often play a supporting role in essays, newspaper articles, and other discursive genres. Fictional and non-fictional narratives follow the same temporal principles.

The key to narrative advancement is the dynamism of events. Recall that dynamism involves successive stages in time. Events such as winning a race take only a moment, while durative events have a run-time that varies with the event. Closing the door has a short run-time; walking to work is longer; building a house has a long run-time. When an event occurs in a narrative context, we assume as a default that it takes the standard run-time, unless there is information to the contrary. Events are bounded when they have reached the end of their run-time or when an explicit stopping time is given.[2]

Narrative time advances with bounded events, and explicit temporal adverbials; it fails to advance otherwise. This is the basic finding of narrative discourse dynamics (Hinrichs 1986, Kamp & Rohrer 1983, Partee 1984). The generalization ignores other interpretations: simultaneous events, flashbacks, changes of scale, and changes of order.[3] Sentences express bounded events when

---

2. This oversimplifies somewhat: adverbials can give an explicit bound that is less than the full run-time of an event.
3. Narrative sequence is the default, in this view. Departures from the default are usually signaled by adverbials or other cues. Another approach takes sequence as one type of "discourse relation" and change of scale, causation, etc., as different discourse relations; see Chapter 11 for discussion.

they have an Event verb constellation and the perfective aspectual viewpoint, conveyed by the simple verb form, e.g. "Mary walked."[4] Event sentences with the progressive *be+ing*, a type of imperfective viewpoint, convey ongoing Events, e.g. "Mary was walking." Ongoing events and states are unbounded. These points are discussed in Chapter 4.

The examples below illustrate passages of the Narrative Discourse Mode; each has sentences of bounded and unbounded Events. The bounded Events advance narrative time, marked with arrows →:

(5)   Narrative passages
        a. 1 → I slipped outside into a shock of cool air and → ran down the pier.
            2 Several small boats were rocking lazily to and fro in the water. 3 → I
            unfastened the rope to one, → paddled out toward the "Republic," → then
            hauled myself hand over hand up a rope ladder to the topgallant bulwark,
            over onto a broad empty deck.
        b. 1 → When I got to Harry's Waldorf Towers apartment, they were winding
            up the meeting downstairs. 2 → Harry appeared about a half-hour later, →
            greeted me warmly, → went immediately to the telephone.

In (5a) the bounded events of S1 and S3 advance narrative time; in (5b) the *when*-clause of S1, and the events of S2, advance the narrative.

Unbounded situations – ongoing events and states, including perfects – do not move time. In the fragments above, ongoing events are expressed in S2 of (5a) and the main clause of S1 in (5b). We interpret the unbounded situations as simultaneous with a time previously established in the text.

The preceding passages are from novels; (6) offers an example of a completely different type of narrative. The passage is from a book of detailed history and analysis concerning events in the Middle East during and after the First World War.

(6)   → Townshend became aware in the autumn of 1918 of rising peace sentiment
        and, like Newcombe, → he decided to give Events a push.
            When Townshend learned that the Talaat ministry had fallen, → he arranged
        an interview with the new Grand Vizier, and on → 17 October went to the
        Sublime Porte carrying some notes that he had sketched out to indicate the
        sort of peace terms that might be asked by Britain. His notes suggested that
        Britain would be willing to leave the Ottoman Empire in possession of Syria,
        Mesopotamia, and perhaps even the Caucasus, so long as these regions were
        allowed local autonomy within a restructured empire that would resemble a
        confederation of States.

4. The interpretation of perfective sentences is slightly different for the types of events known as
   Activities: they are focused as a bounded unit. The unit need not coincide with the endpoints of
   the Event; see Chapter 5.

> → Townshend offered to help Turkey obtain generous terms along these lines → and offered to make immediate contact with the British authorities. → The Grand Vizier told him that it was a crime for the Ottoman Empire to have made war on Britain, and that it was Enver's fault. → He accepted Townshend's offer of help in securing honorable peace terms without letting Townshend suspect that he would accept whatever terms he could get.
> → That evening Townshend met with the Minister of the Marine.

The perfective event clauses and time adverbials advance the narrative.

Inference can also advance narrative time. When a narrative changes place, the reader often infers that there has been a change in time. The fragment in (7) illustrates, from a novel. Banks' activities and perceptions are recounted in the first paragraph. In the second paragraph another person appears in another place, *there*. We infer that time and place have moved, and that Banks has arrived at his destination.

(7)   1 Banks dropped Richmond off at a pub near the West Pier and carried on along Marine Drive, parking just beyond the closed fun-fair. 2 He buttoned up his raincoat tight and walked along the road that curved around the headland between the high cliff and the sea. 3 Signs on the hillside warned of falling rocks. 4 Waves hit the sea-wall and threw up spray onto the road.

   5 Tony Grant was already there, leaning on the railing and staring out to the point where sea and sky merged in a uniform grey. 6 He wore a navy duffle coat with the hood down.

The paragraph break at S5 suggests a change of direction, and the adverb *already* conveys Banks' expectation that he was to meet Tony Grant. Readers of this passage in the novel know that Banks had a destination, which supports the inference of advancement.

Tense is usually unchanging throughout a narrative; conventionally, past is the narrative tense. Tense in this mode actually conveys continuity rather than temporal location. The inferences of temporal advancement are based on aspectual information – the dynamism of bounded Events in sequence – and to explicit time adverbials. These points will be explicated in Chapter 5.

2.2.2   *Description: static, with spatial advancement*

Descriptive passages tend to focus on specifics: particular objects, people, mental States, as the rhetorician Cairns noted in 1902. Time is static or suspended. There are no significant changes or advancements. The entities introduced in descriptions are usually states, ongoing events, atelic events. Description is predominant in travel writing; it appears in fiction, and most other genres.

Descriptive passages progress spatially through a scene.

(8)   Description
  a. We were in an impressive and beautiful situation on a rocky plateau. It
    was too high for grass, there was very little earth and the place was littered
    with boulders, but the whole plateau was covered with a thick carpet of
    mauve primulas. There were countless thousands of them, delicate flowers
    on thick green stems. Before us was the brilliant green lake, a quarter of a
    mile long, and in the shallows and in the streams that spilled over from it
    the primulas grew in clumps and perfect circles.
  b. An example of this kind of diversity is Eleventh Street between Fifth and
    Sixth Avenues in New York, a street admired as both dignified and interest-
    ing to walk on. Along its south side it contains, going west, a fourteen-story
    apartment house, a church, seven three-story houses . . . a three-story apart-
    ment house with a candy and newspaper store at street level. While these
    are nearly all residential buildings, they are broken into by instances of ten
    other uses. Even the purely residential buildings themselves embrace many
    different periods of technology and taste, many different modes and costs
    of living. They have an almost fantastic array of matter-of-fact, modestly
    stated differences: different heights at first-floor levels, differing arrange-
    ments for entrances and sidewalk access.[5]

These descriptive passages introduces states and events of different kinds. Time
doesn't advance, at least not significantly.

In passages of the Description mode the reader progresses spatially from
one part of a scene to another. For instance, in the first sentences of (8a) we
tour the rocky plateau from the boulders to the flowers; then to the lake and
its subsidiary streams, following the gaze of the describer. In (8b) the passage
progresses along the buildings of Eleventh Street.

Typically in description there is a locative phrase with scope over the material
that follows, as in these examples. I also assume a tacit durative time adverbial
for descriptive passages. When there is a change of time in description, there is
also a change of scene. The information that tense conveys is anaphoric: the time
of description is that of a time established earlier in the text. The Description
mode is discussed further in Chapter 5.

2.2.3   Report: deictic advancement
Reports give an account of situations from the temporal standpoint of the reporter. They are, like narrative, mainly concerned with events and states. The

---

5. The sentence listing the buildings on Eleventh street is too long to repeat here: it continues for
most of a page along these lines: "a five-story house, thirteen four-story houses, a nine-story
apartment house, five four-story houses with a restaurant and bar at the street level, a five story
apartment, a little graveyard, and a six-story apartment house with a restaurant at street level;
on the north side, again going west . . ."

significant difference between these modes is that, in Reports, the relation to Speech Time determines temporal advancement. Situations are related to Speech Time, rather than to each other. This is the deictic pattern of temporal advancement.

Reports conform to the basic speech situation, in which the speaker is central. This centrality is signaled by adverbials such as *here*, *now*, *last week*, which take Speech Time as their orientation, or anchor. Such forms are known as "deictic." "Deixis" is the term for linguistic forms that are anchored to the time of speech. The present tense conveys that a situation holds now, the past tense conveys that a situation precedes now. In (9a) the adverb *here* in S1 reinforces the sense of the deictic center.

(9)   Report
        a. 1 A week that began in violence ended violently here, with bloody clashes in the West Bank and Gaza and intensified fighting in Southern Lebanon. 2 Despite the violence, back-channel talks continued in Sweden. 3 Israeli, Palestinian and American officials have characterized them as a serious and constructive dialogue on the process itself and on the final status issues. 4 News accounts here say that Israel is offering as much as 90 percent of the West Bank to the Palestinians, although it is difficult to assess what is really happening by the bargaining moves that are leaked.
        b. 1 At his news conference here, even before he took questions, Schroeder implicitly challenged the official US explanation for the bombing of the Chinese embassy in Belgrade – that target analysts relied on a faulty street map – by renewing his demand for a formal NATO inquiry into the bombing.
          2 Diplomats say that Schroeder, who just returned from China, was angry that a trip he had long planned to herald his chairmanship of the European Union was transformed into an official apology for the embassy bombing.

Reports progress with changes in temporal and spatial location. Frequent changes of tense are common. For instance, the situations S1–2 of (9a) are located in the past, at different spatial locations ("here," "Sweden"). In S3–4 time advances to the present. The fragment of (9b) has a complex temporal analysis, beginning in the past, moving to the present (in the second clause of S1) and then back to the past. The situations are not related to each other.

In passages of the Report mode, the order of events does not determine the interpretation. Rather, the standpoint of the reporter is the organizing factor, as Caenepeel observes (1995:231).

Summarizing, the temporal discourse modes are Narrative, Description, and Report. Passages in these modes progress as temporal or spatial location advances. Advancement is conveyed by aspectual viewpoint and situation type, tense and time adverbs, and by spatial information.

2.3   Text progression in the atemporal modes

2.3.1   Progression as metaphorical motion

In passages of the Argument and Information modes, the entities are mainly General Statives and Abstract Entities. These entities are not dynamic and progression in such texts is neither temporal nor spatial. There is a connection with space, however: generalizing from the spatial domain, I shall say that passages of atemporal modes progress by metaphorical motion.

The atemporal text offers a metaphorical space which readers traverse as they go through the text. The idea can be implemented with the notion of a Primary Referent that is semantically central to a situation. Each clause in a passage has a Primary Referent. When the Primary Referent moves metaphorically from one part of the text domain to another, one has the intuition of metaphorical progression.

The Primary Referent of a clause has a central role in the situation expressed by the clause. In an Event, the Primary Referent is what moves or changes; in a State, a property is ascribed to the Primary Referent. Example (10) gives simple clauses with the Primary Referent phrases underlined:

(10)   a. Mark opened <u>the door</u>.
         b. <u>The door</u> was opened by Mark.
         c. Sarah gave <u>the balloon</u> to her sister.
         d. <u>Louise</u> lives in Peoria.

The Primary Referent is usually the grammatical object in sentences with transitive verbs, and subject in sentences with intransitive verbs. Primacy is determined by event structure, and does not change with shifts of word order and syntax. So, for instance, the Primary Referent is object in the active sentence (10a) and subject in the corresponding passive (10b). The Primary Referent corresponds to the thematic argument role of Theme or Patient in most cases; see Chapter 4 for discussion.

How a domain is organized in the text can affect progression. There are several conventional principles for domains: for instance, they may be organized by hierarchy as in plant and animal taxonomies. Conventional organizing principles include causal relations, chronology, and geography. Example (11), for instance, has a geographical organization (cited in Olman 1998):

(11)   1 Cats also spin a story about how creatures adapt to the world they live in.
         2 Most landscapes hold wild cats indigenous to every continent except Australia and Antarctica. 3 They live in forests, plains, mountains, deserts, snowy steppes. 4 The margay, a small spotted cat of Central and South America, has gymnast-like limbs suited to a life of tree climbing in the rain forest. 5 The

gray-white coat of the snow leopard melts perfectly into the rocky highlands from Siberia through the Himalayas. 6 The slightly webbed front toes of the fishing cat help it dive for prey in the rivers of tropical Asia. 7 The clouded leopard, once found only in Asia's pristine forests, has turned up in habitats damaged by overgrazing and logging. 8 It has adapted to the careless hand of man.

Olman points out that the examples distribute themselves across continents and landscapes, following the rhetorical principle of Comprehensiveness. Understanding the way domains are organized is an interesting and difficult problem.[6]

Linguistic expressions for space and Primary Referents are discussed further in Chapters 5 and 6.

2.3.2   The Information mode

The Information mode gives information, presenting it as uncontroversial. Informative passages introduce mainly General Statives – generics and generalizing sentences – into the universe of discourse. This is the main difference between the Information and Description modes; the latter focuses on specifics, particulars of a single state of affairs. Informative passages predominate in textbooks, journals of information, in-depth studies of particular topics – the examples in this book include discussions of whales, Chinese pottery, and tunnels. Passages of the Information mode often have a supporting role in manuals, newspaper and magazine articles, arguments.

The mode is timeless and progression is metaphorical in the text domain. The text progresses when the metaphorical location of referents changes. The fragment in (12) illustrates; it is from the same article as (1) above. The sentences are all stative. The Primary Referent is underlined in each clause; subscripts indicate that phrases have the same referent:

(12)   1 Humpbacks$_i$ are found in every ocean. 2 Together with blue, fin, sei, Bryde's, and mink whales, they$_i$ belong to the rorqual family of baleen whales. 3 Fully grown females$_j$, which$_j$ are bulkier than the males, can weigh 40 tons and reach lengths of 50 feet. 4 Humpbacks$_i$ tend to favor shallow areas, often quite close to shore, and they$_i$ are among the most sociable of the great whales and the most active at the surface, all of which makes them$_i$ among the easiest to observe.

The Primary Referent is the subject NP in all but one clause in the passage: "humpbacks," "they," "fully grown females," "which," "humpbacks," "they." The last clause has a transitive verb and its object, the pronoun *them*, is the

---

6. This problem is well known in Artificial Intelligence, where knowledge bases must be organized to allow searches from different points of view. See Porter *et al.* (1988), Acker & Porter (1994).

Primary Referent. The limited metaphorical motion is reflected in the interpretation of the passage: it presents a collection of facts about humpback whales.

2.3.3 Argument

An argument passage brings something to the attention of the reader, makes a claim, comment, or argument and supports it in some way. Claims do not have a particular linguistic form: they appear in all sorts of linguistic structures. The assertion of something new, surprising, or tendentious may function as a claim. For instance, one text I examined begins "The American high school is obsolete and should be abolished." In the context of current American life, this is a strong claim. In linguistic terms the sentence is generic, referring to the class of high schools. Determining when a sentence makes a claim is beyond the scope of this discussion.

Passages in the Argument mode are concerned with states of affairs, Facts, and Propositions. They differ in whether the author is strongly present or not: we can think of the extremes as the argument and commentary poles. Texts near the argument pole may not directly involve the author or audience; as in (13). Sentences 1–2 have complement clauses referring to Facts, sentences 3–4 are Generalizing Statives. The Primary Referents are underlined.

(13)   1 <u>The routine transfer of power</u> may not be the most dramatic feature of American democracy, but it is the most important. 2 It separates <u>us</u> [the United States] from the majority of countries in the world, which have still not achieved <u>it</u>. 3 Conceding defeat and going home, or staying on in the minority and allowing the winner to govern – <u>these</u> are not just the elements of good manners and sportsmanship. 4 <u>They</u> are the core of patriotism.

The metaphorical location changes somewhat in the course of this paragraph. In S1 it is "the routine transfer of power" in the United States. The first clause of S2 has the object NP *us* as primary, suggesting the possibility of a shift. The next clause returns to the first location, however, with the Primary Referent the object NP *it* ('the routine transfer of power').

The next example is closer to the commentary pole, partly because of the implicit subjectivity of the predicates "likely," "impossible," etc.; subjective forms are discussed in Chapter 7. Sentences 1–4 have complements referring to Propositions, while S5 is an explicit prediction. As before, Primary Referents are underlined.

(14)   1 It is likely that <u>other new technologies</u> will appear suddenly, leading to major new industries. 2 What <u>they</u> may be is impossible even to guess at. 3 But it is highly probable – indeed, nearly certain – that <u>they</u> will emerge, and fairly soon. 4 And it is nearly certain that <u>few of them</u> – and few industries

> based on them – will come out of computer and information technology.
> 5 Like biotechnology and fish farming, <u>each</u> [of them] will emerge from its own
> unique and unexpected technology. 6 Of course, <u>these</u> are only predictions.

The first sentences have the same Primary Referent, so there is no progression.
At S6 the Primary Referent changes, with metaphorical motion from "other
new technologies" to the more abstract predictions the author is making (the
referent of "these"). When the primary is a quantified NP, as in S4 ("few of
them"), the relevant class is taken as primary.

   This chapter began with an example of a passage that shifted from the Narrative to the Information mode. Another example of a shift in mode, this time
from Argument to Narrative, is given in (15). The fragment is from the same
text as (13) above; the shift occurs at the second paragraph:

(15)   I feel reasonably certain of the final verdict on the current impeachment affair
       because I think history will see it as the climax of a six-year period marred by
       a troubling and deepening failure of the Republican party to play within the
       established constitutional rules.
           It was on Election Night 1992, not very far into the evening, that the Senate
       minority leader, Bob Dole, hinted at the way his party planned to conduct
       itself in the months ahead: it would filibuster any significant legislation the
       new Democratic President proposed, forcing him to obtain 60 votes for Senate
       passage.

In the first paragraph the clauses refer to Facts and Propositions proposed by the
first-person speaker. There is a shift to narration in the second paragraph. The
clauses introduce Events, and the *it*-cleft construction signals that a narrative
is about to begin. It is a typical way of setting the scene in traditional tales ("It
was on a dark and stormy night that . . .").

2.4   *Foreground and background in text passages*

There is a traditional, intuitive distinction between the foreground and the background of a text: foregrounded information is the most important and background material is supportive. The distinction has been discussed mainly for
narrative texts. While the idea of narrative foreground is quite well understood, the concept of background is vague. "Background" simply lumps together
everything that is not foreground. The study of Discourse Modes clarifies by
distinguishing different aspects of a text. I use the factors of situation entity
and progression to give an articulated notion of background. Information is
backgrounded if it fails to contribute to progression; or if it involves entities
that are not characteristic of the current Discourse Mode.

I use this strategy to discuss foreground and background in narrative, and then generalize to the other Discourse Modes.

The foreground of a narrative consists of situations that advance the narrative. The foreground presents the main, sequential events of a narrative, while the background gives supporting and descriptive information. Foreground situations are usually events in sequence presented with the perfective viewpoint, while imperfectives and states are usually background. Hopper (1979) was one of the first to propose this aspectual characterization of foreground and background, which has been widely accepted.[7] The characterization of background can be improved, with some of the insights from the study of Discourse Modes.

I suggest that two kinds of background information can be distinguished: one involves narrative time and the other, types of situation. Typically states and ongoing events are backgrounded in narrative. Both types of situation are related to the time line of the narrative: they are either simultaneous with a bounded Event, or before or after it. In contrast, General Statives or Abstract Entities are off the timeline of a narrative. They are part of the background in another sense.

The generalizing statives and generics of Information discourse, the abstract entities of Argument, give information of a non-narrative kind. For instance, Propositions may provide commentary that supports or subverts a narrative. Shifts in type of entity are also shifts from foreground to background.

The intuition of background and foreground extends to the other modes. One recognizes important material as foreground, and subsidiary, supportive material as background. Foregrounding affects progression. Backgrounding occurs when information does not affect progression, and when entities are not those of the current Discourse Mode.

To illustrate, I give examples of passages of each mode. The passages have foregrounded and backgrounded clauses.

Narrative has a clear line of semantic progression, and shifts from this line are relatively salient. The fragment in (16), for instance, has four background clauses. Three of them (a, b, d) are on the timeline, though they do not advance narrative time; the fourth (c) is off the timeline altogether. The relevant clauses are italicized and lettered.

---

7. Hopper claims that foreground and background also differ in the familiarity status of subjects, type of situation, and function. According to Hopper, there is a strong statistical tendency for foregrounded Events to have familiar, animate subjects, to be punctual rather than durative, to occur in sequence. In contrast, backgrounded situations tend to have less familiar subjects, to be durative or stative, not to be sequential (1979:223).

(16)   Narrative
a Harry did not want to run away. . . . he kept snivelling and burst out, "But I
don't want to!" "Yes, you do" I informed him . . . I kept my little brother awake
by telling him stories and then, already chilly in the night air, we sneaked from
the house, crept past the lit windows where our parents sat reading and ran off
down the road in the dark, the pillowcase with its loose tins banging against
my legs. *b Harry was crying loudly now. c The bush was not then the domestic
bush it has become* . . . And then something happened, the two dogs arrived,
to lick our hands and whine and jump around us. *d We had not remembered
the dogs* . . . we fled into our bedroom and into bed. We giggled and laughed
and shrieked with relief, and the dogs went quietly back to lie in their places
in the lamplight.

Clauses *a* and *b* express a State and an ongoing Event respectively, and *d* is a
past perfect. They are clearly background, since they don't advance narrative
time. (They are important to the story line, however.) Clause *c* is a Generalizing
Stative. It makes a generalization about the bush – the story is set in Africa –
which has nothing to do with the timeline or the story.

Passages of the Description mode are static and within the scope of a tacit time
adverbial. Entities that are dynamic, or located at another time, are part of the
background. Entities not typical of this mode are also part of the background.
Example (17) is a descriptive passage; there is one backgrounded clause, in
italics:

(17)   Description
The valley rose steeply, flanked by gigantic hills, with little terraced fields of
barley, blue vetch and clover half-hidden among the rocks. Here the irrigation
ditches are of a beautiful complexity and *I thought how my children would have
liked them*; the water running swift and silent until it reached a place where
the dyke had been deliberately broken by the "Lord of the Waters," allowing it
to gurgle through into some small property and continue its journey downhill
on a lower level as a subsidiary of the main stream.

The italicized clause is off the static temporal line and involves another type of
entity. The main clause expresses an Event – the author had a particular thought –
and its complement is propositional.

The Report mode relates situations to Speech Time. One would expect that
narrative would be backgrounded in this mode, since it follows a different
pattern of tense interpretation, that of continuity. This expectation is borne out.
The example illustrates: there is a shift to narrative at S4.

(18)   Report
1 The paradox is that the leaders of Ethiopia fought side by side with the
Eritreans to oust the military government of Mengistu Haile Mariam in 1991.

2 For the first two years, the two governments were close friends, so close that they never demarcated the border when Eritrea became independent in 1993. 3 a But tensions grew over personality clashes and economic rivalry, exploding in May 1998 b when Eritrea claimed the Badme border region based on old colonial maps. 4 *Eritrea moved troops into the area.* 5 a *Ethiopia said it was invaded*, b *and a war ignited* that c has defied long peace talks and claimed tens of thousands of lives on both sides.

The narrative fragment consists of the events of S4 and S5a–b; they are related to the Event of S3a ("tensions grew"). The Report mode resumes at S5c, with the present perfect. In this passage the narrative is subsidiary, backgrounded.

The atemporal modes progress metaphorically, and have the deictic pattern of tense interpretation. Specific situations may be backgrounded. For instance, the following Information passage consists of generalizing statives, except for one clause, which is italicized:

(19)   Information
       The motifs [of the moulded pottery] include a large number of different flowers and fruits including the chrysanthemum, which is not found in the carved ware, both the flower and fruit of the pomegranate and melon gourds. To these are added somewhat abstract foliage scrolls and a debased form of key-fret, the only geometric motif in Ting decoration. There are proper fish among aquatic plants and in lotus pools. Finally there are chubby infants, wholly or partially naked. *It seems unlikely that they were incorporated into the decorative vocabulary much before the late twelfth century.* The organization of the surface [of the pottery] is similar to that of the carved ware.

The italicized sentence has a propositional complement, unlike the Generalizing Statives of the other sentences. It presents supporting, backgrounded material.

In Argument, specific Events and States may also be backgrounded. In the passage below, for instance, Sentences 5–6 express a question-and-answer sequence. The sequence departs from the prevailing Argument mode of the passage in the two ways identified above:

(20)   Argument
       1 We in academia must figure out what is really critical to us and what we are willing to give up.
       2 Not all of these choices will be ours alone. 3 Our students, as well as our governments, have changing expectations. 4 Information economies require higher levels of education and more frequent education. 5 More of the new student body may be part time, working and older. 6 *I asked* some students in this new breed what relationship they wanted with their colleges. 7 *They told me* that it should be like the relationship with a utility company, supermarket or bank – their emphasis was on convenience, service, quality and affordability.

8 This group is going to gravitate toward online instruction, with education at
home or in the workplace.

The question and answer of S6 and S7 are Events, one following the other. They
are unlike the entities expressed in preceding clauses, which are more abstract
and deictically organized. At S8 the Argument mode resumes with a general
prediction.

The examples show that with changes of entity there is a change from foreground to background in passages of a given mode. The change is, in effect, to
a different mode. However, we tend to take one or two clauses merely as a shift
from foreground to background.

Summarizing, I have shown two ways in which material may be backgrounded in text passages. They correspond to the distinctive characteristics
of the Discourse Modes. Situations are in the background if they do not advance the time of a passage in the temporal modes; or if they are of a different
type from those of the current Discourse Mode.

2.5   *Rhetorical and linguistic background*

The Discourse Modes have counterparts in the field of rhetoric, the art and
study of using language effectively and persuasively.[8] Since the nineteenth
century, rhetoricians have recognized a group of "forms of discourse." They
are similar to Discourse Modes, though without the linguistic focus. The notion
of Discourse Modes was developed independently of the rhetorical approach.
The similarities between the two are striking and, I think, validate each other.
Before discussing the rhetorical forms of discourse, I'll sketch in the rhetorical
background.

2.5.1   *Traditional rhetoric: background*
Classical rhetoric is a 2,500-year-old discipline that began with the Greek
sophists and Aristotle; it dealt with persuasion in public discourse. Rhetoric
was seen as an art that could be taught, and Aristotle's *Rhetoric* from the mid
fourth century BC was a basic text.

Aristotle says that "rhetoric does not belong to a single defined genus of
subject but is like dialectic . . . its function is not to persuade but to see the
available means of persuasion in each case" (translation of Kennedy 1991:35).

---

8. I thank Keith Walters for helpful discussion of this section. The definition in the text is from the
American Heritage Dictionary of the English Language, 3rd edition, Boston: Houghton Mifflin
Co., 1992.

Aristotle taught that there are three aspects to persuasion: the truth and logical validity of what is being argued (*logos*); the speaker's success in conveying to an audience that he or she is to be trusted (*ethos*); and the emotions that the speaker can awaken in the audience (*pathos*). In the *Rhetoric*, persuasive oratory is organized into categories of political, legal, and ceremonial (praise and censure). Classical rhetoric was further developed by Cicero, roughly from 103 to 46 BC, and by Quintilian in the first century AD. After the first century it was taught off and on in Europe until the end of the eighteenth century.

There was a strong revival of classical rhetoric in nineteenth-century England. Richard Whately's 1828 *Elements of Rhetoric* presents itself as an adaptation of classical rhetoric. Whately discusses the invention, arrangement, and introduction of propositions and arguments. He teaches students how to find suitable arguments to prove a point, and how to arrange them skillfully. Whateley gives a typology of arguments (syllogisms, arguments from example, from testimony, cause to effect, analogy); the appropriate use of arguments; the best arrangement of arguments. Part II treats Persuasion, "influencing the will." Whately's book was reprinted in 1963 and is still cited in discussions of rhetoric.

Modern rhetoric in the United States emphasizes the social and communicative aspects of persuasive discourse (Lunsford & Ede 1984). Rhetorical texts teach students the actual processes of planning, speaking, writing, in addition to classic argumentation. For instance, Edward P. Corbett's *Classical Rhetoric for the Modern Student*, published in 1965 and still reprinted, offers rhetoric as a system for finding something to say, learning how to select and organize material, and how to phrase it in the best possible way. Corbett's main topics are discovery of arguments, arrangement of material, and style.

The text draws on a categorization of discourse types that is close to the Discourse Modes of this book. Corbett recognizes "four forms of discourse: Argumentation, Exposition, Description, Narration" (1965:32). They are not defined or documented, but assumed as part of the toolkit of the rhetorician. For instance, Corbett says that, in expository discourse, one can sometimes organize according to a chronological scheme. But in argumentative discourse, the speaker has to think about things like where to use the weakest argument (1965:314). The notion of forms of discourse has a fairly long history in England and America.

2.5.2 *The rhetorical "forms of discourse"*

The forms of discourse appear in rhetorics of the late eighteenth century, when the field of rhetoric had broadened beyond persuasive oratory. Discourse was classified according to function and content. Scholars attribute the idea to George Campbell; the approach was developed by Alexander Bain (1877), John Genung (1900), and others. Bain and Genung distinguished four forms of discourse: Argumentation, Exposition, Description, Narration. The internal structure of each form is determined by its purpose: according to Genung, there is a "natural movement of ideas appropriate to each kind" (1900:475). Bain and Genung described the main characteristics of each form and tried to teach students to understand and use them effectively. The four forms are used in many texts, including modern texts. The term "form" was later replaced by "mode" in some cases; I will say "rhetorical mode" to avoid confusion with the linguistic Discourse Modes of this book.

The rhetorical modes are strikingly close to the Discourse Modes, allowing for differences across fields. The emphasis in rhetoric is on strategy and effect rather than linguistic features but some of the main insights are the same. Genung differentiates among the rhetorical modes according to what is talked about. Narration recounts Events in sequence; Description portrays observed objects; Exposition explains, classifies, makes clear ideas, terms, or propositions (the "Information" mode of this book); Argumentation seeks to prove the truth or falsity of a proposition and deals with issues of conviction (1900:475). The "kinds of things talked about" that Genung notes are like the entities distinguished as covert linguistic categories. William Cairns, also in this tradition, comments: "Description . . . deals with particular objects . . . the element of time isn't present . . . [In contrast] catalogues of general characteristics are really Exposition because their object is to explain, define, classify, or make clear the meaning of a general term or proposition" (1902:114).

People recognized that forms vary throughout a text: "[the modes] are combined in a great many ways, one helping and reinforcing another" (Genung 1900:475). And Brooks & Warren comment that "frequently in discourse which is primarily intended to explain something or convince us of something, we find bits of narrative used to dramatize an attitude, to illustrate a point, to bring an idea home to us" (1958:265).

The rhetorical modes still appear in relatively recent texts, for instance in *Modern Rhetoric* by Brooks & Warren, published in 1958 and often reprinted since. The book recognizes "the traditional four forms of discourse": Exposition, Argument, Description, Narration. Exposition explains or clarifies by appealing to the understanding. Argument also appeals to understanding, but with a different purpose: to convince the reader of the truth or desirability of something. There is some confusion, mainly terminological, between genre and rhetorical mode. Brooks & Warren distinguish two types of narrative, for instance, according to the purpose of the text. "Expository" or "ordinary" narration aims to give information, to explain (1958:110), while narrative proper appeals to the imagination; there is a difference in intention, and thus in method (1958:231). From the point of view of this book, "narrative proper" and "expository narrative" are both of the narrative type, appearing in different genres. Brooks & Warren's comments can be interpreted as a recognition that rhetorical mode differs from genre.

Many textbooks of composition used the approach of Bain and Genung in the United States from about 1885 until the 1940s. After that expository writing was emphasized in many rhetorical texts, to the exclusion of the other forms. There was also a new emphasis on "process-oriented" teaching that emphasized the writer's intentions and methods, beginning in the 1960s (Connors 1997:251). The rhetorical modes are found less often in texts today, mainly because they did not help students learn to write, according to Connors; see Larson (1984) for a different view.

The approach of rhetorical modes has been strongly criticized, especially as a teaching technique. The pragmatic objection is that it is not effective with students. Theoretically, people objected that it confuses purpose with mode: "The categories [are] supposedly based on purpose or intention. Yet narrative can scarcely be seen as an intention in the same sense as persuasion or exposition might be. We can perceive widely varying intentions in different narratives such as a fictional story, a factual report of Events, a scientific account of a sequence of Events, and a narrative contained within an advertisement" (Britton *et al.* 975:5). There may be just such a confusion in Brooks & Warren's treatment of narrative.

Another point is that different rhetorical modes can be used in pursuit of a single purpose. Faigley & Meyer comment, "an argument against slums might well use descriptions of living conditions in slums, personal narratives of life in slums, and evaluations of housing conditions in slums," and go on to claim that this criticism "refutes" the traditional modes (1983:308). But this is too strong. The problem is rather a confusion between mode and genre. Moreover, the experiments cited in their own work (mentioned above) give evidence that the rhetorical modes have a cognitive basis.

There is indeed a certain confusion in discussions of the rhetorical modes. We are told that they have a particular purpose or intention that determines their character – which suggests that they function at the level of genre. Yet the modes can be used to realize different purposes, in different genres. I think that we can resolve the confusion by clarifying the distinction between genre and mode. The rhetorical modes do not classify by purpose. Rather, they describe texts at the more local level identified in this book as the passage.

The rhetorical Discourse Modes correspond nicely to the linguistically based Discourse Modes of this book. One Discourse Mode, the Report, does not appear in the traditional classification. The importance of Report as a Discourse Mode may be due partly to mass communication, with the pervasive use of newspaper, television, and now internet reports. Moreover, diaries and other personal genres are taken seriously today and they often use the Report type of organization.

Actual texts consist of more than one type or mode of discourse: this is an uncontroversial point on which all agree.

2.5.3   *Other discourse classifications*

Scholars have classified text types according to purpose and other parameters, many of them situational. James Kinneavy works with a "communication triangle" that consists of the speaker, the audience, and the subject of discourse. He posits four general "discourse types or modes" on the basis of their purpose: referential, persuasive, expressive, and literary discourse. For each type, he undertakes to describe the "distinctive nature, distinctive logic, characteristic organizational patterns, and the stylistic features peculiar to the particular aim" (1971:63). Kinneavy notes that actual texts are mixed: "No theory of modes of discourse ever pretends that the modes do not overlap. In actuality it is impossible to have pure narration, etc. However in a given discourse there will often be . . . [a] 'dominant' mode" (1971:37).

Other parameters lead to slightly different classifications. Using two-valued parameters of "involvement–detachment" and "integration-fragmentation," Chafe (1982) proposes a four-way classification of texts. Longacre (1968) takes temporality as a primary parameter. Some discourse is primarily time-oriented, e.g. narrative and procedural, with identification and explanations as peripheral elements. In other types of discourse, temporal factors are subordinate. In later work, Longacre (1983–1996) proposes three two-valued parameters – contingent temporal succession, agent orientation, projection – and develops a broad typology of monologic discourse.

2.5.4   *Linguistic features of texts by genre*

Perhaps the most basic classification of discourse is according to genre. Discourses of the same genre have similar purpose, setting, and participants. They have similar global structures, determined by purpose and the other factors.

It would be natural if discourses of the same genre were similar in linguistic features. But they are not similar in the ways one would expect, as Douglas Biber has shown.

Biber investigated the occurrence of syntactic and lexical linguistic features in samples of twenty-three genres, using a sophisticated computational analysis of a large corpus. He found that the features clustered together into clear categories, or text types. Strikingly, the text types cut across genre categories rather than corresponding to them (1989:39).

The corpus analyzed consisted of contemporary British discourse from the Lund-Oslo-Bergen (LOB) corpus and the London-Lund corpus.[9] The investigators catalogued the occurrence and co-occurrence of such linguistic features as present tense verbs, pronouns, contractions, past tense forms, perfect aspect verbs, *wh*-relative clauses, time and place adverbials, infinitives, modals, nominalizations. They found that the linguistic properties they studied clustered together reliably across texts (Biber 1988, 1989).

Five dimensions of clustering were identified. Biber provides broad interpretive labels for each. The dimensions are: (1) Involved vs. Informational; (2) Narrative vs. Non-narrative; (3) Elaborated vs. Situation-dependent reference; (4) overt expression of persuasion; (5) abstract or not. In each dimension, certain forms have high frequency and others have low frequency. On the dimension of "involved vs. informational," for instance, the high-frequency forms are present tense verbs, private verbs, first- and second-person pronouns, demonstrative pronouns, contractions, *that*-deletion. Low-frequency forms are nouns, prepositional phrases, long words, lexical variation, attributive adjectives.

The analysis results in a set of "text types" that have feature clusters from more than one dimension. Biber proposes eight "prototypical" text types: intimate personal interaction, informational interaction, scientific exposition, learned exposition, imaginative narrative, general narrative exposition, situated reportage, and involved persuasion. Text types do not pattern according to genre. Instead, "texts within particular genres can differ greatly in their linguistic characteristics, e.g. newspaper articles can range from extremely narrative and colloquial in linguistic form to extremely informational and elaborated in form. On the other hand, texts of different genres can be quite similar linguistically: newspaper

---

9. Biber (1989) lists the genres studied as follows – examples of written genres from LOB corpus: press reportage, editorials, press reviews, religion, skills and hobbies, popular lore, biographies, official documents, academic prose, general fiction, mystery fiction, science fiction, adventure fiction, romantic fiction, humor, personal letters, professional letters; examples of spoken genres from London-Lund corpus – face-to-face conversation, telephone conversation, public conversation, debates, interviews, broadcasts, spontaneous speeches, planned speeches.

articles and popular magazine articles can be nearly identical in form"
(1989:6).

Text types and genres are valid and different typologies, Biber suggests.
Genre distinctions are based on essentially nonlinguistic criteria, reflecting
differences in external format and situation. Other efforts to find consistent
linguistic distinctions that correlate with genres have also been unsuccessful.[10]

People have also looked for linguistic correlates of genre-based units. For
instance, suppose that a story consists of a Setting and an Episode; and an
Episode consists of an Event and a Reaction (there are stories with such units).
There might be linguistically identifiable stretches of text that correspond to
these sub-units. Implementing this idea, people have written "discourse grammars" which generate stories and other types of discourse. The grammars are
hierarchical: they start with abstract units and in principle end with the sentences of a discourse (van Dijk 1972, Rumelhart 1975, Thorndyke 1977). There
are two crucial assumptions behind these grammars. One is that an orderly
relation holds between the abstract units of the grammar and the linguistic
units – sentences, clauses, phrases, etc. – that make up the text. The other
assumption is that discourse has certain constraints, so that texts, like sentences, are well formed or ill formed. Neither of these ideas holds up under
scrutiny.

It's plausible that texts would be well and ill formed like sentences; but
in fact constructing a text that is actually ill formed (as opposed to awkward or confusing) is difficult if not impossible. The reason is that almost
any sequence of sentences can be taken as well formed if the receiver supplies
enough inferences.[11] Nor is there a clear, predictable correspondence between

10. For instance, Edward Smith (1985) looked for linguistic features correlating with four very
general text types identified by Longacre (1983/1996): Narrative, Procedural, Behavioral,
and Expository texts. He concluded that genre – purpose – isn't conveyed by linguistic
features.

11. Discourse grammars use phrase structure expansion rules, producing hierarchical structures.
The grammar approach treats a discourse as one big sentence with hierarchically related parts.
Linguists and psychologists developed these grammars in attempting to model the processes of
discourse construction and discourse understanding. In principle, they believed, the units and
relations of a story grammar are psychologically real: "a higher level organization takes
place . . . strings of sentences combine into psychological wholes which account for . . . salient
facts about structure" (Rumelhart 1975:213). In the 1970s, some experimental evidence supporting story grammars was found. Subjects remembered information, for instance, according
to the sub-units posited; but other, more general explanations for these results have been offered
(Garnham 1983, 1985).
  According to Garnham, "The problem is to specify the way in which general semantic
definitions of syntactic categories could be used to compute the category of a proposition.

the units of a story grammar and the linguistic units in which a story is real-ized. For instance, the Reaction part of an Episode may be given by a phrase, a sentence, several sentences, a paragraph, etc. Recognizing such a sub-part usu-ally requires inference. But if this is true, we cannot specify a procedure for going from the abstract "story grammar" to the actual story: no mapping pro-cedure exists.[12]

2.5.5   Other linguistic studies of texts

Linguists have looked for text units that are intermediate between sentence and text. The paragraph is a grammatical unit in the tagmemic framework, in which sentence and paragraph units are essentially the same. Loriot & Hollen-bach (1970) consider paragraphs in Shipibo, a Peruvian language. They argue that there are three sub-systems of paragraph structure in the language; Event–reference ties and object–reference ties, and the ordering of sentences to form paragraphs. Their ideas are similar to those of Halliday & Hasan (1976), dis-cussed below. Paragraphs have been studied extensively in folktales (Dundes 1975). More recently, studies of American Indian and other languages have re-lated linguistic features to properties of a discourse (Woodbury 1987, Goddard 1990, Thomason 1994).

The field of text-linguistics applies linguistic techniques to text analysis (de Beaugrande & Dressler 1981). Onc approach is strongly influenced by gener-ative semantics and logic and focuses on formal rules (Reiser 1978); another attempts to integrate the complex components of texts into a full semiotic the-ory (Petöfi 1978). Text coherence has received a good deal of attention in this approach: researchers try to understand what underlies the intuition that a text is coherent, or incoherent. Answers have focused on the notions of text coherence and cohesion.

Coherence is the network of relations that organize the propositions and concepts of a text. They involve world knowledge that goes beyond the text. These relations are not necessarily made explicit in the text but are inferred by the receiver. The study of coherence has led to procedural accounts with a strong base in psychology (de Beaugrande & Dressler 1981:Ch. 5). Heyrich *et al.* (1989) offers a group of relatively recent studies in the areas of connexity and coherence.

Story grammarians have never noted this problem, let alone attempted to solve it" (1983:150). Garnham suggests that psycholinguists' findings are better explained in terms of referential continuity and plausibility.

12. Apparent violations of a convention are interpreted with additional inferences that make them plausible.

Syntactic correlates to discourse phenomena have been identified at the level of clause and sentence structure. Aspectual viewpoints often convey foregrounding and backgrounding (Hopper 1979), as noted above. There are studies of how syntactic subordination relates to discourse (Matthiessen & Thompson 1988); tense and narrative (Fleischman 1991); grounding and deictic phenomena (Tomlin 1987, Duchan *et al.* 1995).

"Cohesion," or connexity, deals with the connections made in a text at the surface level. Cohesion relates the sentences of a text by a network of grammatical and lexical ties. The term is due to Halliday & Hasan (1976). Cohesion is expressed by coreference; substitution, as when proforms like "do so" stand in for repeated material; ellipsis; conjunction; and lexical relationships.

Lexical cohesion arises when patterns of related words appear in a text. This is perhaps the most interesting contribution of Halliday & Hasan. Lexical cohesion involves "reiteration" of a word, either actual repetition or words that are "systematically" related such as superordinates, synonyms, or near-synonyms. General nouns can function as cohesive agents, operating anaphorically as a kind of synonym (1976:278):

(21)   Reiteration
        a. Accordingly,... I took leave, and turned to the ascent of the peak. The climb was perfectly easy.
        b. Henry's bought himself a Jaguar. He practically lives in that car.

Instances of the same word may be coherent even if the two are not coreferential:

(22)   a. Why does this little boy have to wriggle all the time?
        b. Other boys don't wriggle. Boys always wriggle.
        c. Good boys don't wriggle. Boys should be kept out of here.

Lexical items that appear in similar contexts have a cohesive effect. For instance, in (23) the word "girls" is cohesive:

(23)   a. Why does this little boy have to wriggle all the time?
        b. Girls don't wriggle.

"Girls" is related by complementarity to "this little boy" Halliday & Hasan note that texts may have cohesive "chains" of related words:

        candle ... flame ... flicker; hair ... comb ... curl; sky ... sunshine ... cloud ... rain.

Cohesive features combine in ways that organize a text, according to Hoey (1991). Hoey finds that repetition and other types of lexical cohesion form "networks" that indicate topical sub-units of a text; he focuses primarily on non-narrative texts. Cohesion across genres is studied by Stoddard (1991). Stoddard was interested in cohesion as part of the overall patterning of a text that leads to the perception of "texture." She did a computational study of thirty-five texts of different genres, which showed that cohesive elements differed according to genre. Stoddard interprets this result as evidence that there are definable cohesive networks in texts.[13]

The notion of lexical cohesion has been taken up by computational linguists as a method for identifying units in texts. An algorithm that finds chains of related terms was developed by Morris & Hirst (1991); the chains are used to structure texts according to the attentional/intentional theory of Grosz & Sidner (1986). Another approach, due to Hearst (1997), uses lexical cohesion as the basis for a computation that discovers "sub-topic" structure in texts by a method called "Text Tiling." Text Tiling finds patterns of lexical co-occurrence and distribution, and uses them as cues to segment a text into units with different sub-topics. The units of a text are defined as a function of the patterns of connectivity between its terms (1997:9). Hearst claims that the lexical patterns are helpful heuristic cues to higher-level structures; lexical cohesion alone is not responsible for such structures.[14]

The notion of cohesion is "semantic" and involves the interpretation of one element as depending on another, according to Halliday & Hasan (1976:4).[15] Although intepretation is often triggered by linguistic form, the reader makes the connection. Nevertheless the term "cohesion" is primarily used for overt linguistic devices that relate sentences.

---

13. The contribution of "cohesive factors" to literary texts was studied by Gutwinski (1976). She examined texts by Henry James and Ernest Hemingway for cohesive ties. James and Hemingway are considered to have different styles of writing, and Gutwinski found that their choice of cohesive ties were different. James depended primarily on grammatical cohesion, especially anaphora, whereas Hemingway used lexical cohesion almost exclusively. Gutwinski's study demonstrated that cohesion could be identified and that it contributed to literary texts.
14. Hearst suggests that one can discover a text's structure by dividing it up into sentences and seeing how much word overlap appears among them. The overlap forms a kind of intra-structure; fully connected graphs might indicate dense discussion of a topic, while long spindly chains of connectivity might indicate a sequential account.
15. Halliday & Hasan also claim that cohesion distinguishes a text from an incoherent sequence of sentences. In other words, cohesion is what distinguishes a coherent, well-formed text. Arguments against this strong claim are given in Brown & Yule (1983), Blakemore (1988). For discussion of the relation between cohesion and "coherence" see Stoddard (1991:13ff.) and Sanford & Moxey (1995).

This discussion is intended to provide a context for study of the Discourse Modes. In the next chapter I turn to the topics of communication and inference in the understanding of text passages, and representations in Discourse Representation Theory.

Example sources in this chapter:

(1) and (12) Douglas H. Chadwick, Listening to humpbacks. *National Geographic*, July 1999.

(5a) Charles Johnson, *Middle Passage*, New York: Atheneum, 1990, p. 20.

(5b) Lillian Hellman, *Scoundrel Time*, Boston: Little, Brown, 1976, p. 55.

(6) David Fromkin *A Peace to End All Peace*, New York: Henry Holt, 1989, p. 369.

(7) Peter Robinson, *A Necessary End*, New York: Avon Books, 1989, p. 103.

(8a) and (17) Eric Newby, *A Short Walk in the Hindu Kush*, Victoria, Australia: Lonely Planet Publications, 1958/1998, p. 146.

(8b) Jane Jacobs, *The Death and Life of Great American Cities*, New York: Random House, 1961, pp. 227–28.

(9a) Barak fights on many fronts. *New York Times*, May 20, 2000.

(9b) Kosovo strategy splitting NATO. *New York Times*, May 20, 2000.

(11) Cats. *National Geographic*, June 1997.

(13) and (15) Alan Ehrenhalt, Hijacking the rulebook. *New York Times*, December 20, 1998.

(14) Peter Drucker, The information revolution. *Atlantic Monthly*, October 1999.

(16) Doris Lessing, *Under My Skin*, New York: Harper Perennial, 1994, p. 107.

(18) After a victory, Ethiopia looks toward other fronts. *New York Times*, May 20, 1999.

(19) Margaret Medley, *The Chinese Potter*, London: Phaidon, 1989, p. 114.

(20) Arthur Levine, The soul of a new university. *New York Times*, March 13, 2000.

3 *Text representation and understanding*

Text understanding is a constructive process that results in a mental representation. In this it is rather like vision. Seeing a tiger, for instance, is the result of a process of construction. The perceiver's mind/brain converts information from a pattern of light and dark on the retina to a representation, an interpretation of the object – an image of a tiger (Marr 1982). Inference often plays an important role at the final stages. Similarly, to understand a sentence, one goes from a sound wave or set of marks to a conceptual representation which brings together information of different kinds, some of it supplied by inference and world knowledge. The active nature of understanding informs the approach to text structure and its representation that I take here.

Studies in cognitive science and psycholinguistics provide background information about text understanding and mental models. Mental models are developed in effect with the structures of Discourse Representation Theory.

Section 3.1 discusses the communicative context of language; 3.2 considers some inferences in language understanding; 3.3 relates language understanding to the notion of mental models; 3.4 discusses the analysis of text passages in Discourse Representation Theory, and introduces the rules and structures of the theory.

3.1   *The pragmatic background for discourse interpretation*

Participants in discourse have in common several kinds of knowledge. They may share a general background and specific knowledge about the particular language activity of a given discourse. The participants also share the information that develops in the discourse itself, the common ground or "context set" (Stalnaker 1978). As a discourse progresses, each new proposition is assessed. If it is accepted, the proposition is added to the context set. Thus each sentence as it is processed updates the context.

The dynamic representations of Discourse Representation Theory model the developing common ground. Other dynamic theories include Dynamic

Predicate Logic and Situation Semantics. All of these theories have an essential pragmatic thrust: they take context as crucial for interpreting discourse. They deal with both semantic and pragmatic reasoning and information.

Pragmatics concerns language as communicative action. What a person says usually underdetermines interpretation, yet most communication is successful. Pragmatics tries to account for this apparent paradox. Successful communication results from a tacit negotiation between speaker or writer and receiver, based on shared assumptions about communication. Speakers try to give enough information so that receivers can understand their intentions. In order to do this, receivers must often work out the semantic and pragmatic meanings of a communication.

The now-classical approach of Grice makes a distinction between the semantic and pragmatic meanings of a sentence. Semantic meaning is conveyed by linguistic expressions, while pragmatic meaning adds what a speaker implicates and/or intends when uttering a sentence in a particular context. In principle, sentence meaning is semantic, while speaker's meaning is pragmatic. Grice developed a theory of how intended meaning can be derived from what is said (1975, 1989). He stated a set of basic assumptions, the cooperative maxims that underlie communication. Using these maxims and what they know about the world, people calculate by inference the interpretations intended in a text. In this view, semantic meaning is the input to pragmatic meaning.

Pragmatic interpretations, or implicatures, are not logically entailed by what is said. They can be cancelled, as Grice put it, by additional information. If I say "John and Mary have two children," you will probably infer that two is the total number of children that they have. This is a conversational implicature. I might go on to say more – possibly "indeed, they have four children" and this would cause you to cancel your earlier inference. Entailments, truth-conditions, and the conventional meanings attached to particular words cannot be cancelled and therefore have a different status.

The division of labor between semantics and pragmatics seemed relatively clear at one time; it is currently the subject of active debate.[1] Complete separation of semantics and pragmatics is difficult to maintain, because pragmatic

---

1. Kent Bach, for instance, proposes that "semantic meaning is the conventional meaning of linguistic expressions, while pragmatic meaning is context-dependent, pertaining to utterances and facts surrounding them." In contrast, Levinson argues that conversational implicature plays a role in assigning truth-condition, so that semantics and pragmatics are interwoven in most cases (1999:168).

reasoning plays a role at all stages of interpretation. For instance, pragmatic cues resolve linguistic ambiguity, and determine the referent of a referring expression and the time and place of an utterance – the indexical coordinates. Yet this information is part of sentence meaning. Pragmatics intrudes into semantics, as Levinson puts it, even at the "semantic" level of what is said (2000:164). Nevertheless semantics and pragmatics are different. Semantic reasoning is monotonic, pragmatic reasoning is non-monotonic.[2]

In this book I consider several kinds of information. Conventionally semantic information, for instance, is conveyed by a verb and its arguments expressing aspectual entities such as events and states. Other information arguably involves both semantics and pragmatics – for instance, the principles of narrative text progression, the identification of the Primary Referents of a clause, and the interpretation of subjective expressions. Information based mainly on pragmatic reasoning includes the calculation of metaphorical progression and identification of sentence topics. Throughout the book I attempt to indicate the bases for the interpretations that I posit, and to distinguish inferences of different kinds. Much of the information would have to be included in any account, whether or not it uses the distinctions I rely on here.[3]

3.2   Types of inference

Inference plays a role in understanding discourse at all levels. Much of the reasoning that underlies discourse interpretation requires plausible rather than logical reasoning. Our understanding of such inferencing patterns is still very much a work in progress. What is needed is a theory of pragmatics which draws on information of many kinds, among them lexical semantics, domain and world knowledge, Gricean principles, and general principles of pragmatic reasoning. There is no such theory at the moment.

I set out here some well-known types of inference that people use in understanding sentences and their implicatures. People make inferences constantly and automatically, in the course of linguistic communication. Inferences

---

2. Non-monotonic reasoning involves defaults, and is defeasible. In defeasible systems, an inference or argument may be defeated by additional premises. In contrast, deductive systems are monotonic.
3. Some approaches do not distinguish between semantics and pragmatics, e.g. Relevance Theory, due to Sperber & Wilson (1986) and other publications. Another approach uses a theory of commonsense entailment or "glue logic" for discourse, known as "DICE" (Lascarides & Asher 1993, Asher & Lascarides 1998b).

fill out explicit linguistic material with information which is essential for understanding. Often, in talking and writing, the speaker or writer leaves out what seems obvious, assuming that the receiver will recover it by inference. In a detailed account such things must be made explicit.

Interpretation that goes beyond linguistic forms is an everyday part of language understanding, not an exotic phenomenon. People tend to avoid redundancy – for instance, relying on the receiver's ability to interpret reduced forms. A fully explicit and redundant text is not preferred and may even be confusing. Consider the examples in (1):

(1)   a. John and Mary went to the store and John and Mary bought two large lobsters.
       b. John and Mary went to the store and they bought two large lobsters.
       c. John and Mary went to the store and bought two large lobsters.

(1b, c) are more natural and perhaps easier to understand than (1a), the most explicit. If an unreduced sentence is used it tends to carry a special meaning.[4]

Working out the intended referent of a pronoun often requires inference. There may be more than one possibility. For instance, in the sentence "John said that he was leaving," "he" may refer to John or to another person; in a specific context, one interpretation is usually preferred. In the second sentence of "John saw Thomas. He was wearing a red hat," the first natural interpretation of the pronoun referent is "Thomas"; but other information could override this. In other cases, pragmatic knowledge about the world makes one interpretation more plausible than another. Compare "Mary lent Jane a bicycle. She asked her to be careful with it," and "Mary lent Jane a bicycle. She thanked her." In the first sequence "she" would probably refer to Mary, whereas, in the second, "she" would probably refer to Jane. Normally people use context, inference, and world knowledge to choose the most plausible pronoun referent.

Inferences are often needed to relate things to each other; one common relation is part–whole, illustrated in different ways by the examples of (2):

4. One of Grice's points is that flouting the maxims conveys a special meaning. The maxim of quantity says that one should make one's contribution as informative as required, and do not make it more informative than required for the purposes of the communication. Sentences (1a) and even (1b) would flout this maxim in most situations.

    The additional meanings of unreduced conjunctions are explored by Levinson as examples of "generalized conversational implicature" (2000:148). Levinson argues that generalized implicature is distinct in kind from the implicatures of a particular utterance in context.

(2)   a. i. We checked the picnic supplies.
            ii. The beer was warm.
        b. i. John and Mary went to India last January.
            ii. They flew to Bombay and then took the train to the interior.
        c. i. Mary had an accident driving home from work.
            ii. The steering-wheel was defective.

In (2aii), we infer that "the beer" is part of "the picnic supplies." To understand (2bii) we infer an event, a trip that is implicit in (2bi); the second sentence gives details of that trip. To understand (2cii) one infers that the steering-wheel is part of the car that Mary was driving (2ci) and one posits a car. Inferences like those of (2) are known as "bridging" inferences. Bridging is an obligatory part of comprehension, since the receiver must identify the intended referents for all referring expressions. Experiments show that people make bridging inferences like those above in the course of text understanding (Haviland & Clark 1974). The inferences involve world knowledge, knowledge of the context, logical entailments, and plausible reasoning.

Positing an entity that is not explicitly introduced in the discourse is a general type of inference known as "accommodation." The receiver infers the existence of an entity if it is necessary to do so for coherence (Lewis 1979). In accommodation one accepts the information conveyed by a linguistic form whether or not the form has an appropriate antecedent and adds an entity or presupposition to the common ground.[5] For instance, the definite article *the* pragmatically conveys that the referent of a NP is familiar, either known or identifiable (see Chapter 6). Encountering a definite NP that is not familiar, the receiver accommodates by taking the referent of the NP to be a known individual. Novels often exploit this convention by beginning with a definite NP whose referent cannot be known to the reader. The experienced reader assumes that the individual is to be added to the universe of discourse, and waits for more information. The assumption that the referent of *the N* is familiar is a pragmatic presupposition. In pragmatic presupposition one takes information as uncontroversial in the context or common ground. There are two main uses of the term "presupposition," one "pragmatic" and the other "semantic."

Semantic presupposition is triggered by particular linguistic expressions: they have the conventional meaning that information is known or presupposed. For

---

5. We understand that an entity is added to the common ground. Lewis discussed accommodation in terms of presupposition: "if at time t something is said that requires presupposition p to be acceptable, and if p is not presupposed just before t then presupposition p comes into existence, ceteris paribus" (1979:172). See also Heim (1982).

instance, "Tom stopped running" entails "Tom ran."[6] The contexts of semantic presupposition include the complements of "factive" verbs (*know, regret*); the clefted clause of cleft sentences ("It was the butler that stole the jewels"); temporal adverbial clauses ("John left after calling his mother"). The information in such contexts is treated as familiar, whatever its actual status for the receiver.

The constructive view of language understanding has experimental support from psycholinguistics. In a classic group of experiments, Bransford *et al.* (1972) studied how people understood descriptions of situations that differed slightly, as in sentences (3a) and (3b) below. The situations have somewhat different consequences. From (3a) a person can infer (3c), using spatial knowledge of the world. In the situation described, if the fish swam beneath the turtles, it swam beneath the log. Sentence (3b) does not support such an inference, however, so that (3d) does not follow from (3b).

(3)   a. Three turtles rested on a floating log and a fish swam beneath them.
       b. Three turtles rested beside a floating log and a fish swam beneath them.
       c. Three turtles rested on a floating log and a fish swam beneath it.
       d. Three turtles rested beside a floating log and a fish swam beneath it.

In the experiments subjects were first presented with sentences like (3a) and (3b) and asked to remember them. Later they heard a group of sentences containing the originals and new, slightly different sentences – some of them like (3c) and some like (3d). The subjects' task was to say whether they had heard a sentence before.

Subjects tended to "recognize" sentences that were consistent with the original descriptions, with high confidence. In other words they tended to confuse sentences like (3a) with (3c), but not to confuse sentences like (3b) with (3d). Bransford *et al.* interpret the result as showing that "recognition was primarily a function of the complete semantic descriptions constructed rather than a function of just that information specified by the linguistic input strings" (1972:205). Results like these strongly support the mental model view of sentence representation.

---

6. There are well-known tests for semantic presupposition. The best-known is negation. Semantic presupposition is undisturbed by negation, as in (b), the negation of (a):

   a. Sam stopped running
   b. Sam didn't stop running.

   Both (a) and (b) carry the presupposition that Sam ran. Other tests include embedding under modality, the antecedent test, the test for constancy under illocutionary force.

3.3   Mental models and representations

The Cognitive Science approach has stressed that mental processes are active. Many cognitive scientists hold that the mind is a symbolic system: in this hypothesis, people think and reason by manipulating symbolic representations.[7] One influential version of this view claims that people "translate" or represent external events into internal models.

The mental models approach to texts posits a mental representation which models the state of affairs expressed in the text. The model is constructed from linguistic information about the world, and from inferences triggered by the text (Johnson-Laird 1983). The fact that people make bridging inferences is a central feature of comprehension, and a reason to believe that people construct mental models, according to Johnson-Laird. He comments that "... the explicit content of a discourse is usually only a blueprint for a state of affairs: it relies on the reader to flesh out the missing details ... [the experiments] ... yield conclusions of a sort that would be explicit only in models of situations" (Johnson-Laird 1989:471). Mental models are structurally isomorphic to situations, according to the theory.

The model is constructed incrementally as a text advances. The developing model functions as context for each sentence, and constrains the interpretation of a sentence. For instance, the set of entities in the model limits the set of possible antecedents for an anaphoric expression. Experiments directly positing mental models are discussed in Glenberg *et al.* (1987), Garnham & Oakhill (1989), Oakhill *et al.* (1989), Tardieu *et al.* (1992), and others.

Propositional information is emphasized in other approaches to representation, for instance Graesser (1981), and Kintsch and his colleagues. Van Dijk & Kintsch (1983) define three levels: a surface form representation, a propositional text base, and a situation model. The situation model is similar to the mental model in that it integrates information derived from the text with reader's knowledge. Whether some or all types of representations are needed to model how people understand texts is still under debate. The important point is that representations are essential.

The semantic representations of Discourse Representation Theory are close to the mental models posited by Johnson-Laird and his colleagues. The theory

---

7. Not all agree with this classical view. In the approach of Connectionism, or Parallel Distributed Processing, the mind is not symbolic but rather a network of simple processing units. Connectionist cognitive modeling tries to understand the mechanisms of human cognition through the use of simulated networks of simple, neuronlike processing units. This approach is presented in McClelland & Rumelhart (1986), Bechtel & Abrahamsen (1991), and others. A. Clark (1989) provides cautionary comments.

states construction rules which take the sentences of a text as input and deliver a representation as output. It does not try to account for the actual mental process involved in understanding a text.

3.4   *The analysis of text passages in Discourse Representation Theory*

The representations of Discourse Representation Theory model the developing common ground of a discourse. The theory has two levels. At the first level, a representation of the conceptual meaning of the text is constructed, a Discourse Representation Structure. The Discourse Representation Structure (DRS) contains discourse entities that represent individuals, situations, and times, together with conditions that characterize them. The entities and conditions are licensed by information conveyed in the sentence together with the DRS of the prior discourse, up to that sentence. The conceptual DRS is evaluated by a truth-conditional mapping at the second level of the theory.

The framework is flexible enough to allow for semantically and pragmatically based information. Indeed, both are arguably included in the DRS representations introduced below: "DRSs in fact incorporate the results of pragmatic resolution (most obviously, anaphoric linkages)...There is a common level of propositional representation, a slate on which both semantics and pragmatics can write...it is this representation that is assigned a model-theoretic interpretation" (Levinson 2000:193).

Rules and representations in the Discourse Representation Theory (DR Theory) framework show how the linguistic forms give rise to discourse mode interpretation. The heart of the theory at the first level is the construction rule. The rules interpret linguistic expressions and construct the representation licensed by them. The predictions of the theory are embodied in the rules and the structures that they trigger. The input to the rules is the surface structure of sentences; the output is the discourse entities that are entered into the DRS, together with conditions that characterize them. Thus DRSs embody the traditional notion that linguistic understanding proceeds from linguistic form to meaning. The construction rules represent conceptual meanings, which involve semantic and pragmatic information. I shall assume that both contribute to interpretation.

The second level interprets DRSs within a formal model. This is the truth-conditional component. It provides an embedding function from the DRS to a model-theoretic construct. The model is an information structure, a domain of individuals of various kinds. As expressions of a language can be evaluated relative to a model, so DRSs are evaluated. To assert a sentence amounts to asserting that the world, or the model, accords with the information in the DRS.

The model corresponds to the way some state of affairs might be, a mapping from the DRS to the model and the world. The mapping is stated with rules of functional application: they assign to sentences a denotation or meaning in a model. It is impossible to include everything that is in the world in framing conditions and models. Rather, the information in a sentence focuses on certain situations, entities, locations, and times; the rest of the world is assumed. Thus the models specified are partial models. In this book I work with conceptual representations; the conceptual and truth-conditional levels are discussed in Kamp (1981), Kamp & Reyle (1993).

3.4.1   The linguistic analysis and Discourse Representation Theory

Much of the analysis of this book is stated in the Discourse Representation Theory framework. The formal statements give content to my claims about the linguistic basis of intuitions about discourse mode and subjectivity. Interpretations that can be stated in construction rules differ significantly from those that cannot be stated within the theory, as we shall see.

The interpretations of the Discourse Modes depend on composing information from several linguistic sources. In interpreting aspectual situation types we look at information from the verb, its arguments, and adverbials – the latter sometimes in another sentence. As a composite the semantic features associated with each form determine the situation type of a clause. The composite approach is extended in this book to all types of situation entities, and to temporal advancement as well. Presentational text progression and point of view also require that various factors be taken into account. The construction rules of the theory operate on the surface structure of sentences, and license information in the ongoing Discourse Representation Structure. The rules and structures of Discourse Representation Theory (DR Theory) allow nicely for the composite approach, and for subsequent calculations.

Once entered into a representation, information is subject to further interpretation. Rules calculate temporal advancement by relating the current sentence to the representation already developed. Information of more than one kind is required: temporal advancement depends on the type of entity involved and whether it is expressed as bounded or not in the sentence under interpretation. Both temporal and aspectual information must be integrated to arrive at this kind of text progression. This is the key factor in dealing with text progression in the Narrative and Report modes.[8]

---

8. Rules for calculating narrative progression in the DR Theory framework are proposed in Kamp & Reyle (1993); they are somewhat different in detail from the rules given here.

Description is temporally located but static. Text progression is spatial, following through the scene described. Changes in space are inferred from the lexical information in a passage, supplemented with world knowledge and inference. The static nature of descriptive passages can be accounted for in the DRS, but spatial information is difficult to state in construction rules. The reason for the difference is that spatial information is conveyed lexically, rather than by terms of a closed system (Chapter 5).

In the atemporal modes, text progression is due to changes in the metaphorical location of Primary Referents. Primary Referents can be identified with the Theme/Patient argument in a clause; I will assume that such information is coded and available in surface syntactic structure. Information about Primary Referents is interpreted by construction rule and entered into the DRS. However, determining metaphorical motion depends on pragmatic knowledge, lexical rather than grammatical information. This kind of interpretation cannot be made in the formal theory.

Surface structure presentation involves subjectivity and topic–focus information. Perhaps surprisingly, the forms that convey subjectivity are amenable to a Discourse Representation Theory treatment. I provide formal rules that recognize subjective forms in texts and ascribe responsibility for them to the correct source. The rules are stated for grammatical forms and verb classes that trigger interpretations of subjectivity; see Chapter 7.

Sentence topic and focus, the other surface presentational factors considered here, are problematic for construction rules. I suggest that presentational text progression depends on sentence topics. The principles for identifying the topic of a sentence are almost entirely pragmatic and are difficult to formalize. I do not provide construction rules for topic phrases. These matters are discussed in Chapters 8 and 9.

3.4.2   *Discourse Representation construction rules and structures*
I now give some construction rules and representations of Discourse Representation Theory. They introduce aspects of the theory that will be important in the later discussion. The detailed analysis of Discourse Modes and presentational structure will be developed in later sections of this book.

The theory determines the meaning of a sentence by rule from its morphemes and surface syntactic structure. I assume a phrase structure syntax with generative rules. The surface structures are organized on X-bar theory lines. Inflectional Phrase (IP) is the maximal projection for the sentences in this book. Tense is treated as the realization of I in IP. I use the functional projection Aspect Phrase (AspP) for the simple and progressive verb forms. The subject of a verb is directly dominated by IP; the direct object appears in the Verbphrase (VP) as sister to the verb. For simplicity, I ignore higher projections and other projections that might appear in a more complete structure.

The construction rules of the theory interpret the information in surface syntactic structure and in the already-constructed DRS. Complex structures and dependencies are modeled with sub-structures that are within the scope of operators such as negation, quantifiers, modal subordination. The theory has had notable successes in analyzing referential, scopal, and other phenomena. For detailed accounts see the references in the text.

Rules of the theory applies to hierarchical surface structures with syntactic–semantic features. The structures do not otherwise encode semantic information: there is no level of Logical Form nor an associated semantic structure.[9] The syntactic–semantic features are stated on the relevant syntactic node and percolate to higher nodes in the syntactic tree. The features that I will use in this introduction are NP number, gender, and case; verb class; aspectual viewpoint associated with the simple verb form or the progressive; times and their relations associated with tense morphemes. In discussions later other features are used.

The rules account for the conventional meanings conveyed by a sentence, abstracting away from lexical semantics. Structural constraints on interpretation are modeled in a Discourse Representation Structure with embedded sub-structures. Material within an embedded structure may not be accessible as antecedent for anaphoric expressions.

As an introductory example, I show how entities for individuals and situations are represented for a discourse fragment, following the treatment of Kamp & Reyle (1993). I then add tense and aspectual information. Consider (4):

(4)   Mary read *Ulysses*. It fascinated her.

The figure in (5) gives a simplified syntactic tree representation of the first sentence of this fragment. In the figure, PN = proper name; ∅ = zero, associated

---

9. Logical Form is a semantic level in Principles and Parameters theory and related theories; it is irrelevant to DR Theory, which provides semantic interpretation.

    Syntactic surface structures developed in other syntactic frameworks are also appropriate for the construction rules of DR Theory. Kamp & Reyle (1993) use the syntactic framework and representations of Gazdar *et al.* (1985). The framework is convenient because it is explicit and has a carefully worked out way of dealing with syntactic–semantic features.

in the tree below with the perfective viewpoint; the E subscript on the verb is a feature classifying it as an event verb.

(5)   Mary read *Ulysses.*

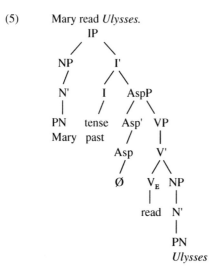

Construction of the DRS proceeds clause-by-clause; in the system of Kamp & Reyle (1993) each syntactic constituent within a clause is interpreted sequentially. The construction rules consist of a triggering configuration and a statement of operations on the DRS. After a constituent is analyzed that constituent is erased, so that when a sentence is fully interpreted only the DRS version of it remains. Entities are introduced into the universe of discourse at the top of the DRS, and conditions are given beneath them in the representation.

In the tree for "Mary read *Ulysses*" the first constituent below the IP-node is NP, the sister of "I"; this is the canonical position for the subject of a sentence. The discourse referent x is introduced for *Mary,* a proper name, with a condition that identifies x as "Mary." The construction rule is sketched in (6). The triggering configurations are given in (6a), the operations in (6b). GEN = gender, a feature on the NP node.

(6)   Construction Rule for Proper Names

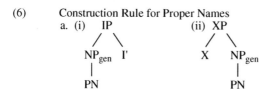

b. (i) Introduce a new discourse referent into the universe of discourse.

    (ii) Introduce a condition placing the discourse referent in parentheses behind the proper name which the PN dominates in the triggering configuration.

    (iii) Replace, in the relevant syntactic structure, the NP-constituent with the new discourse referent.

For the sentence structure in (5) the rule applies first to the configuration in (6ai). The third condition of (b) results in an intermediate structure "x read *Ulysses*," not given here.

The next constituent considered here is the VP; I return to the other nodes later in dealing with aspect and tense information. Rule (6aii) applies to the VP configuration, licensing the entity *y* as *Ulysses* ("reads y"). The highest NP and the VP together license a situation entity *e* and a condition that characterizes it; and the syntactic structure is deleted. The complete rule is not given here; see Kamp & Reyle (1993) for details.

The resulting partial DRS is given in (7): *e* introduces the event of Mary's reading. The information in the DRS consists of the discourse entities, listed at the top, and the conditions, displayed below.

(7)   Partial DRS for "Mary read *Ulysses*."

x y e
1. x = Mary
2. y = Ulysses
3. e: read (x,y)

The figure in (7) follows the standard format for DRSs: a two-tiered box that encloses the entire structure; embedded structures are represented by sub-DRSs, which have the form of embedded boxes.

The tree structure for the second sentence of fragment (4), *It fascinated her*, is like the first except that the NPs are pronouns. For each pronoun, a new discourse referent is entered into the top part of the DRS, together with conditions that identify it. Pronouns may be interpreted as coreferential with an antecedent discourse referent if they agree in gender and number. I assume that the construction rules include a mechanism for agreement. In (8), there is a partial DRS for both sentences of (4); lines 4 and 5 provide that the pronouns are coreferential with their antecedents, the discourse referents *x* and *y*. The entity at the top is *s*, the situation of Mary's being fascinated by *Ulysses*, a state.

(8)   Partial DRS for "Mary read *Ulysses*. It fascinated her."

x y u v e s
1. x = Mary
2. y = Ulysses
3. e: = read (x,y)
4. u = y
5. v = x
6. s: fascinates (u,v)

In (8) the antecedents of the pronouns are available for coreference and there are no other possibilities, so that the DRS identification is licensed.

In some cases the structure of the DRS makes an NP inaccessible as an antecedent for coreference. When an NP is within the scope of a general quantifier or negation, for instance, it cannot serve as antecedent to a pronoun. For instance, the sequence "John doesn't own a car. It is red" is ill formed because the NP *a car* is in the scope of negation and cannot function as an antecedent for the pronoun *it*. The sequence "The elephant is a gentle beast. He is running away from danger" is ill formed for similar reasons. The first sentence is generic, while the second expresses a specific event and the pronoun refers to a specific elephant. This kind of inaccessibility is represented in a DRS with embedded structures. NPs are discussed more fully in Part II; the DRT treatment of coreference is discussed in Kamp & Reyle (1993).

The rules can also be stated with labeled bracketing. The rules can "see" the relevant configuration, as well as features on NPs, verbs, etc. These features are needed anyway in a grammar of the language. Example (9), for instance, gives a labeled bracket version of the rule above.

(9)   DRS Construction Rules for Proper Names
       a. $_{IP}[_{NP}[_{PN}[\ldots]] _{I'}[a\ b]] \rightarrow x = \ldots$
       b. $_{IP}[NP _{I'}[a _{VP}[V _{NP}[_{PN}[\ldots]]] b]] \rightarrow y = \ldots$

The structural description appears on the left side of the arrow; it corresponds to the tree structure in (6). Here only the information relevant to a particular rule is given; variables *a, b* represent other material in the sentence. The rule specifies the relevant phrase structure nodes and, for the NPs in question, the PN feature; the dots represent the actual proper names. On the right side of the arrow is the interpretation, in this case entities *x* and *y* to be entered into the DRS with the proper name as specifying condition. Rule (a) recognizes the subject of a sentence, corresponding to the configuration in (6ai) above. Rule

(b) recognizes the direct object; it corresponds to (6aii) above, though it is more specific. For the fragment in (7), the dots in rule (9a) represent the proper name *Mary*; the dots in rule (9b) represent *Ulysses*. The rules in (9) result in the same DRS as those of (6). I will use rules like (9) throughout the book.

Now we add rules that interpret the aspectual and temporal information of fragment (4), repeated here:

(4)   Mary read *Ulysses*. It fascinated her.

Aspectual information gives the class of the situation entity and the aspectual viewpoint. The sentence "Mary read *Ulysses*" licenses an Event entity in the DRS, because of the E feature on the verb and the proper names in subject and object position; see Chapter 4 for discussion. The E feature on the verb is visible to the rule, as in (10):

(10)   Preliminary construction rule for an Event entity
         $_{IP}[_{NP}]\ _{I'}[a\ _{VP}[V_E\ _{NP}[[PN]]\ b]]] \rightarrow e = $ Event

This rule adds the entity *e* at the top of the DRS and a condition which specifies that the entity *e* is an Event, perhaps of a certain class.

The aspectual viewpoint of the sentence is perfective, because it has the simple verb form rather than the progressive auxiliary. Example (11) indicates very roughly how this interpretation is made. The rule focuses on the simple verb form and the Event verb; it licenses a viewpoint condition in the DRS.

(11)   Preliminary viewpoint rule
         $_{IP}[NP]\ _{I'}[a\ [_{AuxP}[\emptyset]\ VP_E]]\ b]] \rightarrow $ View $= $ Perfective

A more detailed account appears in Chapter 4.

The temporal information in "Mary read *Ulysses*" comes from the past tense morpheme on the verb. The past tense indicates that the event occurred at a time prior to the moment of speech, or Speech Time. This information is given in terms of two times in the DRS, t1 and t2, with t2 prior to t1. The event entity and the viewpoint are located at t2 in this preliminary version of tense interpretation; three times are specified in a more complete account, given in Chapter 5. The left side of the rule specifies that the past tense occurs on the main verb, ignoring the possibility of time adverbials. The past tense licenses the times and conditions as given on the right side; *e* indicates a situation entity, event, or state.

(12)   Preliminary tense interpretation rule
         $_{IP}[[NP]\ _{I'}[_{Tns}[past]\ a\ VP\ b]] \rightarrow $ t1 $= $ SpT; t2$<$t1; e, View at t2

The rules (10–12) add more information to the DRS, as shown in (13). Discourse entities for times are added at the top, t1 and t2. Line 4 specifies that the situation entity is an event, line 5 specifies that the viewpoint is perfective; the next two lines characterize the times, and line 8 locates the event entity at t2.

(13)   Partial DRS for "Mary read *Ulysses*."

x y e t1 t2
1. x = Mary
2. y = Ulysses
3. e: read (x,y)
4. e = Event
5. View(e) = Perf
6. t1 = SpT
7. t2 < t1
8. e at t2

This preliminary account is developed further in Part II.

In actual discourse little is sealed off as semantic, as I note at the beginning of this chapter. Even at the level of reference, semantic information must usually be supplemented by pragmatic inference. The construction rules of DRT cannot choose between possible antecedents of a pronoun, nor arrive at other interpretations based on inference and world knowledge. The simplicity of the examples used here masks this important point. However, it is equally important that structural information excludes certain possibilities.

II Linguistic analysis of the Discourse Modes

4 Aspectual information: the entities introduced in discourse

The Discourse Modes introduce situation entities into the universe of discourse, and have different principles of text progression. The information is conveyed by forms of aspect and temporal location. The two are complementary. Temporal location locates a situation in time, while aspect specifies the internal temporal structure of the situation. This chapter is devoted to aspect; temporal location is discussed in Chapter 5.

The understanding of aspect is the key to the analysis of Discourse Modes, because the situation entities are aspectual in nature. The Discourse Modes characteristically introduce different types of situation entities. Passages of the Narrative and Report modes primarily involve Events and States. The Description mode primarily concerns States and ongoing Events. The Information mode primarily has General Statives; the Argument mode primarily has Abstract Entities, Facts and Propositions, and General Statives. After a brief introduction to aspectual systems, this chapter discusses the concepts of situation entities and their linguistic correlates, and how aspectual information is encoded in Discourse Representation Theory.

Section 4.1 introduces the two components of aspectual systems and discusses Event and State situation types, including shifts of one type to another; 4.2 discusses General Statives; 4.3 discusses Abstract Entities; 4.4 discusses the linguistic correlates for the three major classes of situation type; 4.5 covers aspectual information in Discourse Representation Structures.

4.1   Aspectual categories

4.1.1   The two components of aspectual systems
Aspect is a sub-system of language that conveys information about the internal temporal structure of situations. Aspectual systems have two components, situation type and viewpoint (Smith 1991). The components interact in sentences.[1]

---

1. The two-component theory of aspect is presented in Smith (1997).

Both are relevant to the Discourse Modes. Situation entities realize different situation types, while viewpoints focus all or part of a situation. Together they determine the boundedness of situations, which is essential for temporal progression in the Narrative mode. Situation type indirectly classifies situations into the major categories of Event and State situations, statives, and Abstract Entities. In previous work I have used the term "situation type" for situations and General Statives. I now extend it to include abstract entities as a separate class.

Situation types are idealizations of situations, semantic concepts organized according to their internal temporal properties. They are conveyed by the composite of the verb and its arguments, the "verb constellation." Verb constellations of each class have distinctive distributional properties. Because of these properties, the situation types are covert linguistic categories which are tacitly available to the speakers of a language.

The aspectual viewpoint of a sentence is like the lens of a camera. It focuses on all or part of the situation expressed by a sentence, making the focused information visible. Only visible information is available for semantic interpretation. Viewpoint is important for calculating advancement in the temporal Discourse Modes, because it is one of the factors that determines whether a situation is bounded or unbounded.

Viewpoint and situation type constitute closed "closed systems," within which a choice must be made from a few possibilities. There are two main viewpoints in English, marked morphologically as in most languages. The simple verb form is "perfective," focusing events with bounds ("Mary made a desk"). States are unbounded in the perfective, however ("John knew the answer"). The progressive verbal auxiliary is an "imperfective": it applies only to events.[2] The progressive focuses an open interval, without endpoints: an internal interval of a durative event ("We are building a sandcastle") or a preliminary interval of an instantaneous event ("He is winning the race"). Both are taken as ongoing events. Progressive viewpoints appear in many languages. Other imperfective viewpoints, for instance the French *imparfait*, apply to states as well as events.

The information given by a viewpoint depends on the type of situation entity it focuses. Each class of verb constellation and aspectual viewpoint has an associated temporal schema, and viewpoints focus all or part of the temporal schema. The relationship between situation type and viewpoint is modeled by a

---

2. There is a marked use of the progressive with stative verb constellations, often found in informal speech, e.g. "I'm loving this walk." Such sentences present states as events (Smith 1997).

composite of the schema of each component. The aspectual viewpoint schema focuses all or part of the situation type schema. What follows is a brief account that deals mainly with material relevant to the Discourse Modes; for detailed discussion see Smith (1997).

4.1.2   The Event and State situation types
Classifying situations by temporal properties has a long tradition, starting as we know it with Aristotle, who recognized the distinction between static and dynamic situations. Vendler (1957) and others developed a finer classification of States and types of Events, using three temporal properties. Events and States are typically found in passages of the temporal discourse modes – Narrative, Report, and Description.

Three two-valued temporal features hold of Events and States: dynamic–static, telic–atelic, durative–instantaneous. The feature dynamic–static is most far-reaching, distinguishing states from events. Events take place in time, due to their dynamism; states are specific situations that hold in time. Dynamic situations occur at successive stages. Every stage of an event takes time, and thus involves change of some kind. Instantaneous events consist of a single stage, a point in principle; events with duration have endpoints, changes to and from a state of rest. Telicity involves endpoints: telic events have a goal or natural final endpoint (e.g. *walk to school*). Atelic events have arbitrary endpoints: they can end at any time (e.g. *walk in the park*). In contrast, states are static, consisting of an undifferentiated interval with no structure (e.g. *own the farm, know the answer*).

Clusters of these features distinguish five situation types: States and four types of Events – Activities, Accomplishments, Semelfactives, and Achievements. The types are like Vendler's except that I add the category of Semelfactive, instantaneous atelic events. Semelfactives are sometimes treated as a subtype of Achievements. Semelfactives are a separate class because they have distinctive linguistic properties (Smith 1997).

(1)   Situation types:
       Events: dynamic
            Activities: atelic, durative (*laugh, push a cart, stroll in the park*)
            Accomplishments: telic, durative (*build a house, walk to school, learn Greek*)
            Semelfactives: atelic, instantaneous (*tap, knock, flap a wing*)
            Achievements: telic, instantaneous (*win the race, reach the top*)
            States: static
            States: durative (*know the answer, love Mary, be sick, be in the room*)

Associated with each situation type is a schema that represents its temporal properties. The temporal schema of Events includes either a single point or an initial and final point, depending on the feature of duration. The final endpoint is natural or arbitrary, depending on telicity. The schema for a State does not have endpoints: changes into and out of a state are events in their own right and not part of the state. For simplicity I will sometimes call a verb constellation or sentence by the situation type or temporal feature with which it is associated – for instance, an "event" or "dynamic" sentence.

4.1.3   *Viewpoint and situation type*
In an aspectual system, aspectual viewpoint interacts with situation type, determining the information conveyed by a sentence about the situation expressed. The examples in (2) illustrate two expressions of a dynamic, durative Event with natural endpoints (an Accomplishment). Example (2a) has the progressive viewpoint, (2b) has the perfective. Line (i) of each example gives the situation type schema: I and F_{nat} represent initial and final endpoints, the dots represent internal stages. Line (ii) gives the viewpoint schema, with dots representing the span of the viewpoint. In the composite schema of line (iii), slashes indicate the span focused by the viewpoint.

(2)   a. Informal temporal schema for *They were building a sandcastle*
          i. [They build a sandcastle]   I . . . . . F_{nat} (Event)
         ii. [be+ing]   . . .   (progressive)
        iii. They were building a sandcastle   I. . . . . . F_{nat}
                                                 ////   (composite)
        b. Informal temporal schema for *They built a sandcastle*
          i. [They build a sandcastle]   I . . . . . F_{nat} (Event)
         ii. [Ø]   . . . .   (perfective)
        iii. They built a sandcastle   I. . . . . . F_{nat}
                                                 ////////////   (composite)

The visible span of the viewpoint inherits the properties of the entire situation schema.[3] This correctly provides that we know the situation type of a sentence, independent of whether the viewpoint makes visible all or part of the situation.

---

3. For Activities the precise statement is more complex. Activities are focused by the perfective viewpoint with implicit temporal bounds which may, but need not, coincide with their endpoints. In other words, the temporal boundedness of the viewpoint does not require that an activity terminate.

   The perfective viewpoint focuses a segment that is implicitly bounded. If the activity continues after the implicit bound, the continuation constitutes another temporal segment. The point is delicate but important for understanding the contribution of Activities to discourse. Assertions of continuation may felicitously be made, as in the examples below. The second conjunct of

The schemata illustrate the effects of viewpoint. Perfective event sentences focus Events as bounded, discrete entities, while progressive, imperfective event sentences focus events as unbounded. The distinction between bounded and unbounded situations is important for narrative advancement. Telic events have intrinsic bounds bounds for a situation may also be given with explicit information. Imperfective events and non-dynamic situations are all unbounded, and have certain properties in common.[4] Entities that are static include States, General Statives, and Abstract Entities. Recall their effect in narrative: perfectives advance narrative time, progressives and states do not.

The interpretations are formalized in Discourse Representation Structures by introducing situation entities, temporal intervals, and conditions. The conditions specify the class of a situation entity according to the verb constellation that introduces it. The "visible" portion of the situation is conveyed according to the viewpoint and its interaction with the situation type.

4.1.4   Coercion

There is a standard, basic-level set of associations between situations in the world and idealized situation types. In choices that depart from the standard, the speaker uses derived situation types (Smith 1995a). They are shifted by rule from the basic-level types through a mechanism widely known as "coercion," a term due to Moens (1987). No additional situation types are needed to account for coercion: derived situation types fall into the same classes. Shifts in situation type are triggered by material in the context, often by adverbials. For instance, "Mary knew the truth" is a state sentence. With the adverbial *suddenly*, as in "Suddenly Mary knew the truth," the sentence expresses an event, that of Mary coming to know the truth. Another example is the perfect: in the perfect construction dynamic sentences shift to states, e.g. "We have (already) eaten

each sentence asserts that another segment, or temporal unit, follows the unit presented in the first conjunct (Smith 1999b).

    a. Mary worked and continued working without a break.
    b. Sam rehearsed and kept on rehearsing.
    c. Alice thought about the math problem while Chris drove her to the station, and she kept on thinking about it all morning.

4. States and other static situations are homogeneous, with a uniform part structure. They have the sub-interval property: when a state holds for an interval, it holds equally for any smaller interval of that interval. Progressives, too, have this property.

   In a view that I have characterized as the "strong mereological" approach, states, progressives and Activities all belong to the one global semantic category because of their homogeneity. For discussion see Smith (1999) and the references therein.

dinner."[5] Derived situation types include the basic verb constellation and the triggering adverbial.

Adverbials of duration and completion can also trigger a shift in situation type. Telic verb constellations become atelic with a simple durative adverbial, as (3) shows:

(3)   a. Mary wrote a letter.
        b. Mary wrote a letter for an hour.

The understanding of (3a) is that Mary wrote and completed a letter; that of (3b) is that she was engaged in the activity of letter-writing, but that she did not actually complete a letter. The shift in understanding is due to the different aspectual values of the verb constellation and the adverbial: durative adverbials are atelic. Example (3) illustrates a consistent pattern in coercion. If there is a clash in value between the verb constellation and an adverbial or other form external to it, the external value overrides. This pattern is formalized in Section 4.4 as the Principle of External Override.

The progressive is often treated as an instance of coercion. In this approach the progressive is an operator that applies to events and produces states as a derived situation type (Vlach 1981, Kamp & Reyle 1993). The treatment has the advantage of formally unifying progressives and static situations. But there is a disadvantage: progressives are not entirely like states.[6] For discussion see Smith (1983, 1995b).

I now turn to the two other major classes of entities. They are all static in nature and thus form a super-class with States.

4.2   *General Statives*

General Statives are more abstract than the States considered above, because they do not express particular situations. There are two types, Generic and Generalizing sentences. Generic sentences hold of kinds; Generalizing sentences express a pattern of situations, a generalization or regularity. Example (4) illustrates, repeated from Chapter 2:

5. The "perfect" construction is formed with the verbal auxiliary *have* and a participle. In English there are past, present, and future perfects.

   Perfects are semantically states: one piece of evidence is that they do not advance narrative time. The perfect affects temporal location as well as aspect; see Comrie (1976), Kamp & Reyle (1993), Michaelis (1994).
6. The differences between them are significant: (a) progressives cannot be taken as inchoatives, whereas states can be; (b) progressives are dynamic, whereas states are not; (c) progressives and statives have different co-occurrence properties with adverbials as noted in Glasbey (1998).

(4)   Sentences expressing statives
        a Dinosaurs are now extinct.   Generic
        b The lion has a bushy tail.   Generic
        c Mary speaks French.   Generalizing
        d John always fed the cats last year. Generalizing

Sentences like these are studied in depth in the articles in Carlson & Pelletier (1995).

Generic sentences refer to kinds rather than individuals: in (4b) the subject NP denotes the entire class of lions, not a particular lion or lions. Definite NPs (*the lion*) and bare plurals (*lions*) are the main types of NP that are used as kind-referring. Indefinite NPs, both mass and count, can be used in a "taxonomic" reading, as in "The World Wildlife Organization decided to protect a (certain) large cat, namely the Siberian tiger," an example from Krifka *et al.* (1995).

Generalizing sentences express regularities, not particular facts. Such sentences often have a frequency adverbial (*sometimes*, *always*, *never*). There are a number of special forms which lead to the general reading, e.g. *used to*, the agentive *-er* suffix, the middle voice, present simple tense with an Event verb constellation. Kind-referring NPs can occur in a Generalizing sentence, as in "Potatoes are served whole or mashed as a cooked vegetable." The characterization and examples above are due primarily to Krifka *et al.* 1995; they use the term "characterizing" for the class that I call Generalizing sentences.[7]

Generic and Generalizing sentences are static: they have no dynamism. They are derived by coercion from verb constellations that express specific situations at the basic level of categorization. For instance, the verb, object argument, and adverbial of examples (3c, d) above – "speak French", "feed the cats" – standardly express specific events. In context with a definite NP subject, simple viewpoint, and present tense, however, they have the generalizing interpretation. Similarly, Generic sentences may have event verb constellations, as in "The lion eats meat." Verb constellations that express states at the basic level also appear in General Statives, as in "have a bushy tail."

---

7. Two additional properties of Generic sentences are noted by Krifka *et al.* (1995): Generic sentences with the indefinite article don't express accidental properties. For instance, "polyphonic" is an intrinsic property of "madrigals," but "popular" is an accidental one. The sentence "The madrigal is polyphonic" can be taken as generic or particular. But with the indefinite article, only the ascription of an intrinsic property is acceptable: "A madrigal is polyphonic" is fine, but #"A madrigal is popular" is odd. This is a slightly different version of the characterization by Krifka *et al.*

    Kind-denoting NPs in Generic sentences are only plausible with a nominal that refers to a well-established kind. Thus, "The Coke bottle has a narrow neck" is fine but #"The green bottle has a narrow neck" is odd (indicated by #), on the generic reading.

General Statives are spatiotemporally located in the world: they hold at particular intervals and places, though these coordinates may not be specified in a given sentence.

4.3   *Abstract Entities*

The class of Abstract Entities consists of Facts and Propositions. Conceptually, Facts and Propositions can be distinguished from other entities by the factors of spatiotemporal location and causality. Situations and General Statives are located in the world and have causal powers. Facts are not so located, yet they are contingent for truth on situations being a certain way and arguably have causal powers. Propositions are not located, are not contingent, and do not have causal powers. The linguistic and philosophical aspects of these entities are discussed in Vendler (1967, 1972), Asher (1993), Peterson (1997).

Facts are assessments that we make of states of affairs, abstract or concrete. Facts are not in the world; but they are about the world. They are expressed linguistically as clausal or deverbal arguments of certain predicates, e.g. *matter, amuse, explain, show, indicate* etc., as in these examples:

(5)   a. I know that the German war effort collapsed.
       b. The collapse of the Germans was surprising.

We point out a fact, regret or rejoice in a fact. If there is a dispute about a fact, one challenges by asking, "How do you know?" or "Why are you so sure?" These questions assume that the speaker is in a position to know, or have satisfactory reasons. Questions of fact are empirical questions, although facts are not part of the furniture of the world (Herbst 1956). Facts transcend the limitations of subjectivity: they are "objective," waiting to be discovered (Vendler 1972:82). The class of fact predicates includes mental event verbs (*forget, discover, realize*); emotives (*regret, resent, deplore*); evaluatives (*matter, be significant/important/odd/surprising/mysterious*); psychological verbs (*surprise, amuse, annoy*).

Propositions are the objects of such mental states as beliefs, expectations, and decisions. They are expressed by clausal and deverbal arguments of verbs of propositional attitude and other predicates.

(6)   a. I believe that Mary refused the offer.
       b. Mary's refusing the offer was unlikely.

Since propositions are the mental states of the particular individuals who hold them, they have subjective features. Propositions are referentially opaque: they do not accept substitution of a different expression with the same referent.

This property reveals their subjectivity (Vendler 1972:81). In contrast, facts allow such substitution. The class of propositional predicates includes mental verbs (*believe, fear, hope*); verbs of communication (*say, tell, show, indicate, affirm, deny*); epistemic predicates and others (*seem, appear, be possible/likely/ unlikely/certain/true/consistent*); logical verbs (*entail, imply*).

Sentences that directly express Facts and Propositions cannot be distinguished on linguistic grounds, and so will not be discussed here.

4.4   Linguistic correlates of situation entities

Clauses expressing different types of entities have distinctive linguistic features, which can be used as tests to determine what type of entity is expressed in a given clause.

4.4.1   Situations: the temporal properties

The temporal features of the Event and State situation types have characteristic distributional properties.

The property of dynamism has a close association with the semantic feature of agency. Dynamic events may have agents as sources of energy and volition; States do not have agents, at least not directly. Reflecting this, linguistic forms which are associated with agency occur with event verb constellations but not with statives (Lee 1971, Ross 1972). Imperative sentences, and complements of verbs like *persuade, command*, require event verb constellations. Only an event that is controllable can be commanded or persuaded. For instance, it's natural to say "Wash your car!" or "I persuaded Mary to wash her car"; but odd to say #"Know Greek!" or #"I persuaded Mary to know Greek." Also related to agency are adverbs of manner and instrument.

Adverbs of intention and control are plausible with events, odd with states: compare "John carefully washed the car" and #"John carefully knew Greek." These correlates of agency are semantically based and hold across languages.

There are also two grammatical correlates of dynamism in English: the progressive viewpoint and the pro-verb *do* in the pseudo-cleft construction. Both require event verb constellations, as (7) shows (*indicates ill-formedness):

(7)   a John was washing the car.   (Event)
        b *Kim was knowing the answer.   (State)
        c What John did was wash the car.   (Event)
        d #What John did was know Greek.   (State)

In other constructions the pro-verb *do* appears with both event and state verb constellations. For instance, in verb-ellipsis constructions such as "John knows Greek and Mary does too," "do" is a pro-verb for the State "know Greek."

The interpretation of present-tense events is another correlate of dynamism. Events are taken as generalized, or habitual, in sentences with present tense and the perfective viewpoint. In contrast, similar sentences with state verb constellations express a particular state. The examples in (8) illustrate:

(8)   a Mary swims in the ocean.   (Event)
         b Ellen is in the room.   (State)

Sentence (8a) must be interpreted as generalizing, whereas (8b) expresses a State that holds at a particular time.

The generalizing interpretation of sentences like (8a) is due to a pragmatic constraint on bounded events that prevents them from being located in the Present. In the Present, events must be presented as ongoing, e.g. "John is talking," "Mary is drawing a circle." Event verb constellations are otherwise taken as conveying a general pattern, like "Tom (often) feeds the cat." This constraint, which I call the Bounded Event Constraint, is due to a principle of communication that holds in language generally: speakers follow the convention that communication is instantaneous. The perspective of the Present is incompatible with bounded events, because the bounds would go beyond that perspective; see Chapter 5 for discussion.

Together, these syntactic and semantic properties distinguish sentences with the temporal feature of dynamism, that is, event sentences. The linguistic correlates of telicity and duration do not pertain directly to the Discourse Modes and will not be discussed here.[8] State verb constellations, which are static, do not

---

8. Telicity is not expressed directly in language at the level of a general distributional property, although it is an important conceptual property of Events for human beings. There seem to be no linguistic correlates of it *per se*. The syntactic evidence for a telic Event turns on the notion of completion, which involves the interaction of duration and change of State.

   Verbs and adverbials of completion (*finish, in an hour*) contrast with verbs and adverbials of simple duration (*stop, for an hour*). Telic verb constellations are compatible with completion; in contrast they are odd with forms of simple duration, requiring a special derived interpretation. In contrast, atelic verb constellations are odd with forms of completion, as the examples illustrate:

   a Mary walked to school in an hour.   (telic)
   b Mary finished walking to school.   (telic)
   c ? Mary walked in the park in an hour.   (atelic)
   d ? Mary finished walking in the park.   (atelic)

   These contrasts are semantically based: the notion of completion is intrinsic to a telic Event, irrelevant to an atelic Event. Other tests for telicity involve verbs such as *stop, finish*, verbs of time *take* and *spend* with sentential complements. *Take* is compatible with telic verb constellations, *spend* with atelic verb constellations. The property of duration also has adverbial and verbal linguistic correlates; see Smith (1997).

appear in imperatives, as complements of *persuade*, with volitional and instrumental adverbs, with the progressive viewpoint, or in pseudo-cleft sentences. In present sentences with the simple, perfective verb form they have a specific interpretation.

Verb constellations of the different types are composed and interpreted by rules. The rules are sensitive to features of the verb and its arguments, and to adverbials. These matters are discussed in 4.5, where some compositional rules are presented.

4.4.2   The linguistic correlates of General Statives

Generic and Generalizing sentences are not marked by particular morphemes nor by verb class. Nevertheless, there are a few distributional characteristics that distinguish them. I summarize them briefly.

Generic sentences: Kind-referring NPs appear in these sentences. If an NP is felicitous with predicates that refer only to kinds, such as *die out, be extinct, invent*, it can function as kind-referring. Definite NPs and bare plurals are most commonly used to refer to kinds, as in "The dinosaur is extinct," "Dinosaurs are extinct." Strikingly, indefinite NPs cannot appear as subjects of these predicates: "The lion / lions / will soon become extinct," but #"A lion will soon become extinct" is odd (Krifka *et al.* 1995:9–10).

Generalizing sentences: If a sentence has a frequency adverb such as *usually* or *typically*, or if such an adverb can be felicitously added to a sentence, the sentence is of the generalizing class. The progressive viewpoint in English is limited to dynamic situations; it typically excludes generalizing predicates too. This is not an absolute criterion: one can construct generalizing sentences with the progressive, e.g. "John is calling his sister more these days." Sentences like this often have an explicit or implicit contrast with a different state of affairs.

When set in the Present time, many Generalizing sentences can be recognized by a particular combination of aspectual and temporal factors. Such sentences have an event verb constellation, the perfective viewpoint (the simple verb form) and present tense, as in "Mary speaks French." The generalizing stative interpretation is due to the Bounded Event Constraint. This cue to Generalizing sentences does not apply to generalizations of states, which have basic state verb constellations ("Mary always likes Italians").

Although Generalizing sentences lack the dynamism of particular event sentences, they have some distributional properties of dynamism (Smith 1997). They can appear with forms associated with agency and control, and with pseudo-cleft *do*:

(9)   a. John deliberately plays tennis every Friday.
       b. I persuaded John to play tennis every Friday.
       c. What John did was to play tennis every Friday.

These distributional facts reflect the hybrid nature of Generalizing sentences.

Generalizing sentences are semantically stative. They tend to have dynamic verb constellations and they imply a series of sub-events which are dynamic.

4.4.3   The linguistic correlates of Abstract Entities

The linguistic properties of abstract entities are both semantic and distributional. Vendler was perhaps the first to notice the latter: he found distributional differences between sentences with argument complements that referred to Events and States, Facts, and Propositions (1967, 1972). The key factors are the form of the complement and the main predicate. Complements may take one of several forms in English. Substantives, or deverbal complements, have nominal properties. They appear with determiners, adjectives, and noun plurals, as in "John's clever analysis of the situation." Clausal *that*-complements are sentential, with full verb forms. Gerundives and infinitives are closer to the verbal end of the continuum, as shown by their ability to appear with adverbials, as in "John's cleverly analyzing the situation," "For John to fully understand the situation."[9] Clausal complements also appear after NPs such as *the fact that*, *the idea that*, *the proposition that*, etc.

There is a correlation between the form of a complement and its interpretation. Substantives are associated with situations and *that*-clauses and gerundive complements with Abstract Entities, Vendler showed. For instance, *take place* and *be slow* are situation predicates: both allow a substantive complement but not a gerundive or *that*-clause complement. In contrast the verb *know* is a fact predicate and allows only a *that*-complement. For the two fairly representative predicates, the pattern of grammaticality is this:

(10)   a. The collapse of the Germans occurred yesterday/was slow.
       b. *That the Germans collapsed was slow.
       c. *The Germans' collapsing was slow.

(11)   a. I know that the Germans collapsed.
       b. *I know the collapse of the Germans.
       c. *I know the Germans' collapsing.

---

9. The complement forms of English include the substantive with *-ing*, as in "The collapsing of the Germans," "John's cooking of the dinner," "Mary's analyzing of the situation." These forms have all the properties of substantives; they are not preferred when a morphological substantive is available such as *collapse, analysis*.

The complement of (10a) refers to an Event, that of (11a) refers to a Fact. Thus in the clearest cases complement form and predicate classes together fall into distinct distributional patterns.

However, other patterns are less clear. Certain verbs and predicates are flexible, allowing several kinds of complement. Among the flexible classes are epistemic predicates such as *be unlikely* and psychological verbs such as *surprise, horrify*. The complements of such predicates may be a substantive, gerundive, or a *that*-clause:

(12)   a. The collapse of the Germans was unlikely.
           b. The Germans' collapsing was unlikely.
           c. That the Germans collapsed was unlikely.

(13)   a. The enemy's destruction of the city horrified us.
           b. The enemy's destroying the city horrified us.
           c. That the enemy destroyed the city horrified us.

These sentences are acceptable as paraphrases, as Vendler noted. However, psychological predicates with a substantive may be ambiguous between an Event or fact interpretation. For instance, the clausal subject of "John's singing of the Marseillaise surprised me" may be interpreted either way.

The distributional facts suggest that we must recognize predicates that are clearly eventive, factive, or propositional; and predicates that are flexible. For the latter classes, certain complement types are indeterminate.

To assess the interpretation of a complement, two paraphrase or substitution tests are offered by Peterson (1997). The first test substitutes *That S* for a clausal complement, while the second substitutes an indirect question for a clausal complement. The question is whether the substitutions preserve grammaticality. Together, the two tests distinguish clausal complements that refer to Facts, Propositions, and situations. A clausal complement refers to a Fact if both substitution tests preserve grammaticality, as in (14):

(14)   a. Mary's having refused the offer was significant.
           b. That Mary refused the offer was significant.
           c. What Mary refused was significant.

A clausal complement refers to a Proposition if the first substitution test preserves grammaticality and the second does not, as in (15):

(15)   a. Mary's having refused the offer was inconsistent.
           b. That Mary refused the offer was inconsistent.
           c. *What Mary refused was inconsistent.

A clausal complement refers to an Event or State if both of the substitution tests destroy grammaticality:

(16)   a. Mary's having refused / refusal of the offer was followed by silence.
        b. *That Mary refused the offer was followed by silence.
        c. *What Mary refused was followed by silence.

These tests are quite effective. Peterson found that essentially the same properties support the distinction in such varied languages as Arabic, English, French, German, Hebrew, Hindi, Kannada, and Marathi. On the basis of this data, Peterson (1997) argues that the categories are universally linguistic as well as conceptual.

There are some difficulties in actually applying the tests because not all sentences have the form stipulated. It is often necessary to "normalize" a sentence, to construct a version of the sentence which fits the substitution template.[10] Normalization can be unreliable. Moreover, it's not always clear when a complex nominal has an underlying clausal structure and when it is just what it seems to be, a nominal. Abstract nouns, for instance, are arguably often propositional. In many cases they seem intuitively to involve a proposition, and they occur with predicates that allow sentential complements.

When are we justified in substituting a clause for an abstract noun or complex nominal? In some cases the substitution requires little change, in other cases several are needed, changes that are on the borderline toward reinterpretation. The examples of (17) illustrate with sentences from texts in this study. They require increasingly drastic changes in complement form to arrive at a normalization.

(17)   a   The routine transfer of power may not be the most dramatic feature of American democracy, but it is the most important.
        a' (The fact) that power is routinely transferred may not be the most dramatic feature of American democracy, but it is the most important.
        b   The national outpouring after the Littleton shootings has forced us to confront something we have suspected for a long time: the American high school is obsolete and should be abolished.
        b' (The fact) that there was a national outpouring after the Littleton shootings has forced us to confront something we have suspected for a long time: the American high school is obsolete and should be abolished.
        c   But it was the $10 or $11 price of February 1999, not the one today, that really deserved the headlines.

10. The process that I refer to as "normalization" is called "De-vendlerization" by Peterson (1997:75). Vendlerization is a "pseudotransformation" deriving a nominal sentence via transformation from underlying full sentence structure. De-vendlerization is the reverse, a procedure for obtaining the underlying structure.

c' The $10 or $11 price of February 1999, not the one today, really deserved the headlines.

c" But that the price was $10 or $11 in February 1999, rather than the one today, really deserved the headlines.

In (17a, b) normalization turns the subject nominals into verbal clauses. For (17c), however, more changes are needed. The original is a cleft sentence. The restatement of (17c') removes the cleft, and (17c") gives a *that*-clause version which is arguably the same semantically as (17c). Normalizations like this are often necessary for carrying out the tests proposed by Peterson. Sentence (17c) illustrates the kind of problem that can arise when trying to produce sentences of the right form for the substitution tests. One must decide when the transformation results in a sentence that is appropriately close to the original sentence, and when the result is too far from the original.

Moreover, some classes of predicates don't give the right results with these tests, as Peterson himself points out. The troublesome classes include verbs of communication and conjecture (e.g. *tell, say, show, indicate, guess, predict, estimate*), which are ambiguous between Fact and Proposition readings but permit indirect question substitution. The substitution test predicts that propositional complements exclude the substitution of indirect questions, as in (15) above. Emotive verbs such as *regret, resent, deplore* are also counter-examples: they don't take indirect questions (*"I resent who won the race"), but are expected to do so since semantically their complements denote facts.[11]

Nevertheless the substitution tests are useful and I will assume that, together with distributional classes of predicates, they can usually distinguish complements referring to Facts and Propositions.

There is also a quantification test that distinguishes between types of entities. Asher shows that quantifiers such as *everything, something*, can be used in sentences that express entities of the same class. But they are odd if the entities are of different classes (1993:33). Consider (18):

(18)   a. Everything that happened took an hour.
       b. Everything that John believes is true.
       c. #Nothing John believes takes an hour.

Example (18a) involves Events, and the sentence is good: the main clause expresses an Event and the complement clause refers to Events. Similarly, (18b) expresses and refers to Propositions. But (18c) is odd, even uninterpretable,

11. These verbs are known as "factive" verbs. They presuppose the truth of their complements. Thus, the truth-conditional status of the complement remains under question and negation, e.g. "Did you resent John's winning the race?" "I don't resent John's winning the race." Peterson extends the term "factive" to include a wider range of Abstract Entity complements.

because it expresses an Event and refers to a belief. The belief context and temporal location context are not satisfied by the same kind of entity.

4.5   *Aspectual information in Discourse Representation Structures*

The key to the Discourse Modes is the type of entity introduced in the clauses of a text passage. In the structures of Discourse Representation Theory, situations (Events and States), General Statives, and Abstract Entities are represented as discourse entities of situations, with conditions that characterize them. Discourse entities can be referred to, hence they are also known as discourse referents (Karttunen 1976). The aspectual meaning of a sentence is represented in a Discourse Representation Structure with situation entities, times, and characterizing conditions.

Every clause introduces a situation entity into the developing DRS. Information in the clause licenses a condition giving the situation type of the entity. I will use [e], [s], and [a] for the classes of situation, general stative, and abstract entity respectively. Situation type is determined by compositional rules which take as input the surface structure of a sentence, and produce as output a situation entity of a given situation type; examples will be given directly. The temporal properties of the situation types appear in the DRS as intensional conditions on a situation entity. The properties have a procedural force in sentence interpretation. For instance, if a situation has the property [Telic], the final endpoint made visible by the perfective viewpoint is natural rather than arbitrary. If a situation has the property [Instantaneous] only a single point is focused by the perfective.

Aspectual viewpoint makes visible information about a situation, and may add conceptual meaning; for instance, the progressive has a dynamic sense (Smith 1997). Viewpoint is independent of situation type.[12] To represent this independence, an interval [I], and times [ti, j], are introduced into a DRS with each clause. The interval is the locus for viewpoint information. Information

---

12. This independence is one of the basic ideas of the two-component theory. One argument for it is that the span of a viewpoint does not necessarily coincide with the span of a situation type. For instance, the progressive of an instantaneous Event focuses a preliminary interval that is not part of the Event itself: "He was reaching the top". There are additional viewpoints in other language that have similar properties.

   Another argument is that the viewpoint of a sentence does not obscure its situation type. The situation type of a sentence is available to the receiver whatever its viewpoint. Consider a sentence with the progressive viewpoint "Jane was walking to school." Receivers of this sentence know that only part of the Event is visible, and what sort of Event it is. They know the nature of the final endpoint, although it is not semantically visible and may not occur.

made semantically visible by the viewpoint appears in the DRS as conditions on the interval [I], given in terms of times and the endpoints or internal stages of [e].

4.5.1   *Interpreting situation type*

The situation type of a sentence is determined by the verb and its arguments, the verb constellation. For instance, "John walked to school" expresses a telic event, whereas "John walked in the park" expresses an atelic one. The difference is in the prepositional phrase (PP) complement. The complement is directional in the first case and locational in the second. In other cases the subject or object NP affects situation type: "Mary drank a glass of wine" is telic, "Mary drank wine" is atelic, since no amount of wine is specified. In cases of coercion, adverbials or other forms outside the verb constellation determine the derived situation type. These points are uncontroversial (Verkuyl 1972, Smith 1997).

Compositional rules provide a natural mechanism for interpreting situation type. The important notion is interpretation. By computing the aspectual value of the verb and its arguments, the rules arrive at the situation type of a sentence. They depend on a prior assignment of aspectual values to the constituents of the constellation. The process of determining the aspectual meaning of a sentence or clause involves three stages:

A.   The surface structure representation of a sentence is scanned for the features of the verb constellation, the temporal adverbials, and the viewpoint. The aspectual features of the constituents are assigned in the lexicon. The features relevant to aspectual value include whether or not an NP argument is quantized; whether the verb alone is telic or atelic; the value of complement PPs (locative, directional, etc.) and adverbials.

B.   Compositional rules compute the situation type of the verb constellation and the relevant temporal adverbials, if any. These rules take as input the surface structure of a sentence and produce aspectual information as output. Their output is a situation discourse entity and a condition that identifies it as a situation, General Stative, or Abstract Entity.

C.   The aspectual meanings are stated in the DRS. Situation type information occurs in the DRS in the form of conditions on the situation entity introduced with every clause. In the case of derived rather than basic-level categorization, both levels are preserved by the rules.

Verbs are assigned intrinsic aspectual features in the lexicon. The intrinsic value of a verb is determined by its value in a simple verb constellation with obligatory arguments. Simple constellations have the minimum number of countable arguments that a verb allows. For instance, the verb *walk* may appear in intransitive atelic sentences such as "Mary walked," and in telic sentences such as "Mary walked to school." Since it is atelic and durative in the simpler constellation, *walk* is assigned the intrinsic features [Atelic] and [Dur].

The essential aspectual feature of NP arguments is whether they are countable or uncountable. Proper names are countable; pronouns depend on their antecedents. Common noun NPs are countable when they appear with determiners forming a specific or definite NP, e.g. *an apple, those apples, 3 apples.*

Common nouns are either count or mass. For instance *red* and *flour* are mass nouns at the basic level, while *dog* and *apple* are count nouns at that level. Most nouns can appear as members of both categories. The notions of standard and marked choice are relevant to the multiple categorization in nouns, as they are for verb constellations. The analysis of *apple* as a mass noun and *flour* as a count noun is similar to that of the shifted and derived categories of verb constellations.

As an introductory example, consider the compositional analysis of an Event sentence that expresses an Activity. In (10), line (i) gives the sentence, line (ii) its surface structure feature analysis, and line (iii) the compositional rule. The rule registers the verb features [Atelic, Durative] and the compatible feature of the complement. VCon = verb constellation; NP = NounPhrase, V = Verb, PP = prepositional phrase, Loc = location, Dir = directional.

(19)   i Mary strolled in the park
       ii $_{VCON}$[[NP] $_{VP}$[$_V$[stroll] $_{PP}$[in the park]]]
       iii $_{VCON}$[NP[+Count] $_V$[Atelic, Durative] $_{PP}$[Loc]] $\rightarrow$ $_{VCON}$[$_e$[Activity]]

The output of the rule is a situation entity of the Activity type, as indicated on line (iii). The term [Activity] represents the complex of temporal features – [Dynamic], [Atelic], [Durative] – that characterize the Activity situation type.

I give below a few compositional rules that are slightly more general. They interpret the situation type of a clause by composing the aspectual feature values of its constituents. The rules specify only relevant parts of the sentence. For instance, rule A below composes a simple Activity verb constellation with an atelic verb and a subject or other argument. Sentences with such verbs are atelic whether or not the subject NP is quantized: "Susan laughed" and "People laughed" are both atelic. Therefore the rule does not specify a feature for the subject NP. The feature of the object NP is slightly more complex, due to the variation that exists among verbs, but I shall ignore the problem here. Examples indicate the type of case covered by each rule. Abbreviations: Ct = count, NCt = non-count, Prt = particle, Adv = adverbial, PP = prepositional phrase, Tel = telic, Atel = atelic, Dur = durative, Cmp = completive, ( ) = an optional constituent.

Activity:

A. Atelic verb and compatible (atelic) complement:[13]

[Susan laugh] [Susan push a cart] [Susan stroll in the park]
$_{VCON}$[[NP] $_V$[Atel, Dur] ([NP]) ($_{PP}$[Loc]) ($_{Adv}$[Dur])] → $_{VCON}$[$_e$[Activity]]

B. Telic verb and atelic particle:

[Peter read in *War and Peace*] [Susan work on the report]
$_{VCON}$[[NP] $_V$[Tel, Dur] $_{Prt}$[Atel] NP ($_{PP}$[Loc]) ($_{Adv}$[Dur])] → $_{VCON}$[$_e$[Activity]]

C. Telic verb and uncountable argument:

[Peter eat apples] [Guests visit that clinic]
$_{VCON}$[[NP] $_V$[Tel, Dur] ($_{NP}$[NCt]) ($_{PP}$[Loc]) ($_{Adv}$[Dur])] → $_{VCON}$[$_e$[Activity]]

Accomplishment:

D. Telic verb and countable argument:

[Mary build a sandcastle (in an hour)] [John arise]
$_{VCON}$[$_{NP}$[Ct] $_V$[Tel, Dur] ($_{NP}$[Ct]) ($_{Adv}$[Cmp])] → $_{VCON}$: [$_e$[Accomplishment]]

E. Atelic verb and directional complement:

[They walk to school (in an hour)]
$_{VCON}$[[NP] $_V$[Atel, Dur] ($_{NP}$[Ct]) $_{PP}$[Dir] ($_{Adv}$[Cmp])] →
$_{VCON}$[$_e$[Accomplishment]]

The feature stated in this output is entered as a condition on the entity [e] in the DRS (recall that "Accomplishment" and other situation type labels are shorthand for clusters of features).[14]

Derived situation types are also interpreted by compositional rule. Recall that they are triggered by adverbials or other information in the context. The output

13. There is some variation among atelic verbs. The transitive verb in this example, *push*, allows a specific NP – "Susan pushed a/the cart"; but other verbs become telic with a specific NP as direct object, for instance "walk," as in "Susan walked the dog."

14. The features characterize the situation entity by associating it with the class of Accomplishments. The account of situation types with compositional rules can be explicated in terms of semantic processes, as in Krifka (1989).

of the basic-level compositional rules, together with the feature values of the adverbial (or other form), provide the input to the derived-level rules.

The trigger for a shift in situation type is usually a clash between feature values. Typically the temporal feature of an adverbial clashes with the corresponding feature in the verb constellation, as in example (3b) ("Mary wrote a letter for an hour"). The verb *write* is telic with a quantized object. In this sentence the verb constellation has the aspectual feature [+Telic], while the adverb is a simple durative, with the aspectual feature [−Telic]. The adverb feature value determines the shifted interpretation by a general principle that I call the External Override Principle. The coercion rule for interpreting this sentence is sketched in (20). The verb constellation is already interpreted by a basic-level compositional rule as telic (only the relevant features are stated). The rule interprets the combination of the adverbial and verb constellation, with the output an atelic derived verb constellation (DVCON):

(20)   Coercion rule ("Mary wrote a letter for an hour")
        $s[\text{VCON} [_e[+\text{Telic}]] + {}_{Adv}[-\text{Telic}]] \rightarrow {}_{DVCON}[_e[\text{Activity}]]$

The rule shifts the telic verb constellation, an Accomplishment, to an atelic derived verb constellation, an Activity. The feature value of the adverbial overrides that of the basic-level verb constellation.

The Principle of External Override holds for many derived situation types. The principle can be stated as an alpha rule, sketched in (21). The input to the rule is a verb constellation with a situation type value, and an adverbial or other form. The situation type value is represented by a cluster of temporal features (a,b,f); feature f has a given value, symbolized as α. The adverbial also has feature f, but with the value β. The output of the rule is a derived verb constellation with the feature value of the adverbial:

(21)   Coercion: Alpha rule of External Override
        $\text{VCON}[a,b,f\alpha] + {}_{Adv}[f\beta] \rightarrow {}_{DVCON}[a,b,f\beta]$

The output of the rule is the derived situation type value, which will be entered in the DRS as a condition on the situation entity.

Information in the context of a sentence may trigger coercion, a shift of situation type. For instance, a generic or habitual sentence may be within the scope of an operator in a preceding sentence. The time and space adverbials of the Description mode are similar. They have scope over the clauses of the description and may trigger situation type shifts. See Chapter 5, 5.3.5.

Situation type information is represented in a DRS with a situation entity and conditions that characterize it. For instance, (22) presents a partial DRS for

"Mary read a book." A compositional rule will interpret the situation entity as an Event. The type of event, Accomplishment in this case, is not included here; identifying an event is sufficient for Discourse Mode interpretation. Individual entities x and y represent *Mary* and *a book*; the entity e represents the Event. The entity e is introduced into the top section of the DRS; the conditions on lines 1–2 specify further.

(22)   Partial DRS for "Mary read a book"

> x y e
> _____
> 1. e: = read (x,y)
> 2. e ∈ {Event}
> 3. x = Mary
> 4. y = a book

The curly brackets in line 2 indicate that the entity e belongs to the concept of an Event with the intensional properties of that concept.[15] Partial DRSs will be developed further, with additional information, in later sections of this book.

4.5.2   *General Statives: interpreting situation type*

The class of General Statives consists of Generalizing and Generic sentences. Most are derived by coercion from basic-level situation types, except for Generic sentences with kind-referring predicates such as *extinct*.

The strongest linguistic correlates for Generalizing sentences are frequency adverbs (*usually*, etc.) and the simple present tense. The frequency adverbial type is interpreted by a variant of rule (20), which provides that a frequency adverbial shifts any verb constellation to a General Stative. The input to the rule is a basic-level verb constellation; the output states that the resulting derived verb constellation expresses a General Stative, notated as St and General:

(23)   Generalizing rule (Frequency)
         $_S[[_{VCON}] + _{Adv}[Frequency]] \rightarrow _{DVCON}[_{St}[General]]$

The label [General] stands for the features [Static, Generalizing, Durative]. All states are durative. This rule ignores the case of *used to*, a special verb form that conveys a past pattern of events in English. The form could be added as an optional feature of the input verb constellation. The rule in (23) does not

---

15. The temporal properties of a situation entity concept are intensional; they are realized as the situation unfolds in time. The DRS account of aspectual information follows Smith (1997); it differs in certain respects from that of Kamp & Reyle (1993).

interpret Generalizing sentences without a frequency adverbial. The possibility of adding a frequency adverbial cannot be stated here: construction rules deal only with the actual forms in a surface structure.

The main type of Generalizing sentence has the simple present tense and an event verb constellation, such as "John walks to school." These too involve coercion, a shift of situation type. The coercion rule recognizes a composite of an event verb constellation, the present tense, and the simple verb form (conveying the perfective viewpoint). Together these factors license the interpretation of a sentence as Generalizing, by the Bounded event Constraint. The input to the rule is a sentence with an interpreted verb constellation, itself the output of a compositional rule. Schematically, the rule looks like this: it specifies only that the basic-level verb constellation is eventive, that tense is present, and that viewpoint is perfective (the simple verb form). Tns = tense; View = viewpoint:

(24)   Generalizing rule (simple present)
$$s[_{VCON}[Event] + {}_{Tns}[present] + {}_{View}[Perf]] \rightarrow {}_{DVCON}[_{st}[General]]$$

I do not State rules for interpreting Generic sentences. The interpretation of generic sentences on syntactic grounds is notoriously difficult; rules would look for a kind-referring NP and certain verb classes.

4.5.3   Abstract entities in a Discourse Representation Structure

Abstract Entities are interpreted by compositional rules that interpret information about predicate class and complement form. Generally, *that*-clauses and gerundive complements refer to Facts or Propositions in the context of fact and propositional predicates, and flexible predicates. This information suffices for many clear cases, although it is not always enough to distinguish complements that refer to Abstract Entities from those that refer to Events; some verb classes and complement forms are indeterminate (4.4.3 above). The form of a clausal complement may affect the determination of verb class. For instance, *think* is a stative verb of propositional attitude with a *that*-complement, e.g. "John thought that the earth was flat." With an *about*-PP as complement, however, the verb is dynamic, and allows a gerundive complement ("John thought about Mary's winning the race"). Since neither seems more basic than the other, I will tentatively assume that there are two verbs *think*.[16]

---

16. Whether there are two lexical entries for *think* in its different senses, or one is more basic than the other, is a question about the lexicon and compositional rules generally. The difference in dynamism between the verb constellations *NP thinks that S* and *NP thinks about NP* can't be attributed to the complements. *That*-complements appear in some verb constellations that are dynamic ("John was saying that he will leave early") and *about*-PPs appear in some that are static ("The book is about the war").

The first rules interpret sentences with verbs that clearly involve reference to Facts; if they have an object complement, it is a *that*-clause. The rule specifies the class of Fact predicates (Fact); the main sub-classes are noted above in 4.3. The complement may have the form of a *that*-clause or gerund; other possibilities are ignored here. COMP = complement; Ger = gerund.

(25)   Fact rule: object complement
        $_S[[NP] + _V[Fact] + _{COMP}[thatS/Ger]] \rightarrow _{VCON}[[_e[State]] + _{COMP}[_a[Fact]]]$

This rule will interpret sentences, "I know that Mary refused the offer," and "I resent Mary's winning the race."

The main classes of fact predicates with subject complements are evaluative and psychological verbs. Both classes are flexible, allowing complements of all types. *That*-clause and gerundive complements refer to Facts in the context of these predicates. The rule specifies that the main verb be of the class of situations, correctly allowing both State and Event main verb constellations; psychological verbs like *surprise* may be dynamic. Eval = evaluative verb.

(26)   Fact rule: subject complement
        $_S[_{COMP}[thatS/Ger] + _V[Eval] + X] \rightarrow _{VCON}[_e[Situation]] + _{COMP}[_a[Fact]]$

Other subject complement forms are ambiguous: they also have a situation (Event or State) interpretation with these predicates, as noted above. The situation interpretation of these predicates is sketched in (27). Substantive complements are NPs, as provided in the rule. The linguistic expressions after the predicate of interest are unspecified (X). Subst = substantive complement; Psych = psychological verb.

(27)   Fact/Situation rule: subject complement
        $_S[_{NP}[Subst] + _V[Psych, Eval] + X] \rightarrow _{VCON}[_e[State]] + _{COMP}[[_eEvent/_aFact]]$

In a general treatment of English, we might dispense with the situation interpretation rule. Instead, there might be a default rule providing that the default interpretation of a complement is reference to a situation.

Rules for interpreting complements that refer to Propositions are similar. The rule in (28) is written for verbs of mental state (V_{ME}) and communication (V_{COM}). The rule encodes the association of *that*-clauses and gerundives with an Abstract Entity interpretation in the context of such verbs.

(28)   Proposition rule: object complement
        $_S[[NP] + _V[ME/COM] + _{COMP}[thatS/Ger]] \rightarrow _{VCOM}[[_e[State]] + _{COMP}[_a[Prop]]]$

Propositional predicates with subject complements are epistemic predicates, and logical verbs (*entail, imply*). The rule for interpreting them is like the others except for the specification of the verb class, here Epist = epistemological verb, Log = logophoric verb.

(29)   Proposition rule: subject complement
        $_S$[$_{COMP}$[thatS/Ger] + $_V$[Epist, Log] + X] → $_{VCOM}$[[$_e$[State]] + $_{COMP}$[$_a$[Prop]]]

4.5.4   Viewpoint information in the DRS

The contribution of aspectual viewpoint is modeled in a DRS with a temporal interval [I] and associated times that are introduced with every clause. The viewpoint morpheme – simple verb form or progressive auxiliary – licenses the introduction of [I] in the DRS. Associated with each viewpoint is a formal semantic statement which is represented in the DRS interpretation. The viewpoint of the clause is located at this interval, and the visible information is specified as a property of the interval.[17]

The perfective viewpoint makes visible the endpoints of events. This information is given by specifying times within the interval [I] at which the endpoints occur. [I] consists of instants, the first is [t_i], the last is [t_j]. The initial and final endpoints of the entity e are indicated by $I(e)$ and $F(e)$ respectively. One viewpoint condition states that $I(e)$ occurs at [t_i] and $F(e)$ occurs at [t_j]. The other viewpoint associates the interval with the concept of a perfective viewpoint. The structure in (30) adds viewpoint information to the partial DRS for "Mary read a book." The sentence has the perfective viewpoint. The entities introduced include [I] and specified times; the conditions on lines 3–6 specify the visible information, as licensed by the viewpoint information in the sentence.

(30)   Partial DRS for "Mary read a book."

x y e I t_i t_j
1. e: = read (x,y)
2. e ∈ {Event}
3. {Viewpoint (I,e) = Perfective}
4. $t_{i,j}$ ∈ I
5. t_i = $I(e)$, t_j = $F(e)$
6. t ∈ I, t ≥ t_i, t ≤ t_j
7. x = Mary
8. y = a book

---

17. This follows the treatment of viewpoint in Smith (1997). In another DRT approach, viewpoint might be treated as a trigger for a sub-DRS in which all or part of the situation is visible (Patrick Caudal p.c.).

The viewpoint concept is set off with curly brackets to indicate its special status.

The progressive viewpoint focuses an interval of an Event that does not include its endpoints. This is modeled formally by providing that the interval [I] includes only times after the initial endpoint of *e* and before the final endpoint of *e*.[18] The partial DRS for a progressive sentence is given in (31):

(31)   Partial DRS for "Mary was reading a book."

x y e I t_i t_j
_____
1. e: = read (x,y)
2. e ∈ {Event}
3. {Viewpoint (I,e) = Imperfective}
4. $t_{i,j}$ ∈ I
5. t ∈ I → t > $I(e)$, t < $F(e)$
6. x = Mary
7. y = a book

These DRSs are still incomplete because they do not include information about tense.

The aspectual information that is encoded in a DRS identifies a situation entity for each clause. This information is essential to determining the entities introduced in text passages. Viewpoint information specifies whether an Event is bounded or unbounded, which is essential for calculating temporal advancement.

18. This statement covers the basic progressive meaning which focuses an internal interval of a situation. It does not account for cases where the progressive focuses an interval before a single point, as in "They were reaching the top."

5 Temporal and spatial progression

Time and space are pervasive in human experience and in language; they are essential in understanding the Discourse Modes. Text progression depends on both domains. The temporal modes progress with changes in time and space, while the atemporal modes progress with metaphorical changes of location through the text domain. This chapter discusses text progression in the temporal modes; the atemporal modes are considered in Chapter 6.

The principles for temporal progression are essentially pragmatic, depending on inference about how situations are related to each other and to times. Tense is interpreted in three different patterns. After discussing progression in the modes, I provide the linguistic account that underlies the analysis, and implement it in Discourse Representation Theory. There is a distinct grammatical sub-system for talking about time in English, consisting of tense and time adverbials. The system is a closed one: choice of tense and type of adverbial is limited to a small set of alternatives. In contrast, spatial information is conveyed by lexical means that do not constitute a grammatical sub-system, except for a very few deictic adverbials.

Section 5.1 discusses temporal interpretation in the temporal discourse modes; 5.2 introduces the sub-system of temporal location in English; 5.3 implements the interpretations in Discourse Representation Structures; 5.4 discusses space, and how it differs in linguistic expression from the temporal domain; 5.5 gives the forms and linguistic features of the temporal location sub-system.

5.1   Sentences in context: patterns of tense interpretation

The syntactic domain of tense is the clause: tense appears in some form in every clause of a language with morphological tense. The interpretation of tense requires information from context, however. Tense is interpreted differently according to the Discourse Mode of a passage. There are three patterns of interpretation: Continuity, Anaphora, and Deixis. Recognizing the different discourse patterns challenges the traditional idea that tense is deictic; it also provides a needed supplement to accounts that deal only with narrative advancement.[1]

In narrative passages bounded events advance narrative time. I will use the term Reference Time for the advancing time of a narrative: with each bounded event, Reference Time advances. The notion of Reference Time is explained in 5.2 below. Narrative has the Continuity pattern of tense interpretation. In Description, there is a full Anaphora pattern: time is static, the same as a previously established Reference Time. Tense is interpreted as Deictic in the other Discourse Modes – Reports, Argument, Information – and in texts generally. Deictic tense is oriented to Speech Time; this is the default pattern, as in traditional accounts.

In this section the different patterns will be demonstrated in some detail, and principles proposed to account for them.

5.1.1   Continuity: Narrative mode

Narratives advance dynamically. After the first sentence, the Events and States of a narrative are related to previous events and times in the text, rather than to Speech Time. The narrative fragment in (1) illustrates; it is familiar from Chapter 1. The events and states are indicated with subscripts E and S for each clause:

(1)   Narrative: Events and States related to each other
       1_{E1} She put on her apron, $_{E2}$ took a lump of clay from the bin and $_{E3}$ weighed off enough for a small vase. 2_{S1} The clay was wet. 3 Frowning, $_{E4}$ she cut the lump in half with a cheese-wire to check for air bubbles, $_{E5}$ then slammed the pieces together much harder than usual. 4_{E6} A fleck of clay spun off and $_{E7}$ hit her forehead, just above her right eye.

In the fragment, narrative time advances with perfective event sentences and fails to advance otherwise. I consider the example in detail.

The narrative of (1) conveys a series of events in sequence, E1 (put on apron), E2 (took a lump of clay), etc. There is one State, expressed in sentence 2 (clay was wet), which we understand to hold at the same time as the preceding event, and perhaps to extend before and after it. The diagram in (2) gives a time line for the passage; E indicates an event, S a state; SpT is Speech Time:

1. The need for more than one pattern of tense interpretation is recognized in Caenepeel & Moens (1994) and Caenepeel (1995). They note that some contexts evoke a narrative interpretation, while others are deictic.

(2)   Time line for (1)
       ...t1......t2......t3......t4......t5......t6......t7...... <SpT
          E1   E2   E3   E4   E5   E6   E7
                       S1

All these situations are temporally located at a time prior to Speech Time, following narrative convention. Otherwise the information conveyed by tense is simple continuity. The past tense is not interpreted deictically: if it were, the events would be related to Speech Time rather than to each other. Nor do we interpret the past tense as expressing a series of events successively prior to one another. The continuity function of tense holds for narratives in the present or future as well as the past.

The interpretation can be expressed in two general principles that hold for narrative passages. As a narrative advances it establishes a set of different Reference Times. In clauses that express bounded events, Reference Time advances. In clauses of states and ongoing events, the time is the previously established Reference Time. This is an anaphoric interpretation, limited in narrative to certain types of situations. The two patterns are set out in (3). When tense is past, as in many narratives, we take it that Reference Time (RT) is prior to Speech Time (SpT).

(3)   Temporal interpretation in narrative
       a. Continuity pattern: bounded Events
          E_1.................E_2.................E_3..........
          $RT_1 < SpT$ $RT_2 > RT_1$ $RT_3 > RT_2$
       b. Limited Anaphoric pattern: States, progressives
          E_3......S_1..............
          RT_1 $RT_2 = RT_1$

Temporal adverbials also advance narrative time, of course. This brief account does not consider the relative past tenses, past perfect and future-in-past. They locate situations before and after the current time established in the text. Similar principles are stated by Kamp & Reyle (1993) in a slightly different approach. The continuity pattern also occurs in procedural discourse.

Narrative continuity depends on semantic and pragmatic factors. The interpretation of bounded Events is based on semantic, aspectual information: the class of a verb constellation and the perfective viewpoint. The past-tense morpheme conveys that a situation is prior to Speech Time (in simple sentences; for other cases see 5.5 below). The sequential narrative interpretation itself is pragmatic, and can be cancelled by additional information. Situations may be taken as simultaneous; they may be related by causation or some other factor; or we may infer a shift in level of detail.[2]

Another example of narrative is given below:

(4)   Narrative Entities, progression

1_{S1} Michael White, the mayor of Cleveland, is a Democrat, an African American and the son of a union activist. 2_{S2} And he is at war with his party. $3_{E1} \rightarrow$ First, he backed an end to forced busing. $4a_{E2} \rightarrow$ Then, he supported Republican Governor George Voinovich's radical school choice law, b_{S2} which offers students vouchers at parochial as well as private school. $5_{E3} \rightarrow$ Then, he made city workers compete against private firms for garbage collection, road maintenance and other contracts, prompting union officials to walk out of a speech [that] he gave at the Democratic national Convention. $6_{S3} \rightarrow$ Now, he's allied with the governor again, backing a bill by two Republican State legislators to grant him control over Cleveland's destitute school system and the authority to get "rid of any people who aren't directly tied to the direct education of children." 7_{S4} Arrayed against him are "the teachers' union, the NAACP and just about every elected Democrat in the city of Cleveland."

The passage consists of bounded events and states; there are no ongoing events. The bounded events advance time, here supported by adverbials.

5.1.2   Anaphora: Description mode

In descriptive passages time is static, without dynamism. Tense is anaphoric to a time in the discourse: all the sentences of a given passage have the same Reference Time. There is a sense of progression in such passages, spatial in nature. The text advances as the reader goes from one part of the scene to another.

Usually a locative adverbial appears at the beginning of a description, with scope over the material that follows; such a phrase appears in both passages below.

(5)   Description

a. 1 In the passenger car every window was propped open with a stick of kindling wood. 2 A breeze blew through, hot and then cool, fragrant of the woods and yellow flowers and of the train. 3 The yellow butterflies flew in

---

2. Shifts in level of detail are common, as in "We went on a long trip last summer. First we traveled to India." The second sentence is at a finer level of detail than the first. The inference of shift is triggered by the adverb "first" and based in world knowledge. There may be other interpretations of how sentences are related, more abstract and/or rhetorically based. Such interpretation is usually triggered by additional information in the context. Discourse relations are discussed briefly in Chapter 11.

at any window, out at any other . . . 4 Overhead a black lamp in which a circle of flowers had been cut out swung round and round on a chain as the car rocked from side to side, sending down dainty drifts of kerosene smell.

b. 1 On the big land below the house a man was ploughing and shouting admonitions to the oxen who dragged the ploughshares squeaking through the heavy red soil. 2 On the track to the station the loaded wagon with its team of sixteen oxen creaked and groaned while the leader cracked his whip that reached to the horns of the leader oxen and yelled on a note only they understood. 3 On the telephone wires the birds twittered and sang. 4 The wind sang not only in the wires, but through the grasses, and the wires vibrated and twanged.

To account for the temporal stability of description, I assume a tacit durative time adverbial that has scope over the entire passage.

The situations expressed in these fragments include states and ongoing events. They fit the Anaphoric pattern discussed above. There are events presented with the simple, perfective viewpoint which do not seem to fit, however. For instance, several events – "a breeze blew," "butterflies flew in," "a . . . lamp . . . swung," "the car rocked" – appear in sentences 2–4 of example (5a). The events are all atelic and durative, of the Activity situation type. In this context they are interpreted as continuous, iterative: the lamp swung round and round, the car rocked. This interpretation does not disturb the anaphoric pattern, and is predicted by the formal analysis of perfective Activities. The viewpoint focuses a bounded unit which need not coincide with the beginning or end of an Activity (Smith 1999b). In descriptive contexts such as this, Activity events are taken as continuing.

To reach a better understanding of description, consider (6), a variant of (5b). I have changed the example slightly so that the new sentence 3 has a telic verb constellation ("walk to school"). Strikingly, the Description mode is still undisturbed: the new sentence 3 does not have telic force in this fragment.

(6)   1 On the big land below the house a man was ploughing and shouting admonitions to the oxen who dragged the ploughshares squeaking through the heavy red soil. 2 On the track to the station the loaded wagon with its team of sixteen oxen creaked and groaned . . . 3 A group of children walked to school. 4 On the telephone wires the birds twittered and sang.

In this context the event of walking to school is taken as atelic. This is an instance of coercion, a shift in situation type: the potential telicity of the Event verb constellation is overridden.

The coercion effect can be attributed to the tacit time adverbial of description posited above. Within the scope of a durative time adverbial telic sentences are coerced to atelic, undergoing a shift of situation type. This is part of the general phenomenon of coercion discussed in Chapter 4. Recall that sentences with a telic verb constellation and a durative time adverbial are atelic. For instance, in "Mary read a book for an hour" there is no sense that Mary completed the book – on the contrary. The durative time adverbial overrides the telicity of the verb constellation.

Similarly, "A group of children walked to school" in (6) is atelic under the scope of the tacit durative adverbial of description. The actual duration of such an adverbial is determined by context. The assumed duration is the time in which the perceiver scans the scene and becomes aware of its properties, or simply a period during which the situation is expected to hold.

In Description, the anaphoric pattern of tense interpretation holds for all situations. There are coercion effects due to the tacit adverbial of duration: telic events shift to atelic. Limited and Full anaphoric patterns of interpretation are pragmatic, depending on the notion that what is conveyed is a static description of a scene.

5.1.3 Deictic pattern: Report, Information, Argument
The Deictic pattern of tense interpretation is the default: it holds for the Report, Information, and Argument modes. The deictic pattern is found in discourse generally, including conversation. Like the other patterns, the deictic interpretation can be cancelled by information that relates situations in a different way.

I illustrate for the three modes. Reports give an account of situations and their significance from the temporal standpoint of the reporter. Tense is deictic, with Speech Time the anchor for the deixis. Passages in the Report mode tend to have deictic adverbials as well as tense; for instance, *next year* and *in March* are such adverbials, anchored to Speech Time. This point is important in identifying Report passages, see 5.3.2. A passage in this mode is illustrated here; Events and States are noted as before.

(7)   Report: situations related to Speech Time
        1_S Downtown Austin will have to live for at least several more months with the half-finished shell of the Intel Corp design center. 2_S Intel has postponed a decision on what to do about the project until sometime next year, $_S$ when the semiconductor company has a better reading on the strength of the economy. 3_E Intel decided in March to halt construction on the 10-story center at Fourth and San Antonio streets, as well as other projects around the country, to save money during a chip industry downturn. 4_E Intel took heat from critics $_E$ who called the half-finished concrete skeleton, encircled by a chain-link fence, an eyesore.

The passage begins with a future time, indicated by "will" and the *for*-adverbial; at S2 the temporal location shifts to the present ("has postponed"), and then to another future State. S3 shifts to the past event ("decided"), with a past tense and time adverbial. The events of S4 ("took heat," "called") are also located in the past relative to Speech Time. They need not occur at the same time as the event of S3. The diagram in (8) gives a time line for this passage in terms of Reference Time (RT) and Speech Time (SpT).

(8) Time line for (7)

S_1.................S_2...................S_3..................E_1..................E_2...

$RT_1 > SpT$ $RT_2 = SpT$ $RT_3 > SpT$ $RT_4 < SpT$ $RT_5 < SpT$

This is the typical pattern of Reports.

Passages in the atemporal Argument and Information modes also have this pattern of tense interpretation. Tense is deictic, and may change frequently. The types of entities are noted: F = Fact; P = Proposition; GE = Generalizing Stative. Some of the Abstract Entities posited are due to normalization, following Peterson (1997) (Chapter 4).[3]

Atemporal modes with deictic tense interpretation:

(9) Argument

1_E The press has trumpeted the news $_F$ that crude oil prices are three times higher than they were a year ago. 2_{GE} But it was $_F$ the $10 or $11 price of February 1999, not the one today, that really deserved the headlines.

3_{GE} When inflation is taken into account, $_{GE}$ that 1999 price was the lowest in modern history, $_{GE}$ while oil has gone above today's seemingly high price several times. 4_{GE} And for the past 14 years, at $17.50, oil has been one of the real bargains of the modern age. 5_{GE} The $_P$ low price has been a mixed blessing. 6_{GE} In the United States, we have lost over 500,000 jobs in the oil industry while $_{GE}$ we have grossly increased our dependency on foreign oil; we now import 55 percent of what we use. 7 With little incentive for drillers to find and tap new oil, $_{GE}$ supplies eventually dropped, and in the past year $_E$ the Organization of Petroleum Exporting Countries deliberately dropped its production.

(10) Information

1_{GE} Surprisingly, tunnels are among the most ancient engineering feats. 2_{GE} The earliest were very likely extensions of prehistoric cave dwellings. 3_E The Babylonians, in the twenty-second century BC, built a masonry tunnel beneath the Euphrates River that connected the royal palace with a major temple. 4_{GE}

---

3. For instance, the subject of S5 is interpreted as a Proposition. The subject nominal "the low price" is normalized as clausal, *That the price of oil was low*. The clause then meets the criteria for a Proposition.

The Egyptians, using copper-bladed saws, excavated long passageways and intricate rooms inside soft-rock cliffs. 5_{GE} The Romans built an elaborate network of above- and below-ground acqueducts to carry water. 6_{GE} And they tunneled through solid rock by repeatedly heating it with fire and then cooling it with water, causing the rock face to fracture. 7_S The greatest of those acqueduct tunnels, which eventually drained Lake Fucino in central Italy, stretched more than three miles underground.

The general Deictic pattern of past-tense interpretation is given schematically in (11):

(11)   Deictic tense interpretation
        E_1...............E_2..................S_1..................S_2............
        $RT_1 < SpT$ $RT_2 < SpT$ $RT_3 < SpT$ $RT_4 < SpT$

In the Deictic pattern situations and deictics are oriented to Speech Time.

Summarizing, three patterns of tense interpretation have been demonstrated for non-first clauses of text passages. (I assume that the first sentence of a passage is interpreted by the default deictic principle.) Tense conveys Continuity, Anaphora, or Deixis. Each Discourse Mode has a different pattern:

(12)   Patterns of tense interpretation in the temporal Discourse Modes
        Continuity: Non-first clause, bounded Events, Narrative mode
        Anaphora: Non-first clause, unbounded Events and States, Narrative mode
                   Non-first clause, all situations, Description mode
        Deictic: Default – all other cases

As a background for implementing the analysis in Discourse Representation Theory, I give a brief account of the temporal location system of English.

5.2   *Introduction to the temporal system of English*

Time is a single unbounded dimension, analogous to space though simpler; see 5.3 below. Like space, time requires an orientation point or landmark for location. The speaker is the canonical center of linguistic communication so that the basic orientation points in language are the speaker, the speaker's place (*here*), and the speaker's time (*now*). In sentences out of context, situations are located with respect to Speech Time, which is always the Present. I use capital letters to refer to time, lower case for tense.

I will briefly introduce the temporal forms and then discuss their interpretation. "Tense" is the grammatical category of inflectional verb morphemes that convey information about time. English has two tenses, past and present. The modal auxiliary *will* standardly conveys Future time.[4] Tense is obligatory in the main clause of a sentence. There are complex tenses, the perfect ("Mary has arrived") and the embedded future ("Mary would leave soon"). Temporal adverbials are optional. Locating adverbials specify times ("Mary called at noon"), as do clausal time adverbials ("John left when Mary arrived"). Adverbials anchor either to Speech Time or to a time specified in the linguistic context. The discussion below focuses on tense, although adverbials are included in the summary of the system in 5.5.

The temporal expressions form a closed system, a limited domain from which one of a few possibilities must be chosen. Tense in independent sentences is deictic, anchored to Speech Time. Tense locates the situation in a clause by tacitly invoking two times: the time of the situation expressed, which I will call Situation Time; and Speech Time. Present and past tense, and future *will*, indicate that Situation Time is respectively simultaneous with, before, or after Speech Time. In complex sentences the anchor may be a time other than Speech Time.

There is a third time conveyed by tense, a temporal perspective time. Every tensed sentence takes a temporal perspective or standpoint, known as "Reference Time," following Hans Reichenbach (1947). Reichenbach presents strong arguments for the notion of Reference Time, which I assume here.[5] The centrality of the speaker implies an organizing consciousness that provides a standpoint "from which the speaker invites his audience to consider the Event"

---

4. The modal *will* has present tense, correspondingly the modal *would* has past tense and has a future-in-past meaning. *Would* is also a conditional form, not discussed here. Enç (1991) shows that *will* is a modal not a tense. *Will* with strong stress conveys volition or requirement, as in "I WILL go"; "Bill WILL go."

5. There are three main arguments, for the notion of Reference Time, two of them due to Reichenbach himself. The first involves perfect sentences. Consider the difference between a simple past and a present perfect sentence. Both present an Event that takes place before Speech Time; they have the same truth conditions, yet they contrast in conceptual meaning.

       (i) a Mary arrived.   past
          b Mary has arrived.   present perfect

In both sentences Situation Time (the Event of arriving) is Past.

The notion of Reference Time gives us a way of understanding such contrasts. In past tense sentences, both situation and temporal standpoint are in the past; in present perfect sentences, the situation is past but the temporal standpoint is present. In the perfect, RT is equal to Speech Time. The perfect has an additional aspectual component of stativity, noted in Chapter 2.

Another argument for Reference Time comes from the relations between situations. The context of a clause gives information that locates situations relative to one another. They occur in sequence, or overlap. Using the notion of Reference Time, we can say that overlapping

(Taylor 1977:203). In sentences with the basic tenses, Reference Time is the same as Situation Time. The reader will recognize the term Reference Time from the earlier discussion of text progression.

5.2.1   Simple sentences

I posit a Reichenbachian system in which the tenses and future *will* involve three times: Speech Time (SpT), Situation Time (SitT), and Reference Time (RT). Each tense conveys a relation between SpT and RT, and a relation between RT and SitT. In the simple tenses, SitT and RT are the same. The perfect tenses all convey that SitT is anterior to RT; in the past-in-future, SitT follows SpT (14c).[6]

(13)   a John is here. $RT = SpT; RT = SitT$
       b John arrived. $RT < SpT; RT = SitT$
       c John will arrive. $RT > SpT; RT = SitT$

(14)   a John has arrived. $RT = SpT; RT > SitT$
       b John had arrived. $RT < SpT; RT > SitT$
       c John will have arrived. $RT > SpT; RT > SitT$
       d (i) John said that (ii) Mary would arrive soon.
                          (i) $RT_1 < SpT; RT_1 = SitT$
                          (ii) $RT_2 = RT_1; RT_2 < SitT$

situations share Reference Time and those in sequence do not. This accounts nicely for the difference between the examples in (ii).

   (ii) a Mary was phoning the police when John arrived.
        a' Mary entered the room. John was smiling.
        b Mary phoned the police when John arrived.
        b' Mary entered the room. John smiled.

Thus the notion of RT provides a locus for relating situations in a principled manner, explicated in a DR Theory framework in Hinrichs (1986).

   A third argument for RT concerns the phenomenon of shifted deixis. As is well known, some deictic adverbials such as *now*, *in 3 days*, etc., which normally anchor to the moment of speech, can anchor to a Past (or Future time):

   (i) Mary sat down at the desk. Now she was ready to start work.

In such contexts the shifted *now* suggests Mary's perspective. The notion of RT is the anchoring point for this perspective. These arguments show that Reference Time is indispensable to an understanding of the temporal information conveyed in sentences. Reichenbach and others use the term Event Time for what I call Situation Time. The system as Reichenbach stated it must be modified and extended (Smith 1980, Comrie 1985, Hornstein 1990, Kamp & Reyle 1993). I will assume these adjustments. The account given here is similar but not identical to that of Kamp & Reyle (1993).
6. There are future perfect sentences in which the situation must precede RT but need not precede SpT, e.g. in "The Prime Minister will have burned the documents by Thursday," as noted in connection with (14) above.

The tenses in (14b–d) are "relative" tenses because they depend on another clause for interpretation: the main clause provides the anchor RT for the embedded clause. Temporal adverbials, if they appear in a clause, specify RT.

This relational information is the semantic meaning of a tense, associated with the tense morpheme in the lexicon. In multi-clause sentences, one clause may be dependent temporally on another, as in (14d).[7] Formally, the tenses have two semantic features, A and B, which give the relation between times associated with a given tense. The features provide what Kamp & Reyle call the "two-dimensional theory" of tense. The A feature relates Reference Time to Speech Time; the B feature relates Reference Time to Situation Time.

Tense interpretation interacts with aspectual information. Recall that the perfective viewpoint focuses events as bounded, while the progressive focuses events as unbounded. States are also unbounded. The property of boundedness is crucial for the way aspect relates to temporal location. Bounded events are totally included in the Situation Time, whether it be a moment or an interval ($e \subseteq SitT$); unbounded events and states overlap or surround it ($e \; 0 \; SitT$). For instance:

(15)   a. Lee built a sandcastle.
       b. Mary is working.

We understand the event of (15a) as taking place within SitT, here an interval.[8] The ongoing event of (15b) overlaps SitT: it holds at an interval that includes the SitT interval. For concreteness I give a semi-formal statement for the two sentences.

(16)   Lee built a sandcastle.
      E: bounded event
      $RT < SpT, RT = SitT$
      $E \subseteq SitT$

7. There are several possible relations between the temporal information of a main clause and other clauses in a sentence. Tenseless complements and adjuncts share the time of the matrix clause. Tensed complements may be dependent on a time established in the main clause for either RT or SitT. In the former case, an adverbial in the dependent clause may specify the time of SitT. The past perfect and future-in-past *would* typically appear in a complement clause, as in (13d). Relative clauses may be temporally dependent or independent of the main clause. See Smith (1981), Ogihara (1989).
8. By convention, SpT is an instant. I will assume that RT and SitT may be moments or intervals, depending on adverbial and situation information in the sentence. Both are needed in a semantic account of the temporal system (Kamp & Reyle 1993:501).

(17)   Mary is working.
        E: unbounded event
        RT = SpT, RT = SitT
        E 0 SitT

The construction of DRS representations is discussed in 5.3 below.

The interaction of temporal location and aspect excludes bounded events located in the Present, at Speech Time. This is an important, non-accidental, gap in the paradigm. It is due to a pragmatic constraint on bounded events: they cannot be located at Speech Time. Events in the Present must be presented as ongoing, e.g "John is talking," "Mary is drawing a circle," or as Generalizing Statives that involve a general pattern, e.g. "Tom often feeds the cat."

The constraint barring bounded events in the Present results from the Bounded Event Constraint, a general principle of communication. The explanation for the constraint is at once pragmatic and semantic. In taking the temporal perspective of the Present, speakers are limited by a tacit convention that communication is instantaneous. The perspective of the Present time is incompatible with a bounded event, because the bounds would go beyond that perspective. As Kamp & Reyle put it:

> A present tense sentence describes an eventuality as occurring at the time at which the sentence is uttered, and thus at a time at which the thought is being entertained which the sentence expresses. So the thought must conceive the eventuality as it appears from the perspective of the time at which it is going on. A sentence which describes something as going on at a time – in the sense of not having come to an end when that time is up – cannot represent something as an event. For the event would have to be entirely included within the location time and thus would not extend beyond it. (1993:536–7)

Due to this constraint, all simple present tense sentences express unbounded situations. Almost the same notion is called the "punctuality constraint" in Giorgi & Pianesi (1997:163).[9] There are well-known exceptions, notably performatives ("I christen this ship the *Queen Elizabeth*") and sports-announcer reports ("Now Jones throws the ball to third base") and narratives entirely set in the present. Another type, less well-known, appears in literary and many other

---

9. I thank Nina Hyams for pointing out the similarity of Giorgi & Pianesi's constraint to the one stated here. The Bounded Event Constraint is realized differently across languages. In Russian, for instance, the perfective present conveys Future time reference. In French the present is imperfective in meaning. The Bounded Event has consequences for temporal interpretation in languages without tense; see Smith & Erbaugh (2001).

kinds of commentary, including scientific journals ("Here the author creates an interesting metaphor").[10]

5.2.2   Sentences with complement clauses

Complement clauses function as the subject or object arguments of certain verbs. We might expect that the temporal advancement principle would apply to complement clauses as in independent sentences. But it does not. Rather than advancing time, most complements present situations that overlap those of the main clause, as in (18):

(18)   a. Lewis knew that the race was over.
        b. Lewis saw that the race was over.
        c. Lewis succeeded in winning the race.
        d. That Mary won the race surprised Lewis.

In these cases the lower clause does not advance narrative time. Main and complement clauses have the same Reference Time. There are two other relations between main and complement clause. The complement may receive its Reference Time from the main clause, or the complement may relate temporally to Speech Time. The determining factors are the tenses and modal *will* of main and complement clause, although adverbials also contribute to interpretation.

When the main-clause verb expresses communication, the complement clause indicates a previous event or overlapping open situation. The examples illustrate: in (19a) an ongoing event is expressed in the complement, (19b) is a variation in which the complement clause has a bounded Event.

(19)   a. When I got to Harry's Waldorf Towers apartment, *his secretary said they were winding up the meeting downstairs.* Harry appeared about a half-hour later, greeted me warmly, went immediately to the telephone.
        b. When I got to Harry's Waldorf Towers apartment, *his secretary said Harry (had) left.* Harry appeared about a half-hour later, greeted me warmly, went immediately to the telephone.

When the clause of communication expresses a bounded event, the event precedes the communication itself. The reason lies in the Bounded Event Constraint. Since communication is taken as instantaneous, a bounded event reported by a verb of communication must precede the communication itself. (In some dialects, including mine, the past perfect is needed in such contexts.)

---

10. The literary examples can be seen either as Generalizing Statives, or perhaps as stage directions that are invoked afresh each time the work is read. I thank Robert Brown for bringing these examples to my attention.

The contribution of direct quotation is somewhat different. Direct quotations are often presented in narrative as events, events that form a conversation. I cannot explore the matter here.

Dependent clauses include relative clauses, condensed clauses, adjunct clauses. Relative clauses also contribute to narrative advancement (Depraeterre 1996); the other types of dependent clauses do not.

Summarizing, the interpretation of tense for single sentences is deictic, oriented to Speech Time. Tense conveys information about the relation between three times, Speech Time, Situation Time, and Reference Time. The relations are given by A and B features associated with each tense in the lexicon. Bounded events and states are included in the Situation Time interval; unbounded events (and other static situation entities) overlap the Situation Time interval. Complement clauses may be dependent or independent of the main clauses. With main verbs of communication, bounded events in the complement precede the time of the main clause.

5.3   *Tense interpretation in Discourse Representation Theory*

The construction rules of Discourse Representation convert the information conveyed by tense into entities and conditions which are encoded in the Discourse Representation Structure (DRS). Featural information associated with the temporal morphemes is given in 5.5.

Linguistic context often provides information that is essential for interpretation. This is true for interpretation of tense: it depends on the Discourse Mode of the passage. I will assume that a minimal passage consists of two clauses and that two clauses can establish a Discourse Mode. Additional conventions are needed for the different modes; they are given below.

Tense interpretation requires assessment of the entities in the linguistic context. Further, we require a way of adapting the information associated with tense morphemes to the different patterns of interpretation. The class of situation entity and temporal advancement appear in the DRS; there is no specific notation of Discourse Mode.

The temporal interpretation of a clause has two stages in Discourse Representation Theory. At the first stage, construction rules interpret the information conveyed by temporal morphemes and encode it in the DRSs as temporal entities and their relations. The second stage consists of calculating the times and relations in the context of the developing discourse. The calculation must take into account the entities already present in the DRS, minimally those that are introduced in the immediate context.

5.3.1   *Principles for tense interpretation*

The basic, deictic pattern of tense encodes in a straightforward manner the information associated with tense and modal *will*. Tense licenses the introduction into a DRS of three times, t_{1-3}. They are associated with notional times in the conditions of the DRS, on the convention that t_1 = Speech Time, t_2 = Reference Time, t_3 = Situation Time. Each tense has an A and B feature, which states the relations between the times that are conveyed by that tense. The features trigger the appropriate conditions on the times. If there is a temporal adverbial, it appears as a specifying condition in the DRS.

The deictic pattern relates a sentence to SpT according to the A and B features associated with it. The principle applies to single sentences and as a default to other sentences, unless another principle applies. The interpretation of tense for passages in the Narrative and Description modes requires a departure from the deictic pattern. The three principles for these modes are Continuity, Limited Anaphora, and Full Anaphora.

The principles of interpretation need information about the entities encoded in the DRS in the immediate context of a given clause. DRSs do not distinguish between sentences, but the information can be recovered. Each clause introduces a new cluster of times t into the DRS. I will distinguish the times associated with independent clauses by subscript, for instance t_{1-3a}; t_{1-3b}; t_{1-3c}. All entities introduced by a clause are grouped together with the subscripted times. Thus two independent clauses will enter three times differentiated as t_a, t_b, into the DRS, ensuring that the entities associated with each set of times will be recoverable. This information will be stated as a contextual constraint on the relevant construction rule. The constraint will look at the situation entities introduced in the sentences that precede a clause under interpretation.

The different principles are discussed and stated in the following sections. I begin with single sentences, which have the deictic pattern of tense interpretation.

5.3.2   *Single sentences*

The interpretation of single sentences follows the deictic pattern of tense interpretation, summarized in (20).

(20)   Deictic Tense Principle
        Applies to present or past tense, or modal future *will*.
        For a sentence S involving three times: t_1 = SpT.
        Feature A: t_2 is related to t_1 according to the tense;
        Feature B: t_3 is related to t_2 according to the tense.

In this sketch I provide an example of a surface structure, a construction rule, and a temporal DRS.

The example interprets a sentence and its surface structure; IP=Infl Phrase; AspP=Aspect Phrase:

(21)   Mara put on her apron

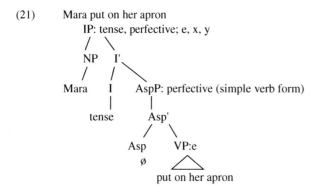

This sentence has past tense, the perfective viewpoint, the participants *Mara*, *her apron*.

Information arises as follows: the IP is associated with a situation entity *e*, and with a tense. The situation entity is interpreted by compositional rules. The tense licenses the introduction of three times in the DRS, and conditions stating the A and B features associated with it. The AspP is associated with the perfective or imperfective viewpoint, depending on whether the verb has the simple form or an auxiliary; the participants appear in the highest NP and the VP, and percolate to the top of the tree. This discussion focuses on temporal location information.

The temporal location construction rule for sentences like (21) is given in (22). The statement covers only simple tenses but could be extended to the perfect tenses and the future-in-past. I include an optional temporal-locating adverbial.

(22)   Temporal location construction rule: single sentences
        $S[\ldots [tense/will]\ldots,\ _{Adv}(TLoc)\ldots] \rightarrow t_1, t_2, t_3; A, B;$
        (condition on t_2)

The times are automatically interpreted by general convention as conditions in the DRS: $t_1 = SpT$, $t_2 = RT$, $t_3 = SitT$. If realized, the adverbial specifies t_2 (RT), as in "Mara put on her apron at noon." The rule gives rise to the DRS in (23):

(23)   Temporal DRS for "Mara put on her apron at noon."

t_1 t_2 t_3 x y e d
1. e: put on (x,y)
2. $t_1 = $ SpT
3. $t_2 < t_1$
4. $t_2 = d$
5. $t_1 = $ SpT
6. d = at noon
7. e $\subseteq t_3$
8. x = Mara
9. y = her apron

Tense is deictic in this single sentence. The tense features are on lines 3 and 5: the A feature for past tense is $t_2 < t_1$; the B feature $t_2 = t_3$. Line 7 specifies that the event is included in the Situation Time interval, since the viewpoint is perfective. Other information is omitted, for simplicity.

The DRS above illustrates the deictic interpretation of tense, which as the default applies to single sentences. I now consider temporal information in text passages. Temporal interpretation requires construction rules and principles for temporal advancement. I will concentrate on the latter.

5.3.3   Narrative passages

The Discourse Mode of a passage is largely determined by the types of entity introduced into the Discourse Representation Structure. Narrative introduces particular events and states into the universe of discourse. However, the Report mode tends to introduce the same entities, so that it is necessary to have a way of distinguishing them. The Report mode can be recognized quite reliably by the presence of deictic adverbials. Report passages typically have spatial and temporal deictics that are anchored to Speech Time, whereas narrative passages do not.[11] Simplifying, I will assume that narrative passages do not have deictics. The narrative interpretation of tense arises in the context of at least one preceding narrative clause.

The Narrative mode of tense interpretation in DR Theory requires a principle of Continuity and a principle for Limited Anaphora. The Continuity

---

11. Shifted deictics sometimes appear in narrative, e.g. "Mary had been working all afternoon; she was tired now." The decitic *now* is anchored not to Speech Time but to the Past time of the first clause. See Chapter 9. Shifted deictics are not dealt with here.

principle advances narrative time with bounded events, and/or time adverbials. I'll work through the principles with the narrative fragment of (1), repeated here as (24):

(24)   Narrative: Events and States related to each other
       $1a_{E1}$ She put on her apron, b_{E2} took a lump of clay from the bin and c_{E3} weighed off enough for a small vase. 2_{S1} The clay was wet. 3 Frowning, a_{E4} she cut the lump in half with a cheese-wire to check for air bubbles, b_{E5} then slammed the pieces together much harder than usual. $4a_{E6}$ A fleck of clay spun off b and $_{E7}$ hit her forehead, just above her right eye.

The principle applies when a clause and its immediate context have event and state entities, which will be notated as entities of type e.

The first part of the rule for continuity is a contextual constraint that looks at a clause and the immediately preceding context for the appropriate entities. The times and entities of a clause are associated by letter subscript; recall that clauses themselves do not appear in the DRS. The relevant entities are of type e, events and states; the entity of the clause being processed is subscripted with "n" for times t_n. The entities of preceding clauses are identified as $n-2$, $n-1$, and associated with temporal entities t_{n-2} and t_{n-1} in the DRS. The principle applies to non-first sentences of a narrative passage:

(25)   Contextual condition for Continuity principle
       In the context of times t_n of the DRS, entity of type e_n; the situation entities are e_{n-2} and/or e_{n-1} and no deictics are associated with entity e_n.

The condition requires that the clause being processed have an entity of type e; that preceding clauses have entities of the same type; and that there are no deictics. Thus in (23), clause 1a is first, so the condition is applicable to clause 1b: it is clause n, with an entity of type e; the preceding clause 1a has times t_{n-1} and an entity of type e. Advancing in the passage, clause 1c will be clause n and clauses 1a and 1b are clauses $n-2$, $n-1$ respectively. Both have entities of type e so the rule applies.

The Continuity Principle provides for an advancement of RT with bounded events. The principle has the form of a rule which advances the narrative from one Reference Time, RT_x, to a later time, RT_y, indicated by the symbol $>$:

(26)   Advancement Principle
       With RT_x immediately preceding; if e is a bounded event:
       $RT_y > RT_x$

This rule applies to the passage in (24). The first application is to clause 1b: the rule says that the RT of "[she] took a lump of clay from the bin," RT_y, is later than the RT of the first clause: $RT_y > RT_x$. RT_y is the updated Reference Time. The rule applies in the same fashion to the next clause, "[she] weighed off enough for a small vase," and so on.

The full Continuity Principle also has a clause providing that a temporal adverbial can advance narrative time, stated in (27):

(27)   Continuity Principle for non-first sentences
       Condition: In the context of times t_n of the DRS, entity of type e_n; the situation entities are e_{n-2} and/or e_{n-1} and no deictics are associated with entity e_n.
       a. With RT_x immediately preceding; if e is a bounded event:
          $RT_y > RT_x$
       b. If associated with entities t_n there is a temporal locating adverbial that indicates a time t_x later than the time associated with entities t_{n-1}
          RT_y advances to time t_x.

The Limited Anaphora Principle applies under the same conditions as the previous principle, but only to State and unbounded Event entities:

(28)   Limited Anaphora Principle
       In the context of temporal entities t_n of the DRS, entities of type e_n; if the situation entities associated with t_{n-2} and/or t_{n-1} are of type e; and no deictics are associated with entities t_n. With RT_x immediately preceding; if e is a state or unbounded event: $RT_y = RT_x$

These principles are stated for clear cases that do not require inference. Adverbs of the locating type advance narrative time for all situations.

I illustrate the principles in a DRS for a narrative fragment of three sentences; the first two introduce Event entities into the universe, the third introduces a State. The times introduced by the sentences are subscripted a–c. The situations e are numbered 1, 2, 3; e_1 and e_2 are Events, e_3 is the State. The entities appear at the top of the DRS.

(29)   1. Mara put on her apron.
       2. She took out a lump of clay.
       3. The clay was wet.

t_{1a} t_{2a} t_{3a} e_1 x y t_{1b} t_{2b} t_{3b} e_2 z w t_{1c} t_{2c} t_{3c} e_3 u

1. $t_{1a} = SpT$ (Principle of Deixis)
2. $t_{2a} < t_{1a}$
3. $t_{2a} = t_{3a}$
4. $e_1 \subseteq t_{3a}$
5. x = Mara
6. y = her apron
7. e_1: put on (x,y)

8. $t_{2a} < t_{2b}$
9. $t_{2b} > t_{2a}$ (Principle of Continuity)
10. $t_{2b} = t_{3b}$
11. $e_b \subseteq t_{3b}$
12. z = x
13. w = a lump of clay
14. e_2: take out (z,w)

15. $t_{2c} < t_{1c}$
16. $t_{2c} = t_{2b}$ (Principle of Limited Anaphora)
17. $t_{2c} = t_{3c}$
18. s 0 t_{3c}
19. u = w
20. e_3: be wet (u)

The individual and situation entities are introduced by compositional rules like those stated in Chapter 4. The rules provide the conceptual aspectual information that classifies the entities as Events and States, and the viewpoint as perfective in each clause. This information licenses the conditions on lines 4 and 11 that an event is included in t_3, or SitT (perfective, bounded); or on line 18 that it overlaps t_3, or SitT (unbounded simple State). The tense interpretation is the result of a calculation within the DRS.

This DRS provides two RTs (t_2) for the three sentences: the first is specified as prior to SpT on the deictic interpretation, line 2; the second follows the first by the principle of advancement, line 9. The third RT is equal to the second by the Principle of Limited Anaphora, line 16. The events are included in the intervals of t_3 (SitT), lines 4 and 11; the State overlaps t_3, line 18. Again, other aspectual information is omitted.

5.3.4   Description: Full Anaphora

The hallmarks of descriptive passages are an adverbial of location in the first clause, with scope over the following material; I posit a tacit time adverbial as well. The entities in a descriptive passage are states, ongoing events (in the progressive) or atelic events. The time adverbial triggers coercion of telic events to atelic events, as in Chapter 4. After the appropriate entities are entered into the DRS, the principle of Full Anaphora applies.

The compositional construction rule for Description applies to the first sentence of a descriptive passage. The sentence has an initial adverbial of space which locates the scene. The rule constructs a tacit durative time adverbial. The adverbial introduces an entity *mt* into the DRS and triggers a condition identifying it as a durative amount, here unspecified. The entity *mt* follows Kamp & Reyle's account of durative adverbs (1993). The durative adverbial serves as a coercion trigger for this sentence and subsequent sentences of the passage.

(30)   Construction rule: first sentence of a Description passage
        In a clause *n* with temporal entities t_n: the situation entity in *n* is unbounded or atelic, of type *e*:
        $S[_{Adv}[Loc] + e + tense] \rightarrow$
        $t_{1n}, t_{2n}, t_{3n}; A, B; adv, mt$

The locating adverbial introduces an entity *adv* into the DRS and triggers a condition locating the situation at that place.

Non-first sentences do not require a special construction rule for temporal interpretation: they introduce times in the usual way. Coercion rules will apply as usual. They must have access to the unspecified adverbial of duration in the context. Non-first sentences of Description fall under the Full Anaphora Principle of tense interpretation because of the entities they introduce and the DRS context in which they are interpreted. The DRS must contain a space adverbial and a durative time adverbial without amount specification, which have the relevant sentence in their scope. I invoke here a general principle of discourse continuity: between the initial Descriptive sentence and the sentence in question, the context must not contain a time or space adverbial, or a bounded event. These would interrupt the continuing scope of the Description passage.[12]

The Full Anaphora Principle is stated in (31).

(31)   Full Anaphora Principle
        In the context of temporal entities t_n of the DRS, if the situation entities associated with t_{n-2} and/or t_{n-1} are unbounded or atelic, and locating and temporal conditions obtain:

12. Recognizing changes in continuity, when scope is interrupted, is discussed further in Chapter 7. Stating the possibilities in detail is quite complex: for instance, description typically has space adverbials that fall within the scope of the initial space adverbial, so that one does not want to block every space adverbial in descriptive contexts.

If the situation entities of n are unbounded and atelic entities of type *e*.
RT_x immediately preceding: $RT_y = RT_x$

The diagram in (32) presents a DRS for the simplified first three sentences of the Descriptive passage in (5a) above. The passage occurs in a narrative context. By the principle of limited anaphora the first RT is the same as the preceding RT. The times introduced with each clause are notated with subscripts "a"–"c."

The first clause introduces a state; the next two situations are perfective Activities. In this context they are bounded, but the bounds do not coincide with the initial or final endpoints of the events. The notation of inclusion (lines 11, 17) applies to the bounded units focused by the perfective viewpoint. The duration of the states is greater than or equal to the amount *mt* of the tacit time adverbial (lines 4, 12, 18).

(32)   a. In the passenger car the windows were propped open.
        b. A breeze blew through.
        c. The yellow butterflies flew in at the window.

---

t_{1a} t_{2a} t_{2a-1} t_{3a} e_1 x adv mt t_{1b} t_{2b} t_{3b} e_2 y t_{1c} t_{2c} t_{3c} e_3 z w

---

1. $t_{2a} = t_{2a-1}$ (Principle of Limited Anaphora)
2. $t_{2a} = t_{3a}$
3. $e_1 \ 0 \ t_{3a}$
4. $dur(e_1) \geq mt$
5. x = the windows
6. e_1: prop open (x)
7. adv = in the passenger car
8. e_1 at adv

9. $t_{2b} = t_{2a}$ (Principle of Full Anaphora)
10. $t_{2b} = t_{3b}$
11. $e_2 \subseteq t_{3a}$
12. $dur(e_2) \geq mt$
13. y = a breeze
14. e_2: blew through (y)

15. $t_{2c} = t_{2b}$ (Principle of Full Anaphora)
16. $t_{2c} = t_{3c}$
17. $e_3 \subseteq t_{3c}$
18. $dur(e_3) \geq mt$
19. z = yellow butterflies
20. w = the window
21. e_3: fly in (z,w)

5.3.5   *Report: temporal advancement*

In Reports, tense is oriented to Speech Time. It is not obvious how to understand the deictic interpretation of tense for sequences of sentences. One approach would posit an advancing Speech Time and a series of communications. With the convention that communication is instantaneous, at each clausal unit the text would advance by a moment (ignoring embeddings). Advancement would be linear. There is something right about this, but it pertains to shifts in the focus of attention during reading, rather than interpretation of sentences in text passages.

I take a different approach that emphasizes the function of RT: Reference Time is the locus for advancement. In the following example, I apply the principle for deictic interpretation to the Report mode. RT may shift back and forth from Speech Time with each clause, because RT is calculated at each clause. To see this, consider the Report passage below, repeated from Chapter 2.

(33)   1 A week that began in violence ended violently here, with bloody clashes in the West Bank and Gaza and intensified fighting in Southern Lebanon. 2 Despite the violence, back-channel talks continued in Sweden. 3 Israeli, Palestinian and American officials have characterized them as a serious and constructive dialogue on the process itself and on the final status issues. 4 News accounts here say that Israel is offering as much as 90 percent of the West Bank to Palestinians, although it is difficult to assess what is really happening by the bargaining moves that are leaked.

S1 has an RT prior to SpT, indicated by the past tense. S2 is also in the past tense. The event expressed, of continuing talks, is not related to the event of S1 in any direct way. The present perfect tense of S3 shifts RT from the Past to SpT. The rest of the passage proceeds in the same fashion.

No additional construction rules or principles for calculating advancement are needed for the Report mode. The deictic principle is applied anew for each clause. I analyze formally a simplified version of this rather complex fragment. The simplification does not substantially affect the temporal advancement of the text.

(34)   Simplified Report fragment
        a. A week ended violently.
        b. Back-channel talks continued in Sweden.
        c. Officials characterized them as a serious dialogue.
        d. Israel is offering as much as 90 percent of the West Bank.

t_{1a} t_{2a} t_{3a} e_1 x t_{1b} t_{2b} t_{3b} e_2 y z t_{1c} t_{2c} t_{3c} e_3 u v w t_{1d} t_{2d} t_{3d} e_4 s t

1. $t_{1a} = SpT$
2. $t_{2a} < t_{1a}$
3. $t_{2a} = t_{3a}$
4. $e_1 \subseteq t_{3a}$
5. $x = week$
6. e_1: end (x)

7. $t_{1b} = SpT$
8. $t_{2b} < t_{1b}$
9. $t_{2b} = t_{3b}$
10. $e_2 \subseteq t_{3b}$
11. $y = back\text{-}channel\ talks$
12. $z = in\ Sweden$
13. e_2: continue (y)

14. $t_{1c} = SpT$
15. $t_{2c} < t_{1c}$
16. $t_{2c} = t_{3c}$
17. $e_3 \subseteq t_{3c}$
18. $w = officials$
19. $u = y$
20. $v = serious\ dialogue$
21. e_3: characterize (w,u,v)

22. $t_{1d} = SpT$
23. $t_{2d} = t_{1d}$
24. $t_{2d} = t_{3d}$
25. $e_3\ O\ t_{3c}$
26. $s = Israel$
27. $t = 90\ percent\ of\ the\ West\ Bank$
28. e_4: offer (s,t)

Aspectual information is omitted since it does not affect the calculation of temporal location in the Report mode.

This completes the sketch of temporal advancement in the Discourse Modes. Description passages advance spatially, as the description covers different parts of what is described. The spatial domain, as we will see directly, is not a closed system. Spatial advancement may be conveyed in several ways and can't be calculated by rule as temporal advancement can.

5.4   Spatial information in language

Space is like time in some ways: both require an orientation point to locate an entity in the domain. Linguistically too space and time are closely related.

Linguistic expressions treat time as metaphorical space. For instance, we talk of the past as "behind" and the future as "ahead"; and say "the coming year," "the fast-disappearing year," etc. (H. Clark 1973, Fillmore 1975). Here and in many other cases, similar linguistic expressions are used for time and space. There are temporal and spatial adjectives, adverbs, and propositions; and temporal and spatial complements to verbs.

Nevertheless space and time are expressed differently in language. Temporal location is conveyed by tense and a relatively small set of prepositions, adverbs, and adjectives. Information about spatial location, on the other hand, is conveyed by many verbs, adverbials, and adjectives. These differences in linguistic expression are due to the structure of the domains themselves, and to humans' knowledge of them.

I will discuss three ways in which the domains differ for humans: directness of perception and cognition, relative complexity, and relation to volitional action.

Space can be experienced directly through various channels, as Freksa (1992) notes. Humans perceive space by visual, tactile, and acoustic means; and indirectly through other senses as well. According to Freksa: "Physical space plays a central role in cognition as the domain in which physical events take place and as reference domain for the interpretation of non-spatial concepts." Time, however, is not perceived directly by senses. We are just beginning to understand its role in cognition (Damasio 2002). Time in Western culture is a human construct that is conceived on the metaphor of space (Friedman 1993).

The domains differ in complexity. Space has three dimensions and therefore objects can be located in space in more than one way. Using one dimension, we locate an object with a reference point; using two dimensions, with a reference line; using three, with a reference plane. English has linguistic expressions for all three dimensions. For instance the prepositions *at*, *on*, *in* differ precisely in the dimensions they express. To say "John is on the grass" treats grass as two-dimensional, while "John is in the grass" treats it as three-dimensional (Fillmore 1975).

There is an additional level of complexity for space, that of orientation. We often think of spatial location in terms of a canonical set of orientations such as "front" and "back." The human body provides the basic orientations, as documented in H. Clark (1973). These orientations are often extended to objects in the world. By extension concrete objects have backs and fronts (e.g. a house), tops and bottoms (e.g. a box); and locations involve internal or external relations such as *within*, *on top of*, *above*, *below*. With all these resources the location of a given entity, or describing a spatial configuration, may be quite complex. Think of an Italian landscape painting with a cathedral atop a hill and rocks spilling down toward the right side. To explain its spatial structure would involve all three dimensions and more than one orienting perspective.

In contrast, the temporal domain is one-dimensional. Because of its relative simplicity, the possible temporal relations between entities can be enumerated and calculated. In linear time any two events have exactly one out of thirteen qualitatively distinct relationships to each other, ignoring orientation (Allen 1983). If we add orientation, there are twenty-six possible relations between objects, Freksa (1992) has calculated. Nothing so simple as this is possible for space.

People engage directly with space by volitional action, whereas their inter-action with time is often involuntary.[13] The role of volition brings out a crucial difference between the domains. Events involving space are agentive, usually following an active choice by the agent. One decides to cross the street, hang a picture, take out the garbage, deliver a message. The passing of time is often parasitic on facts about particular events: crossing a narrow lane takes less time than crossing a wide boulevard. Again, maintaining rather than changing a given state of affairs is often voluntary; the passage of time is concomitant, a secondary effect of the decision to maintain the state. The contrast is not perfect: there are a few cases in which time is directly and volitionally involved in an event, e.g. one may deliberately walk or hold one's breath for a long or a short time.

Languages typically have rich verbal resources for talking about space. Spatial information is encoded directly in many verbs. For instance, in verbs like *hang* the spatial factor makes an essential contribution. English has a set of many prepositions which also convey spatial information. There only a few temporal verbs (*pass the time, take an hour, spend an hour*, and the aspectual verbs *begin, start*, etc.).

Most verbs with a strand of temporal meaning involve projected situations and attitudes. Classes of verbs with a temporal component include verbs of Future Having (*advance, guarantee, owe*, etc.), verbs of Future Situation (*propose, plan, arrange for*, etc.); verbs of Wish and Desire (*want, covet, need, yearn*, etc.); verbs of Future Events (*predict, expect, foretell*, etc.); verbs of Future Prevention (*preclude, prevent*, etc.); and verbs of Past Events (*resent, realize*, etc.). Levin (1993) provides detailed lists.

Strikingly, the main factor for these verbs is modality, not time. They involve attitudes, plans, or factive meanings, many with a discrepancy between the current state of affairs and other states of affairs. They are only indirectly

---

13. I thank Jocelyn Cohan for helpful comments on volition.

temporal. There are few temporal analogues to verbs with spatial meanings, which are directly concerned with space – traversing it in various ways, directionality, spatial configuration.

These points may explain an otherwise odd fact about spatial and temporal phrases and coercion. In coercion, an adverbial triggers a shift in the aspectual value of a basic-level situation type. For instance, a basic-level Activity clause denotes a non-specific atelic event which is not explicitly bounded (35a). When a prepositional phrase is added, the resulting clause denotes a bounded, specific event (35b–c):

(35)   a. They walked.   (no explicit bound)
        b. They walked for three miles.   (bounded)
        c. They walked for an hour.   (bounded)

In these examples the spatial and temporal PPs function in the same way, providing an explicit bound to the event. With other prepositions, however, there is a difference between the contribution of the spatial and temporal adverbials. Compare (36a–b): the spatial PP adds the component of telicity, the temporal PP does not:

(36)   a. They walked to school.   (telic: change of state)
        b. They walked until noon.   (bounded)

In (a) the event involves arrival at a new location, a change of state. But we don't think of (b) this way: we do not conceive of an event of walking-until-noon as an arrival, or as involving a new state. There are grammatical correlates to this conceptual difference. Sentences like (36a) pass tests for telicity, whereas sentences like (36b) do not.[14] The grammatical and conceptual differences show that a spatial bound constitutes a *telos* whereas a temporal bound does not.

Although every concrete entity has a spatiotemporal location, we have seen that there are important differences between the domains of time and space. These differences give an explanation for the fact that aspect and temporal location can be expressed linguistically through a closed system, while spatial location cannot.

5.5   *Features of temporal expressions*

The temporal value of a clause is conveyed by temporal expressions and the syntax of the clause. The information is based on features associated with each

---

14. Tests for telicity include felicitous co-occurrence with verbs and adverbs of completion (*in an hour, finish*) and ambiguity with *almost*.

temporal expression. This section discusses the features needed in a systematic account of English. The features indicate the relational meaning of a form and the systematic possibilities for its interpretation. To develop the system, we need to consider several kinds of information.

There are three types of features: Relational, Orientation, and Role features. Relational features give the value of a temporal expression, based on its lexical meaning. For example, the past tense, the adverb *before*, and the verbal auxiliary *have*, all have the value of anteriority, $<$; *now* and the present tense have the value of simultaneity, $=$; *after* and the modal *will* have the value of posteriority, $>$.

Orientation features give the anchoring possibilities for an expression. Tenses are more limited than other temporal forms. The tenses orient to Present or Future, but not to a Past time. In simple sentences, both past and present tenses orient to Speech Time (SpT), as we have seen. There are other interpretations for tenses in complement clauses. If the main clause has a non-Past time both tenses orient to that time, as in (37); each has its consistent relational value:

(37) a. Mary thinks that she is a candidate.
　　 b. Bill says that he won the election.
　　 c. Bill will say that he won the election.
　　 d. Mary will announce that she is a candidate.

However, (38) shows that neither tense orients to a Past time:

(38) a. Mary said that she is a candidate.
　　 b. Mary said that she was a candidate.

The main clause of (38a) is past; the complement clause, with present tense, orients to SpT, not a time simultaneous with the main clause. In (38b), main and complement clause both have past tense; the complement clause indicates the same time as the main clause, not a time anterior to it.[15] The sequences

---

15. The complement clause may have a relative tense, which conveys a SitT other than RT; the perfect indicates that SitT precedes RT (a), the future-in-past that SitT follows RT (b):

　　 a. John said that Mary had left.
　　 b. Mary said that John would leave.

　Neither of these cases advances narrative time.
　　A very different view of the relation between main and complement clauses is presented in S. Thompson (2001), which argues that the main clauses of traditional analysis express speaker stance toward the content of the clause. The discussion focuses on examples from conversational English.

of tenses in (37–38) show that both tenses have an Orientation value of Nonpast.

Most adverbials, and *have* and *will*, are flexible in orientation. We need an Orientation feature to account for them. There is also a class of deictic adverbials which orient only to Speech Time (SpT); they require a feature that specifies this. The Orientation features are thus Nonpast, Flexible, SpT.

Locating adverbials contribute to the specification of either Reference Time or Situation Time. Their Role depends on the context in which they appear: the combination of temporal expressions, and syntactic structure, determine the interpretation of a clause.

(39)   Types of Locating adverbials
    a. Rigid deictics: yesterday ($<$), tomorrow ($>$)
    b. Flexible deictics: three days ago, in three days, next week
    c. Flexible: on Tuesday, before Mary left
    d. Overt Dependent: three days earlier
    e. Anaphoric: then, at that time
    f. Calendar: June 19, 1984.

With appropriate adverbials it is possible to construct a sentence which relates to a Past anchor time, yet indicates a time in the Future.[16]

Tense and adverbials may contribute to RT or SitT, as the examples illustrate:

(40)   a. Mary called on Tuesday.
    b. Mary called yesterday. She was excited.
    c. Last week, Keith comes up to me all of a sudden and laughs.
    d. Bill said that Keith was leaving in three days.

---

16. The sentence below illustrates this possibility. Assume that it is uttered on a Tuesday, which is two days after last Sunday:

> Bill confessed last Sunday that he would resign in a week.

The complement clause has the same RT as the matrix, the Past time of "last Sunday"; the adverbial *in a week* specifies a time following, a time that is in the future of the RT and of the time of speech. The interpretation is shown below:

> S_1[Bill confessed last Sunday S_2[that he would resign in a week]]
> ..../.............../.............SpT........./......................
> S_1: $RT_1 = SitT_1$ S_2: $RT_2 = SitT_1$
> last Sunday $SitT_2 > RT_2$
> SpT: Tuesday
> $SitT_1$: last Sunday, two days earlier
> $SitT_2$: a week from last Sunday = Saturday

In (40a), the tense indicates RT which precedes SpT; in the second sentence of (40b), the tense continues the RT which is previously established. In (40c) the adverbial specifies RT prior to SpT, whereas in the complement of (40d) the adverbial specifies SitT. These interpretations are made by construction rules using feature information.

Auxiliary *have* has the relational value of anteriority with the same flexibility. It may contribute to either RT or SitT: thus *have* indicates SitT in (41), and RT in (42).

(41)   a. Mary has arrived.
           b. Mary had already arrived.
           c. Mary will have arrived.
           d. auxiliary *have*: $SitT < RT$

(42)   a. Last Sunday John left the country. On Friday he had closed his bank account, and had rented his house; at his office, he had emptied all the drawers and shelves; then he (had) told his staff to take a holiday, and (had) made his final arrangements.
           b. auxiliary *have*: $RT_2 < RT_1$

In a narrative, a fragment like (42a) might be a flashback.

We now discuss Role features in connection with future *will*, a modal with the relational value of posteriority. Unlike the other temporal expressions of English, *will* has only one role: it always contributes to RT. A feature associated with *will* provides for a single Role. This analysis, or something like it, is necessary within the Reichenbach framework (see Ogihara 1996 for a different view). Clauses with *will* always allow auxiliary *have*, and thus an additional time; (43) illustrates:

(43)   a. Mary will have already arrived.
           b. Mary says that in three days she will have finished her project.
           c. Mary said last Sunday that in three days she would have finished her project.

These clauses involve three different times: t_1, $RT > t_1$, $SitT < RT$ (the latter indicated by auxiliary *have*). Note that sentence (43c) involves four times altogether, since the main clause sets a Past orientation time for the complement. A Role Feature limits the role of *will* to RT. The proposed features are summarized in (44).

(44)   Features for Temporal Expressions in English

	Relational			Orientation			Role
	<	=	>	Flexible	SpT	Non-Past	
present tense		+				+	
past tense	+					+	
aux *have*	+			+			
modal *will*			+	+			RT
Locating adv							
at – o'clock		+	+				
– ago	+			+			
yesterday	+				+		

The rules of the construction algorithm automatically have access to these features. They will be listed in the lexical entries for temporal expressions. (Since no working theory of the lexicon has been given, I do not provide actual lexical entries.)

Summarizing, this section provides the basis for the interpretation of English temporal location in Discourse Representation Theory.

This chapter has outlined the temporal location system of English and shown how tense is interpreted in the different Discourse Modes.

Example sources in this chapter:

(1) and (23) Peter Robinson, *A Necessary End*, New York: Avon Books, 1989, p. 182.
(4) Peter Beinart, The pride of the cities. *New Republic*, June 1997.
(5a) Eudora Welty, *Delta Wedding*, New York: Harcourt, Brace, 1945, p. 1.
(5b) and (6) Doris Lessing, *Under My Skin*, New York: Harper Perennial, 1994, p. 116.
(7) Intel delays downtown decision. *Austin American-Statesman*, December 15, 2001.
(9) Robert Mosbacher, Cheap oil's tough bargains. *New York Times*, March 13, 2000.
(10) Jim Collins, How it works. *US Airways Magazine, Attaché*, May 2001.
(19) Lillian Hellman, *Scoundrel Time*, Boston: Little, Brown, 1976, p. 72.
(33) A year after victory, Barak fights on many fronts, *New York Times*, May 20, 2000.

6 *Referring expressions in discourse*

This chapter discusses the contribution of referring expressions to discourse. I first consider in detail the notion of Primary Referent. The Primary Referent is central in a situation, and the key to atemporal text progression. The discussion will complete the linguistically based characterization of the Discourse Modes. With the Discourse Mode analysis fully developed, I turn to other aspects of referring expressions in texts.

Referring expressions convey information by their form. This is possible because the class of referring expressions in a language belong to a closed system. There are a limited number of terms, of which one must be chosen. Choice of a term has contrastive force that may go beyond lexical and referential meaning. Referring expressions give information about the familiarity status of the referent, and signal either continuity or change of direction in a discourse. Within the narrower range of simple and reflexive pronouns, the choice of a pronoun conveys additional, more subtle, notions. These matters are pragmatic in nature.

Section 6.1 discusses Primary Referents and how to determine the primary referring expression in a clause; 6.2 considers referring expressions and closed systems, focusing on pronoun forms and meanings; 6.3 discusses the familiarity status of referring expressions, and their patterns of use in texts; 6.4 considers referring expressions and Discourse Representation Theory.

6.1   *Atemporal text progression and Primary Referents*

6.1.1   *Determining the Primary Referent*

Progression in text passages of the atemporal modes proceeds by metaphorical motion. A Primary Referent that is semantically central is identified for each clause of a passage. Each referent is located metaphorically in the semantic domain of the text. When the Primary Referents in successive clauses are in different locations, the receiver has the intuition of metaphorical motion.

The idea of a semantically central referent is based on our intuition of what is salient and most significant in a situation. For events, the entity that moves or changes is most significant. For states, it is the entity whose location is maintained or asserted. These intuitions are cognitively based, having to do with properties of the situation in the world. Motion, stability, and change of state are important, and psychologists have shown that human children recognize them very early (Gelman 1990, Leslie 1994). The notion of Primary Referent is quite close in spirit to Talmy's notion of Figure, a cognitive–semantic category borrowed from Gestalt psychology. The Figure of a motion or location event sentence is "a moving or conceptually movable point . . . that functions as a variable in the situation" (1978:628). The notion of Primary Referent is also close to Gruber's "pivot of the situation," which he identified as the Theme (1965:29).

The Primary Referent is determined by the components of a situation, and does not depend on the surface form of a sentence. For instance, in both "George broke the glass" and "The glass was broken by George" the Primary Referent is "the glass," though it is the direct object in the active, subject in the passive.

The full range of situations can be conceptualized with a set of primitives, components that provide a basis for analysis. The components organize events and states in terms of causal structure, spatial location, and motion. All components need not be expressed in every clause. Example (1) is based on Talmy (1985) and Croft (1991):[1]

(1)   Cause, Object, Motion, Ground, Path, Final State;
       Means, Manner, Instrument

In a motion event an Object traverses a Path, perhaps toward a Final State; the Cause may be explicit or implicit. Certain states locate an Object in terms of a Ground or other components. These notions can be extended to all domains, following the localist principle that spatial notions are fundamental and applicable generally. The insight, due to Gruber, is that "the formalism for encoding spatial location and motion, suitably abstracted, can be generalized to other semantic fields" (Jackendoff 1990:25). Motion and location, then, may be literal or metaphorical.

---

1. These components are sometimes presented in a way that expresses causal order, as in Croft (1991:185). The components are also useful in understanding the way linguistic expressions in different languages express events. Patterns of realization across languages are explored in Talmy (1985). Croft focuses on linguistic universals and syntactic categories.

   There is another, somewhat different approach to the basic components of situations, due to Hale & Keyser (1993), Erteschik-Shir & Rapoport (in press), and others. These scholars propose a small set of components which are related directly to underlying semantic–syntactic structure.

Elaborating these ideas, I give criteria for determining the Primary Referent of clauses that express situations of different kinds. Example (2) deals with event clauses; states are discussed directly below. The example sentences are taken from an Argument passage in this study; the Primary Referent expressions are italicized.

(2)   Criteria: Primary Referent of Events
        The Primary Referent is that entity in an event which
        a. Undergoes a change of state
           The high school outsider becomes *the more successful adult.*
        b. Is causally affected by another participant
           The national outpouring has forced *us* to confront the situation.
        c. Doesn't exist independently of the event
           High school students present and past have come forward with *stories about cliques and an artificial world.*
        d. Moves or otherwise changes
           Young people mature substantially earlier in the late 20th century than they did when the high school was invented.

There is some overlap among the criteria: a referent which undergoes a change of state (a) is often causally affected by another participant (b) and changes in some way (d). However, there are cases for which all four criteria are needed.

The domain of states requires more discussion. The Primary Referent in state sentences can often be determined with the localist principle: the entity whose location is asserted is the Primary Referent. By the localist principle, all cases in which a property is ascribed to an entity are locational. Positional sentences are basic, with *x is at y* the prototypical state. But the principle is not always easy to put into practice. When two entities are involved, it may not be clear which one is the Primary Referent. In other cases the metaphorical extension is delicate. Additional criteria are needed to supplement the general localist principle.

Criteria for determining the Primary Referent of states are listed in (3). Following the list is a discussion of how they apply to the main classes of states, and to special problematic cases. The examples are from texts in this study; Primary Referent expressions are italicized.

(3)   Criteria: State Primary Referent
        The Primary Referent is that entity which is
        a. Literally or metaphorically located
           Dragons are usually arranged almost heraldically round a conceptual center point.

b. Dependent on the situation for existence
The predominant output was *the white ware* with transparent ivory toned glaze which made the kilns famous.
c. Figure relative to a Ground
A group of kilns is northeast of Ch'ang-an, the capital city of the T'ang dynasty
d. Has a property ascribed to it
The most important kilns are *those at Tao-chu in Shensi.*

More specific criteria are applied before the general. Criterion (d), for instance, holds of the subject in any state sentence.

I distinguish three classes of state: states of location, including position and possession; mental states of thought, belief, feeling, perception, communication; states of composition and identification, and property ascription. The criterion of literal and metaphorical location nicely applies to the first two classes. Consider first states of location. With positional states, the located entity is the Primary Referent (underlined): for instance in "The lamppost is on the corner," the Primary Referent is "the lamppost." For states of possession, the possessed entity or concept is the Primary Referent and its metaphorical location is the possessor, as in "John has a book," "Mary has an idea." Mental states, the second class, fall under the rubric of extended possession. The contents of mental states are possessed by the person who holds them, as in "John likes strawberries," "Mary thinks that Lee is here."

Compositional and identificational states can be analyzed with the criteria of dependence and possession. For example:

(4)   a. We are truly a spoiled society.
        b. Oil has been one of the real bargains of the modern age.
        c. The committee consists of eight people.

In (4a–b) the concepts denoted by the predicative NPs are the Primary Referents; they depend for their existence on the subject NPs.[2] In (4c) the referent of "eight people" is the primary, by possession.

The third criterion applies in location sentences when one entity is located in relation to another, known as Figure–Ground sentences. Consider (5):

2. The NPs in these examples are predicative: the sentences have only one referent. They can be conjoined with adjectives: "Mary considers John competent in semantics and an authority on unicorns" (Partee 1987:119). In uncertain cases, the possibility of conjunction with an adjectival predicate is a good test for the function of an NP. By this criterion the post-copula NPs in (3b–c) are predicative. The subject NP of (3d) is also predicative: there is only one referent in the sentence, the kilns at Tao-chu in Shensi. The formulation of this criterion is similar to a criterion for Theme role in Dowty (1991).

(5)   a. Harry is near John.
        b. Harry resembles Aunt Mabel.
        c. The bike is near the house.
        d. The house is near the mountain.

The sentences seem symmetrical: if John is near Harry, then surely Harry is near John. But in fact one entity functions as the Ground for locating the other, the Figure. To show this we look at different types of cases, following Talmy (2000). For (5 a–b) either NP is plausible as the subject: "John is near Harry," and "Aunt Mabel resembles Harry" are good sentences. Often, however, the alternative realization is semantically peculiar. The alternatives of (5c–d) are peculiar (indicated by #):

(6)   a. # The house is near the bike.
        b. # The mountain is near the house.

Pairs like this show that factors other than location play a role in what makes an acceptable Figure. (6a–b) are odd because a bike is not a plausible reference point for locating a house, nor is a house plausible as a reference point for locating a mountain. Although the relation between the referents is apparently symmetric, one is usually more appropriate than the other as Ground.

The relative size and stability of the referents determine what is appropriate as Figure and Ground. These are points about the world, not about the grammar.[3] In Figure–Ground sentences the subject phrase gives the Primary Referent. An alternative structure is inversion ("Near the house is a bike"). Nothing quite like the active–passive alternation exists for sentences with the copula. The non-canonical existential *there* construction has the same constraint, strikingly. For instance, "There is a bike near the house" is good, whereas # "There is a house near the bike" is odd indeed. Inversions and existential *there* sentences are discussed in Chapter 9. I think that the evidence is strong that the notion of Figure is semantically based in these cases (*pace* Dowty 1991). Yet, since it appears in subject position, the Figure conflates semantic event structure and pragmatic presentation.

3. Talmy lists the main factors: the Ground is usually (i) more permanently located; (ii) larger; (iii) geometrically more complex; (iv) more familiar/expected; (v) of lesser concern or relevance; (vi) more immediately perceivable; (vii) more backgrounded once Figure is perceived; (viii) more independent (Talmy 2000: I, 315).
    Almost identical criteria are proposed by Polinsky in a discussion of Figure and Ground in Tsez, a language of the Caucasus, that belongs to the Nakh-Daghestanian family (1996). She argues that Figure and Ground involve the interface between conceptual structure and syntactic–semantic structure. The similarities suggest that the Figure–Ground distinction may be coded similarly in many languages.

Certain State sentences do not have a semantically Primary Referent. There are two types: sentences with symmetric predicates such as *similar* (7a), and sentences that literally identify a referent (7b–c):

(7)   a. Sam is similar to Lee.
        b. Clark Kent is Superman.
        c. Cicero is Tully.

These appear to be truly symmetrical: neither referent is primary. In such sentences the subject position involves a particular perspective, as Talmy points out. In these, unlike the Figure–Ground cases, either referent can appear as subject.

Equational clauses and clauses with symmetric predicates have no referent that is primary in the semantic sense. In such cases the subject referent functions as Figure, a referent that is presentationally primary.

The notion of Primary Referent corresponds closely to the concept of Proto-patient role proposed by Dowty (1991). The Proto-patient thematic Role is like the traditional thematic Role of Theme, augmented with the Role of Incremental Theme.[4] The syntactic arguments that realize this Role are patients rather than actors, effects rather than causes. In transitive sentences, the direct object usually expresses this Role; in sentences with the copula, the subject expresses it. Dowty takes a prototype approach to the notions of Agent and Patient/Theme. He assembles a cluster of properties which are characteristic of each. In a given sentence, the Proto-patient is the argument that has the most Patient properties; the Agent argument has the most Agent properties. Dowty's approach is semantic, based on the structure of events and states rather than surface structure. His discussion focuses on "the Argument-selection problem," seeking principles that language uses to determine, for each argument of an n-place relation denoted by a predicate, which argument is expressed by which grammatical relation.

The Primary Referent of a clause is usually also its Proto-patient argument. I will use this fact in writing construction rules for determining the Primary Referent for Discourse Representation Theory. I assume that information about Proto-patient, or Theme, is available in the underlying syntactic structure of a sentence, and in surface structure. In principle then, most clauses have a

4. The Incremental Theme argument of a talic predicate participates in a homomorphican from the structured theme argument denotations to the structured event (Dowty 1991, Krifka 1989).

Primary Referent. The criteria given have been used successfully to identify Primary Referents in an informal study.[5]

There is a syntactic notion of prominent argument that may seem related to Primary Referent. It is not: the two are quite distinct. The "prominent argument" relates syntactic structure to argument structure. For instance, Grimshaw (1990) claims that the subject is prominent syntactically because of its position as an external argument. The Agent and Cause roles that are typically realized by subjects are also prominent, according to Grimshaw, in argument structure and event structure respectively. The subject is also regarded as prominent in Speas (1990), who makes a different proposal. For Speas, thematic roles originate in positions in lexical conceptual structure. The syntactic realization corresponds to a thematic hierarchy, and follows the Universal Thematic Association Hypothesis (UTAH) of Baker (1988). Prominence in the thematic hierarchy corresponds to syntactic prominence, Speas suggests; Agents are associated with the prominent subject position. In contrast, the Primary Referent proposed here is associated with the outcome or motion of a situation, not the agent/cause.

In determining the Primary Referents in a text I proceed on a clause-by-clause basis. For clauses with a sentential complement, the Primary Referent is decided as usual. If the event or state expressed by the complement is the Primary Referent, the internal Primary Referent is noted as another level of structure. In complex sentences each clause is treated separately, see Chapter 9.

6.1.2   Primary Referents in text fragments

I now give a sample analysis of the clauses of an atemporal text passage in terms of Primary Referents. I then state construction rules for determining the Primary Referent of a clause, using the notion of Proto-patient/Theme.

The passage in (8) is a fragment in the Information mode. The Primary Referents are underlined for all tensed clauses, and a brief explanation of each choice given in (9). Clauses without an underlined phrase have no decidable Primary Referent. The passage appears at the beginning of a magazine article:

(8)   1 The largest and most complex highway-engineering project in American history has been making <u>headlines</u> over the past several months. 2 Boston's central artery project, known as the Big Dig, has become <u>nightly news fare</u>,

---

5. An informal study ascertained that the criteria can be applied. The members of a seminar on this material were given two texts and asked to identify the Primary Referent of each clause. They agreed in most cases.

thanks to the massive cost overruns and steadily growing complaints of mis-management and corruption. 3 Overshadowed by scandal, <u>the work itself</u> – whose scale and ambition are truly mind-boggling – continues almost as a matter of course.

4 The heart of the project is <u>an eight-to-ten-lane highway</u>$_i$. 5 <u>It</u>$_i$ is being built below ground to relieve the legendary traffic pressure caused by Boston's two major arteries$_i$, <u>which</u>$_i$ converge downtown awkwardly near the harbor, skyscrapers, and historic buildings. 6 Threading 35 lane-miles of tunnel through Boston's 3-D maze of subway lines and building foundations, all without drastically disturbing the normal routines of surface life, is <u>an engineering plan</u>$_i$ that$_i$ borders on the fantastic. 7 In some places <u>the tunnels</u> are 120 feet deep. 8 The first two frequently asked questions on the project's official Web site are "What are you building?" and "Are you nuts?"

9 Surprisingly, tunnels are among <u>the most ancient engineering feats</u>.

The first two sentences have "headlines" and "news fare" as Primary Referents: there is little change in metaphorical location from one to the other. At S3 the Primary Referent is "the work itself," at Sentences 4 and 5 "the highway," and, at the relative clause, the relative pronoun referring to "Boston's major arteries." At S6 the fantastic nature of the plan is primary, at S7 "the tunnels" is Primary Referent; S8 has no distinguishable Primary Referent; at S9 "ancient engineering feats" is primary. This sequence corresponds quite well to one's intuition of progression in the text, I think.

The reason for each choice of Primary Referent is listed very briefly in (9). For sentences with more than one clause, the clauses are lettered *a*, *b*, etc.:

(9)   Justification of choices of Primary Referents in (8)
       S1) referent dependent on the situation for existence
       S2) referent dependent on the situation for existence
       S3) referent that moves/changes in the Event
       S4) referent dependent on the situation for existence
       S5) *a*, subject NP, referent come into being
              b, relative clause, referent located
       S6) referent dependent on the situation for existence
       S7) referent has a property ascribed to it
       S8) equational, no single Primary Referent
       S9) referent dependent on the situation for existence

Although in S8 there is no semantically Primary Referent, the subject is presentationally primary; see Part III for discussion.

6.1.3   Primary Referents and Discourse Representation Theory
Primary Referents can be identified by construction rules on two assumptions. The first is that the Primary Referent of a clause coincides with the Theme/Patient Role. I also assume that the argument realizing this role can

be identified by semantic and syntactic factors that relate event structure and argument structure. I will not try to state them here, so that this construction rule is something of a promissory note. The enterprise, however, does not seem hopeless. There is general agreement as to which argument realizes the Theme/Patient role, although people do not agree on how to state principles of argument selection. By hypothesis, then, an argument in the surface structure of a clause has a semantic–syntactic feature that codes Patient/Theme information from Event structure.

The construction rule identifies the argument with the Theme/Patient feature (T/P) as Primary Referent. The information about Primary Referent will appear as a condition on the entity in the Discourse Representation Structure. I state the rule below and illustrate for the first sentence of (8), simplified:

(10)   Primary Referents in the DRS
         a. Construction Rule
            $[\ldots{}_a[+\text{T/P}].\ldots\ldots] \rightarrow a = \text{Primary Referent}$

The rule applies to the sentence "The project made headlines over the past months," as shown below. The NP "headlines" is the Primary Referent since it is the direct object of a transitive change-of-state verb (notated as V_t for telic), and results in the DRS shown in (11b). In (11a), the input to the rule is a surface structure with an NP subject, a transitive verb (V_t), as NP object specified as [+T/P]. "X" and "Y" indicate irrelevant material.

(11)   a. $_{\text{IP}}[\text{NP}_{\text{VP}} \text{ X}[V_t \text{ }_{\text{NP}}[+\text{T/P}] \text{ Y}]] \rightarrow \text{NP} = \text{PriRef}$
         b. *The project made headlines over the past months*

t_1 t_2 t_3 x y e d
1. e: made (x,y)
2. $t_1 = S_pT$
3. $t_2 < t_1$
4. d = over the past months
5. $t_2 = d$
6. $t_2 = t_3$
7. $e \subseteq t_3$
8. x = the project
9. y = headlines
10. y = Primary Referent

The sentence is first in the DRS, with the deictic interpretation of the past tense that locates the situation before SpT. The adverb specifies t_2, RT. The event is perfective in this version of the sentence and included in t_3, SitT.

The Primary Referent is the first step in determining atemporal text progression. The next step, more daunting, requires additional pragmatic calculation. Recall that atemporal text progression occurs when metaphorical motion has taken place. I suggested that metaphorical motion proceeds on analogy with space, through the semantic terrain of a text. We know from the discussion in Chapter 5 that spatial information is not conveyed by a grammatically closed system. Morever, often the metaphorical motion in question will be only indirectly spatial. To fully understand these matters we needed a way of accessing and organizing many kinds of general information. We do not have a formal account of how such calculations might be made at present. Perhaps the wide-ranging approach sketched in Asher & Lascarides (1998) would eventually be able to handle them.

The factors that determine text progression of atemporal text passages are not grammatically signalled. Therefore the presentational aspect of such texts, and the discourse relations that organize them at a more abstract level, take on more importance. In the Information and Argument modes, discourse relations may be an important part of atemporal text progression; see Chapter 11 for some discussion.

6.2   *Referring expressions*

The next sections of this chapter are concerned with referring expressions as members of closed systems, and the kind of information that they convey. I discuss the choices available in English, and the significance of a particular choice. There are a number of possibilities for referring to people or other entities: proper names, noun phrases with lexical content, and pronouns of different types. I will be interested here in contrasts between the grammatical forms, e.g. pronouns and lexical NPs, ignoring lexical content.

6.2.1   *Closed systems*
Closed systems in language consist of a relatively small set of forms that contrast with each other. Besides the semantic information that the forms code directly, they have a systematic meaning: choice of form A conveys that form B is not appropriate, or less so. Patterns of one form rather than another can convey continuity in a text.[6]

---

6. Closed systems were extensively studied by linguists of the Prague School. Roman Jakobson, for instance, discussed the meanings of their terms as conveying positive and negative values, symmetry, and contrastive information (1957). I have proposed a somewhat different approach

Referring expressions are closed systems, and pronouns are an important subsystem. There is a very limited set of possibilities in English. Some findings from other languages are pertinent to understanding the uses of English pronouns. As a background for the discussion I make brief comments about noun classifiers in Mandarin, proximate–obviative pronoun systems, and switch reference systems.

The forms of closed systems are often obligatory at the level of the sentence, so that the grammar would predict that they appear in all relevant syntactic contexts. It turns out, however, that extra-grammatical factors affect their appearance.

In a study of noun classifiers in Mandarin Chinese, Erbaugh (1986) makes this point quite dramatically. Classifiers (CLs) are a closed set of morphemes. They appear in principle in NPs when a noun is preceded by a numeral or a demonstrative, e.g. *yiwei lao xiansheng* (an old CL gentleman), *yi pi ma* (one CL horse); there are two types, general and sortal classifiers. Erbaugh's study of classifiers in spoken Mandarin showed that sortal classifiers did not always appear in such contexts.

Sortal classifiers were not predictable on a grammatical basis, Erbaugh found: their use depended on genre, familiarity, and discourse structure.[7] In relatively formal speech situations and narratives, classifiers were most frequent. They tended to appear in NPs that introduced new scenes or characters at event boundaries. In casual conversation they introduced new topics or new concrete objects, but they did not occur often. Erbaugh's work shows these are used in discourse according to extra-grammatical factors, although they are in principle obligatory at the sentence level.

Similarly, certain types of pronouns are used to convey discourse meanings. Proximal–obviative systems have contrasting pronominal morphemes with a referential meaning. They signal whether a subject NP is coreferential with a nearby antecedent. The proximate morpheme indicates coreference with a nearby NP; the other obviates this reference, indicating as antecedent a less

---

to closed systems which distinguishes between semantic and pragmatic information (C. S. Smith 1991). Semantic information is associated with a linguistic form in the grammar of a language, while contrastive information about that form is part of the pragmatic knowledge of the speaker.

7. Erbaugh showed films and asked subjects to narrate the story, using the "Pear Stories". She also collected examples of informal narratives, conversations, letters. There are additional subtleties in the use of classifiers: for instance, Chu notes that the general classifier can be used instead of "a specific one to express a casual attitude" (1983:17).

   The Sino-Tibetan languages, including Mandarin, tend to have measure classifiers and special classifiers. Mandarin also has a general classifier *ge* which may appear with any noun at all.

proximate NP.[8] The NPs are usually third person and animate. Systems of this kind are found in Algonquian languages such as Fox, Plains Cree, Blackfoot.

The notions proximate and obviative have discourse interpretations. The notion "proximate" is often metaphorical: proximate forms tend to be used for characters of importance in the discourse. There are several patterns.[9] In narrative with a consistent central character, the proximate form is often used to refer to that character throughout. Proximate forms are also used at the boundary of a discourse unit, for instance the beginning of a new episode. More generally, "proximate" is predictable, neutral, unmarked. "Obviative" is marked and conveys a referent that is special in some way. The extended, metaphorical distinction between proximal and obviative explains many uses of English stressed and unstressed pronouns, and simple and reflexive pronouns as well.

Another type of system, known as switch reference, has a pronominal morpheme on the verb which indicates whether the subjects of main and dependent clauses are the same or different. The Same Subject morpheme (SS) in principle indicates that the subjects are the same; the Different Subject (DS) indicates that they are not. Switch reference morphemes are obligatory at the level of sentence grammar, like noun classifiers. Also like noun classifiers, the morphemes do not appear in every relevant context, and they usually have discourse meanings beyond the referential. Switch reference morphemes are primarily used to convey information about temporal and other relations between the situations in the main and dependent clauses. Languages with switch reference systems include West African languages, American Indian languages, Papua New Guinea languages.

The main use of switch reference is to indicate semantic relations between situations. Often switch reference morphemes function as temporal connectives. In temporal sentences the SS morpheme conveys that the situations in dependent and matrix clauses are simultaneous, the DS morpheme that they are sequential.[10] These morphemes may also indicate logical or epistemic relations

---

8. Obviation refers to a form indicating the less salient of two third persons "to obviate confusion," according to Voegelin & Voegelin (1975:385). Hopi, Algonquian languages, Hokan languages, Yup'ik Eskimo, and many others have contrasting forms which indicate coreference and non-coreference between NPs in certain syntactic environments (Jacobsen 1967, Voegelin & Voegelin 1975). The term "obviation" was proposed by Cuoq.

9. See for instance Frantz (1966) on Blackfoot, Wolfart (1973) on Plains Cree – all Algonquian languages. Goddard (1990) and Thomason (1994) discuss Fox. Both Frantz and Wolfart note that the proximate form has the pragmatic use of indicating a referent which is familiar, the current topic of the discourse: currently in focus, in the sense of discourse focus.

10. When the referential and non-referential meanings of switch reference morphemes clash, the non-referential meanings override. This leads to what Stirling calls "aberrant" uses of the

between clauses, such as causality or reason. Discussing Amele, a language of Papua New Guinea, Roberts (1988) observes that switch reference is used to indicate changes in all the deictic features of discourse: speaker/hearer, world, time, and place.

Discourse considerations are thus the key to the distribution of switch reference morphemes. Though in principle they keep track of reference, their primary function is to indicate closeness or distance of situations or referents according to temporal and causal factors. Null pronouns in English have some of these same functions; see (18)–(19) below.

6.2.2   Pronouns

Across languages pronouns take many forms: there are null pronouns, clitic pronouns, strong pronouns, stressed and unstressed pronouns, reflexive pronouns, possessive pronouns. Some languages have special pronoun forms with specific functions. For instance, there are pronouns that convey reference to an antecedent subject of consciousness, known as "logophoric." Not all types are available in all languages. If a language doesn't have a pronoun form with a dedicated function, other forms may be pressed into service to fulfill it. There are no specifically logophoric pronouns in English, yet the subject-of-consciousness meaning may be conveyed with the English reflexive pronoun. In what follows I will consider stressed and unstressed pronouns, reflexives, null

morphemes. In aberrant DS cases, the morpheme appears when clauses differ in time, place, or some other situation parameter, even though they have coreferential agentive subjects. The examples below illustrate for time. The clauses have the same subject in all three examples. The SS morpheme is grammatical in (a) but ungrammatical in (c); the DS morpheme is grammatical in (b).

(a) Magau t-r-va   (kani) m-augIn
    Magau Fut-sg-come   (and)   SS-eat
    Magau will come and eat
(b) Magau r-n-va   (kani) t-r-augIn
    Magau 3sg-Pf-come   and   Fut-3sg-eat (zero DS)
    Magau has come and will eat (later)
(c) *Magau r-n-va   (kani) t-m-augIn
    Magau 3sg-Pf-come   and   Fut-SS-eat

Example (a) is a typical case of Switch Reference: the second clause has the SS morpheme and is not differentiated in tense from the first clause. In (b) the clauses have different tenses and the second clause has the DS morpheme. The ungrammatical (c) is like (b) except that the second clause has the SS morpheme. What this contrast shows is that having coreferential subjects is not a sufficient condition for the SS marker in Lenakel: the clauses must have the same tense as well. Stirling interprets this and similar examples as showing that the SS marker is primarily used to convey that Events are closely related.

pronouns, and possessive pronouns. Reciprocal and relative pronouns are not discussed.

When used felicitously, pronouns refer to entities that are already known or established in a discourse. The antecedent for a pronoun is mainly determined by pragmatic factors.

6.2.2.1 Stressed and unstressed pronouns

Pronouns refer to an entity in a discourse, or in the immediate context; in the former case they depend on an antecedent for interpretation. There are some grammatical constraints on the possible linguistic antecedents for a pronoun. I will assume the constraints here. I deal only with referential pronouns.[11] The antecedent to a pronoun may be in the same sentence or farther away, within the constraints of grammaticality and agreement.

The unstressed pronouns of English indicate neutral coreference with a relatively salient antecedent entity. Stressed pronouns convey additional meaning. The contrast is similar to that between proximate and obviative pronouns. However, in English the obviative, non-neutral meaning is emphatic or contrastive. The examples illustrate for sentences with two clauses, each containing an NP and a pronoun. In (11a–b) the pronoun is unstressed, and understood as coreferential with the NP in the main clause. The pronoun in (11c) has strong stress (indicated by capitals) and suggests a referent other than the NP. Subscripts give the preferred interpretations:

(11)   a. When he_i works, $John_i$ doesn't drink.
        b. When $John_i$ works, he_i doesn't drink.
        c. When HE_j works, $John_i$ doesn't drink.

The referent of the stressed pronoun in (11c) is presented in contrast with "John," the nearest possible antecedent.[12] Emphasis and focus are discussed in Chapter 8.

---

11. I assume the grammatical constraints on possible pronoun reference as stated in Government Binding Theory. The main constraint is that a pronoun may not be coreferential with an antecedent that is higher in the structure of the same clause, a c-commanding antecedent (Chomsky 1981).

    Non-referring uses of pronouns include quantifier contexts in which pronouns are variable rather than referring expressions ("Everyone that has a donkey likes it"). These sentences are known as "donkey sentences."

12. One can construct examples which have a sentence-internal referent for the stressed pronoun:

    Although $[his_j \text{ colleagues}]_i$ think that $they_i$ understand $John_j$, HE_j doesn't think that $they_i$ do.

    The pronoun in the main clause must be stressed, because the NP "his colleagues" sets up a contrast set suggesting the focal interpretation of the pronoun. The example shows that the

Context decides whether a given antecedent is plausible for a pronoun. In certain contexts, the plausible antecedent appears in a different sentence. For instance, (12) supplies a context for (11c), in which the pronoun is taken as coreferential with an antecedent in the preceding sentence:

(12) a. My parents are coming to spend a week with us next month.
      b. Dad$_i$ is a strict teetotaler; he$_i$ doesn't like to be around alcohol.
      c. When he$_i$ visits, John$_j$ doesn't drink.

In this context the antecedent for "he" in (12c) is "Dad," the referent of the pronoun in the preceding sentence. Context may also affect the interpretation of a stressed pronoun. In the context of (13a) the pronoun in (13b) is taken as coreferential with "John":

(13) a. John$_i$ insists that Tom$_j$ and Bill$_k$ abstain from drinking on the job.
      b. After all, when HE$_i$ works, John$_i$ doesn't drink.

Here "John" is contrasted with the proximate antecedents in the preceding sentence. This account does not deal with those contexts in which pronouns are inaccessible for coreference.

The unstressed pronoun in English indicates neutral coreference with an antecedent. The referent may be nearby, literally proximate; the referent may also be familiar or predictable, metaphorically proximate. The stressed pronoun is obviative, indicating contrast or emphasis, with a referent that is not necessarily proximate. Pronoun antecedents are also discussed in 6.3.2 below.

6.2.2.2 Reflexive pronouns

Reflexive pronouns indicate coreference between two arguments of a verb, as in "Mary washed herself," "The doctor asked John about himself." Reflexives in English are grammatically constrained. In the Binding Theory the constraint is a locality condition, requiring that a reflexive have a local c-commanding antecedent (Chomsky 1981). However, there are many reflexives that do not obey this condition. They either have an antecedent in the same sentence that does not c-command, or an antecedent in a sentence that is quite far away. I will call such reflexives "Locally Free Reflexives" following C. L. Baker (1995); they are also known as "long distance reflexives."

Locally Free Reflexives (LFRs) may convey that their antecedent is a subject of consciousness, in addition to coreference. This is a logophoric meaning. The term was coined by Claude Hagège for pronouns "which refer to the author

---

information for focal reference can be presented in more than one way; I shall not explore the possibilities here.

of a discourse or participant whose thoughts are reported" (1974).[13] Reflexive pronouns with a logophoric function appear with verbs of communication and mental state when the subject of main and complement clauses is the same. They attribute the contents of the complement clause to the speaker or another antecedent. Pronouns indicating an internal self and/or responsibility for thought and communication occur in many languages. The Japanese pronoun *zibun* is a well-known example: it indicates an internal self in certain contexts (Kuno 1972, Kuroda 1973).

English does not have a direct counterpart of the logophoric pronoun, since the reflexive doesn't appear in the subject position of tensed clauses. Reflexives that indicate a subject of consciousness, however, appear in other logophoric contexts, as (14) illustrates:[14]

(14)　　a. This paper was written by Ann and myself.
　　　　b. But Rupert$_i$ was not unduly worried about Peter's opinion of himself$_i$.
　　　　c. It angered him$_i$ that she should have the egotism to try to attract a man like himself$_i$.
　　　　d. Lucie$_i$ boasted that the chairman invited her husband and herself$_i$.

In (14a), the reflexive has no overt antecedent and is taken to refer to the speaker of the sentence. Here and in other contexts, the reflexive alternates with the ordinary pronoun form so that use of the reflexive represents a choice. Reflexives that function similarly appear in other languages, e.g. Dutch *zich*, Icelandic *sig*.

Locally Free Reflexives (LFRs) may also convey "empathy," suggesting the viewpoint of the antecedent in the situation expressed, as Kuno points out (1972, 1987). The empathy meaning arises for LFRs in contexts that do not directly express communication or mental state, as in (15):

---

13. Hagège compared the African languages with Latin and Japanese. Typically logophoric pronouns are third person in subject position, but some languages are more flexible (Stirling 1993). Some languages have a special pronoun form for non-subject cases, including the West African languages Igbo, Gokana, and Ewe (among others).

　　The term "logophoric" has a general and a more specific use. Very generally, a logophoric pronoun attributes a connection of some kind between a pronoun and its antecedent, a connection that is not licensed by the grammar, that is, the constraints of the Binding Theory (Reinhart & Reuland 1993).

14. Cantrall (1969), Ross (1972) noticed that when they alternate with ordinary pronouns, reflexives convey the consciousness or point of view of their antecedent. Sources of the examples: Ross 1970 (a); (b), is quoted in Zribi-Hertz (1989); c–d, Reinhart & Reuland (1993).

　　Other cases of LFRs include "My husband and myself would like to invite you to dinner" (Keith Walters, pc).

(15)   a. Max pulled the blanket toward himself.
         b. Lucie likes pictures of herself.

According to Kuno, these reflexives indicate the point of view or "camera angle" of their antecedent: the speaker thus empathizes with that person. Neither example falls under Binding Theory principles. In (15a) the reflexive and its antecedent are not coarguments of the verb; (15b) is a "picture noun context" – picture nouns have been problematic for the Binding Theory (Reinhart & Reuland 1991).

Locally Free Reflexives may also indicate emphasis, contrast, or intensification. The clearest cases of emphasis have strong stress, conveyed by capital letters in this example from Zribi-Hertz (1989):

(16)   Joyce$_i$ is just holding herself together... Her$_i$ defenses are well inside HERSELF$_i$, not where mine are, outside in clothes, hair, etc.

Contrastive uses may involve explicit or implicit comparison. There is also an "intensive" LFR. It has a contrastive meaning and requires that the antecedent be prominent in the discourse, according to C. L. Baker (1995). This use of the reflexive is primarily found in British English; Baker's study is based on the novels of Jane Austen. Example (17) illustrates.

(17)   Sir William Lucas, and his daughter Maria, a good humoured girl, but as empty-headed as himself, had nothing to say that could be worth hearing, and were listened to with about as much delight as the rattle of the chaise.

                                                            (*Pride & Prejudice* 188)

Baker observes that the antecedent to the LFR "himself" in this example, Sir Willliam Lucas, cannot be explained as a subject of consciousness, empathy, or contrast; but that the antecedent is prominent in the discourse. Discourse prominence, according to Baker, is due to a character's role as Agent or Patient, of high importance or rank, or the primary topic of concern.[15] A similar intensive use also occurs with the [NP+reflexive] form, e.g. "The president himself opened the door," found in British and American English.

This section has identified several interpretations of Locally Free Reflexives, in addition to their referential meaning. In the logophoric meaning, the antecedent of the LFR is responsible for the thoughts, feelings, or sayings expressed in a clause. The empathy use implies the point of view of the antecedent.

---

15. Baker's account is based in part on Ross (1970), Moyne (1971) on reflexives, and a suggestion of Ferro (1993) that "self" may function as a focus marker. According to Baker, in American English the difference between intensive and non-intensive contrast has been neutralized.

The emphatic use highlights the antecedent of the reflexive, and the contrast use involves explicit or implicit comparison with another entity. The intensive use, typical of British English, both contrasts and highlights. Recall that LFRs can always be replaced by an ordinary pronoun, since they are not subject to grammatical constraints. They represent the choice of the writer and carry special meanings.

6.2.2.3   Null pronouns

Null pronouns have no morphology and thus the minimal amount of coding material. Null pronouns appear as subjects in limited contexts. They are possible in conjunctions, in nominals, in the complements of certain verbs.[16] They also appear in temporal clauses (18a), purpose clauses (18b), and participial adjunct clauses (18c–d).

(18)   a. Before leaving the room with Gabriel she signalled to Mr Browne by frowning and shaking her forefinger on warning to and fro.
       b. In order to confront dictators of his kind we must set aside the misleading lesson of our victory in the cold war, achieved by huge military expenditure on a deterrent strategy.
       c. Punctuated by the most spectacular busts in economic history, the boom continued in Europe for thirty years.
       d. Ethiopian troops are pressing deeper into Eritrea, denying with every step that they plan any long-term invasion of their neighbor and once-tight ally.

The situations in these sentences are tightly bound by their syntax. I will refer to such clauses as "condensed clauses," following Jespersen (1940). Condensed clauses appear in argument and adjunct positions.

Sentences with condensed clauses present situations as a single syntactic unit. The semantic meaning mirrors the syntactic presentation, as in (19):

(19)   *Searching with insatiable curiosity for underlying explanations,* both did far more than discover new facts or solve circumscribed problems, such as the structure of DNA: they synthesized knowledge from a wide range of fields and

---

16. There are also lexically determined null subjects, as in the following examples. The possibilities depend on the verb.

       a. Mary wanted ø to win the race.
       b. Mary wanted herself to win.
       c. Mary wanted John to win.
       d. Mary tried ø to win.
       e. *Mary tried herself to win.
       f. *Mary tried John to win.

    Note that there is a close relation between the situations in main and complement clauses.

created new conceptual frameworks, *large parts of which are still accepted today.*

This fragment, presented as a unit, contains two condensed clauses and two full clauses, both with conjoined VPs.

Strikingly, condensed clauses with null pronouns in English appear in almost the same syntactic environments as the Same Subject morphemes of switch reference systems. They use the two closed systems that allow anaphoric dependence, tense and referential expressions. Condensed clauses have the effect of presenting situations as tightly bound, just as the corresponding Switch Reference cases do. This semantic discourse effect follows from the syntax.

Choices from the closed system of referring expressions also convey information about the familiarity or unfamiliarity of the referent.

6.3 The familiarity status of referring expressions

Speakers and writers have a choice among linguistic forms when they refer to a person or other entity. The possibilities include names and titles (*Samuel Barnes, the Secretary*), NPs with the definite article (*the cat*), NPs with the indefinite article (*a cat*), demonstrative (*this cat, that cat*), NPs with additional lexical material (adjectives, relative clauses, prepositional phrases), pronouns (*he, they*), and anaphors (*herself*). The choices reflect assumptions about what the receiver knows, assumes, and can infer. Following Grice, I assume that the speaker or writer presents information in a way that will enable the receiver to arrive at the intended message.

Referring expressions may introduce a new entity or refer to a familiar one. In a model of an ongoing discourse, a referring expression is taken as an instruction either to add an entity or to find the relevant antecedent in the Discourse Representation Structure. New entities are introduced with an identifying condition; if the referring expression indicates that an entity is familiar, the DRS is searched for an antecedent with which it is coreferential.

The distinction between familiar and new entities is reflected in the forms and use of the articles in referring expressions. Typically in English, the indefinite article introduces new and unfamiliar entities into a discourse, while the definite article indicates entities that are familiar, readily available to the receiver in the discourse context. This was recognized in early work of Discourse Representation Theory by Kamp (1981) and Heim (1982). The sequence in (20) illustrates:

(20)   I saw a cat. The cat was sitting on a fence, watching a bird.

The NP "a cat" refers to a hitherto-unknown cat, and we understand it as an instruction to introduce a new entity into the DRS. The definite NP "the cat" refers to a particular, identifiable cat – the one introduced in the preceding sentence. If one were constructing a DRS for (20), the definite article would be taken as an instruction to search for the antecedent entity and establish a link between the antecedent and the NP in question. I ignore generic reference to kinds.[17]

"Familiar" and "New" are both susceptible to further distinctions, as Prince has stressed. Entities may be new in more than one way. An entity that is New in a discourse may be "Brand-new" or "Unused." Brand-new entities are totally unknown to the receiver, while Unused entities are known but not active or salient at the time of the utterance. They are in the receiver's long-term memory or background knowledge. The subject NPs of (21) illustrate, from Prince (1981):

(21)   a. A guy I work with says he knows your sister.
        b. Noam Chomsky went to Penn.

The new entity in (21a) "a guy I work with" is quite different in status from "Noam Chomsky" in (21b), as Prince points out. The former is Brand-new. The latter is Unused, familiar – to the linguist at any rate – but not necessarily active. The proper name can refer successfully only if the receiver is already somewhat familiar with its referent.

The category of "familiar" entity can also be made more precise, Prince shows.[18] An NP with the definite article may refer to an entity actually available in the discourse context; or to an entity that is readily inferrable in the context. Example (22) illustrates:

(22)   I got on a bus yesterday. Unfortunately, *the driver* was drunk.

Although no driver has been introduced, we have no difficulty inferring the presence of one from the NP "a bus" in the preceding clause. This is a bridging inference, based on our general knowledge that buses have drivers. Inferred

---

17. Both types of articles can convey reference to kinds:

    The lion is a mammal.
    A lion is a mammal.

18. The full set of Prince's categories of Assumed Familiarity:

    New   → Brand-new, anchored & unanchored; Unused
    Inferrable → Noncontaining; containing (from relevant set)
    Evoked   → Textually; situationally

entities tend to have the definite article, as in the example. Definite possessives can also be taken as familiar if their possessor is familiar, as in "A man came in. His daughter was with him," from Barker (2000).

The simplest adequate account has three main classes of familiarity status, classified as New, Evoked, or Inferrable (E. Prince 1981). Inferrable entities arise from background knowledge and a trigger in the text, as the referent of "the driver" in (22) is triggered by the mention of "a bus" in the preceding sentence. Prince's categories are based on the assumption that writers choose forms based on their understanding of receivers' knowledge and expectations.

Evoked entities are familiar, usually coreferential with an entity already introduced in the text. The distance between the entity and its antecedent may be great or small. The antecedent may be in the same or a preceding sentence, in which case the entity is already in the focus of attention, present in the consciousness of the receiver. The antecedent may also be relatively far away.

The forms of referring expressions differ in amount of coding material and content. Thus the unstressed pronoun *he* is shorter and has less content than a full NP such as *the man* or *the man standing by the window*. Expressions that have the least information tend to be used when their antecedents are nearby and/or salient in the text. For instance, if the antecedent of an entity is nearby, a pronoun is commonly used to refer to it. When the antecedent is further away, people tend to use referring expressions that are more informative.

Drawing on these and other observations, Ariel (1990) gives a ranking of referring expressions that links coding material, or amount of information, and accessibility. Accessible referents are near, or easily found, in the text. The rank of an expression correlates with how much information it conveys. Null forms and unstressed pronouns are at the low end of the scale, with a minimal amount of coding material. In the middle are demonstrative NPs (*this X*, *that Y*) and stressed pronouns. At the high end of the scale are full names and long definite descriptions. According to Ariel, each expression signals the reader to search for an entity with accessibility indicated by its ranking on the scale.

Evidence from text counts supports Ariel's ranking. Pronouns are predominantly used for short distances, anaphoric demonstratives are used in cases of intermediate distance, and definite descriptions refer to antecedents that are relatively far away (1989:70). Ariel notes that this conforms with the principle of relevance proposed in Sperber & Wilson (1986). The correlation between form and accessibility is supported by psycholinguistic research, e.g. Marslen-Wilson *et al.* (1982), Garrod & Sanford (1985).

The main factors in a text that make an antecedent more or less accessible, Ariel claims, are (i) distance from the referring expression; (ii) number of competitors for the role of antecedent that agree in gender, number, and other features; (iii) topicality; (iv) whether there is a frame for identifying the antecedent (1989:65).

The correlation between linguistic form and information is further developed by Gundel *et al.* (1993). They propose a ranking of referring expressions according to the "cognitive status" of the receiver. Cognitive status includes location in the text and in memory, attentional state, and position on the givenness hierarchy. There are six degrees of status. Referring expressions of English appear at each degree. The ranking is given in (23), with the different ranks numbered for clarity; the pronoun *it* stands for all unstressed pronouns:

(23)   Cognitive Status (Gundel *et al.* 1993)

6	5	4	3	2	1
in focus >	activated >	familiar >	uniquely	> referential >	type
it	that, this,	that N	identifiable	indefinite[19]	identifiable
	this N		the N	this N	a N

The ranks are implicationally related. The implicational ranking relates a form to all others that are below it on the hierarchy. For instance, if an expression of rank 4 is licensed, so are expressions of ranks 1–3.

In using a particular form a speaker "signals that the associated cognitive status is met and . . . that all lower, less restrictive statuses have been met" (Gundel *et al.* 1993:184). The implicational relations may explain how people understand expressions from the lower end of the scale used to refer to relatively familiar entities. Such reference often appears in discourse when there is a change of direction (see 6.3.2 below). Gundel *et al.* give similar rankings for

---

19. The hierarchy in (22) has a definite and indefinite use of the demonstrative *this*. In the definite use, the NP is coreferential with an antecedent, as in the toy example below:

    A man walked into the room. This man was wearing a red hat.

    The indefinite use introduces a new element into the universe of discourse:

    There was this guy I saw yesterday who was wearing a red hat.

    The second use is common in speech and informal writing, as Keith Walters has pointed out to me.

the referring expressions of other languages. The rankings in (23) relate nicely to Prince's classes of familiarity status. Expressions from rank 6 to 3 are Evoked or Inferrable; 1 and 2 are New.

The work reviewed above emphasizes the receiver rather than the text. There is evidence that a text-based approach may be sufficient, even preferable, to the receiver-based one. Prince (1992) looked at both approaches in a study of referring expressions in a single written text. She asked whether hearer-based or discourse-based categories were the most relevant and best predictor of pronoun form. Comparing the cognitive status for the receiver and text status of the entities, she found that the two overlapped in many cases. When they did not overlap, "discourse-old" and "discourse-new" were better predictors of the form of referring expressions than the corresponding categories "hearer-old" and "hearer-new" (Prince 1992). The work of Birner & Ward (1998), discussed in Chapter 8, also bears out this finding.

6.3.1   *Patterns in discourse*
There are two main patterns of coreference in discourse: continuity and shift. Pragmatic factors such as the familiarity status of a referring expression, syntactic structure, and the distance and importance of an antecedent play a role in maintaining continuity. Shifts are indicated by referring expressions that break continuity.

6.3.1.1   Continuity
Texts have referential continuity when each sentence refers back to entities in the sentence that immediately precedes it, according to Sanford & Garrod (1981). The simplest kind of continuity is conveyed by a chain of pronouns after an entity is introduced. Example (24) is a constructed example from Kameyama (1985):

(24) Max_i is a chemist. He_i is 30 years old, and he_i lives in San Francisco.

The pronouns keep the entity at the same level of focused attention. If the chain of pronouns is broken by an intervening sentence, the result can be odd and difficult to interpret, as in (25), from Sanford & Garrod (1981).

(25)   The little $puppy_i$ trod on a $wasp_j$. The $puppy_i$ was very upset.
        It_j started to buzz furiously.

Examples like this have led people to seek the conditions for felicitous continuity.

The interpretation of a pronoun is affected by syntactic structure, especially parallel structure. In sentences with parallel structures, people interpret as coreferential NPs that have the same grammatical function. Consider the examples below:

(26)   a. Bill$_i$ talked to Tom$_j$ and he$_i$ talked to Mary.
        b. Bill$_i$ talked to Tom$_j$ and HE$_j$ talked to Mary.

The natural interpretation of (26a) has "Bill" as antecedent for the pronoun, although both nouns in the first conjunct are possible.[20] Strong stress on the pronoun conveys the other interpretation unambiguously, as in (26b); it also adds a sense of contrast. The principle of parallelism is very strong, overriding the factor of proximity. For instance, "Tom" is nearer to the pronoun in (26a), but the parallel interpretation remains. From a procedural point of view, parallel syntactic structures are an instruction to the reader to look for a certain connection between them; the antecedent–pronoun link serves this function (Blakemore 1988). Parallelism affects pronoun interpretation similarly in other languages.

There are other patterns of continuity as well. General principles for continuity in discourse are stated in Centering Theory, which models connections between referents in discourse (Walker *et al.* 1998).[21] The theory works with "centers," semantic entities in an ongoing discourse model. The referring expressions of a sentence comprise a set of ranked forward-looking centers (Cf). The highest ranked is a backward-looking center (Cb), which links the sentence to previous discourse. The Cfs are potential backward-looking centers for other utterances.

The notion of grammatical salience is the key to the ranking of centers. Salience is determined by a hierarchy of grammatical relations: subject > object > second object. The "preferred center" is the Cb. The Cb represents

20. The effects of parallelism can be increased or mitigated by the lexical properties of the main verb. For instance, note the differences in the pairs below:

    a. Fran$_i$ won the money from Helen$_j$ because she$_i$ was a skillful player.
    b. Fran$_i$ won the money from Helen$_j$ because she$_j$ was a careless player.
    c. Helen$_i$ punished Cathy$_j$ because she$_j$ confessed to shoplifting.
    d. Helen$_i$ punished Cathy$_j$ because she$_i$ disapproved of shoplifting.

21. Centering Theory developed from a computational model of local attention and coherence, where coherence was understood in terms of the links between sentences of short discourses (Joshi & Weinstein 1981, Grosz & Sidner 1986, Walker *et al.* 1998: Ch. 1). Psychological studies, e.g. Brennan (1995), Gordon & Chan (1995), give evidence that supports the model. See also studies in Walker *et al.* (1998).

a discourse entity that the sentence centrally concerns – a notion similar to discourse topic (see Chapter 7). Pronouns and grammatical subjects are key factors in English centering transitions (Kameyama 1998).

The theory focuses on pronouns, following the generally accepted notion that pronouns are used to refer to entities readily available in a discourse. If there is a pronoun in a sentence, it is the Cb, the backward-looking center. Indeed, only if the Cb is realized as a pronoun does it contribute to the coherence of the discourse (Gordon & Chan 1995).

Centering Theory identifies strategies for the transition from one sentence to another. For instance, the strategy "Continue" predicts that the same Cb appears in two utterances. The pronouns in (26) above exemplify this pattern. It is the most highly preferred, according to the theory, because it maximizes continuity. Other strategies hold when sentences have different Cbs. For instance, in "Smooth shift" the pronouns have different referents. Example (27) gives a constructed fragment which exemplifies this strategy, from Walker *et al.* (1998). The subscripts indicate the interpretation.

(27)   a. Jeff$_i$ helped Dick$_j$ wash the car.
        b. He$_i$ washed the windows.
        c. He$_j$ buffed the hood.

The change in pronoun referent is said to be less preferred. Centering Theory models expectations of continuity, assuming a simple, linear progression. I return to the topic of continuity in Chapters 8 and 9.

The distance between a referring expression and antecedent also affects continuity. When the two are near each other, relatively uninformative expressions are expected; more informative expressions are predicted when greater distance is involved.

6.3.1.2   Referring expressions and discourse organization

The organization of a text also affects the form and interpretation of referring expressions. The form of a referring expression may signal continuity, or a break in continuity. Breaks in continuity may coincide with new themes or episodes, or, more locally, with changes of direction or point of view.

The clearest distinction is between full NPs and pronouns. Full NPs are often used where pronouns would have been possible, and indeed expected in a simple continuity account. The full NPs occur at points where the discourse shifts in some way. In a study of four written narratives Fox found many such examples. The full NPs coincided with "the structural organization" of the text

(1987a:167). An illustrative example from Fox is given in (28). The change from "she" back to "Susan" demarcates a new unit in the text, indicated graphically by the paragraph indentation.

(28)   The four flights up to her floor seemed longer than usual to Susan$_i$. She$_i$ paused on several occasions, because of a combination of physical fatigue and mental effort.
        Susan$_i$ tried to remember if Bellows had said succinylcholine was among the drugs found in the locker.

The choice of form, a full NP (*Susan*) at the beginning of the second paragraph signals the functional structure of the narrative. Fox (1987b) documents similar patterns in discursive prose. Similarly, Clancy (1980) observes that full NPs are used at episode boundaries in narratives based on the "Pear Story" films, in both English and Japanese.

These findings have experimental support from work in psycholinguistics. In studies of production and comprehension, Vonk *et al.* (1992) looked at pronouns and full NPs in text fragments. They found that when NPs were more specific than necessary to recover an antecedent, the NPs had a discourse structuring function. Pronouns were related to thematic continuity, full NPs triggered or signalled shifts in theme.[22] The authors interpret these findings as showing that the full NP functioned as a signal to set up a new chain of information in the discourse representation.

Other referring expressions have the same pattern: the fuller, more informative expression indicates a shift in the discourse. For instance, the pronouns *it* and *that* differ. The pronoun *it* is neutral and *that* is deictic, indicating non-proximate reference. In a study of oral apartment descriptions, Linde (1979) found that the two appeared systematically according to whether their referents were in the same or different discourse unit. *It* was used when the referent was in the same unit; *that* when the referent was in a different unit.

Another prediction of the linear continuity account is that a long gap between mentions of a referent triggers a full NP. One might predict that pronouns,

---

22. These patterns also appear in other languages. In an oral Polish narrative with a main protagonist, reference was made with null pronouns when continuous and predictable. Null pronouns are the Polish equivalent of unstressed ordinary pronouns. Overt pronouns appeared when there was narrative discontinuity, changes in speaker perspective, and contrast between foreground and background (Flashner 1987). Similarly Clancy (1980), in a study of spoken English and Japanese narratives, found that people tended to use full NPs to mark discourse boundaries, point-of-view changes, and episode changes. See also the articles in Givón (1979).

which have little coding material, are not strong enough to access an antecedent that is relatively far away. This prediction has been disconfirmed. In a study of narrative, for instance, Fox found that pronouns are used for a particular character over relatively long stretches of text "until another character's goals and actions are introduced, unless those goals and action are interactive with the first character's" (1987a:162). In sum, what matters is discourse continuity. In texts with one central character, reference to that character may be made at any time with an ordinary pronoun, even if there have been significant interruptions (Whitaker & Smith 1985).

Similar findings have been documented for non-narrative English discourse. Hinds (1977) examined the use of pronouns and full NPs in newspaper articles. He found that the choice between them depended on the structure of the text. Nominal and pronominal reference were sometimes used to convey different degrees of prominence, with nominal reference indicating "semantically prominent" information. Hinds found that nominal expressions tended to appear at discourse peaks.

Summarizing, the form of a referring expression encodes the familiarity status of a referent. In discourse, anaphoric expressions convey referential continuity. Fuller expressions are used to convey discourse shifts, and expressions that code unfamiliarity tend to appear at discourse boundaries.

6.4   *Referring expressions and Discourse Representation Theory*

Discourse Representation Theory developed a landmark procedural approach to referential expressions.[23] The referential expressions of an ongoing text are interpreted as instructions to introduce a discourse entity into the universe of discourse, with a condition that identifies the entity. Conditions indicate that an expression is coreferential with an entity in the discourse context, or specify the entity in the wider context. The bare bones of the approach are laid out in Chapter 3. I return to the topic here, with comments on how the material of this chapter relates to the theory. For more complete accounts see Kamp (1981), Heim (1982), Kamp & Reyle (1993).

An important insight of Discourse Representation Theory is that referring expressions have different functions according to their forms. One class of referring expressions introduces new discourse entities into the context, another

---

23. The approach of Discourse Representation Theory was a significant advance over earlier theories such as the referential theory of indefinites and an alternative, the quantificational theory.
    The discussion below necessarily omits many important points, among them varieties of pronoun reference and plurals.

introduces discourse referents that are coreferential with entities already there. These classes correspond, more or less, to the distinction between new and familiar referents. In some cases a referring expression has the form associated with familiar referents, but the context does not contain an appropriate antecedent. The receiver accommodates by assuming or inferring such an antecedent.

Proper names and indefinite NPs license the introduction of new entities into a DRS; pronouns and certain other NPs refer to entities that are already in the context.[24] In certain contexts coreference is impossible, as noted in Chapter 3. The theory recognizes this by stating structural accessibility conditions. (This notion of accessibility is different from accessibility based on distance in a text.) In conversation, pronouns may refer to an entity in the context; they refer to discourse entities in a written text.

Anaphora in the DRS is thus a relation that holds between a discourse entity and a pronoun or other referring expression. This is the standard Discourse Representation Theory account. The work on referential expressions discussed above suggests that the standard account should be augmented slightly. Expressions that refer to familiar entities should include NounPhrases with demonstrative (*that*, *this*), and null pronouns which are interpreted by rule. Expressions that introduce new identities should probably include referential indefinites ("this N"), although it is not easy to distinguish them from nominals of the same shape referring to "activated" referents.

Reflexive pronouns in syntactically bound contexts require additional conditions, as Kamp & Reyle point out. Reflexives do not alternate with simple pronouns in such contexts. To convey a coreferential meaning a reflexive form must be used. For instance, in "Jane washed her," "her" cannot be interpreted as coreferential with the subject "Jane." Coreference can only be expressed with the reflexive "Jane washed herself." These conditions are straightforward in principle, although actually stating them is complex.

Locally Free Reflexives do alternate with simple pronouns and thus require a different treatment. Two questions arise, one specific to the class and the other general to pronouns. The specific question is whether the special quality of LFR should be encoded in the DRS. The mechanism for such encoding exists: a special feature could be introduced that would allow for the

---

24. Proper names are linked to entities in the world by an external anchor. The external anchor for a discourse referent x is a function which maps x into some real individual a. The anchor constrains the mechanism used for truth-conditional verification of a sentence (Kamp & Reyle 1993:248).

appropriate interpretation. There is also a subjective use of LFRs, which has a different treatment. I will propose that such reflexives be associated with a discourse entity as a Responsible Source in the DRS; see Chapter 9 for details.

Discourse Representation Theory provides a mechanism for interpreting referring expressions, and states the structural and semantic conditions for one referential expression to be coreferential with another. Entities are either "new" or "familiar" and their definition is based on the developing DRS for a text. New entities have no antecedents in the DRS; familiar entities have antecedents in the DRS. The current theory does not deal with inferred entities. However, proposals for bridging and other inferences are put forth in Asher & Lascarides (1998).

The pragmatics of successful reference are not within the purview of the theory. When more than one antecedent is structurally possible for a referring expression, the theory does not have principles for the best or most likely choice. But there is no incompatibility between the pragmatic material discussed above and Discourse Representation Theory. Rather, pragmatics provides an indispensable complement for the structural approach of the theory. Finding the appropriate antecedent for a pronoun or NP depends on several factors, as we have seen. In addition to relative familiarity status, continuity and discourse organization play a role. The contrastive meanings associated with closed systems, and the resulting discourse meanings, also belong to pragmatic interpretive principles that go beyond the structural information of a construction rule.[25]

As an example of how referential entities are treated in the theory. I give a DRS for a simplified version of an example discussed above, given here as (29). The proper name "Bellows" is at the top level of the DRS because the reference of proper names is independent, not contingent on information in the sub-DRS. The *if*-clause is a sub-DRS that encodes the information after "tried to remember" in the third sentence; this treatment roughly follows that of Asher (1993).

(29)   1 The four flights up seemed longer than usual to Susan$_i$. 2 She$_i$ paused on several occasions.
        3 Susan$_i$ tried to remember if Bellows had found drugs in a locker.

---

25. In a more complete account of the pragmatics of discourse, pragmatic principles for contrastive meanings might be stated. I proposed such principles for contrastive meanings in aspectual viewpoint systems in C. S. Smith (1997).

(30)   Schematic partial DRS for (29)

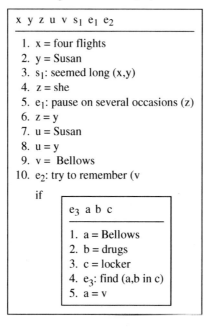

x y z u v s_1 e_1 e_2

1. x = four flights
2. y = Susan
3. s_1: seemed long (x,y)
4. z = she
5. e_1: pause on several occasions (z)
6. $z = y$
7. u = Susan
8. $u = y$
9. v = Bellows
10. e_2: try to remember $(v$

if

e_3 a b c

1. a = Bellows
2. b = drugs
3. c = locker
4. e_3: find $(a,b$ in $c)$
5. $a = v$

The discourse entities are licensed by the proper names, pronouns, and Noun-Phrases. In this case there is only one possible antecedent for the pronoun "she": Susan. The second instance of the proper name is taken as coreferential with the first. This is a matter of pragmatic interpretation, indeterminate in the DRS.

Example sources in this chapter:

(8) Jim Collins. How it works. *US Airways Magazine, Attaché*, May 2001.
(18a) James Joyce, "The Dead," In *Dubliners*, 1916; reprinted London: Penguin Books, 1982, p. 185.
(18b) Tony Judt, Tyrannized by weaklings. *New York Times*, April 5, 1999.
(18c) Peter Drucker, The information revolution. *Atlantic Monthly*, October 1999.
(18d) After a victory, Ethiopia looks toward other fronts. *New York Times*, May 20, 2000.
(19) Jared Diamond, A tale of two reputations: scientific contributions of Charles Darwin and Sigmund Freud. *Natural History*, 2001.

III Surface presentational factors

7 *Subjectivity in texts*

In all Discourse Modes and genres, one finds passages that suggest a particular voice. They convey a sense of subjectivity, a point of view toward propositional information. "Point of view" is familiar as a literary term referring to presentation of the mind of a fictional character in narrative. More generally, point of view is "the perceptual or conceptual position in terms of which narrated situations and events are presented" (G. Prince 1987:73). Linguists now use the term for expressions of speech and thought, evidentiality, perspective, and other indications of an authorial or participant voice. "Point of view" is used almost interchangeably with "perspective" and "subjectivity." I shall use the latter term as more general. Subjectivity is conveyed by grammatical forms and lexical choices.[1]

Three traditions come together in the area of subjectivity. One is deixis and its linguistic expression. Deixis is a general term for the centrality of the here and now in language. The study of deixis takes as basic the canonical speech situation with Speaker and Addressee, and explores its linguistic ramifications. The second tradition involves evidentiality, indications of the source and reliability of information. Evidentiality is a relatively new term for the semantic field of attitude toward knowledge, a kind of modality. Linguistic resources for this vary strikingly across languages. Finally, subjectivity conveys the contents of mind and personal perspective; here linguistic study is complemented by a strong literary tradition. The area is a vast one and I intend this chapter as an introduction, by no means a complete account. I will give the grammatical underpinnings of subjectivity, the bare bones.

Subjectivity arises primarily in discourse contexts. It is expressed by grammatical forms at the sentence level: verbs and their complements, adverbials, tense, modals, aspectual viewpoint, anaphors. Often a subjective form has scope

---

1. Some of the material in this chapter was presented at a symposium at the University of Oslo in December 2000: "Information Structure in a Cross-linguistic Perspective." I would like to thank the audience for their questions and the discussion; I also thank Cathrine Fabricius-Hansen for helpful comments.

beyond a single sentence. To interpret the forms of subjectivity we determine their scope and identify the mind responsible: the Responsible Source.

I suggest a composite account of subjectivity in Discourse Representation Theory, using rules that look at subjective forms in a sentence and in the context. The rules assign the role of Responsible Source to a participant in the text situation or to the author. The interpretation is encoded in the Discourse Representation Structure, using the technique of subordination. The Responsible Source is associated with an embedded sub-structure that encodes the relevant information.

The major categories of subjectivity are communication, contents of mind, evidentiality/evaluation, and perception and perspective. I do not consider lexical choice. Particular words in a sentence often suggest the mind of the speaker/writer or a participant in the text situation. For instance, the following sentence appeared in a recent newspaper article about the political campaign being prepared in the United States: "The Republicans and Democrats have concocted their message for the coming campaign." The word "concocted" suggests a skeptical attitude of the writer rather than a straightforward recounting of facts. I will not deal with this kind of subjectivity.

As with the discussion of Discourse Modes, I try to provide an armature for the complex and subtle notions conveyed by texts.

Section 7.1 discusses subjectivity and objectivity, and the notion of Responsible Source; 7.2 considers communication; 7.3, expressions of the contents of mind; 7.4, evaluation and evidentials; 7.5, perception and perspective; 7.6 formalizes the interpretation of subjectivity; 7.7 summarizes.

7.1   Responsibility for subjectivity

When a sentence expresses a point of view, or takes a particular perspective, we need to identify the person/mind responsible. Ascribing responsibility is part of the interpretation of a subjectivity. There are some systematic ambiguities as to whether the author or a participant in the text situation is responsible. I will sketch a general account.

There is a prior question, however, which I take up first. It is reasonable to ask whether we can recognize certain sentences as subjective and others as objective. I think that we can. In making the case I draw on insights about the genre of narrative fiction.

The linguistically oriented study of subjectivity begins, perhaps, with Kuroda's (1973) observations about Japanese fiction. The Japanese language has different forms for subjective and other expressions of mental state. To express one's own sadness, for instance, a person uses a subjective adjective with a first-person pronoun; to report the sadness of another, a verb and a third-person subject. What Kuroda noticed is that the subjective forms appear in third-person narrative fiction, where they would not, strictly speaking, be expected. In these fictional contexts the subjective forms directly render a character's mental state; they do not function as linguistic communication.[2] Kuroda calls this use the "non-reportive" style, distinguishing it from the "reportive" style typical of communication (1973:384). Although lacking forms like these, English too can convey expressions of mental state. In fact, there are English expressions that correspond to Kuroda's reportive and non-reportive styles. Banfield argues that represented speech and thought, which are typical of fiction, are non-reportive (1982:12). Subjectivity can also be expressed with deictic pronouns and verbs of mental state. Lyons notes that English has distinct forms for "experiential" and "non-experiential" expressions (1982:107).

In fact, English has ways of expressing subjectivity in sentences of all genres and modes. The linguistic forms that convey subjectivity include verbs of mental state and perception, modals and evaluative adverbs, and others discussed below. Sentences that lack these forms are neutral or objective in our conventional understanding, which posits a Responsible Source and a point of view for every sentence. I do not have space here to explore competing views.[3] The force of the subjective and objective is unique in fictional narrative, however.

The fictional world of a story or novel can be known to the reader only from the text. The functions of sentences with and without subjective elements reflect this. Certain sentences of a fictional narrative are objective, in the sense that we accept them as true information about the fictional world. These are sentences

2. Kuroda's examples include sentences with the subjective adjective forms and third-person subjects. The following, for instance, has the subjective adjectival form for "sad":

> Yamaderra no kane o kiite, Mary wa kanasikatta.
> Hearing the bell of the mountain temple, Mary was sad.

Sentences like this are odd, even ungrammatical in isolation. In a narrative context they are taken to express a character's point of view directly.

3. This view has been developed primarily for narrative. For instance, Genette (1980) says that strictly objective narration is impossible, and that all narrative is subjective, or "focalized," although in different ways. He makes an important distinction between the "one who sees," (the narrator), and "one who speaks."

There is surely something right about the idea that the speaker/author is present in all genres, cf. Palacas (1993). In an account that included expressive lexical items, one might want to posit a Responsible Source for all cases.

The distinction between subjective and objective sentences may not hold for all languages. Some languages have obligatory morphemes which code subjective information for evidentiality in all sentences; see Willett (1988).

with no elements of subjectivity. Subjective sentences filter information through the lens of a character's perspective. They give information about the character as well as about the fictional world. Banfield (1982) makes this point at length; see also Bruder & Wiebe (1995), Galbraith (1995). To understand fiction, then, it is important to distinguish subjective and objective sentences.

The convention of subjective and objective sentences is not limited to fiction, however: it holds quite generally in discourse. For "objective sentences" – those without linguistic forms associated with subjectivity – we assume that the author is the responsible source. We ask whether such sentences are true but not, usually, who is responsible for them. What is unique to fiction is the understanding of "objective" sentences as true. Subjective sentences can be identified by their linguistic forms; I discuss the forms and their interpretations in later sections of the chapter.

Let us assume that sentences expressing the contents of a mind, or a particular perspective, are subjective. For such sentences the question arises: to which mind do we ascribe the material that is expressed or reported? There are clear cases. In a belief report such as "Mary believed that John was sick" we ascribe the belief expressed in the complement clause to Mary. In the sentence "Mary unfortunately may win the race" we ascribe responsibility for the modal and the adverbial commentary to the speaker, not to Mary. Indirect speech is systematically ambiguous: responsibility for the content may rest with the reporter or with the original speaker.

To interpret expressions of subjectivity we must find the source, the person responsible. Texts can be seen as creating the basic communication situation with a Speaker/Author, Addressee, and the speaker's communication. This situation provides the possibilities for sources of subjectivity. I use the term Responsible Source for the mind to which responsibility is ascribed. The possibilities depend on the type of subjective expression involved. In some sentences the Author is the Responsible Source. In others the source is in the communication itself, a participant in the text situation. Usually it is the human referent of a subject NP or evidential PP. I will refer to this mind as the Subject. The Subject is often distinct from the Responsible Source, unless only first-person reference is involved. Compositional rules for determining the Responsible Source are given below. One source of responsibility can account for the varied interpretations of subjectivity.[4]

---

4. The view that only one Responsible Source in needed accords with much recent work. In her discussion of narrative and represented speech, Banfield (1982) formulates syntactic principles for attributing expressive elements to a unique subjectivity. Stirling (1993) takes a similar approach in the Discourse Representation Theory framework. She posits a single Validator role,

In the next few sections I discuss the main types of expression that lead to the interpretation of subjectivity: communication, mental states, evaluation, perception and perspective. The examples of text passages come from texts in this study.

7.2   *Expressions of communication*

Linguistic communication is by definition due to the speaker/author, a sentient being. The category includes direct address from writer to reader, and communication by participants in text situations. The latter comprises quoted speech, represented speech, and indirect speech. Quoted speech is often referred to as "direct" speech. I use the term "quoted" here as one of several kinds of direct communication.

Verbs of communication introduce quoted speech, indirect speech, and represented speech. Quoted speech reproduces what was said, in principle faithfully. Indirect speech reports what was said. There is always the possibility that the report is not entirely faithful. Actually both direct and indirect speech almost always involve the speaker/author, as Tannen (1989) points out.[5] The third type, represented speech, presents what was said or thought: it is neither a report nor a reproduction. It is closest of the three to Kuroda's "non-reportive" speech. The different types have characteristic patterns of deixis.

Quoted and indirect speech are illustrated first; the examples were chosen to bring out the role of deictic elements. Verbs of communication are sometimes optional in fiction.

(1)   Quoted speech and thought
    a. "I am getting ready for the party this afternoon."
    b. $Mary_i$ said "I_i am excited."
    c. $Mary_i$ told me_j yesterday at the station,"I_i will meet you_j here."
    d. $Mary_i$ asked "Do I_i have to go?"

(2)   Indirect speech and thought
    a. $Mary_i$ told me_j yesterday at the station that she_i would meet me_j there.
    b. $Mary_i$ asked whether she_i had to go.

which is associated with the appropriate sentient being. Speas and Tenny (2001) posit a single interpretive role, the Evaluator, in a semantically based syntactic approach. In contrast Sells (1987) argues that three roles are necessary to account for logophoric expressions; for discussion see Stirling (1993). Sanders & Redeker (1996) also posit a single Responsible Source, using the framework of cognitive linguistics.

5. The line between quoted and reported speech is sometimes difficult to draw, in a discussion of real and constructed dialogue and quotation. Tannen (1989) notes that the context for quotation and report always informs what is said. She claims that even seemingly "direct" quotation is really "constructed dialogue," primarily the creation of the speaker rather than the party quoted (1989:99). I am grateful to Keith Walters for pointing out this book to me.

Quoted speech typically is introduced by a verb of saying and a direct representation of what was said, as in (1). Person, tense, and other deictics are anchored to the first-person speaker and the here and now, as in the original or imagined utterance.

Indirect speech does not present exactly what was said. In reports of indirect speech, pronouns, tense, and deictic adverbials must shift away from the deictic center. Compare for instance (1c) and (2a), from Banfield (1982). In (1c) the complement reproduces Mary's utterance, with pronoun *I*, future *will*, and deictic *here*. In (2a) the deictic forms are shifted: the pronoun is *she*, the deictic is *there*. The tense is past, in concord with the tense of the main clause verb.[6] Indirect speech is syntactically constrained: constructions that appear only in main clauses, such as questions and exclamations, are blocked unless they have other forms. Examples (1d) and (2b) illustrate direct and indirect questions. Complementizers typically appear, e.g. *that* and *whether* in (2a–b).

There is a systematic ambiguity in indirect speech. It may present precisely what was said, or a recoding by the reporter, as in the classic example of (3):

(3)   Oedipus said that his mother was beautiful.

This sentence could be used to report an utterance of Oedipus in which the speaker identifies a person as his mother and says something about her (the "de re" reading). It could also be used to report exactly an utterance of Oedipus, "My mother is beautiful" (the "de dicto" reading). The truth of the sentence depends on both the interpretation and what was actually said: it might be true on the *de re* but not on the *de dicto* reading. Epithets and evaluative terms are ambiguous in the same way; see example (10) below.

Deictic expressions in the lower clause may be oriented to the reporter, as in (4):

(4)   a. John said that Mary was leaving tomorrow.
       b. John said that Louise is pregnant.

The deictics convey that the reporter has recoded all or part of what was said.[7] In (4a) "tomorrow" relates the leaving to Speech Time rather than to the past time of John's utterance. In (4b) the clauses have different tenses. The sentence

---

6. Tense concord is also known as "sequence of tense." Tense and person concord is required in English, but not in all languages. Japanese and Navajo, for instance, do not have shifted person markers nor tense concord in the complements of communication verbs; Russian does not have sequence of tense, Amharic does not have sequence of person (Schlenker 1999).
7. Deictic adverbials vary: some can shift orientation to any deictic center, others are oriented only to the here and now, as noted in Chapter 5. *Tomorrow* and *yesterday* are rigid adverbials that do not shift.

conveys that John's utterance about Mary's pregnancy was made in the past; and that the reporter relates the pregnancy to the time of speech. This type of sentence is known as a "double-access" sentence; see Ogihara (1996), Abusch (1997), Giorgi & Pianesi (1997).[8]

Verbs of communication are a distinct syntactic class. They allow a direct object complement which expresses the actual communication and an indirect object referring to the addressee ("X said Y to Z"). The class includes the verbs *say, ask, request, command, declare, confess, advise, insist, claim, shout, read, sing, remark, observe, note, swear, promise, announce, pray,* and many others. Manner-of-speaking verbs such as *shout, scream, whine, whisper, holler* have special properties (Zwicky 1971).

Given the close relation between them, we might attempt to derive indirect speech from direct speech. However this approach cannot work. The argument turns on two points: firstly, not all indirect speech reports have plausible counterparts in expressions of direct speech; and secondly, the ambiguity between *de re* and *de dicto* readings arises only for indirect speech (Partee 1973, Banfield 1982).

Communication in discourse may take the form of represented speech or thought, which has some features of quoted and some of indirect speech. Represented speech maintains the syntax of actual, or quoted speech, but tense and pronouns are shifted as in indirect speech; (5) illustrates:

(5)   Represented speech and thought
        1 He then took from his waistcoat pocket a little paper and glanced at the headings he had made for his speech. 2 He was undecided about the lines from Robert Browning, for he feared they would be above the heads of his hearers. 3 Some quotation that they would recognize from Shakespeare or from the Melodies would be better. 4 He would only make himself ridiculous by quoting poetry to them which they could not understand. 5 They would think that he was airing his superior education. 6 He would fail with them just as he had failed with the girl in the pantry. 7 He had taken up a wrong tone. 8 His whole speech was a mistake from first to last, an utter failure.

After S1, the sentences have shifted tense and person. The narrator would think of himself as "I," would represent the future with "will," the past with "took." The locutions of direct speech and thought are rendered directly, as in Sentences 6–7.

---

8. Cathrine Fabricius-Hansen notes (p.c.) that the reporter is responsible for the temporal description but not for the claim. Example (4b) would not necessarily be false if Louise were not pregnant at the time of the report, as is shown by the felicity of the following:

    (i) John said that Louise is pregnant but in fact she isn't.

It is the claim that John is reported to have made that would be false.

Represented speech is not syntactically embedded: it renders untouched syntactic structures which appear only in main clauses. Such structures include exclamations, direct questions, topicalization, elliptical fragments, and a few other constructions. Represented speech is also known as "narrated monologue," *style indirect libre*, and *erlebte rede*. Literary studies include Hamburger (1973), Cohn (1978), Genette (1980).

Represented speech and thought are not limited to fiction, as the passage in (6) illustrates; it is from an article in the *New York Times* cited in Wiebe (1991):

(6)   Looking at the more severely affected countries, experts are wondering where the saturation point will be. Where will the infection rate level off as most of those engaging in riskier behavior fall prey: 30 percent? 40 percent?

The second sentence presents a represented thought or utterance: the direct questions are due to the experts, not to the writer.

Although the forms of these communications are at the sentence level, they are not limited to a single sentence. The scope of the subjective form may extend over several sentences, so long as continuity is maintained. This sense of continuity is discussed in connection with examples (18) and (19).

Direct address to the reader in the form of questions, imperatives, and deictic *you*, also appear in texts. They address a communication to the reader, creating the canonical deictic situation. The source is the author and the addressee is the reader; (7) illustrates:

(7)   Those are rather windy thoughts, but I have had a hard time escaping them the last few weeks as I've tried to make some sense of the Events surrounding President Clinton, Congress and impeachment. What will people say about all this 20 years from now? Will they quiz each other on the minutiae of the Starr report, as they do on the contents of the Warren report? Or will posterity simply conclude that one of the two political parties, having lost an election, saw an opportunity to nullify it and proved too weak to resist the temptation? You may find that a difficult question. I don't.

The writer is the source of subjectivity in this text. The reader may also be addressed directly, as in the last sentences of the fragment above.

7.3   *Contents of mind*

Expressions of mental states such as thoughts, beliefs, and attitudes convey the contents of mind. Typically they have verbs like *think* and *believe*; complements express the object of thought or belief. The same deictic conventions hold for complements of mental verbs as for indirect speech, as (8) illustrates:

(8)   a. We thought that Bella was in New York.
       b. Mary$_i$ believes that she$_i$ won the race.

In (8b), which expresses a belief, the main and complement clauses have coreferential subjects. The coreference relation between subjects in clauses of thought and communication triggers a logophoric interpretation, discussed in Chapter 6.

The person who holds a belief is responsible for it. But belief sentences are also reports by the writer and have the possibility of recoding. The writer's presence is sometimes suggested by evaluative expressions and epithets, which are vague as to source. For instance, epithets such as "that fool," "that idiot of a doctor," "a peach of a girl" can be ascribed to the believer or to the reporter, as in (9):

(9)   a. Sam thinks that his beloved cat should have only fresh fish.
       b. Mary believed that that fool Kevin wanted to run the committee.

On one reading, the epithets "beloved cat," "that fool" are part of the reported beliefs. There is also a reading in which the reporter designates the cat as beloved, Kevin as a fool. This reading is salient in (9b) because of the deictic *that*.[9]

Sentences with clauses referring to propositions have an additional dimension of subjectivity. Recall that propositions are subjective, ascribed to the person holding them (Chapter 4). Clauses referring to Facts are not subjective in this way. Nominals of communication and mental state are similar to verbs in subjectivity. For instance, the interpretation of "Mary's belief that John won the race" is not significantly different from the corresponding tensed clause.

7.4   *Evaluative and evidential subjectivity*

Different attitudes and degrees of commitment may be expressed by participants in the text situation, or to the writer as participant or intruder. The linguistic

---

9. The interpretation is my own; Banfield claims that epithets in clauses of indirect speech and thought are attributable only to the speaker (1982:54).

   Epithets are lexical items whose full interpretation entails a reference to the speaker. In the embedded clause of indirect speech, however, they only express the state and attitude of the reporting speaker, according to Banfield, who suggests two classes:

   a. Epithets: fool, bastard, etc.
   b. Evaluative adjectives: the poor girl, that damned Faustus, etc.

   Banfield claims that these forms constitute a well-defined, "non-classificatory" class that can be distinguished with a lexical feature.

expressions are evaluative and evidential adverbs and adjectives, modals, and parenthetical expressions. Attitudes are ascribed to participants in the text situation when they appear within the scope of subjective expressions.

Adverbs can be divided into classes according to their semantic relationship to the situation and speaker/writer. One class gives the speaker's attitude toward what is said (*frankly, honestly*); another conveys the speaker's evaluation of the text situation (*fortunately, surprisingly*). Evidential adverbials express the speaker's commitment to a proposition (*clearly, allegedly, seemingly, probably, possibly*); *likely* is an adjective of the same type. Adverbs like these can appear in various positions in a sentence: they are also called "parentheticals."

(10)   a. *Surprisingly*, tunnels are among the most ancient engineering feats. The earliest were very likely extensions of prehistoric cave dwellings.
   b. Most of us don't suffer as a result of Darwin's having eventually attributed too much scope to the process termed sypatric speciation than it actually deserves. But a powerful man's mistaken ideas about women have *certainly* caused suffering.
   c. The rest of the space was taken up by fancy notepaper, glass paperweights, fluffy animals and fridge-door magnets shaped like strawberries or Humpty Dumpty. In the back, *though*, the setup was very different.

(11)   a. The predominant output was the white ware with transparent ivory toned glaze which made the kilns famous. The other wares were a soft, dark brown or dense black glazed type, a white ware and a group of lead glazed earthenwares.
   The kilns *clearly* specialized in the production of the porcellanous ware.
   b. Sooner or later, oil prices are *likely* to drop. But prices at today's levels have their advantages.

The adverbs of (10a–b) and parenthetical of (10c) express attitude and evaluation. The adverb and adjective of (11) express evidentiality; they are sometimes called "speaker-oriented" forms. These expressions are attributed to the speaker as Responsible Source. The adverbs are classified as Speech Act, Evaluative, and Evidential adverbs by Cinque (1999). Cinque presents a semantically based syntactic account of these expressions: he posits a syntactic projection for each class according to their possible positions in a sentence.

Many evaluative and evidential adverbs have corresponding adjectives. They differ in the Responsible Source, reflecting a different syntactic status. The speaker is always the source for adverbs, which are external syntactically and semantically to the sentence. Evaluative adjectives, however, function as the main predicate. They are associated with an experiencer, explicit or implicit. This allows more than one interpretation of responsibility; (12) illustrates:

(12)   a. Darwin accepted the postulate of "blending inheritance" (the fusion of a
              mother's and father's characteristics in their off-spring), even though his
              own experiments on pigeons refuted it. Much more *surprising* are two other
              errors.
          b. One thing the experts are *certain* of is that this species, depleted by whaling
              and not protected throughout its range until 1966, is showing signs of a
              comeback.
          c. For a big-city mayor to be so at odds with his party would *seem peculiar*.
              Except that it's happening everywhere.

In (12a), we infer that the author is responsible for evaluating the situation
as surprising. But in (12b) the experts hold the evaluative attitude. Example
(12c), though vague, includes the author. The modal contributes to the interpretation of subjectivity; modals are discussed below. The verbs *seem, appear,
suggest* have the same range of interpretation. The speaker is responsible for
the evaluation unless a text participant is explicitly mentioned. For instance, a
variant of (12c) has a sentence-internal interpretation: "For a big-city mayor to
be so at odds with his party seemed peculiar to the voters." Another difference
between evaluative predicates and adverbials is that verbs and adjectives can
be questioned, whereas adverbs cannot. The related "psychological" verbs, e.g.
surprise, frighten, annoy, etc., are not subjective in the sense developed here:
they do not require that responsibility be ascribed to a mind.

  Discourse salience, evidentiality, and "performativity" must all be considered in understanding evaluative predicates and adverbials, according to Nuyts
(1993). He suggests that evaluatives may be "performative" or "descriptive."
When used performatively, the speaker/author is an active participant in the
evaluation. They are descriptive when they report evaluation that is part of the
text situation.

  Evidentiality is the semantic domain of speaker commitment to what is said.
In English, evidentiality is expressed by adverbs and adjectives, as above; and
by verbs and modal auxiliaries.[10] I will sketch here how modals fit into an
account of evidentiality. I cannot offer a full account here of the contribution of
modals to interpretation, nor of the domain of modality; I ignore conditionals
and the modal aspect of generics.

  Strictly speaking, modality has to do with necessity and possibility: modal
forms express the necessity or possibility of a proposition. More abstractly, they
express a certain way the world might be, and involve a modal relation and a

---

10. Some languages have highly developed sub-systems for evidentiality, see Chafe & Nichols
    (1986), Willett (1988), Dendale & Tasmowski (2001) for surveys. Kamio (1994) discusses
    Japanese.

conversational background for interpretation (Kratzer 1981). There is a useful distinction among modals between the "epistemic," expressing possibility and necessity, and the "deontic," expressing the will in action in the sense of volition, permission. In English the same forms, modal auxiliaries, are used for both types of meaning, leading to systematic ambiguity.

Modals of evidentiality express the position of the speaker toward the propositional content of the clause. In contrast, modals that pertain to the internal proposition are not evidential. Certain modals have both the internal and speaker-related interpretation. *Must*, for instance, has three interpretations in (13), an example from Lyons (1977). The first is internal, the other two are evidential:

(13)   Alfred must be unmarried.

On the internal interpretation *must* functions like the modal operator of logical necessity on the proposition; it does not express the position of the speaker. The evidential interpretations can be paraphrased as "I (confidently) infer that Alfred is unmarried" *and* "Alfred is obliged to be unmarried." The two interpretations correspond to the distinction between epistemic and deontic modality. The epistemic interpretation ascribes confidence to the speaker. It is "subjective," qualifying the speaker's commitment to the proposition that Alfred is unmarried. The deontic interpretation in this sentence is "objective': it indicates that, according to the judgment of the speaker, there is a mathematically computable chance that the proposition is true.

Subjective and objective modality differ in how the speaker participates in the evaluation. For instance, on the subjective *must* reading of (13) the speaker expresses commitment to an evaulation. The objective interpretation is a factual assertion expressing the speaker's judgment about content (Lyons 1982).

Three classes of modals are recognized in Verstraete (2001): internal, epistemic, and deontic. Internal modals concern ability and volition and pertain directly to the proposition expressed. Epistemic modals are evidential and subjective. Deontic modals may be subjective or objective, for instance, "Alfred may be unmarried" is ambiguous between the speaker's subjective assessment and an "objective" assessment of circumstances. Such an assessment, although objective, is due to the speaker and therefore also evidential.[11]

11. Subjective and objective evidentials are distinguishable by the criteria of behavior under interrogation and in conditional contexts, and surface ordering, according to Verstraete (2001). Verstraete may not share my interpretation of objective modal interpretation as evidential. Nuyts (1993) distinguishes subjective and objective evidentials by their availability for negation, and other criteria. His work is based on a study of adverbial and adjectival expressions in a corpus of Dutch discourse. He suggests that the English forms can be explained along similar lines.

The following examples illustrate the classes: (14) has a modal of ability, internal to the proposition. Sentence (15), repeating (12c), has a subjective, evidential modal; the modals of (16) are evidential and ambiguous between the subjective and objective interpretations.

(14)   Gabriel went to the stairs and listened over the banisters.
He *could* hear two persons talking in the pantry.

(15)   For a big-city mayor to be so at odds with his party *would* seem peculiar. Except that it's happening everywhere.

(16)   a. In Belgrade, Yugoslav President Slobodan Milosevic . . . insisted . . . that the details must be negotiated directly with the United Nations. That *would appear* to fall short of Western conditions for halting the eight-week bombing campaign.
         b. For the body to operate properly, it is crucial that diverse hormones and receptors produce distinct effects on cells. To achieve such specificity, receptors *must* engage in somewhat different behavior.
         c. Bass rumbles that could have issued from the lowest octave of a cathedral pipe organ gave way to plaintive moans and then to glissandos like air squealing out of a balloon when you stretch the neck taut. With the notes building into phrases and the phrases into repeated themes, the song *may* be the longest – up to 30 minutes – and the most complex in the animal kingdom.

The preferred reading of (16a) is the subjective, the writer's assessment. Example (16b) has only an objective interpretation, (16c) is ambiguous between subjective and objective assessment. When a modal appears in the complement clause of a verb of saying, responsibility is ascribed to the subject, as in (17):

(17)   Allied divisions over using ground troops in Kosovo burst into the open on Wednesday when Germany's chancellor declared that his country *would* block NATO from fighting a land war.

Similarly, when a modal is within the scope of a mental State verb, the Responsible Source is the subject of the verb.

Context is often essential in interpreting expressions of subjectivity: the Responsible Source may be in a preceding sentence. For instance, a mental state verb holds over subsequent sentences unless it is interrupted by another subjective indicator or a change of time or place. Example (18) gives a simple example, a variant of (12a); the evaluative *was clear* in S2 is in the scope of *believe* of S1.

(18)   1. Darwin believed in the postulate of "blending inheritance."
         2. It was clear that the mother's and father's characteristics fused in their offspring.

The predicate "be clear" in S2 implies an evaluator, and in the uninterrupted context of S1, the evaluator is Darwin. Uninterrupted contexts maintain subjective continuity.

So long as continuity is not interrupted, a subjective form may have scope over later sentences. Interruptions consist of (a) change of time; (b) change of place; and (c) other candidates for Responsible Source. These criteria can be stated formally in terms of time and place information, and whether a sentient being is introduced into the universe of discourse. Modals and some adverbials are limited in scope to the sentence in which they appear, unlike other subjective forms. Stretches of text that are uninterrupted in this sense have "subjective continuity."

To illustrate these points I present a rather long text fragment. There is one participant in the text situation, Sir Mark Sykes. The fragment has expressions indicating communications of Sykes', his mental state, and evidentials that suggest the author as Responsible Source. The subjective forms are marked according to their source: triggers for Sykes as Responsible Source are underlined; triggers for the author as Responsible Source are in bold; triggers for other Responsible Sources are in italics.

(19)   1 Sir Mark Sykes **seems** to have started <u>worrying about</u> the Syrian problem the year before in the context of pledges he <u>intended</u> Britain to keep to her allies – and her allies to keep to her. 2 <u>His concern</u> was that Syrians <u>might</u> not accept the Sykes–Picot agreement and the terms outlined by Sir Henry McMahon to the Sherif Hussein. 3 In 1917 he <u>asked</u> the Arab Bureau [of Britain] to set up a meeting for him with Syrian Arab leaders in Cairo, **apparently** in order to arrive at an agreement with them that would be consistent with the secret accords with France and with the Hejaz – accords whose existence, however, he <u>could</u> not reveal to them. 4 He <u>claimed</u> he had succeeded; in his own hand he <u>noted that</u> "The main difficulty was to manoeuvre the delegates into asking for what we were prepared to give them, without letting them know that any precise geographical agreement had been come to." 5 The "precise geographical agreement" **must** have meant the Damascus–Homs–Gana–Aleppo line that was to be the westward frontier of Arab independence in Syria under the agreement with al-Faruqi in 1915 and with France in 1916.

    6 But reports arrived from various quarters that the Ottoman government *might* be planning to pre-empt Arab nationalism by granting autonomy to Syria immediately. 7 That *would* leave Britain in the awkward position of sponsoring the claims of King Hussein as against an indigenous Arabic leadership in Damascus that threatened to be far more popular in the Syrian provinces.

The list in (20) summarizes the interpretation, giving the trigger for subjectivity; the Responsible Source (RS), and the scope of the subjective expression. The

RS is the Author or the Subject, Sykes unless otherwise stated. I discuss an issue of scope at the end.

(20)   Interpretation of subjectivity in (19)

S1: "seems," evidential verb: RS Author; scope, S1 or through S7; "worry about," mental state: RS Subject; scope, S1 or entire fragment; "intend," mental state: RS Subject; scope, rel. clause headed by "pledges";

S2: "concern," mental state: RS Subject; scope, *that*-clause in S2; "might," evidential modal: RS Subject; scope, *that*-clause in S2;

S3: "ask," communication: RS Subject; scope, subsequent clauses of S3; "apparently," attitude adverb: RS Author; scope, subsequent clauses of S3; "could," ability modal: no RS; internal to rel. clause headed by "accords";

S4: "claim," "note," communication: RS Subject; scope, clauses in S4;

S5: "must," evidential modal: RS Author; scope, rest of S5;

S6: "might," evidential modal: RS "reports"; scope, S6, possibly S7.

S7: "would," evidential modal: RS Author, Subject, or "reports"; scope S7.

There are three candidates for the Responsible Source of the modal in the last sentence. The first is the Author; the second is "reports," Subject by extension, though not a sentient being. On this reading the evidential is contained in the reports and the scope of "reports" is S6 and S7. The third possible source for "would" in S7 is Sykes, the Subject of the mental State verb "worry about" in S1 of the fragment.

The entire fragment is concerned with Sykes' worrying about a complex situation. The verb "worry about" in S1 has uninterrupted scope through S7 because continuity is maintained. The fragment does not introduce a Responsible Source that competes with Sykes, nor does it contain any deictic shifts indicating a difference in the situation.

Evaluation may take other forms as well. Sentence connectives such as *yet*, *anyway*, *still*, *but*, for instance, convey the author's view of relations between situations. There are also idiomatic forms, e.g. *after all* as in "So he is coming after all! (despite our expectation to the contrary)" from Cinque (1999). Like other lexical expressions, cases like this are beyond the scope of this discussion.

Compositional rules for subjective interpretations like those given above are presented in 7.6.

7.5   *Perception and perspectival sentences*

We recognize certain sentences as expressing a perspective that filters information through a particular mind. Such sentences depart from the objective stance, in which perspective is transparent. The central examples of perspectival sentences involve perception, usually by a participant in the text situation. In other cases, a particular perspective is indicated without reference to perception. The linguistic forms of perspective include reflexives, deictics, and forms of direction or location.

7.5.1   *Perception*

Linguistic presentation of perception may be direct, contextual, or inferred. The most straightforward cases are reports of direct perception, in which a verb of seeing, hearing, etc., introduces a complement which expresses the percept, as in (21):

(21)   a. John saw that the sun was shining.
       b. John saw Mary walk to school.
       c. John saw Mary walking to school.

The examples illustrate the three forms of perception verb complements in English: propositional, a "bare" or "naked" infinitive, or gerundive. First-person reports of perception are subjective, expressing the perspective of the reporter as a participant, including the "unreliable narrator" of fiction. Not all perception verb sentences convey direct perception. Complements with *that* convey not perception but inference from evidence. For instance, if John saw mud on Mary's shoes and reasoned that the mud was due to her having taken a walk, one could say "John saw that Mary (had) walked to school." Complements with a different tense from the main clause are also interpreted this way, e.g. "John sees that Mary walked to school."[12]

Less direct but very clear are perception verb sentences that immediately precede another sentence expressing the percept. Example (22) illustrates:

(22)   Gabriel smiled at the three syllables she had given his surname and glanced at her. She was a slim, growing girl, pale in complexion and with hay-colored hair.

The subject of the first sentence is the perceiver; the second sentence conveys what is perceived. Sentences that convey perception in this way are "perspectivally situated" (Caenepeel 1989);[13] they tend to occur in narrative contexts.

---

12. In a full account of direct perception sentences, one might distinguish perceivable situations from those that can only be inferred, e.g. "Mary saw John thinking about the race." Such distinctions would help to separate the extended meanings of *see, hear, feel* from the meaning of direct perception. The extended meaning of *see* would be something like "understand," "infer", while that of *hear* would be "have been told that"; etc.

13. According to Caenepeel, perceptual reports or perspectively situated sentences are always stative (state or progressive event sentences, in our terms). She claims that events – that is, event verb constellation with the perfective viewpoint – are impossible or awkward as perceptual

The progressive viewpoint is hospitable to subjective interpretation. In traditional terms, the progressive and other imperfective viewpoints take an "internal perspective" on a situation, whereas the viewpoint of perfectives is external (Comrie 1976). More formally, the progressive focuses an interval that is internal to an ongoing event; thus its formal meaning is compatible with the interpretation of an experiencing mind. Shifted deictics are clear linguistic evidence for the internal, subjective interpretation. They are good in progressive imperfective sentences, somewhat limited in perfectives:[14]

(23)   a. 1 Mary had been working hard all day. 2 Now she was ready to stop.
        b. 1 Mary had been working hard all day. 2 Now she stopped.

S2 in (23a) suggests Mary's perspective. The tense of both clauses is past; the complement clause has the deictic adverb *now*, which is normally anchored to Speech Time; the situation is a state. S2 in (247b), however, is indeterminate between the perspective of Mary and that of the narrator. Oppositions such as perfective and imperfective often have the pragmatic function of marking what is traditionally referred to as "point of view" in narrative (Fleischman 1991:26).

There are also contexts of inferred perception, when the situation implies a percept due to our knowledge of the world. As with indirect perception more than one sentence is needed. The examples in (24) illustrate:

(24)   a. 1 I sipped my drink and nodded. 2 The pulse in his lean grey throat throbbed visibly and yet so slowly that it was hardly a pulse at all. 3 An old man two-thirds dead and still determined to believe he could take it.
        b. 1 One night in November 1961, Alice went into the tub room to put some clothes in her old wringer washing machine. 2 a When she turned on the light, b there was a rat the size of a small cat sitting on the machine.

reports unless there is a contingency relation between the event and the focalizing sentence. In a contingency relation, the situation of the perspectivally situated sentence is contingent on the immediately preceding situation.

However, events are acceptable as perceptual reports in extended, continuous situations of perception:

a. 1 John looked out the window. 2 Birds flew back and forth and the church bell tolled loudly.
b. John looked out the window. Mary threw the ball to Sue and Bill played in the sandbox. The neighbor's dog arrived and trotted around the yard.

Of course, not all sequences with a verb of perception preceding a sentence of an unbounded situation express a percept. The second sentence may indicate an entirely different situation:

c. John looked out the window. The children were playing quietly in a corner of the room.

14. This is particularly clear in French: the *imparfait* past tense allows shifted deictics more freely than the perfective past tenses (Banfield 1982, Smith 1991).

Both fragments set up a situation with the subject referent of S1 as participant. In (24a), we take the sentences after S1 to express the percept of the narrator as he talks to the old man. The adverb *visibly* supports, but it is not essential. S2 might be "The pulse in his lean grey throat throbbed so slowly that it was hardly a pulse at all"; the inference of perception remains. Example (24b) has a subtle and more complex subjectivity. In S2a, Alice turns on the light. World knowledge tells us that she is in a position to see the room, and S2b by implication presents her percept. The possessive *her* in S1 is oriented toward the subject, Alice; see the discussion of example (28) below.

Inferred perception is difficult to establish formally since it depends on inference and world knowledge. It is beyond the scope of compositional rules. Other kinds of perception can be recognized at the level of grammatical form.

There is an additive effect in sentences which suggest but do not require subjective interpretation. With one such form, the suggestion may be weak; with two or more, it is stronger. Examples in (25) illustrate. In these examples, consider whether the reporter or Mary is the source of the question.

(25)   a. Mary played in the sandbox. Huge storm clouds covered the sky. Was it going to rain?
         b. Mary was playing in the sandbox. Huge storm clouds were covering the sky. Was it going to rain?
         c. Mary was playing in the sandbox with her brother. Huge storm clouds were covering the sky. Was it going to rain?

In (25a) the direct question is the only subjective element; in (25b) the preceding sentence has the progressive, which invites a subjective interpretation. The example with the strongest subjective interpretation is (25c), which also has a possessive phrase oriented to Mary. I do not have a formal account of inferred perception. It depends on pragmatic factors as well as linguistic form.

7.5.2   *Particular standpoints*

Perspective may be suggested by forms that indicate the standpoint of a participant, or the reporter. The notion of standpoint has a literal basis in the world. From a particular location, a person sees in a certain way: if I say that the tree is nearby, it is because of my position in space. If I say that the bank is around the corner and you say it is across the street, we can both be right if we are standing in different places (Mitchell 1986:1). The notion of standpoint can be extended to situations in which one talks as if one were in a location; and metaphorically to attitudes and views that are not grounded in space.

Perspectival examples have reflexive pronouns, deictics, the progressive, and other expressions that suggest a particular standpoint. Example (26) illustrates with reflexives, based on examples from Ross (1970), Cantrall (1969), Kuno (1987):

(26)   a. This paper was written by Ann and myself.
       b. They$_i$ heard the stories about themselves$_i$.
       c. Mary$_i$ put the blanket over herself$_i$.

The perspective of the reflexives' antecedent is suggested in these sentences. In (26a) the speaker must be the antecedent of the reflexive, and is plausible as participant.[15] In (26b–c) the subjects "they" and "Mary" are the reflexives' antecedents; the reflexives locate the stories and blanket from their standpoint or perspective. The reflexives are Locally Free Reflexives (LFRs), not syntactically conditioned.[16]

When they convey a particular perspective, reflexive pronouns represent a choice between two possible pronouns. To see the contribution of the reflexive, compare the sentences of (27). Both are grammatical; the choice of pronoun affects interpretation:

(27)   a. John$_i$ pulled the toy toward him$_i$.
       b. John$_i$ pulled the toy toward himself$_i$.

15. Cantrall was perhaps the first to note the perspectival use of the reflexive. Cantrall presents many examples, among them the following sentences. Cantrall asks us to imagine that they describe a photograph which portrays a group of standing women who have their backs to the camera:

    a. The women$_i$ were standing in the background, with the children behind them$_i$.
    b. The women$_i$ were standing in the background, with the children behind themselves$_i$.

    In (a) the children are located from the perspective of the speaker; in (b) they are located from the perspective of the women. As Zribi-Hertz notes, the sentences provide empirical evidence that the reflexive is correlated with an "internal" point of view – that of a discourse protagonist as opposed to the speaker (1989:704).

    Examples like (27a) led Ross (1970) to suggest that all sentences have a higher clause in underlying structure with a first-person pronoun and a verb of communication in the present tense. The overt reflexive pronoun would be coindexed with the covert first-person pronoun. Zellig Harris reached the same conclusion on a different basis (in Harris 1982), as Bruce Nevin has pointed out to me.
16. Syntactically conditioned reflexives are obligatory in certain contexts; they are defined in Government Binding Theory with the notions of c-command and locality of domain. The Binding Theory requires that the antecedent c-command a reflexive if it is within the domain of the relevant governing category (Chomsky 1981). The Binding Theory as stated has been the subject of much critical comment. Reinhart & Reuland (1993) offer an extensive revision in the same general framework.

Example (27b), with the reflexive, suggests the perspective of John as he pulls the toy, (27a) does not. Other uses of Locally Free Reflexives are discussed in Chapter 6.

According to Kuno (1987), the reflexives in these examples convey an "empathy perspective" in which the reporter takes the perspective of another person.[17] Empathy may be conveyed by other means as well. For instance, consider the descriptions of the participants in "Accompanied by his son, the informant went out to investigate." The writer expresses empathy with the informant by describing him independently and the son dependently, as Sanders & Redeker (1996) observe.

Possessive pronouns may also suggest perspective, often of a participant. In English this is due to the limited resources of the language. Possessive pronouns have no reflexive alternant. There is only one form, with the potential for a possessive, reflexive, or perspectival reflexive reading. The examples in (28) show possessive pronouns suggesting the perspective of the antecedent: (28a) is from Kuno (1987), (28b) from Hirose (2000):

(28)   a. John criticized his brother.
        b. Kazuo lost a book that he borrowed from a friend of his.

17. Perspectival LFRs have been identified in many other languages, among them Japanese, Scandinavian languages, and Italian. Kuno (1987) offers a survey of perspectival and logophoric phenomena across languages.

   Hirose gives examples of two uses of *zibun*, perspectival and logophoric. The logophoric involves access to consciousness, the perspectival does not; his term for the latter is "point of view." Hirose says that in the logophoric example (a) Kazuo is aware that he is shy, because he says so. On other other hand in example (b), Kazuo does not have to be aware that the book he lost is the one he borrowed from his friend. This is shown by the fact that (c) is not contradictory (2000:1646). The examples are reproduced with Hirose's abbreviations and translations. TOP = topic, COP = copula, QUOT = quotative, STAT = stative, NOM = nominative case, ACC = Accusative case, NEG = negation.

   a. Kazuo wa   zibun wa   tereya   da   to   itteiru
      K.   TOP self   TOP shy.person COP QUOT say-STAT
      Kazuo$_i$ says that he$_i$ is shy.
   b. Kazuo wa   zibun ga   tomodati karita hon   o   nakusit
      K.   TOP self   NOM friend   from borrowed book ACC lost
      Kazuo$_i$ lost a book that he$_i$ borrowed from a friend.
   c. Kazuo wa   zibun ga   tomodati karita hon   o   nakusita ga, sono
      K.   TOP self   NOM friend   from borrowed book ACC   lost but that
      hon ga tomodati kara karita mono da to wa kizuite-it-nai. book NOM friend from
      borrowed thing COP QUOT TOP realize-STAT-NEG
      Kazuo$_i$ lost a book that he$_i$ borrowed from a friend but he has not realized that the book is the one he borrowed from a friend.

   Hirose says that "zibun" in examples like (b) and (c) conveys "point of view," whereas in (a) "zibun" is logophoric.

The perspectival reading of the possessives is relatively weak in these examples. They can be read as simply giving information about the relationship of the participants, or as conveying the perspective of the antecedents John and Kazuo. If they appeared in a narrative context, however, the perspectival readings might be stronger.

Recognizing differences in strength among the relevant examples, Kuno posits a continuum of "degrees of empathy." At the high end of the continuum the reporter totally identifies with a participant; in the middle the identification is partial; at the low end the reporter manifests a total lack of empathy with participants. Perspective may also be suggested by adjectives or epithets that would be expected from the participant, e.g. "John talked to Mary about his beloved cat."

Deictic adverbials can indicate the perspective of a participant. When a deictic neutrally anchored to Speech Time is reanchored to the past or future, a personal perspective is suggested strongly. Compare (29a) with (29b–c):

(29)   a. Mary lost her watch three weeks ago.
        b. Mary had lost her watch three weeks ago.
        c. Mary packed her clothes. She would be leaving soon.

In (29a) the deictic "three weeks ago" is anchored to the time of speech; there is no subjectivity. But (29b–c) suggest the perspective of Mary, the sentence subject, with deictics anchored to a past time.

The rather delicate interpretation of perspective can be partially accounted for by compositional rules. Reanchored deictics can be recognized by rules which look at the tense and deictic adverbial in a clause. If the two are not in accord – for instance, a past tense and Speech-Time-oriented deictic – and there is an appropriate Responsible Source, then the deictic is perspectival. Locally Free Reflexives (LFRs) could in principle be recognized by a rule with access to the principles of the Binding Theory. If a reflexive has no Binding Theory antecedent, it is an LFR. However, it need not be perspectival: recall that LFRs have other functions, noted in Chapter 6. I will not state a compositional rule for perspectival LFRs.

7.6   Formalizing the interpretation of subjectivity

7.6.1   The approach

More than one linguistic form contributes to subjectivity. This diversity is essential to the composite analysis. Example (30) gives the forms that contribute to a subjective interpretation in alphabetical order:

(30)   *Linguistic forms contributing to subjectivity*
         Communication verbs
         Deictic adverbials: place, time
         Direction and location PPs
         Epithets
         Evaluative verbs and adverbs
         Evidential adverbials, adjectives, and verbs
         Experiencer predicates
         Possessive pronouns
         Progressive viewpoint
         Propositional complements
         Situation type: State and activity sentences

The list is not complete but it gives a sense of the many and varied forms involved. Among the forms ignored here are conditionals and counter-factives; the subjunctive; conjunctions such as *yet*, *anyway*; verbs and PPs with a deictic component such as *come* and *go*, *toward* and *away from*. Forms of comparison and evaluation also indicate subjectivity (Hunston & Thompson 2000); since they are conveyed lexically they are beyond the scope of this discussion.

The interpretation of subjectivity requires that a Responsible Source be identified. To account for subjectivity in Discourse Representation Theory, I write a set of construction rules that introduce the Responsible Source as a conceptual role. The rules associate this role with the appropriate individual entity, on the one hand, and with a sub-structure of the representation on the other. The output of the rule is encoded in the Discourse Representation Structure (DRS).

The construction rules recognize as Responsible Source either the Author or the Subject, a sentient being in the text situation. When the Author entity is needed, a special discourse entity is constructed by the rule. The Subject is usually the subject of a sentence, but may also be the direct object or the object of a preposition. In clauses with subjective forms the rules look for NPs that have the feature [+human] in appropriate syntactic relation as candidates for Subject. Most of the features of subjectivity are needed anyway in a grammar of English, e.g. the noun feature [+human]; the verb classes of communication, mental state, and perception; pronoun forms; modals; tense, etc.

Subordinate structures in a DRS model the relation between the Responsible Source and the relevant material. The information in the scope of a subjective form appears in a sub-DRS. This correctly identifies subjectively introduced information, and provides a special status for it. The approach is consistent with treatments of propositional attitude verbs and modality in Discourse Representation Theory since the mid 1980s by Kamp (1985), Roberts (1987), and

Frank & Kamp (1997). I also draw on the DR Theory account of logophoricity in Stirling (1993). All of these analyses use subordination: material in the scope of mental state verbs, modal operators, and other forms of subjectivity appears as a sub-DRS. The mental space theory of Fauconnier (1985) takes essentially the same approach.

Thus, for instance, a mental state verb will trigger a sub-DRS. The subject of the verb is identified with the role of Responsible Source. This appears as a condition in the DRS. The information in the complement of the verb is in a sub-DRS that is associated with the Responsible Source.

Before introducing the compositional rules, I give two examples of DRSs with expressions of subjectivity. The first DRS interprets a sentence with the mental state verb *believe* and a complement clause: "Mary believes that John won the race." By rule, the main clause subject is interpreted as Subject and Responsible Source; the resulting condition is entered in the DRS (lines 3, 4). The contents of the belief appear in a sub-DRS associated with the verb. In a belief sentence like this, individuals are independent of the sub-DRS. The individual "John" therefore appears at the top of the DRS and as a discourse referent *a* in the sub-DRS. In the sub-DRS *a* is identified with John as a condition (line 6). The DRSs are radically simplified, including only the relevant information.

(31)   Mary believes that John won the race

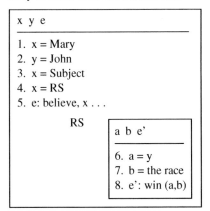

In some other types of subjectivity all the individuals within the scope of the subjective form are independently posited and thus appear at the top of the DRS.

The next DRS interprets a sentence with a modal, for which the Author (A) is Responsible Source (RS). The Author is introduced as a discourse entity at the top of the DRS, and is interpreted as RS (lines 2 and 3).

(32)   Mary may win the race.

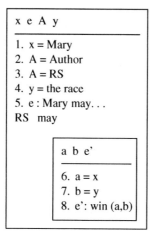

The material within the scope of the modal is within the sub-DRS, as in the previous example. However in this case both individuals in the sub-DRS, "Mary" and "the race," are posited independent of the modal operator. The formal interpretation of the modal would also be included in a complete DRS. Additional DRS interpretations of subjectivity will be presented in Chapter 10.

7.6.2   Compositional rules
This section presents compositional rules for interpreting subjectivity that result in DRSs like those above. The rules are organized into the categories of subjectivity introduced in this chapter: communication, contents of mind and evidentiality, perception, and perspective.

7.6.2.1   Rules for subjectivity I: communication
These rules interpret quoted speech, indirect speech, and direct address to the audience. Represented speech is not included. For quoted speech, the rule recognizes as Responsible Source the sentient being to which the quote is attributed: Rule 1. For indirect speech, recall that recoding by the Author is always a possibility. The rule recognizes two Responsible Sources, the Author or the person whose communication is reported, the Subject. Indirect speech typically

has a verb of communication; a *that*-complementizer introducing the complement; the past tense in main and complement clause; shifted pronouns and adverbials. Together, these forms trigger the interpretation of indirect speech.

I give only the basic rule: Rule 2. The rule does not provide for special cases. Special interpretation cases include logophoric clauses, where the Subject is coreferential with the subject of S2; and clauses where the deictic forms in S2 are proximal rather than distal; and the interpretation of double-access sentences, with the past tense in the main clause and present tense in S2. Other rules would be needed for sentences where the Subject is not in subject position.

Direct questions, imperatives, and direct addresses to the audience introduce the entity Author as Responsible Source. This constitutes the interpretation of subjectivity. The rules use the abbreviations in (33); they allow for verbs or nominals of the classes discussed above, for instance, the verb *believe* or the nominal *belief*:

(33)   Abbreviations
         Animate NP picked out by rule = NPx
         Referent of NPx, usually subject or experiencer = Subject
         Speaker/Author = Author
         Responsible Source = RS
         Ability, obligation modal = Modc
         Communication verb or nominal = V/Ncom
         Evidential evaluative modal, verb, adverb, adjective V/Mod/Adj/AdvE
         Mental State Verb or nominal = V/Nme
         Perception verb or nominal = V/Npe

The rules are listed below. Each rule has 3 parts: (a) a verbal statement of the surface structure that the rule recognizes, with examples in italics; (b) the formal rule itself – X, Y indicate optional additional material that is not relevant to a rule; (c) a statement of the interpretation the rule makes.

Rule 1: Quoted Speech
(a) Subject (NPx) is subject of V_{COM}, quotes in complement clause, Subject = RS
    Kim said "I'm ready to go home." Kim said "John went home."
(b) S1[NPx V_{COM} ["X"]] → Subject = NPx; Subject = RS (S2)
(c) Rule 1 interprets NPx as Subject, and Subject as the RS for the quoted material.

Rule 2: Indirect Speech
(a) NPx subj of V_{COM}, complement clause, Subject and/or Author = RS
    Kim said that he was ready to go home.

(b) S1[NPx V$_{COM\ tns}$[past] S2[that [X.$_{tns}$[past] (Adv[+distal])]]]]
    → Author; Author = RS (S) Subject = NPx; Subject = RS (S2)
(c) Rule 2 interprets NPx as Subject, introduces the entity Author, and interprets both Author and Subject as RS.

Rule 3a: Direct Question

(a) Question form not involving a text participant: Author = RS
    What will happen in five years time? Will anyone remember this incident?
(b) S [(WH) aux NPx Y Z] → Entity Author; Author = RS (S)
(c) Rule 3a recognizes a direct question, introduces Author, and interprets Author as RS.

Rule 3b: Direct Imperative

(a) No surface subject, no text participant: Author = RS (S)
    Think about this carefully.
(b) S [e $_{tns}$[e] (aux) V X] → Author; Author = RS (S)
(c) Rule 3a recognizes a direct imperative, introduces Author, and interprets Author as RS.

Rule 3c: Direct Address

(a) 2nd-person pronoun; Author = RS
    You may find that a difficult question. Everybody's worried about George Bush except you.
(b) S [X $_{NP}$[2nd p] Y] → Author; Author = RS (S)
(c) Rule 3c recognizes a sentence containing a 2nd-person pronoun in subject or another syntactic position, introduces the entity Author, and interprets Author as RS.

7.6.2.2   Rules for subjectivity II: contents of mind and evidentiality
These rules interpret sentences with verbs of mental state; and sentences containing evaluative, evidential, and modal expressions.

The last rule accounts for cases where a subjective form has no Responsible Source in the sentence, but there is a relevant RS in the prior context. If continuity is maintained so that the form is within the scope of V/NME verb in the preceding context, the RS for that verb is also the RS for the sentence in question.

Rule 4: Mental state

(a) Subject (NPx) is subject of V$_{ME}$, Subj = RS
    John believed that the earth is flat.
(b) S1[. . . NPx V/N$_{ME}$ . . . S2[(that) . . . (modal) . . .]]
    → Subject = NPx; Subject = RS (S2)
(c) Rule 4 interprets NPx as Subject, and interprets Subject as the RS for S2, the clausal complement. If there is a modal in the complement, the Subject is RS for that modal.

Rule 5: ModalE

(a) V/ModalE not in the scope of V/N$_{COM}$; entity Author; Author = RS
  The earth may be flat. Mary may be very clever. Mary may think that she is clever.

(b) S[. . . NP V/NM . . .] → Author; Author = RS (S)

(c) Rule 5 introduces the entity Author, and interprets Author as RS for the sentence. The rule doesn't need to know whether there is a potential Subject in the clause.

Rule 6: V/Mod$_C$

(a) NPx sentient being, subj verb/NP, Modal$_C$, Subject = RS
  John could not see the ship on the horizon. RS: John

(b) S[. . . NPx Mod$_C$[VP]] → (Mod$_C$(VP))

(c) Rule 6 interprets the modal as modifying the VP. Such modals are internal, with no RS and without intertriggering a sub-DRS.

Rule 7: Evaluative/Evidential + Experiencer

(a) Subject (NPx), PP obj of V/Adj$_E$; Subject = RS
  It seemed to John that Mary had left. That Mary left was surprising to John.
  It seemed an anomaly to John.

(b) S[NP . . . Adj/V$_E$. X PP[to NPx]] (Y) → NPx = Subject; RS = Subject (S)

(c) Rule 7 interprets the NPx of a *to*-PP as experiencer subject and RS in the context of an evaluative or evidential predicate.

Rule 8: Evaluative/Evidential

(a) Adj/V$_{EX}$; no experiencer subject or PP; Author = RS
  It is evident that the earth is flat. Evidently, the earth is flat.

(b) S[NP . . . Adj/V$_E$ . . .] → Author; Author = RS (S)

(c) Rule 8 introduces the entity Author, and interprets Author as RS for the sentence.

Rule 9: Evaluative/Evidential Adverbial

(a) Adverb$_E$; entity Author; Author = RS
  Obviously, the earth is flat.

(b) S[{Adv$_E$} NP {Adv$_E$} vp[X . . .] {Adv$_E$}] → Author; Author = RS (S)

(c) Rule 9 introduces the entity Author, and interprets Author as RS for the sentence. The braces give the three main positions for adverbs of this class: initial position; before the VP; final position. Only one position is filled, so the braces mean "choose one."

Rule 10: Contextually Licensed V/Mod$_E$, No Candidate NPx for Subject

(a) In the scope of V/Nm$_E$ in the context.
  Darwin believed in the postulate of "blending inheritance." It was clear that the mother's and father's characteristics fused in their offspring.

(b) [S-[NPx Vme X] Y S[NP V/Advex X]]
Condition: in a context without adverbs of time or place, or a new sentient being
→ Subject S- = RS (S)

(c) Rule 10 applies if no potential RS appears in a sentence and a subjective form is within the scope of V/Nme in the context, and there is nothing that interrupts continuity (see the comments on example (19)). The rule interprets the RS for V/Nme as the RS for the sentence in question.

7.6.2.3 Rules for subjectivity III: perception and perspective

These rules deal with sentences that present direct and contextually licensed perception, and particular standpoints or perspectives. I do not include inferred perception, which is based on pragmatic inference rather than linguistic form; nor empathy perspectives with LFR reflexives or other forms. LFR reflexives are excluded because they can express emphasis and contrast as well as subjectivity; the interpretations that I have developed are not sufficiently delicate to distinguish these cases.

The rules for perception are similar to those for contents of mind. There are some differences. Perception involves a different class of verbs, and some rules require that the situation expressed be unbounded (a state, a progressive, or a perfective Activity). The rules do not interpret this notion; I assume that it would be available as part of the general principles for interpretation. Rule 11 is like Rule 4 above, ascribing the contents of the complement clause to the Subject; but the complement is limited to certain forms that convey direct perception. Rule 12, like Rule 10a, gives a contextually licensed interpretation, requiring a situation without endpoints, stated as a disjunction.

Rule 13 interprets sentences with perspectival subjectivity. The rule recognizes shifted deixis: it applies to sentences that have past tense and a deictic that neutrally anchors to Speech Time. The rule allows for all kinds of situations, rather than limiting the possibilities as Rule 12 does.

Rule 11: Direct Perception

(a) Subject = NPx subj of Vpe, complement clause, Subject = RS
John saw Mary opening the door

(b) Conditions: S2 does not contain *that*, nor tense.
S1[... NPx Vpe ... S2[NP V(ing) X]] → Subject = NPx; Subject = RS (S2)

(c) Rule 11 interprets NPx as Subject, and interprets Subject as the RS for S2, the clausal complement.

Rule 12: Contextually Licensed Perception

(a) No candidate NPx for Subject; in the scope of VPE in the context. The situation must be unbounded.

Gabriel glanced at Mary. She was a slim, growing girl.

(b) Condition: the context has no adverbs of time or place, nor a new sentient being.

[S-[NPx VPE X] Y S[e/s unbounded]] → SubjectS = RS (S)

(c) Rule 12 applies if a sentence is within the scope of a VPE verb in the context, and there is nothing that interrupts continuity.

Rule 13: Perspective, Shifted Deictic

(a) Sentences indicate the perspective of NPx.

Mary was tired now. John would be leaving in three weeks. Mary had lost her watch a week ago.

(b) S[NPx tns[past] Deictic[SpT]] → Subject = NPx; Subject = RS (S2)

(c) Rule 13 interprets NPx as Subject, and interprets Subject as the RS for S2, the clausal complement.

These rules indicate the interpretation of subjectivity in Discourse Representation Structures.

7.7   Summary and conclusion

Sentences have a dimension of subjectivity when they express a point of view, or take a perspective on a situation. Communication sentences involve public events, while contents of mind and evaluation express private events or mental states. The perspectival category includes perceptual reports and indications that a situation is viewed from a particular standpoint. Perspective is conveyed by verbs of perception, indirect cues that perception is involved, reflexives that are not syntactically conditioned, and deictics.

In interpreting subjectivity we ascribe responsibility for a clause to the Responsible Source, either the Author or the Subject participant in the text situation. Perspectival sentences suggest the perspective of a participant in varying degrees; in the weaker cases, we may ascribe the perspective to the author.

The subjective interpretation may extend over several sentences, so long as subjective continuity is maintained. Subjective continuity is interrupted by changes of time or place, or introduction of a new candidate for Responsible Source.

Compositional rules recognize expressions of subjectivity and ascribe them to the appropriate Responsible Source. Subjectivity is encoded by embedding in the DRS.

Example sources in this chapter:

(5), (14), and (23) James Joyce. "The Dead." In *Dubliners*, 1916; reprinted London: Penguin Books, 1982, pp. 179, 182, 177.

(7) Alan Ehrenhalt, Hijacking the rulebook. *New York Times*, December 20, 1998.

(10a) Jim Collins. How it works. *US Airways Magazine*, Attaché, May 2001.

(10b), (12a) and (19) Jared Diamond. A tale of two reputations. *Natural History*, February 2001.

(10c) Peter Robinson, *A Necessary End*. New York: Avon Books, 1989, p. 181.

(11a) Margaret Medley, *The Chinese Potter*. London: Phaidon, 1989, Ch. 5.

(11b) Robert Mosbacher, Cheap oil's tough bargains. *New York Times*, March 13, 2000.

(12b) Douglas Chadwick, Listening to humpbacks. *National Geographic*, June 1999.

(12c) and (15) Peter Beinart, The pride of the cities. *New Republic*, June 1997.

(16a) and (17) Kosovo strategy splitting NATO. *New York Times*, May 1999.

(16b) John Scott & Tony Pawson, Cell communication. *Scientific American*, June 2000.

(19) David Fromkin, *A Peace to End All Peace*, New York: Henry Holt, 1989, p. 329.

(24a) Raymond Chandler, *The Long Goodbye*, Boston: Houghton, 1964, Mifflin, p. 64.

(24b) J. Anthony Lukas, *Common Ground*, New York: Knopf, 1985, p. 149.

8 *The contribution of surface presentation*

Sentences that differ in arrangement and sentence accent also differ in meaning, although their propositional content may be the same. As Bolinger puts it, discussing the difference between active and passive (1977:9):

> The classical case is the passive voice. If truth value were the only criterion, we would have to say that *John ate the spinach* and *The spinach was eaten by John* are the same. They report the same event in the real world. The same entities are present, in the same relationship . . . Linguistic meaning covers a great deal more . . . [it] expresses, sometimes in ways that are hard to ferret out, such things as what is the central part of the message, what our attitudes are toward the person we are speaking to, how we feel about the reliability of our message, how we situation ourselves in the Events we report, and many other things.

The meanings that Bolinger talks about involve the way a text presents information, its presentational structure.

Surface structure presentation instructs the receiver about how to organize the information in a sentence. The sentences of a text are not undifferentiated wholes, nor simple linear arrangements of words. I adopt the approach to presentation originally put forth by Prague School linguists and further developed in recent years. This approach uses the notions of communicative dynamism, topic–comment, and focus–background, to understand the internal organization of sentences and how they are deployed in texts. Although "topic" is notoriously difficult, I hope to show that it contributes an important dimension to the analysis of sentences and texts.

The writer's choices of how to present material are influenced by assessment of what is accessible to the receiver. The familiarity status of information is a key factor. This notion was introduced in Chapter 6, where it was shown that the forms of referring expressions used in a text tend to correlate with familiarity of the referent. Familiarity status concerns whether information is discourse-old or discourse-new, hearer-old or hearer-new. What is new to the discourse needn't be new to the hearer; but discourse-old is also hearer-old.

The distinction between discourse-old and discourse-new information is most useful, as noted in Chapter 6. Familiarity status is intertwined with the notions of topic and focus, and imposes constraints on an important class of non-canonical syntactic structures.

Language allows propositional information to be presented in different ways. For instance, in English one may choose an active sentence such as "Mary drew a circle" or its passive counterpart, "A circle was drawn by Mary." The object may be preposed, as in "A circle Mary drew"; or "extracted" in a pseudo-cleft or cleft sentence, "What Mary drew was a circle," "It was a circle that Mary drew"; etc. These sentences express the same proposition, yet they convey somewhat different messages. The study of presentation explores the differences. Linear order, syntax, morphology, and prosody are the linguistic factors that vary in presentation.

Choices of structure and prosody depend on the speaker's intent and assessment of the receiver's current state of knowledge and attention. The main factors in presentation are the topic–focus structure of a sentence and the familiarity status of information. They are independent, but coincide in many cases: topics tend to be familiar, while focused information tends to be new.

In this chapter I discuss the notions of topic and comment, focus and background for English. They lead to different but overlapping partitions of a sentence; I will argue that both are needed. The discussion of topic is most extensive since it is key to presentational progression as I develop it. The terms "topic" and "focus" and the ideas behind them appear in one form or another in many studies. I do not offer a full account of different theories of presentation, or information packaging as it is sometimes called. Nor do I present a complete theory of my own. Accomplishing these goals would require detailed discussion of prosodic information, and of languages of different structural types. Both are beyond the scope of this book. This chapter discusses canonical sentences, and contrast and emphasis; non-canonical, or marked, syntactic structures are discussed in Chapter 9.

There is a sense in which receivers progress through the passages of a text according to the topic and marked focus of its sentences. This "presentational progression" complements the text progression of Discourse Modes discussed in Part II of this book. The duality of progression contributes to the richness of texts.

Section 8.1 gives introductory comments on presentation; 8.2 discusses topic–comment; 8.3 considers Focus–Background; and 8.4 presents a combination of the two, in dual partitioning; 8.5 concludes.

8.1   *Presentational factors*

Sentences have a dynamism of their own. There is a progression in the sentence from its starting point to the end. The beginning is the point of departure, from which the receiver continues on to the final phrase, the goal of the sentence as a communication. This linear development is called 'communicative dynamism' by linguists of the Prague School: "The first element has the lowest degree [of dynamism] . . . the reader progresses from the beginning to successively more dynamic elements of the sentence" (Daneš 1974).[1] The least dynamic element tends to be information that is familiar. The most dynamic element is new, or significant in an unexpected way. It is known as the focus phrase, and receives the main sentence accent. This is a general pattern across languages. Variations on the basic pattern convey subtly different messages.

The information in a sentence is organized in terms of a topic – what the sentence is about – and a focus phrase that carries the most significant information. This organization is reflected in the linear order of most sentences. The linear order reflects the communicative dynamism of a sentence, going from least to most dynamic, with topic phrase at the beginning and focus phrase at the end. The pattern reflects the psychological principles of primacy and recency. The speaker or writer initiates a sentence with shared information. This enables the receiver to establish a mental address to which the new information that arrives later can be directed (Prideaux 1993:54).

The approach assumes a basic systemic order in language. I take it that the neutral, canonical order in English is [X-Subject-Verb-(Object)-(Y)]. "Object" denotes subcategorized complements of the verb; "X" denotes parentheticals and sentence adverbs that appear at the beginning of a sentence (Rizzi 1997, Cinque 1999); "Y" denotes other adverbs and optional adjuncts. Non-canonical sentences are marked structures that depart from the neutral. I will assume that sentences with non-canonical order arise by movement, though I do not state

---

1. The Prague School is a general term referring to a group of linguists in Central Europe who worked in the structuralist tradition, first in the 1930s and early 1940s, later in the 1960s and 1970s. Their ideas are enjoying something of a resurgence; see Hajičová *et al.* (1995), Hajičová *et al.* (1998). The notion of topic and comment can be traced to Henri Weil, a French classical scholar who published in 1840, to German scholars of the late nineteenth century, and to Mathesius; see Firbas (1974) for discussion.

   The approach presented here owes a great deal to the latter-day Prague School but is not identical with it. I recognize both topic and focus phrases in most sentences, whereas the traditional partition consists of focus and background.

movement rules here.[2] When a phrase is displaced to the end of the sentence it becomes the focus phrase and receives the sentence accent, by the "ordering principle" of Hajicová and Sgall (1987). Alternatively, another phrase may be highlighted with a contrastive accent.

In the spoken language, prosody is an important cue to the topic and focus phrases of a sentence. The intonation center, or sentence accent, occurs canonically on the rightmost stressable unit of the sentence, the focus phrase.[3] The scope of the accent is indeterminate: it may be limited to a single phrase or extend to larger constituents. I assume that prosodic structure is a reflex of semantic and pragmatic information (cf. Gussenhoven 1983, Erteschik-Shir 1997, Steedman 2000, and many others). Prosody will not be discussed, since this study is devoted to written texts.

The status of information as more or less familiar plays an important role in presentation. The familiarity of a referent is often coded by morphology: pronouns tend to have referents that are familiar and definite NPs to have identifiable referents. For discourse reasons a definite NP may be used for a referent that is already familiar, as noted in Chapter 6.

The notions of topic and comment, focus and background, represent different partitions of a sentence. Topic–comment recognizes a topic referent, what the sentence is about; the rest of the sentence is comment. The focus–background partition distinguishes the main contribution of a sentence in a focus phrase, and the rest of the sentence functions as background for that focus. To cover the full range of possibilities, both are needed. The apparent contradiction between them is resolved with dual partitioning. I discuss each of these matters in turn.

8.2   *The topic–comment partition*

The topic of a sentence is what the sentence is about. In the topic–comment partition, a referring phrase and its referent are singled out as the topic; the remaining part of the sentence is comment. Speakers have intuitions about sentence topics, although there are some unclear cases. The intuitive notion of topic is necessary for languages like English. Some languages have a syntactic topic

2. Movement rules are implied by the notion of a canonical sentence order. Grammatical rules that move phrases to non-canonical positions are essential to the approach of transformational generative grammar.
3. The typical pitch contour of sentence accent is high and falling, written H^*+L in Pierrehumbert's (1980) notation (an A accent in Bolinger's system, 1972). Many sentences have a secondary intonation peak, typically with a rising pitch contour, written $L+H^*$ (Bolinger's B accent). These notational systems do not bear on the question of how stress and intonation relate to the syntactic and semantic components of the grammar.

position, e.g. Hungarian and Mandarin Chinese; others have topic morphology, e.g. Japanese and Korean.[4] Topics in such languages may differ from topics in English.

Subsequent sections discuss the notion of aboutness (8.2.1); the position of topic phrases in sentences (8.2.2); sentences without topics (8.2.3); different notions of topic (8.2.4); and determining sentence topic in texts (8.2.5).

The notion of aboutness organizes the information conveyed by a sentence. We understand that a sentence says something about X, the topic referent. Thus the topic determines how the truth of a sentence is assessed: we ask "Is it true of X[topic] that Y?" The topic phrase is canonically the subject of a sentence, as in (1):

(1)   A. Beavers build dams.
       B. Sue visited her cousin last week.

People tend to understand (1a) as saying something about the class of beavers and (1b) as saying something about Sue, unless there is information to the contrary.

The topic–comment partition mirrors the classic division of a sentence into "subject" and "predicate," also known as "theme" and "rheme." The subject and predicate are distinct syntactic constituents in traditional accounts. The division determines interpretation: a sentence makes a comment about the subject referent, and the comment is expressed by the predicate. The topic of a sentence indicates how the information it conveys should be added to the developing mental model of the discourse.

The context of a sentence usually points to a particular topic interpretation. The pairs in (2) present different contexts for the second sentence; in both "Mary" is topic, the subject of immediate concern.

(2)   a. i. What did Mary wear?
          ii. Mary/she was wearing an enormous hat.
       b. i. I saw Mary yesterday at the movies.
          ii. Mary/she was wearing an enormous hat.

Questions and answers like (2a) are often used to demonstrate sentence topics. The felicity of this pair contrasts with another in which Mary is not topic of the second sentence, for instance a cleft sentence like "It was MARY who wore an enormous hat."

4. Studies show that languages with syntactic topics differ substantially from those without them; cf. Li & Thompson (1976), Kiss (1986), Portner & Yabushita (1998), Vallduví & Vilkuna (1998), etc.

Paraphrase can test and support the intuition that a given phrase is topic. With paraphrase tests, one recasts a sentence with an explicit introductory phrase and the putative topic phrase (*as for, speaking of*). The result is felicitous if the phrase in question is indeed the topic. For instance, supporting the intuition that the (ii) sentences are about Mary, one can say "As for Mary, she was wearing an enormous hat" and "Speaking of Mary, she was wearing an enormous hat." Both are reasonably felicitous. Another paraphrase test uses a verb of saying, as in "He said about Mary that she was wearing an enormous hat" (Gundel 1974, Reinhart 1982). There are well-known difficulties with paraphrases as actual tests for topic; they are both too weak and too strong.[5] Nevertheless the tests can be helpful in illustrating and identifying the topic of a sentence.

8.2.1   Aboutness

The intuition of aboutness is often taken as primitive. Strawson and Reinhart, however, offer useful discussions.

The notion of aboutness explains how the information of a sentence is understood and assessed in context, according to Strawson. Aboutness relates a sentence to a matter of concern in the context: "We do not, except in social desperation, direct isolated and unconnected pieces of information at each other, but...intend to give or add information about what is a matter of standing

---

5. Reinhart gives the following pairs. Only the first is felicitous:

> Felix is an obnoxious guy. Even Matilda can't stand him.
> Felix is an obnoxious guy. As for Matilda, even she can't stand him.

The second pair is odd because the topic that is structurally identified does not correspond to the intuitive aboutness topic.

The paraphrase tests are too weak because they work for non-topics; too strong, because they aren't always appropriate for a topic. Moreover, *as for* phrases do not always introduce the topic referent of a sentence, as the fragment below illustrates. Under discussion are various types of fuel, listed early on as natural gas, nuclear power, and coal. The phrase of interest is italicized:

> Despite current capacity and price problems, clean-burning natural gas should be recognized as America's best source of energy for the future . . . All Americans should support construction of the proposed transcontinental natural gas pipeline, following the route from Alaska's north slope to the 48 States.
> *As for nuclear power*, we have not yet solved the intractable problem of where to store the thousands of metric tons of nuclear waste scattered across the country.

Here "as for" introduces a very general referent ("nuclear power") that signals a change in the direction of the discourse. But the introducing phrase is not coreferential with any referent in the following sentence. It's more like a discourse or "Chinese-style" topic: "As for fruit, I like watermelon" (Li & Thompson 1976). The example shows that *as for* does not always introduce a sentence topic.

current interest or concern" (1964:97). Statements are assessed as information about their topics. In determining the truth of an assertion, the topic plays a key role: one asks whether an assertion is true with respect to its topic. On the one hand, a topic has an anchor in context. On the other, the topic organizes the understanding and assessment of a sentence.

The concept of common ground adds another dimension to the notion of topic, as Reinhart shows. The common ground consists of the "context set" of propositions, the information of a developing discourse. This can be a large body of information. If unstructured, it would be difficult for a person to use. Reinhart suggests that the context set is organized along the lines of a subject catalogue in which sentence topics are referential entities which classify propositions. In constructing the context set, "the two procedures, assessing and storing information, are relativized to topics" (Reinhart (1982):24). The idea appears in various guises in later work on topic.

In this approach sentences have many potential topics. The propositional information of a sentence may be relevant to context in different ways, each corresponding to a different topic interpretation. The sentences of (3) illustrate, from Reinhart (1982). The first, (a), presents an assertion; (b–c) give different topic interpretations of (a), each with an introductory topic phrase and additional reinforcing material:

(3)   a. It's no wonder that Carter is considering withdrawing the American athletes from the Olympic games.
        b. As for the Olympic games, it's no wonder that Carter is considering withdrawing the American athletes from them (because they are such a farce).
        c. As for Carter, it's no wonder that he is considering withdrawing the American athletes from the Olympic games (because he is such a hard-liner).

Reinhart formalizes her proposal for multiple potential topics in terms of possible pragmatic assertions. In a given context one assertion is selected from the set.

The topic of a sentence affects truth-conditional semantic interpretation. A definite NP triggers a presupposition of existence when it is the topic and subject of the sentence, but not otherwise (Strawson 1964, Hajičová 1971):

(4)   a. The king of France is bald.
        b. Yesterday Prague was visited by the king of France.

Example (4a) presupposes that there is a king of France. Example (4b) has no such presupposition, as standard tests such as denial and questioning show.

Another point is that, in sentences with complex quantifiers, the phrase in topic/subject position has an interpretation not available to other phrases.

(5)   a. Everyone in this room knows at least two languages.
       b. At least two languages are known by everyone in the room.

The wide-scope reading for "at least two languages" is available for (5b) but not for (5a). These phenomena are well known, but not always ascribed to topicality.

Other evidence that sentence topics affect semantic interpretation comes from work in formal semantics. In *if/when* sentences with adverbials of quantification, the topic phrase determines which indefinites are bound by the adverbial (Chierchia 1992).[6] The notion of sentence topic is part of the interpretation of quantifiers, according to Partee (1991) and Büring (1999). Topics are modeled as a presupposed salient set of alternatives, arrived at by constructing implicit questions by von Fintel (1994) and McNally (1998). In a study of Japanese, Portner & Yabushita argue that topics affect semantic interpretation in computing entailments, implicature, and certain scopal phenomena (1998). Their work is suggestive, though Japanese topics differ from English topics in more than one way.

Sentence topics are often demonstrated with question–answer pairs. As in (2a) above, the topic of a sentence is clear in the context of a particular question.[7] The observation has been generalized as a basic organizing principle of texts. Following this principle, one looks for the question that a sentence answers in a given context. If no question actually appears in a text, the analyst constructs an implicit question. For instance, van Kuppevelt uses implicit questions to construct an interpretation "which does not differ in acceptability and coherence" from a text without them (1995:116). He claims that the approach gives an operational way of characterizing topics.

8.2.2   Topic phrases in sentences

Typically, the topic referent of a sentence is in subject position and represents familiar information. The subject of a sentence is prominent positionally and

---

6. Chierchia (1992) integrates the treatment of NPs with the theory of generalized quantifiers. He outlines the "proportion problem," which concerns the scope of the quantificational determiner in "donkey sentences" and conditionals, and the scope of quantificational adverbials in *if/when* sentences.

7. The question approach to topic was used by Daneš (1974), as well as Vennemann (1975), and others. For the latter two the topic is identified with one of the presuppositions defined by a question.

grammatically. As first element it links directly to what precedes and by extension to the common ground; it is the starting point for the communication of a sentence. The subject is usually the perspectival center, the reference point from which the material of the sentence is presented. All sentences of English have a subject, usually overt. The last element in the sentence is prominent positionally, and tends to carry the sentence accent. There is empirical evidence from psychology for the prominence of the subject (Brennan 1995), and for the claim that people pay attention to beginnings and ends of sentences.[8]

Subjects are salient from a grammatical point of view. Syntactically, subjects have a cluster of well-known properties. They determine nominal case marking and verbal agreement; they can be omitted under conjunction; they control coreference in multi-clausal constructions. Semantically, the referent of the grammatical subject phrase is pragmatically presupposed. Typologically, languages can be divided into "subject" and "topic" languages (Li & Thompson 1976).

The study of grammatical voice has traditionally focused on subjects. Voice deals with verbal alternations that indicate participants' roles in a situation, as in active, passive, and other constructions. The voice of a sentence conveys the subject's status vis-à-vis a situation or action, whether the "principal effects of action devolve upon the subject or the object" (Klaiman 1991:3).[9] In other words, voice makes prominent the thematic role of a subject. For instance, when the agent is salient the cause of the event is prominent; when the patient

---

8. When subjects in experiments hear a series – of digits, syllables, words, a long sentence or series of sentences – they tend to remember the material that begins and ends the series (Neisser 1967:222).

   Brennan (1995) studied people's choice of referential expressions. She found that speakers mentioned entities as full NPs in subject position before referring to them with pronouns. New entities tended to be introduced as full NP objects. Experimental subjects tended to use pronouns to express the most salient entity in a scene. Brennan's study was done in the context of Centering Theory (see Chapter 6). Subjects' behavior was taken as evidence for a Centering Theory account of pronoun use, rather than a simple knowledge-based strategy. The latter would predict that pronouns be used for all familiar entities.

   Linguists who worked with this and related pragmatic notions include Firbas (1964), Hockett (1958), Strawson (1964), Halliday (1967), Kuno (1972), Dahl (1974), Hajičová (1971), Daneš (1974), Reinhart (1982), Davison (1984), Fries (1983), Vallduví (1992), Lambrecht (1995), Vallduví & Engdahl (1996), and Erteschik-Shir (1997).

9. Cross-linguistic studies of voice are concerned with variations in such constructions as active and passive, middle, anti-passive, inverse. Klaiman (1991) identifies other approaches to voice. "Posttraditional linguistics" takes voice as being concerned with the mapping from logical to grammatical structure, and not associated with participants or viewpoint. For Philippine and Mayan languages there are "pragmatic voice" alternations which signal assignment among nominals of a certain pragmatic status.

is salient, the event or its result is prominent. The active–passive, and other alternations, change pragmatic perspective, as Givón (1993) puts it. The perspective varies according to what aspects of a situation – cause, process, and result – are prominent in a sentence. This view is reminiscent of Grimshaw's (1990) notion of aspectual prominence, and is different from the perspectival notion of subjectivity discussed in Chapter 7.

There is a strong tendency for topic and subject to coincide in texts as well as single sentences. The empirical correlation will be discussed and examplified in Chapter 10. But the topic phrase is not always the sentence subject. To show this, we need a context that clearly determines a given phrase as topic. Example (6) illustrates: note the third clause of B's answer. The example is from Erteschik-Shir (1997):

(6)   A. So tell me about the earth. What do you know about the earth?
       B. *It*'s round, *it*'s a planet, the moon goes around *it*.

In the last clause of B's answer, the topic phrase is the pronoun object of the preposition.

The topic referent must be an individual of some kind: an entity or a concept. In the case of sentential subjects, the referent is the event, state, or other entity expressed by the subject clause. Sentences with quantified subject phrases have no direct topic referent. In such cases, the topic is the domain of quantification, the class referred to in the quantified phrase. For instance:

(7)   a. All the humpbacks in a given region sing the same song, which is constantly evolving.
       b. No person could survive without precise signalling in cells.

The topic referent in (7a) is the class "humpbacks in a given region," the topic referent of (7b) is the class of "persons," and so on.

Topic referents tend to be familiar or readily inferrable from the discourse context. The topic referent, however, needn't be familiar. Example (8) illustrates: the referent is identified by his connection to the speaker and is unknown otherwise. The example is based on Prince (1981):

(8)   A man I know had a really surprising experience.

Intuitively, the sentence is "about" the referent of the subject NP.

The examples demonstrate that neither familiarity nor subject position is a defining property of a sentence topic in English.

8.2.3 *Sentences without topics*

Not all sentences have a topic. Sentences without topics simply offer a situation to the receiver. They are unpartitioned wholes, all-focus sentences, rather than predications about a particular referent, as in (9):

(9)   a. There are yellow flowers.
        b. God exists.
        c. It's raining.

These sentences are known as "thetic." In contrast, "categorical" sentences express a judgment or predication about a referent (Kuroda 1973, Sasse 1987; "neutral descriptions" in Kuno 1972). Thetic sentences can answer questions such as "What happened?" or "What is there?" that do not single out any referent as the locus of aboutness. Lambrecht notes that the construction of (9a) functions to introduce a new entity into the discourse (1994:39). Thus (9a) is presentational. (The term "presentational" is used both for the family of constructions that function in this way and for the factors of topic and focus.)

The entities introduced in presentational sentences become part of the universe of discourse. As such they are relevant to the developing information of a text.

The thetic–categorical distinction is expressed overtly only by accent in English. The subject receives the sentence accent in thetic sentences, the H+L* contour. Categorical sentences have the H*+L contour in the predicate and may have a secondary accent, the L+H* contour, on the subject. The examples illustrate, from Chafe (1976); small capitals indicate sentence accent, as usual; italics here indicate the secondary accent. The sentences of (10) are thetic, those of (11) are categorical:

(10)   The BRITish are coming.
        The BUTTer melted.

(11)   *Mary* is SINGing.
        The *butter* MELTed.

Subject accentuation, as in (10), signals that the situation be taken as a whole. The dual accentuation of the sentences in (11) distinguishes an element denoting an individual. The accents on the subjects are secondary, while the verbs have the stronger sentence accent. In texts, the interpretation of a sentence as thetic or categorical is determined by contextual cues since the intonational factor is not present.

8.2.4   *Notions of topic*

The term "topic" and its meaning are often seen as problematic. One reason for the difficulty is terminological. The term has been used for distinct notions, and different terms have been used for the notion of topic. The main ideas are the initial position in a sentence, familiar information, and aboutness.

"Theme" and "topic" are sometimes used almost interchangeably to refer to the phrase in initial position in a sentence. The initial phrase is the starting point of the sentence, and tends to convey familiar information. According to the Prague School, "The theme is that which is known or at least obvious in the given situation and from which the speaker proceeds" (Firbas 1964).[10] The theme–rheme structuring of a sentence is thus based on the two factors of position and familiarity status. Theme or topic in this sense is developed further in the work of Firbas (1974), Gundel (1974), Kuno (1976), and others. Difficulties arise when the factors of initial position and familiarity status are combined, as pointed out by Daneš (1974), Chafe (1976) and Fries (1983).

"Theme" refers to the initial constituent of a sentence in the work of Halliday (1967) and in systemic linguistics. The theme is the point of departure for the message, and is often what the sentence is about, especially in simple sentences. The unmarked theme is the subject of a declarative sentence, for instance "John" in "John saw the play yesterday." Marked themes are non-subject phrases in initial position, as in "The play John saw yesterday" and "Yesterday John saw the play" (1967:212). Halliday's notion of theme has a relatively weak component of aboutness. The theme includes some phrases that do not refer, and do not have the aboutness relation to the clause. "Theme" fails to account for phrases in other positions that bear the aboutness relation to the sentence; but it was not Halliday's intention to characterize them.

The term "topic" is discourse-functional for Givón (1983): it refers to a dimension that includes "backgroundiness, predictability, continuity." This notion of topic is non-discrete, with differences of degree according to the structure of a sentence. For instance, in a sentence such as "John, we saw him yesterday," the initial phrase "John" and the subject "we" both have some degree of topicality. Givón defines topicality in terms of anaphoric accessibility and "cataphoric persistence" – whether a referent recurs in a text and its thematic importance and activation. Highly topical referents tend to have antecedents in preceding clauses and to recur in subsequent clauses (1983:10).

---

10. The definition is a translation from Mathesius. Most definitions of theme are derivable from this one, according to Fries (1983).

The aboutness notion of topic is developed in Lambrecht (1994), and somewhat differently in Erteschik-Shir (1997). Even closely related uses of "topic" represent the tip of different theoretical icebergs. The difference between these theories is beyond the scope of this discussion.

The term "topic" is also used at the discourse level. "Discourse topic" is another kind of aboutness, a supersentential notion. Unlike sentence topics, discourse topics are not always expressed directly. There is often no linguistic expression that denotes the theme, or topic, of a discourse or discourse unit. Often the discourse topic must be inferred or constructed.[11]

The problematic nature of aboutness has led some linguists to a limited version of this notion (Vallduví & Engdahl 1996, Walker *et al.* 1998).[12] Others have argued that sentence topic be abandoned, notably Sperber & Wilson (1986). However, I shall rely on the aboutness notion of sentence topic, using the approach of multiple cues discussed below. In this view, the topic phrase of a sentence denotes a topic referent; the sentence is about that referent.

8.2.5   *Determining the topic phrase of a sentence*
The topic phrase is typically the subject in canonical S-V-O sentences, and the topic referent is typically familiar information. But the topic phrase need not

---

11. Topics in conversation can be derived, according to Keenan & Schieffelin. They claim that any discourse has a single proposition which represents the discourse topic (1976:338). The listener establishes the discourse topic by reconstructing the semantic relations between referents. Chafe argues that discourse topics are aggregates of semiactive information that segment a conversation into larger chunks than intonation units (1994:135).

    For written texts, van Dijk suggests that a discourse topic proposition can be constructed for the whole (1972:37). His account is based on an analysis of the propositions that underlie the text. The result is a complex proposition that is entailed by the joint set of propositions of the text. Van Dijk's approach has been influential in text studies that focus on memory and cognition. It is not relevant here because it departs immediately from the text in seeking the underlying propositions. Moreover, construction of the propositional analysis is difficult at best, as Garnham (1983) argues.

    Discourse topics for several sentences at once have also been proposed. For instance, Asher & Lascarides (1998) present the following sentence sequence:

    I've just arrived. The camel is outside.

    To make sense of the pair, Asher & Lascarides suggest that the receiver recovers the discourse topic notion of "transportation," which correctly links the sentences.
12. One type of limited topic is the "backward-looking center or Cb" of Centering Theory: see the discussion in Section 6.4. The backward-looking center is defined in terms of grammatical relations and pronouns. In many ways the Cb is a return to the two-factor notion of theme proposed by Mathesius. Another limited topic is the operationally defined "Link" of Vallduví & Engdahl (1996).

be the subject of a sentence in discourse, and the topic referent may be new. Given these difficulties, the question arises as to whether the topic of a sentence can be reliably identified. Both Smith (1991) and Vallduví (1992) argue that there is no structural or "operational" test for topic. I think that this is correct. Yet I am committed to the position that intuitions about sentence topic are mostly reliable, and that sentence topics have semantic and pragmatic effects in discourse.

How then does one decide on the topic phrase of a sentence in the context of other sentences? I suggest that the intuition of topic is based on a set of cues. Subject position is the default; it may be overridden by other cues in the sentence and its context. There is the possibility of tension between sentential and discourse factors. Cues may reinforce each other, or one cue may override. Occasionally cues conflict and the intuition of aboutness is weak. In actual texts the topic phrase of a sentence is usually the subject phrase, as noted above.

Within a sentence, the subject position is salient because of its linear position, the grammatical relation of subject, and the typical familiarity status. Also relevant are accent and morphology; topic phrases do not bear sentence accent except in the marked case of contrastive topics. Topic referents tend to be familiar, and familiar referents tend to be coded with pronouns. Thematic role is another factor. Agent and experiencer arguments tend to appear in subject position, with some exceptions, e.g. the psychological verbs *surprise, amuse, annoy*, which encode the experiencer as object.

Discourse factors may also affect the intuition of aboutness. One factor is continuity. Topic phrases maximize local or global continuity. Local continuity identifies as topic the phrase that is coreferential with an immediately preceding topic phrase.[13] Global continuity identifies a topic phrase that is coreferential with other topic phrases in the context. Syntactic parallels in sentence structure, and changes of direction in the text, are also relevant.

In context, and in sentences that depart from the canonical S-V-O structure, these factors may not converge. Therefore they must be considered as potentially separate cues to the topic of a sentence. Criteria for sentence topics are listed in (12):

(12)   Topic cues
        An NP may be the topic phrase of a sentence if it
        a. is the subject of a sentence;
        b. is a pronoun;

---

13. Local continuity is most highly ranked in Centering Theory. Other "strategies" are recognized but considered less preferable, as Haihua Pan has pointed out to me.

    c. realizes the agent or experiencer argument of the main verb;
    d. is coreferential with the topic phrase in the preceding sentence;
    e. is coreferential with a topic phrase in the context;
    f. is coreferential with a phrase in the context;
    g. is lexically related to other material in the context;
    h. is in a parallel grammatical position with an NP in the context.

NPs with sentence accent or other focus cues are not candidates for topic. The criteria usually function together, but in some cases they clash, as we will see. When a sentence has more than one clause, the clauses are analyzed sequentially in left-to-right order. This treatment is justified in Kameyama (1998); the alternative is to take the main clause first.

In applying the criteria, the natural strategy is an additive one: the phrase to which the largest number of these criteria applies is the topic. The topic phrase must be integrated into the organization of the whole sentence. Recall that every sentence has a focus phrase, canonically in the predicate.

The criteria and principles are applied to a text fragment in (13), part of it already presented in Chapter 5. Topic phrases are italicized. The immediately preceding sentence concerns a large project in Boston; the definite NP in S1 refers to working tunnels in that project. I give in (14) the cues used for determining each sentence topic; the letters before each cue refer back to the list of criteria in (12).

(13)   1 In some places *the tunnels* are 120 feet deep. 2 In some particularly delicate places *the road-work* passes within just a few feet of skyscraper foundations or beneath construction projects. 3 *The first two frequently asked questions* on the project's official Website are "What are you building?" and "Are you nuts?" 4 Surprisingly, *tunnels* are among the most ancient engineering feats. 5 The *earliest [tunnels]* were very likely extensions of prehistoric cave dwellings. 6 *The Babylonians*, in the twenty-second century BC, built a masonry tunnel beneath the Euphrates River that connected the royal palace with a major temple. 7 *The Egyptians*, using copper-bladed saws, excavated long passageways and intricate rooms inside soft-rock cliffs. 8 *The Romans* built an elaborate network of above- and below-ground acqueducts to carry water.

(14)   Criteria used for sentence topics
    S1: (a) subject; coferential with earlier NP
    S2: (a) subject; (g) lexically related context (*the tunnels – road-work*);
        (h) parallel
    S3: (a) subject
    S4: (a) subject; (g) lexically related context (*the tunnels – tunnels*)
    S5: (a) subject; (f) coferential with earlier NP
    S6: (a) subject; (c) agent; (g) lexically related context (*earliest*)

S7: (a) subject; (c) agent; (g) lexically related context (*earliest*); (h) parallel
S8: (a) subject; (c) agent; (g) lexically related context (*earliest*); (h) parallel

The topic phrases are all subjects; there are no non-canonical syntactic structures. The object NPs are the focus phrases in the last three sentences: "a masonry tunnel," "long passageways and intricate rooms," "an elaborate network."[14] These phrases pertain to the theme of the passage and might be taken as topics. But topic–focus organization precludes such an interpretation: the object NPs are focus phrases. The semantic notion of Primary Referent applies to these NPs: they are the Primary Referents in their clauses. Each is the result of the event expressed in the sentence. There is an interesting tension in the passage between topical and semantic progression.

Although sentence topics can usually be identified, there are some unclear cases. They arise when the criteria for topics result in a clash. For instance, consider clause 2b in the familiar fragment of (15); the first four clauses are familiar from previous examples. Clause 2b has pronouns as subject ("she") and object ("it"), both are coreferential with material in the immediate context.

(15)   1a She put on her apron, took a lump of clay from the bin and weighed off enough for a small vase. 2a The clay was too wet, b so she wedged it with a flat concrete tray, c which absorbed the excess moisture.

The subject pronoun of clause 2b realizes the agent role, and is in subject position, so by the additive strategy "she" would be the topic phrase. Now consider the two continuity principles. By local continuity, we take the object pronoun "it" as topic because its referent is topic of the previous clause. The global continuity principle looks at other sentences in the passage. S3 and S4 have "she" as topic phrase, so by global continuity "she" would be topic in S2b. The sentence organization does not resolve the problem: the verb "wedge" is the focused phrase. The most satisfactory analysis is simply to say that in clause 2b both pronouns are part of the background; see the next section below. In my judgment the uncertainty of cases like this does not compromise the many clear cases of sentence topics and the importance of the notion.

The cues to sentence topic are pragmatic in nature. Coreferentiality and lexical relatedness are probably the most important, and neither can be stated in a construction rule of Discourse Representation Theory. The other cues are difficult to formalize as well. Therefore I do not give construction rules for topic or presentational progression. I have argued that sentence topic is needed

14. I thank Pascal Denis for helpful discussion of these sentences.

for conceptual and truth-conditional calculations within the DRS; and for further pragmatic interpretation. I assume that topic information must be part of enriched Discourse Representation Structures that allow further pragmatic interpretation.[15]

8.3   *The Focus–Background partition*

The focus phrase represents the speaker's "declared contribution" to the common ground (Gussenhoven 1983:383). Focus is conveyed with sentence accent and/or syntactic structure.

Canonically a sentence progresses from the starting point toward the focused material, which bears the sentence accent. Every sentence has a focus. Focus in this sense is "informational": it is distinct from contrastive focus, discussed below. Focus is robust because it has a clear linguistic correlate of accent in the spoken language, and often position in the written language. Section 8.3.1 introduces focus phrases; 8.3.2 considers focus and semantic interpretation; 8.3.3 discusses contrastive and emphatic focus; 8.3.4 concludes.

8.3.1   *Properties of focus phrases*

The focus may be the smallest phrase that bears the sentence accent, or a larger phrase.[16] The scope of sentence accent is often indeterminate since the predicate accent allows more than one interpretation. Example (16) illustrates for sentence (1a) discussed above, an example from Sgall *et al.* (1986). The sentence has three focus interpretations for successively larger phrases. Sentence (16a) gives

15. Recognizing sentence topics in a DRS does not necessarily provide for sentence topics as an organizing factor of information in the common ground, or context set. Organizing potential is one of Reinhart's arguments for aboutness, and a feature of Vallduví & Engdahl's procedural account of Links. I do not wish to make the stringent requirement that the context set be organized in any particular way. Rather, I suggest that organization by topics is a potential feature of organization in memory. It may be best not to limit information access, as Portner & Yabushita (1998) point out. People are able to organize large amounts of information in multiple ways, according to what question is being answered or what kind of task is involved. For instance, research on word access shows that people can search their word memory by first sound, alphabetically by first letter, according to taxonomic meaning, functional meaning, etc. (Forster 1979). In the current theory the information that makes up the context set is structured only in DRS terms.

16. There is an extensive literature on focus and sentence accent, especially contrastive focus. Semantic analyses of focus operators are given in Rooth (1992) and Krifka (1991). Although they differ in some respect, they agree on the points that I rely on here. See also Horn (1991), Fauconnier (1985), and Bosch & van der Sandt (1999).

   Stress and intonational highlighting mark focus in cases where the topic–focus articulation cannot be read off the syntax; they also mark strong contrast or exhaustiveness.

the schematic surface structure, (16b–d) the focus interpretations. Sentence accent will be indicated with small capital letters; it should not be confused with contrastive stress, which will be written with large capitals ("JOHN saw Mary" vs "John saw MARY").

(16)   a. Beavers build [DAMS].
        b. [Beavers build] ᵣ[DAMS].
        c. [Beavers] ᵣ[build DAMS].
        d. ᵣ[Beavers build DAMS].

The accented NP is the focus in (16b); the VP predicate is the focus in (16c); the entire sentence is focused in (16d). I use the terms "argument focus" and "predicate focus" for the first two cases and the term "all-focus" for the third (from Vallduví 1992, Lambrecht 1994). Sentence (16d), which is all-focus, is a thetic sentence. The notion of focus is a relational one, internal to a given sentence. On the argument focus interpretation of (16b), for instance, *dams* is the focus relative to the other information in the sentence.

Different focus interpretations arise in different contexts. The argument focus reading of (16b) is natural in a discussion of what beavers build, or in answer to a question about the building habits of beavers. The predicate focus reading would be natural if one were discussing what beavers do. For the sentence focus reading imagine the sentence uttered "out of the blue," perhaps by a child imparting a newly learned fact.

The focus of a sentence is its contribution to a discourse. The focus is a matter of presentation in that it "reflects the speaker's decision as to where the main burden of the message lies" (Halliday 1967:204). The speaker presents the focused material as relating to the background in the sentence. Standard examples of focus–background structures in the literature are question–answer pairs, where the question clearly determines a particular interpretation. Example (17) is from Prince (1986):

(17)   a. What did she give to Harry?
        b. She gave the SHIRT to Harry.

The question provides the background for the answer, making it clear that the focused phrase provides the contribution to the discourse. In the context of the question the background is shared knowledge. Typically, the background represents what is salient or inferrable in the discourse at the time of utterance, or what the speaker assumes to be so.

This notion of focus should not be confused with other meanings of the term. It is used for "center of attention" in psychology, computational linguistics, and artificial intelligence. The attentional focus of a sentence is often taken to be its topic phrase, it has the opposite meaning from the linguistic term "focus." Another meaning is focus of contrast, discussed below.

The Focus–Background partitioning of a sentence need not correspond to its syntactic structure. The background material may be discontinuous. For instance, the argument–focus partitioning of "Beavers build dams" has the subject and verb as background [Beavers build –], not a constituent in syntactic structure. In "She gave the SHIRT to Harry," the background is also discontinuous [She gave – to Harry]. Surface structure does not relate directly to the background–focus partition in such cases.

8.3.2   *Focus and semantic interpretation*
Formal accounts of the Focus–Background partition treat the relation between the parts as that of a variable to an open proposition (Prince 1986, Rooth 1992). The background part of a sentence is an open proposition with a variable, which is instantiated by the focus. In modelling this partitioning one replaces the focus phrase with a variable; the result is an open proposition.

The semantic interpretation of a sentence may be affected by focus. Sentences with different focus phrases sometimes have different truth-conditional meanings, as in the following examples from Gundel (1999):

(18)   a. The largest demonstrations took place in PRAGUE in November 1989.
        b. The largest demonstrations took place in Prague in NOVEMBER 1989.

If the largest demonstrations of November 1989 were in Budapest rather than Prague, (18a) would be false because "Prague" is focused in the first example. Under the same circumstances (18b) would not be false.[17] "Prague" is part of the background, not the focus, in the sentence. Another example shows the interaction of focus with negation, from Hajičová & Sgall (1987):

(19)   a. This time our defeat wasn't caused by Harry.
        b. This time Harry didn't cause our defeat.

In (19a) the defeat has taken place: it is presupposed, part of the background. Example (19b) has no such presupposition: the sentence is compatible with a situation in which we were not defeated. The difference follows from their background–focus structure, according to Hajičová & Sgall (1987). In (a) "our defeat" is part of the background, whereas in (b) it is the focus phrase. There

---

17. If one assumes a three-valued logic, (18b) would have no truth value, as Neil Smith points out (p.c.).

is some difference of opinion about the source of these intuitions of truth and falsity.

The semantic consequences of background–focus are further adduced by Partee (1991). Partee relates the distinction to tripartite semantic structures that represent the contribution of quantifiers and other operators to a sentence. The tripartite structure consists of a Restrictor, Nuclear Scope, and Operator. The Operator applies to the Nuclear Scope in the context provided by the Restrictor. The Restrictor and Nuclear Scope in such structures correspond to the background–focus distinction. The focused phrase of a sentence functions as Nuclear Scope, and the background functions as Restrictor. This and other interactions of focus and semantics are addressed in Hajičová, Partee & Sgall (1998).

Focused material need not convey information that is new in familiarity status to the discourse, or to the receiver. What is essential is that the focus add to the receiver's apprehension of the information, relative to the rest of the sentence. The fragment (20) illustrates; consider the status of "sedimentation," the focus phrase in the last sentence (Daneš 1974:111):

(20)   Sedimentary rocks: Most of historical geology has to do with sedimentary rocks and their organic remains . . . Events in earth history are recorded mainly in terms of differing kinds of SEDIMENTATION.

The focus phrase "sedimentation," far from being new, is fully recoverable from the context, as Daneš notes. It has a unique function in this sentence, however.

Examples of another kind also show that focused information need not be new to the discourse; (21) is from Lambrecht (1994), (22) from Gundel (1999). In each case the relevant example is B's answer to A's question:

(21)   A. Where did Sam$_i$ go last night, to the movies or to the restaurant?
        B. He$_i$/Sam$_i$ went to $_F$[THE RESTAURANT].

(22)   A. Who called?
        B. Pat$_i$ said $_F$[SHE$_i$] called.

Reference to the focus phrase referent appears in the same sentence (22), or in the preceding question (21), so that it cannot be regarded as new. The focus phrases supply information that completes the background open propositions, which are [– called] and [Sam went to –]. Thus, focus–background is a sentence-internal relation established for a particular sentence.

The main cues to focus are sentence accent and linear or syntactic position. Position is particularly important in writing, where the only other cue is typographical indication of contrast, usually italics or capital letters. In certain syntactic structures the focus phrase appears in a special position. Example (23) illustrates focus preposing, from Hannay (1991):

(23) a. Did you get wet?
      b. ₍[Bloody SOAKING] I was.

In other structures, the syntax highlights or focuses a constituent. The examples illustrate: (24a) is a cleft, (24b) a pseudo-cleft, and (24c) a presentational sentence. The accent falls on the syntactically focused constituent.

(24) a. It was ₍[THE BUTLER] who took the necklace.
      b. What the butler took was ₍[THE NECKLACE].
      c. There were ₍[SWANS] on the lake.

Non-canonical structures are discussed in Chapter 9.

8.3.3 Contrastive and emphatic focus

Contrastive focus and its close relation, emphatic focus, add an additional dimension of meaning to the information in a sentence. I will consider the difference between contrast and emphasis as conveyed in writing with capital or italic letters. I'll refer to them both as "strong focus."

Contrast and emphasis are often put into a single category of "contrast-or-emphasis," but they differ semantically and pragmatically. The sentences in (25) give an idea of the kinds of examples to be discussed:

(25) a. Sue danced with BILL. (imagine that)
      b. Sue danced with BILL. (not Tom)
      c. Sue even danced with BILL. (of the possible people)

8.3.3.1 The relation between contrast and emphasis

Contrast and emphasis both single out an entity or property from a set of relevant possibilities. The two differ in how the singling out is presented. In simple sentences out of context, such as "Sue danced with BILL," the stressed phrase can be interpreted as emphatic or contrastive. On the emphatic meaning, the dancing is interesting, surprising, unexpected, or noteworthy in some way. The contrastive meaning involves choice of a more pointed kind.

Contrast depends on a choice among alternatives. But not all choices are the same. The more specific the alternatives, the more contrastive the effect. Bolinger comments: "As the alternatives narrow down, we get closer to the standard idea of contrast" (1961:87). He illustrates with the examples in (26):

(26)   a. Let's have a PICnic.
        b. Where'll we have it? Let's have it in the PARK.
        c. Can we all go? No, MARY can't.
        d. Bring some hotdogs. I don't like hotdogs, I like HAMburgers.

The alternatives increase in specificity. Example (26a) suggests a general contrast between picnicking and anything else the group might do. Example (26b) implies other places where a picnic might be held, but does not state them. Example (26c) offers a clear set of alternatives (*we all*). Example (26d) states alternatives and sets up an opposition between them. This is the strongest type of contrast, where one alternative is chosen and others rejected.

The difference between contrast and emphasis can be explained with a continuum, a gradient scale of choice and alternatives. At the weakest end of the scale is emphasis (26a); explicit contrast between alternatives is in the middle (26c); at the strongest end is "oppositional contrast" (26d).

Emphasis arises when strong stress is used to draw attention to a particular referent, rather than to the choice of that referent over alternatives. (27) makes this clear:

(27)   Sherlock Holmes to the butler:
        The murderer is YOU.

The example is from Lambrecht, who comments that Holmes needn't have had alternative suspects in mind to utter the sentence (1994:287). The focus is emphatic, adding strength to informational focus, but does not change the interpretation of a sentence.

8.3.3.2   Types of contrastive focus

Contrast is at the middle of the scale or continuum of choice, and oppositional contrast is at the strong end. Oppositional contrast rejects the non-preferred alternative. Contrastive focus singles out a particular referent in preference to alternatives. The relevant alternatives are explicit, or inferrable from the context. Strong stress is the simplest type of focus operator. It conveys a contrast between the focused phrase and the relevant set of alternatives. For instance, consider "Sue danced with BILL" on the contrastive meaning. Contrastively the sentence conveys that Sue danced with Bill rather than with others. The semantic interpretation is that focus triggers a partition of a sentence into background and focus, with a set of alternatives. The focus applies to the background rather than to the other alternatives (Krifka 1991, Rooth 1992). This type of interpretation is set out schematically in (28):

(28)   Focus structure of *Sue danced with BILL*
         Background: Sue danced with –
         Focus: Bill
         Focus operator: strong stress
         Alternatives: everyone, Mats, Manfred, Bill, etc.

Focalizing particles such as *even, only, also,* convey contrastive focus. These particles trigger and contribute to contrastive interpretation; strong stress is not needed in their presence. Different particles relate focus and background to their alternatives in a particular way. For instance, *only* conveys that there is no relevant alternative to which the background applies. *Even* conveys that there are alternatives to the focused choice which are more probable, more expected, than the one that actually appears.

Focus that involves clear alternatives is often exhaustive, or "identificational," according to Kiss: "Identificational focus . . . identifies the exhaustive subset of the set [of potential candidates] for which the predicate phrase holds" (1998:245). Kiss contrasts this type of focus with information focus, which every sentence conveys. Information focus merely marks the nonpresupposed nature of the information it carries, according to Kiss.[18] By this criterion, some sentences with contrastive meaning do not have identificational focus. For instance, "Sue danced with BILL" does not necessarily mean that Sue danced with no person other than Bill. In contrastive contexts, however, focus constituents express identificational focus in English, according to Cohan (2001).

Phrases with strong stress tend to be focus phrases. Topic phrases, however, may also be contrastive. The alternatives are often explicitly parallel, as in (29) from Vallduví & Engdahl (1996):

(29)   Where can I find the cutlery?
         a. THE FORKS are in the CUPBOARD . . .
         b. but I left THE KNIVES in the DRAWER.

Contrastive topics like these have the aboutness property, rather than the semantic properties of focus phrases (Lambrecht 1994:291).

---

18. In Hungarian informational and identificational focus phrases are associated with different structural positions. Kiss lists six differences between the two kinds of focus. The first is given in the text. The next two differences are these: (2) the type of constituent that can function as information focus is not restricted, but certain types of constituents cannot function as identificational focus; (3) information focus does not, but identificational focus does, take scope. The other differences are more technical (1998:248).

I now return to the contrast continuum. Contrast and oppositional contrast differ in how the focused element relates to alternatives. In contrast, a choice is preferred to its alternatives. In oppositional contrast, a choice is opposed to its alternatives and the alternatives are rejected. I present below some fragments from discursive texts with focus operators. The focus phrases are italicized.

(30)   Contrast
        a. Chimpanzees engage in what might be called "trickle-down" provisioning of meat to females and their offspring. *Only those females and their young who are in the vicinity of the killsite when the meat is being devoured* will have a chance of gaining access to it.
        b. There is another difference between intelligence and other traits. Height and weight and speed and strength and *even conversational fluency* are real things: there's no doubt about what's being measured. Intelligence is a much murkier concept.

In (30a) background knowledge enables the reader to provide reasonable alternatives to the focused phrase; in (30b) the alternatives are explicitly given. The fragments illustrate the main functions of focus particles in texts: *only* limits a category or domain, while *even* extends the range. The fragment in (31) presents oppositional contrast

(31)   Oppositional Contrast
        The desirability of segregating dwellings from work has been so dinned into us that it takes an effort to look at real life . . . In an article about Harlem we find "We've got hills and views of both rivers . . . and it's the only close-in area that doesn't have any industry."
        Only in planning theory does this make Harlem an "attractive piece of real estate." From the time of its . . . beginnings, Harlem never was a workable, economically vigorous residential district of a city.

The contrast is oppositional because, in addition to a chosen alternative, there is an alternative that is explicitly rejected.

The alternatives to contrastive focus may be nearby, or relatively far away in the context. The information may appear in the same syntactic phrase, a neighboring sentence, or in a paragraph segment other than the one in which the focus-phrase sentence appears. Contrast occurs in text at the level of the phrase or sentence; it may also function as a discourse relation or a higher-level organizing principle. There are lexical ways of indicating opposition, for instance with phrases such as *rather than, instead of*, and others; see Smith (1998) for further discussion.

8.3.3.3 Summary and comment

The partitioning of a sentence into focus and background has roots in the work of Daneš, Firbas, and other scholars of the early Prague School, and Halliday. The ideas are developed further in recent work by Hajičová and her colleagues. In another tradition, Chomsky (1971), Jackendoff (1972), and Rochemont (1986) discuss focus and presupposition, and related distinctions. Prince (1981, 1986) elucidates the notions of background and focus. Much current work on the interface between different parts of the grammar uses the notion of focus because it involves phonology, semantics, syntax, and pragmatic interpretation.

There is more than one type of focus. Informational focus appears in all sentences: it is the contribution that a sentence makes to a discourse. Strong focus is emphatic or contrastive; it is indicated by italics or capital letters in writing, heavy stress in speaking, or by focus operators. Traditional terminology varies. For Halliday (1967) and Daneš (1974) the distinction presented here as focus–background is known as theme–rheme. Sgall, Hajičová, and the current Prague School use the term Topic–Focus Articulation, or TFA. Their term "topic" is like "background" as presented here; the background is not structured, so that a particular topic phrase and referent is not always identified.

There is an enormous literature on focus, in phonology, syntax, and semantics. In this brief introduction I have introduced the key ideas, with comments of my own on contrast and emphasis. The notion of focus balances that of sentence topic; it is a necessary prerequisite for the dual partitioning of sentences.

8.4   *Dual partitioning and the representation of topic and focus*

The approaches of Background–Focus and topic–comment are complementary ways of dealing with presentational factors. The two partitionings distinguish different aspects of how information is organized, and they hold simultaneously for most sentences. The topic–comment and Focus–Background partitions each select a particular phrase, leaving the rest of the sentence unorganized. In the topic–comment partition, the comment has no internal structure. Similarly, the Focus–Background partition gives no internal structure to the background.

Yet many sentences have phrases that are neither topic nor focus. Consider the simple transitive sentence "The girl broke a VASE," for example. The subject is the topic phrase ("the girl") and the object is the focus phrase ("a vase"). The verb is neither topic nor focus, on the narrow interpretation of focus. Yet the verb should be integrated into the organizational structure of the sentence. Dual partitioning allows a way of doing this (Dahl 1974, Vallduví 1992).

In dual partitioning, the first partition recognizes a "Focus phrase" and an optional "Ground." The focus phrase receives the sentence accent, the H*+L contour. The Ground is optional because there are all-focus sentences without a Ground, as in example (10). The second partition divides the Ground into "Link" and an optional "Tail." The Link has the L+H* secondary sentence accent, optional in subject position. The Link corresponds roughly to the notion of topic.

The differing types of partitioning are most explanatory for different cases. The topic–comment partition applies to sentences with a topic phrase which is evidently the locus of aboutness. Focus–background is useful for answers to questions and for sentences in which a focus phrase is clearly set off from the background. But, as Vallduví points out, the focus–background partition fails to account for the "informational split" in a sentence with a preposed phrase such as "To Harry she gave the SHIRT." No function is recognized for the preposed phrase (1992:51).

Dual partitioning allows information of both kinds to be represented. Taking this approach, Vallduví & Engdahl (1996) give a procedural account of how presentational structure organizes information. They rely on an adaptation of the File Change Semantics of Heim (1982). In understanding a sentence the receiver updates the developing context of a discourse in terms of "file cards" for referents. The way information is presented gives instructions for the update in terms of Link, Focus, and Tail. The Link phrase of a sentence indicates a locus of update, while the Focus adds information to the relevant file card in the common ground. The Tail of a sentence, if there is one, further specifies the update.

The dual partitioning scheme is set out in (32) and exemplified in (33), with a strong accent on the verb.

(32)   Sentence = {Focus, (Ground)}
        Ground = {Link, Tail}

(33)   The president H A T E S chocolate.
        {$_G$(The president – chocolate) $_F$(hates)}
        {$_G$($_{LINK}$(The president) $_{TAIL}$(chocolate))}

Analyzing this sentence into Focus and Ground, the discontinuous material ["the president – chocolate"] is the Ground; the Focus phrase is "hates." Within the Ground, "the president" is Link, "chocolate" is Tail. The Link functions as an instruction for updating the common ground, the locus of update "the president," with a further condition specified by the Tail (Vallduví & Engdahl 1996:468–70).

Links are structurally encoded by position and accent, an operational definition. Vallduví & Engdahl claim that Link phrases appear in subject and non-subject position. In non-subject position they have the secondary sentence accent. Secondary accent is optional in subject position, as noted above (1996:473). Vallduví and Engdahl suggest that the operationally defined "link" should replace aboutness topics. The account is attractive but empirically inadequate. An important difficulty is that pronouns do not have a secondary accent, and most non-subject topic phrases are pronouns. For instance, a non-subject topic pronoun appears in the third clause of example (6b) above: "It's [the earth's] round, it's a planet, the moon goes around it." The example is far from trivial: pronouns are very common as recurrent topic phrases in text, and are not accented.[19]

I adopt the dual-partition approach, but with the aboutness notion of Topic instead of the operationally defined Link of Vallduví & Engdahl. The Ground consists of Topic and Tail. The topic phrase referent is the locus of aboutness for the sentence; the Tail consists of material that is not included in the Focus.

(34)   a. Sentence = {Focus, (Ground)}
       b. Ground = {Topic, (Tail)}

Simple intransitive sentences (e.g. "The girl fell") are exhaustively partitioned by Topic and Focus; others have a Link as well. All-focus, thetic sentences have no Ground.

How does presentational structure relate to grammar and to the representation of discourse? It is clear that presentational structure interacts with semantic as well as pragmatic interpretation. Some theories have a level of syntactic structure from which the semantic effects of focus are derived, with some underspecification, as in the dependency grammar of Hajičová & Sgall (1987). Erteschik-Shir (1997) proposes an informational level of grammar that affects semantics and phonology. Combinatory Categorial Grammar has a level of information structure which includes syntactic and prosodic information; in this architecture there is no distinct level of surface syntax (Steedman 2000:126). Others argue that a pragmatic component deals with the "information structure" of topic and focus (Vallduví 1992, Lambrecht 1994).

Since focus is associated with semantic operators, including negation, it is directly relevant to truth-conditional representation. Some evidence is cited

---

19. In fact, the treatment of unstressed pronouns is problematic in this account. Vallduví & Engdahl (1996) assimilate them to null pronouns, treating both types as a single class. Although this has a certain appeal for a general, cross-linguistic account, I do not think that it is correct for English.

above; see also Hajičová, Partee, & Sgall (1998). Rules and representations for focus are beyond the scope of this work.

8.5   Conclusion

The notions of topic and focus organize the information within a sentence. The topic phrase of a sentence gives the referent that the sentence is about; the focus phrase gives the main contribution of the sentence to a discourse. Dual patterning is needed to account for the full range of cases.

The familiarity status of information is a key factor in presentation, both within and across sentences. Within the sentence, familiar information tends to appear first; and topic referents tend to be familiar. Focus phrases may convey informational, emphatic, or contrastive information.

In the next chapter I look at surface presentational factors in non-canonical sentences, and discuss whether and how to represent them in Discourse Representation Theory. The account of presentational progression is developed further in Chapter 10.

Example sources in this chapter:

(13) Jim Collins, How it works. *US Airways Magazine, Attaché*, May 2001.
(15) Peter Robinson, *A Necessary End*, New York: Aron Books, 1989, p. 182.
(30a) Terrence Deacon, *The Symbolic Species*, New York: Norton, 1997, p. 393.
(30b) James Fallows, *More Like Us*, Boston: Houghton Mifflin, 1989, p. 153.
(31) Jane Jacobs, *The Death and Life of Great American Cities*, New York: Random House, 1961, p. 175.

9 Non-canonical structures and presentation

Canonical sentences furnish the background for variation. I consider here structures that play off this background with different word orders and syntactic structures. Non-canonical structures have special force, because of their features and because they depart from the basic case. Writers choose structures. I assume that choice is based on assessment, not necessarily conscious, of how a structure affects interpretation in a specific context.

Sentence-internally, non-canonical structures highlight or downplay the material in certain positions. Syntax may enhance connectedness between sentences by placing information that is familiar to a discourse first in a sentence. A given structure may allow or block a topic relation with the following sentence. Changes in direction may be conveyed by sentences that lack such connection, and by breaks in the syntactic pattern. Thus syntactic patterning affects the organization and progression of discourse passages.

This chapter concentrates on non-canonical structures that affect topic and sentence connectedness, the main factors of presentational progression. I draw on discussions in the literature of a variety of constructions. Together they give a sense of the different tools that the language makes available. I will also look briefly at multi-clause sentences, and will discuss paragraphs as text units.

The interpretations involve inference. Semantic presuppositions are close to the linguistic forms: they are triggered by particular structures, such as cleft sentences and temporal clauses; and by particular forms such as the focus particles "only" and "even." Pragmatic presuppositions of familiarity status and linking inferences depend on context, world knowledge, and convention. Topics are determined by a combination of cues including syntactic position, lack of sentence accent, and coreference. Most of these cues are pragmatic in nature.

Section 9.1 introduces non-canonical constructions; 9.2 discusses non-canonical constructions with arguments; 9.3 discusses adjunct preposing; 9.4 considers multi-clause sentences; 9.5 discusses paragraphs; 9.6 comments on presentational information in Discourse Representation Structure.

9.1   *Non-canonical constructions*

These constructions affect the topic potential of a sentence and its connection to context, the main factors in presentational progression. Some structures affect the verb and its arguments, others affect adjuncts. In the first class are non-canonical subject constructions, inversions, preposing, and postposing. The second class consists of structures in which adjuncts are preposed from their canonical rightward position. This is not an exhaustive list of non-canonical structures: it ignores particle shift, the many types of conjunction and ellipsis, and others.

Phrases that are displaced to the beginning or end of a sentence are in positions of prominence. Clefts highlight a phrase syntactically, while sentences with empty subjects highlight a non-subject phrase. Structure-based factors of presupposition and strong, identificational focus are also relevant. Informational focus, a feature of all sentences, is not.

The effect of a non-canonical construction is often to place information that is familiar at the beginning of the sentence, where the canonical structure would have it later. In fact, the felicity of a construction in context often depends on the placement of familiar information. At the beginning of a sentence it can link directly to the preceding text, maintaining continuity. The familiar phrase also functions as starting point for the sentence.

The notion of a link or connection between sentence and context is intuitively plausible, but the basis for one's intuition is not always clear. I draw on a formal approach to linking developed by Ward & Prince (1991). Discourse entities are linked to context by their relation to a constructed set of entities. The construct is a partially ordered set of entities evoked directly or by inference in the context, a "poset." The link entity is ranked with other entities in the poset according to formal relations; they include relations such as part-of, attribute-of, prior-to, etc.; the standard set relations; the identity relation. The poset must be salient in the context. ("Link" in this sense should not be confused with that proposed by Vallduví in connection with the topic–focus partitioning of sentences.)

Discourse entities are linked through the poset construct to the context. For instance, consider the underlined preposed phrase in a sequence from Prince: "This I don't call cooking, when you go in that refrigerator and get some beans and drop them in a pot. And <u>TV dinners</u>, they go stick them in a pot and she say she cooked." The referent "beans" has already been evoked when the receiver encounters TV dinners. "In the absence of any explicitly evoked set to support 'TV dinners,' the entity evoked by beans is construed as an alternate member of a set available by inference, the set of 'fast-food home-cooked foods' " (1997:7). Here the relation between the referents is alternate members of the poset. Another example: "I walked into the kitchen. <u>On the counter</u> was a large book." The first sentence with "kitchen" evokes the poset "elements of a house," ordered by the part-of relation; the referent of the preposed phrase "the counter" is related to this set as part-of the kitchen.

If no salient poset can be inferred, there is no linking relation.[1] The non-canonical structure of preposing depends for felicity on poset linking. If a sentence does not have a poset link to the context, preposing cannot occur. For instance, in "I walked into the kitchen. <u>On the jacket</u> was a large book," there is no salient or inferrable poset that relates "kitchen" and "jacket," and the sequence is infelicitous (Birner & Ward 1998:19–20). The notion of "poset" linking accounts for many inferred entities in the literature. I will use "poset linking" as a technical term for this type of connectedness between the sentences of a discourse. These examples show that the term "familiar information" includes material that is either explicitly mentioned or inferrable in the context.

For each structure considered below, I discuss how it differs from the canonical pattern; its topic potential; structure-based particulars, if any; and the role of familiarity status in its use. The examples are from texts in this study.

9.2   *Argument constructions*

9.2.1   *Non-canonical subjects*
Syntactic structures with non-canonical subjects include the passive, existential *there*-sentences, cleft and pseudo-cleft sentences, and extraposition sentences. The variety is striking and suggests that such structures are useful in discourse.

The passive. This is the classic case of a non-canonical structure. Subject and object arguments are displaced, and the simple active verb form is replaced by the passive auxiliary. The surface subject is the logical or underlying object; the underlying subject appears optionally in a postposed *by*-phrase.

---

1. The notion of posets is due to Hirschberg (1991) and has been further developed by Ward & Prince (1991), Birner & Ward (1998).

   A partially ordered set is any set defined by a transitive partial ordering relation R, a relation which is either reflexive and antisymmetric, or irreflexive and asymmetric (Hirschberg 1991). Ward & Prince give as an example of the first type the relation "is-as-tall-or-taller-than"; as an example of the second the relation "is-taller-than." The discourse entity is related to the poset by a ranking in which the entity represents a lower or higher value, or alternate value.

   In the terminology of Birner & Ward (1998), the linguistic material that is related to the context is the "link" and the poset that relates link and prior context is the "anchor." The relation between link and anchor, the "linking relation," is always a poset relation.

The derived surface subject is often the topic phrase of a sentence. In fact, the traditional function of the passive is to present as subject a phrase that would canonically be in object position. There are two main reasons for using the passive construction: "a greater interest in the passive subject . . . or to facilitate the connection of one sentence with another" (Jespersen 1924/1965:168; see also Creider 1979, Davison 1984).

The full passives in the texts of this study all have the surface subject as topic. In most of them the topic phrase is linked to the prior context via a related poset. There are several types of connectedness, as the examples in (1) illustrate.

(1)   a. There were protests that Freud was unworthy of even being honored by an exhibition. *A corresponding exhibition on Darwin would have been protested only by creationists.*

    b. Dynamite was something new, and it gave engineers their most powerful tool for tunneling through *hillsides that couldn't be opened by digging from above.*

    c. Despite the often cavalier attitude toward teaching in college, at least physicists know their physics, mathematicians know and love their mathematics, and *music is taught by musicians*, not by graduates of education schools, where the disciplines are subordinated to the study of classroom management.

In (1a), the surface subject is linked to the indefinite NP "exhibition" in the preceding sentence by an inferred poset of "exhibitions." In (1b) the passive is a relative clause on the head noun "hillsides," which functions as link and antecedent by identity. In (1c) the passive is parallel to other clauses in the sentence and is linked by a poset of "subjects taught" to the context.[2]

---

2. A recurrent question is whether the length and complexity of a phrase – known as "heaviness" – is a factor of importance in non-canonical constructions. The heaviness of the underlying subject does not appear to be a determining factor in the use of a passive, as the following examples show:

    The peals of laughter which followed Gabriel's imitation of the incident were interrupted by a resounding knock at the hall-door.

    He would only make himself ridiculous *by quoting poetry to them which they could not understand.*

In the first example the surface subject is long and complex; in the second the postposed material is long and complex. They are from the same text. To determine the importance of the factor of heaviness would require a large, corpus-based study.

Hawkins (1994) argues that heavy phrases in sentence-final position are relatively easy for receivers to understand; postponing them to the end of a sentence may be helpful for speakers as well: cf. Arnold *et al.* (2000). Thus the heaviness of a phrase might lead to the use of a non-canonical structure which would move it toward the end of a sentence.

Using the notion of link developed above, Birner & Ward (1998) discuss the familiarity status of passive surface subjects and *by*-phrases. They propose a familiarity status requirement couched in relative terms: the subject referent of a passive must be at least as familiar, in context, as the referent of the *by*-phrase (1998:199). This requirement accounted for all full passives found in an extensive corpus. It also accounts for most of the passives in this study.[3] Birner (1996) compared the familiarity status of the subject and *by*-phrase NPs in passives in an earlier corpus-based study. In that study too she found that the surface subject referent was always as familiar as the *by*-phrase in the context. Summarizing, the surface subject of a passive tends to be the topic phrase, and has information that is relatively familiar in the context.

Psycholinguistic experiments have often used the passive in studies of sentence processing because of its clear relation to the active form and its greater surface complexity.[4] Gordon & Chan studied pronouns and full NPs in passive and active sentences presented in short constructed contexts. They consider surface structure factors and thematic roles and conclude that the passive allows for "optimal discourse organization" by maximizing continuity based on surface form and syntactic relations. The semantic factor of thematic role was less important (1995:229). Their conclusion supports the approach of this book, in which presentation is separated from semantics.

The short passive, without an agent, is much more common than the full passive in spoken and written discourse. Corpus studies from 1966, 1979, and 1987 found that 80–83% of the passives were agentless (Svarthvik 1966, Givón 1979, S. Thompson 1987). Birner & Ward (1998) also found that short passives

---

3. There are some passives which appear to be counter-examples to Birner & Ward's generalization. In the example below, the surface subject information may be less familiar than the *by*-phrase. The passive appears in the third sentence.

> There was only one important exception, one new product, in those first fifty years: the steamboat, first made practical by Robert Fulton in 1807. It had little impact until thirty or forty years later. In fact, until almost the end of the nineteenth century *more freight was carried on the world's oceans by sailing vessels than by steamships.*

"Freight" is perhaps evoked in the context by "impact" but this does not seem like a salient poset. However, "sailing vessels" is a link to the context via a poset "ships" to which both sailing vessels and steamboats belong.

4. Psycholinguistic experiments showed that reversible passive sentences in isolation took longer for subjects to process than actives (Gough 1965). This result was taken to mean that passives are more complex in processing. However, processing time was reduced when passives were presented in the context of previous mention of the subject referent of the passive (Turner & Rommetveit 1968, Davison & Lutz 1985). When passives and actives were presented in context, few processing differences were found by Gordon & Chan (1995).

are more frequent than full passives. In the texts in this study, short passives are also more frequent than full passives.

Existential there. In this construction the underlying subject is displaced to the predicate with *there* as the surface subject and the copula as main verb. The displaced phrase receives the sentence accent. *There*-sentences are all-focus, thetic rather than categorical, and therefore have no topic phrase. Given the lack of a topic phrase, the displaced-subject entity is the locus for presentational progression.

Sentences of this type present new entities. As Lambrecht puts it, "the sentence expressing the thetic proposition introduces a new element into the discourse without linking ... to an established topic or to some presupposed proposition" (1994:144). Example (2) illustrates:

(2)   Products made in the new factories differed from traditional products only in
         that they were uniform, with fewer defects than existed in products made by
         any but the top craftsmen of earlier periods.
             There was only one important exception, one new product, in those first fifty
         years: the steamboat, first made practical by Robert Fulton in 1807. It had
         little impact until thirty or forty years later.

In this example "there" introduces the "one exception," which is not prepared for in the preceding text. The entity introduced by the displaced NP is the point of the message, not the starting point (Hannay 1991:138). In addition to the verb *to be*, verbs of appearance or emergence such as *appear, come, exist* are found in this construction; some researchers treat sentences with the latter class of verbs as a distinct type of construction (Birner & Ward 1998).

There is a strong requirement on familiarity status in existential *there*-sentences: the entity presented must be hearer-new or discourse-new. Typically the displaced NP in a *there*-sentence is indefinite. However, it need not be. Felicitous examples with definite NPs are often cited, e.g. "There strode into town the ugliest gunslinger alive." In an extensive discussion, Birner & Ward show that definite NPs can appear in *there*-sentences when they refer to a hearer-new discourse entity. They suggest that the frequency of indefinites results from the strong requirement that the referent be new (1998:120ff).

Cleft and pseudo-cleft. These constructions syntactically highlight a phrase by extraction. The extracted, "clefted phrase" is introduced with the main verb *to be*, and followed by a "cleft clause" that has a missing element, similar to a relative clause. *It*-clefts have expletive *it* in subject position; *wh*-clefts, also known as "pseudo-clefts," have a *wh*-phrase as subject.

Cleft sentences semantically presuppose the material in the cleft clause; they cannot be directly questioned with felicity and are unaffected by question or negation of the main clause. These are the standard tests for presupposition. Clefts suggest a set of alternatives, and in positive sentences introduce an entity that satisfies the predicate of the cleft clause. Canonical sentences that correspond to clefts are cognitively synonymous, but do not have these semantic properties. Cleft sentences are derived states due to the main verb *to be*, and have the discourse properties of states. *Wh*-clefts are essentially equative, according to Heycock & Kroch (1999). In spite of their complex surface structure, *wh*-clefts (also known as pseudo-clefts) behave like canonical sentences, even in their potential for connection between sentences.

The topic and focus of *it*-clefts depend on sentence accent and context. If unaccented, the clefted phrase is often the topic phrase, as in (3a). If the clefted phrase receives the sentence accent, it is the focus, as in (3b–c):

(3)   a. The newly hatched *Formica* workers . . . forage for nectar and dead arthropods, regurgitate food to colony members, remove wastes and excavate new chambers. When the population becomes too large for the existing nest, *it is the 3,000 or so Formica slaves that locate another site and physically transport the 2,000 Polyergus workers, together with eggs, larvae, pupae and even the queen, to the new nest.*

       b. we sometimes use the stated intentions of dictators against them while rallying world opinion. But to what end? When Stalin engineered the worldwide peace movement in the early 1950s, or Slobodan Milosevic promises to allow "peace-loving" Albanian refugees to return, *it is our own intentions and our own public opinion that these dictators are reflecting and manipulating.*

       c. The truly revolutionary impact of the Information Revolution is just beginning to be felt. But *it is not "information" that fuels this impact. It is not "artificial intelligence." It is not the effect of computers and data processing on decision-making, policymaking, or strategy.*

The topic phrases in (3b–c) are *these dictators* and *this impact*; the referents of both phrases are familiar from the context.

Two main types of *it*-clefts are recognized, according to whether the clefted phrase is topic or focus. I will call them "comment-clauses" and "topic-clauses," following Hedberg (1990). In comment-clause clefts such as (3a), the clefted phrase is the topic and the clause the comment. The sentence accent falls within the cleft clause. Comment-clause clefts are often used with a backgrounding effect in discourse, Prince (1978) notes. In topic-clause clefts like (3b–c) the clefted phrase is the focus and receives the sentence accent; the topic phrase appears in the cleft clause. Topic-cleft sentences are natural answers to questions; they may also indicate contrast. And because the information in the cleft clause of a topic-cleft is familiar, the cleft clause may often be omitted. Fragment (3c) exemplifies both contrast and the omission of the cleft clause.

Traditionally, clefting is felicitous when there is a prior basis for the presupposed information. Thus cleft sentences are natural answers to questions, with the sentence accent on the extracted constituent. For instance, "Is it JOHN who writes poetry? No, it is BILL who writes poetry" (Chomsky 1971, Jackendoff 1972). Neither point, however, holds generally. Clefts often appear with no prior basis; and they allow more than one placement of the sentence accent.

In fact, new information often appears in the presupposed, clefted clause; this is perhaps the most frequent use of clefts according to Prince (1978). It may seem contradictory that a syntactic structure implying presupposition is used to present new information. But there is no contradiction. Rather, the clefted clause conveys pragmatically that the presupposed information is to be accepted as shared knowledge. Receivers automatically assume the information in the clefted clause, without engaging in a process of accommodation. Thus the notion of presupposition that is relevant for clefts does not require mutual knowledge (Delin 1995).

It-clefts also appear in a third use, where the clefted phrase gives information that sets the stage for the situation in the cleft clause. In this case both topic and focus phrase fall within the cleft clause. The example in (4) illustrates, repeated from Chapter 2. The cleft phrase sets the scene:

(4)   I feel reasonably certain of the final verdict on the current impeachment affair because I think history will see it as the climax of a six-year period marred by a troubling and deepening failure of the Republican party to play within the established constitutional rules.

   It was on Election Night 1992, not very far into the evening, that the Senate minority leader, Bob Dole, hinted at the way his party planned to conduct itself in the months ahead.

The clefted phrase is adverbial here; both topic and focus phrases of the sentence are in the cleft clause. The cleft sentence suggests a story to experienced readers. There are fairy tales, for instance, that open in a similar way: "It was a dark and stormy night when the beautiful princess stole out of the castle." The sense of fairy tale is bolstered in this text when later one comes upon the sentence "The Republicans were already on the road to further adventure" (the full text is given in Appendix A). Other adverbial functions of *it*-clefts, especially of a temporal nature, are discussed in Delin & Oberlander (1995).

In discourse, *wh*- and *it*-clefts have different distributions and functions. The *wh*-cleft clause represents "given information, assumed to be in the hearer's consciousness"; the *it*-cleft clause tends to "mark the information in the *that*-clause . . . as known" (Prince 1981:904). In *wh*-clefts, the clefted information is often familiar or inferrable, as in (5a). It may also, however, be new, as in (5b):

(5) a. Underwater they [humpback whales] can blast out at 170 decibels – louder than a jet's roar. They also make all kinds of lower intensity social sounds. I wish I knew what they were talking about. *What I like about humpback research is the way it lets your imagination roam free.*
   b. The difference between Giuliani's and Dinkins's anticrime policies is not that Giuliani hired more cops: Dinkins hired 7,000 new police in his final years in office. *What Dinkins would not do, according to celebrated former New York police chief William Bratton, was to reorient policing around a universal standard of nonviolent deviancy.*

It-cleft sentences are more frequent in the texts in this study than *wh*-clefts.

Extraposition. In Extraposition a sentential subject is postposed, with expletive *it* in subject position. Choice of this structure affects the possible topic phrases of a sentence. Since the expletive subject is not a denoting expression, it cannot be the topic phrase. However, the topic phrase may be the direct object, if there is one; the situation or proposition of the extraposed clause; or a phrase in the extraposed clause. In some cases Extraposition sentences may not have a topic phrase (see Chapter 10, ex. 7).

The extraposed clause is pragmatically presupposed, as are subjects generally. The presupposition attached to the clause allows this construction to be used to present information as uncontroversial, much as the *it*-cleft construction is used.

Familiarity status is the main factor in extraposition. Sentential subjects that are postposed invariably convey new information, as in (6).

(6) a. When people try to get a message from one individual to another in the party game "Telephone," they usually garble the words beyond recognition. *It might seem surprising, then, that mere molecules inside our cells constantly enact their own version of telephone without distorting the relayed information in the least.*
      Actually, no one could survive without such precise signalling in cells.
   b. "The only intention we have is to weaken the forces that have occupied our country and to regain our sovereignty. That is all." A week after Ethiopia started an offensive that it says is aimed at ending the two-year-old war, *it is now clear that the whole of Eritrea could become a battlefield.*

The information in the moved clauses is discourse-new. Plausible topic phrases in (6a–b) are the referents of clauses and/or their subjects: "mere molecules inside our cells" and "the whole of Eritrea." Transitive verbs also occur with extraposition, as in "It surprised Mary that John left early." In such sentences the direct object may be the topic phrase.

Extraposition is a discourse requirement for sentential subjects with discourse-new information. For sentential subjects with discourse-old information, extraposition is possible but not required. The generalizations are due to Miller (2001), who examined sentential *that* and infinitival VP clauses in a large corpus. He found that extraposition was chosen when the predicate of the sentence was not discourse-new and when the sentential subject provides the topic of the subsequent sentence in the text. Similar conclusions for inversion were reported in Birner (1994).

Extraposed clauses tend to be relatively "heavy," that is with many words and/or syntactic nodes. However, not all heavy clauses are extraposed if the information they express is discourse-old or inferrable, Miller (2001) notes. Example (7) illustrates:

(7)   The kilns clearly specialized in the production of the porcellanous ware. It is characterized by the extreme whiteness and hardness of the body, which may be translucent. *That the kilns confined themselves very largely to the production of bowls, basins, dishes and plates*, is evident from the immense waster heaps in the vicinity of the kilns and from the predominance of these shapes in collections all over the world.

The sentential subject is relatively heavy. Examples like this show that familiarity status rather than heaviness is the determining factor in extraposition.

Summarizing, sentences with non-canonical subjects vary in topic possibilities. For passives, the surface subject is the topic phrase. Cleft constructions have an expletive subject; the topic may be the clefted phrase itself, or a phrase in the clefted clause. Extraposed sentences have a postposed topic phrase. Existential-*there* sentences are thetic, with no topic phrase. All have strong requirements on the familiarity status of the displaced phrase.

9.2.2   Inversion

The subject is displaced to the right of the verb in inversion constructions, and a phrase from the predicate appears in initial position. There are three main types. In subject–auxiliary inversion the first auxiliary and subject are inverted; other verbs follow. Quotation inversion preposes the entire quoted phrase, with the subject and verb following. In predicate inversion a phrase from the predicate is preposed. The first two are illustrated in (8); I discuss the third type below.

(8)   a. It is true that the filibuster has a long and disreputable Senate history, and
           that . . . it has been used more by Democrats than by Republicans. But *only*
           after 1992 did it become the centerpiece of opposition conduct toward an
           elected President.
        b. The whale . . . was visible 40 feet below, suspended head down in pure
           blueness with its 15-foot-long arms, or flippers, flared out to either side
           like wings. *"That's the posture humpbacks most often assume when they*
           sing," Darling said.

The function shared by all inversions is highlighting of the inverted phrase, which occurs initially, in the canonical subject position. This is particularly clear with auxiliary inversion. In (8a) the inverted phrase "after 1992" is a strong focus phrase, with the focus operator "only"; the topic in (8a) is the subject, the pronoun ("it," coreferential with "the filibuster"). Green notes that quotation inversion tends to put new information first and "gets the non-quote part of the sentence out of the way of the reader" (1974:591). The topic phrase of (8b) is the subject of the quoted sentence. In contrast, some inversions put familiar information in the initial position of a sentence.

    Predicate inversion is another inversion construction. It has an argument phrase from the predicate in initial position, followed by the verb; the subject is displaced to the right of the verb. Familiarity status is the key factor in this type of inversion, Birner & Ward (1998) show. The preposed phrase must represent information that is more familiar, or discourse-old, than the information of the displaced subject. This is almost the same constraint that they propose for passives. The difference is that, with predicate inversion, familiar information appears in the initial position of a sentence rather than as grammatical subject. Example (9) illustrates:

(9)   a. Darwin accepted the postulate of the fusion of a mother's and father's char-
           acteristics in their offspring, even though his own experiments on pigeons
           refuted it. *Much more surprising are two other errors*: he failed to acknowl-
           edge the reality of species as non-interbreeding sets of populations, and . . .
           that new species originate predominantly through geographic isolation.
        b. The brown-headed cowbird does the same. Each bird has evolved so that
           it produces eggs that match those of its chosen baby-sitter.
           Even more varied than these avian parasites are the slave-making ants.

In (9a) the adjective phrase with "surprising" is more familiar in the discourse context than "two other errors." The sentence is presentational, with no topic phrase. The preposed PP in (9b) is linked to the context: "these" is coreferential with the subjects of the preceding clauses "each bird" and "it."

Locative inversion is a sub-type of predicate inversion with the same relative constraint on familiarity status. Example (10) illustrates. The fragment is from a book chapter in which Europe and the Cro-Magnons are both introduced earlier and are thus familiar.

(10)   The evidence for a localized origin of modern humans, followed by their spread... seems strongest for Europe. Some 40,000 years ago, *into Europe came the Cro-Magnons*, with their modern skeletons, superior weapons, and other advanced cultural traits.

The preposed phrase refers to *Europe*; mentioned in the prior sentence, it is more familiar than the post-verbal phrase. The topic structures of such sentences vary according to context. Here the inverted phrase functions as the topic; Coopmans calls such phrases "topicalized adverbial PPs" (1989:735). Bolinger notes that the initial phrase in locative inversions often has an almost visual "staging effect" (1977:94). Locative inversion may also be presentational, with no topic phrase. The verb of such sentences is the copula or one of a small set of motion verbs.

Predicate inversion also applies to existential-*there* sentences.

(11)   No other group of adults young or old is confined to an age-segregated environment, much like a gang in which individuals of the same age group define each other's world.
In no workplace, not even in colleges or universities, is there such a narrow segmentation by chronology.

The displaced subject is the focus phrase. The familiarity status requirement for *there*-inversion is the same as for such sentences generally: the dislocated phrase must be discourse-new.

The topics of inversion structures vary. In subject–auxiliary inversion and quotation inversion, the topic is often the inverted surface subject. In predicate inversion the sentence may be presentational, with no topic phrase; or the inverted phrase may be the topic phrase.

9.2.3   Argument preposing and postposing
Argument preposing structures have an initial, pre-subject phrase that is displaced from its canonical position in the predicate. In that position, a non-subject phrase is salient: it is adjacent to the preceding context, first in the sentence, and highlighted by virtue of its non-canonical position. The main preposing constructions are Topicalization, Focus Preposing, and Left-dislocation. They

tend to occur in speech rather than written texts. Examples are relatively rare in the texts in this study; the only ones found were in narrative fiction, which mimic the patterns of speech. The argument postposing constructions are Right-dislocation, Dative Alternation, and Heavy NP Shift.

In *Topicalization*, an argument of the verb or the entire verb phrase is preposed to initial position. The preposed phrase must be linked to the context in the strong sense of linking developed above.

(12)   "Why, what am I a-thinking of!" said Toby, suddenly recovering a position as
         near the perpendicular as it was possible for him to assume. "I shall forget my
         own name next. It's tripe!" *Tripe it was*; and Meg, in high joy, protested he
         should say, in half a minute more, that it was the best tripe ever stewed.

In this example the preposed NP "tripe" is linked by identity to the context.

The preposed phrase need not be the topic of a sentence, so that the term "Topicalization" is something of a misnomer. However, preposed arguments are often topics. In topicalizations from the corpus of Birner & Ward (1998), the preposed phrase was topic in over 75 percent of the examples. Contrast was also a significant factor, accounting for 49 percent of the examples. (Birner & Ward 1998 do not consider the relation between these factors.)

Focus Preposing has a preposed argument phrase that receives the sentence accent and is the focus phrase of the sentence. The preposed phrase presents new rather than familiar information, as in (13):

(13)   It was the voice of this same Richard, who had come upon them unobserved,
         and stood before the father and daughter, looking down upon them with a
         face as glowing as the iron on which his stout sledge-hammer daily rung. *A
         handsome, well-made, powerful youngster* he was; with eyes that sparkled
         like the red-hot droppings from a furnace fire.

Both Topicalization and Focus Preposing structure the propositions they represent into a focus and focus frame (Partee 1991, Prince 1986). The open proposition conveys that an entity has a certain attribute; the focus represents the value of that attribute.

Left-dislocation has an initial phrase followed by a full sentence. The phrase is coreferential with a pronoun in the sentence and may function as the topic, as in: "My grandmother, *I remember when she used to work*" (from Prince 1997). The familiarity status of the preposed phrase varies: it may express information that is familiar and linked to the context, or discourse-new. In the latter case the coreferential pronoun tends to appear in a position that is not favored for discourse-new entities, often an embedded subject as in the grandmother example. Prince (1997) suggests a processing account of the structure:

Left-dislocation simplifies the processing of a sentence by moving a discourse-new referent from a disfavored to a more favorable position.[5]

Right-dislocation is formally the mirror image of left-dislocation: it has a pronoun subject and a final unaccented phrase coreferential with the subject. But the construction differs, predictably, in the familiarity status of the sentence-final phrase. The right-dislocated phrase tends to express information that is familiar, as in (14):

(14)   Miss Kate and Miss Julia were there, gossiping and laughing and fussing, walking after each other to the head of the stairs, peering down over the banisters and calling down to Lily to ask her who had come.
         It was always a great affair, the Misses Morkan's annual dance. Everybody who knew them came to it.

This construction is used when the topic referent is relatively salient, but not enough to be identified with a pronoun alone, according to Lambrecht. Right-dislocation signals to the receiver that the topic referent will be named at the end of the sentence (1994:203). The two dislocation structures are sometimes used in speech to maintain reference to a topic and thus maximize discourse continuity, according to Givón (1983).

Dative Alternation and *Heavy NP Shift* are rightward-movement constructions that move phrases to the right in the predicate of a sentence. In Dative Alternation, a direct object phrase is moved over an indirect object and the preposition is deleted: for instance, "We gave a book to Mary" alternates with "We gave Mary a book."[6] In Heavy NP Shift, a long and/or complex direct object or complement is moved over another phrase in the predicate. The phrase that is moved is the focus phrase, receiving the sentence accent. In English this accent may hold for the smallest phrase or for successively larger phrases.

(15)   a. Dative Alternation
         First, he backed an end to forced busing. Then, he supported Republican Governor George Voinovich's radical school choice law, which offers

---

5. Prince discusses Left-dislocation cases in which the pronoun rescues what would otherwise be an island violation. These constructions occasionally occur in writing; there were none in the texts in this study – for instance: "There are always GUESTS who I am curious about what THEY are going to say." Prince notes that this marginally acceptable sentence would be impossible with a gap in the position of the pronoun. Right- and Left-dislocation in French are discussed in Lambrecht (1994).

6. There are several differences between canonical Dative sentences and the Dative Alternative construction. The alternation is possible only for sentences with certain verbs; Gropen *et al.* (1989) attempt to characterize them on semantic grounds. Green (1974) shows that the two structures may have different entailments: "I taught Latin to the students" entails that they learned Latin, whereas "I taught the students Latin" does not have such an entailment.

students *vouchers at parochial as well as public schools*. Then, he made city workers compete against private firms for garbage collection, road maintenance and other contracts.
b. Heavy NP Shift
Reasonable people may differ on the quality of the evidence Mr. Starr has accumulated ... But his appointment in the first place is impossible to defend. Republicans selected *as independent counsel* a lawyer who was already involved in consultations with a plaintiff suing the president in a civil dispute.

Since the rightmost phrase in a sentence receives the accent, these constructions result in a focus phrase that would canonically be in another position. Thus the discourse function of postposing is to introduce a marked focus phrase (Hajicová and Sgall 1987; see also Erteschik-Shir 1979).

Familiarity status is an important factor in non-canonical constructions, as the foregoing discussion has established. Yet in rightward movement the heaviness of the moved phrase also seems to be significant, cf. Hawkins (1994). Often, but not necessarily, the moved phrases in the Dative Alternation are relatively heavy; the rightmost phrase in (15a), for instance, is longer and more complex than the one that precedes it. The Heavy NP Shift construction by definition involves a heavy phrase.

The relative importance of heaviness and familiarity status in Dative Alternation and Heavy NP Shift is studied by Arnold *et al.* (2000). The authors examined instances of these constructions in a corpus consisting of parliamentary debate transcripts from Canada; they also elicited dative sentences experimentally. Heaviness was measured by number of words; familiarity status was coded as given, inferrable, or new. Arnold *et al.* asked which factor better accounted for the sentences in which movement did and did not occur. Both factors were relevant, they found: the phrases that appeared in rightmost position tended to provide new information and to be relatively heavy.

Summarizing, non-canonical constructions that involve the verb and its arguments highlight by position and syntax. Topic possibilities vary. No topic phrase occurs in existential-*there* sentences or in some inversion constructions. The topic phrase is the subject or leftmost phrase in passive, some clefts, some inversions, some argument preposings. The topic phrase is in rightward position in extraposition, some clefts, some inversions. To determine the actual patterns of use would require a large-scale study.

What these constructions have in common is that they change phrases with familiar information from canonical to non-canonical positions. All but two constructions position relatively familiar information to the left and relatively new information to the right. The exceptions are subject–auxiliary inversion and quotation inversion.

The next two sections are devoted to discussion of non-argument preposing and multi-clause sentences. These constructions do not involve the topic and focus organization of a sentence. Rather, they offer a choice about how to deploy information. Non-argument preposing affects the familiarity connectedness of sentences in texts. Multi-clause sentences present the situations expressed in the clauses as closely related.

9.3   *Non-argument preposing: Adjuncts*

Adjuncts canonically appear after the arguments in a clause. They may be preposed to initial position, or to other non-canonical positions. In initial position, adjunct phrases are highlighted and function as starting point for a sentence. Preposed adjuncts do not affect the internal organization of the clause. They contrast with preposed arguments in their connection to context.

There are no familiarity constraints on preposed adjuncts. Connections of all kinds, including no connection, are found between a preposed adjunct and the context. Some preposed adjuncts presuppose the information that they express; others do not.

Many types of phrases can be preposed, including adverbs (*frankly, unfortunately, carefully*), locative PPs (*in the garden, at noon*), adjunct PPs (*with little difficulty, in response to the inquiry, like fish farming*), condensed clauses with non-finite verbs (*carrying his briefcase, backed into a corner*), temporal clauses (*when S, until S*), purpose clauses (*in order to S*), and adjunct clauses (*because S, unless S*).[7] Sentence connectives such as *as for, and, yet* belong to a separate category because they appear only at the beginning of a sentence.

Locative and adjunct PPs. Preposed time and place adverbials provide a location – temporal, spatial, or metaphorical – for the situation expressed in a sentence. The examples in (16) illustrate:

(16)   a. But how do circuits within cells achieve this high-fidelity transmission? *For a long time*, biologists had only rudimentary explanations. *In the past 15 years*, they have made great progress in unlocking the code that cells use for their internal communications.

---

7. Quirk *et al.* (1985) distinguish between adjuncts and disjuncts. Adjuncts pertain to the situation in the main clause and allow syntactic processes of focusing with clefts, pseudo-clefts, negation, question, and focusing operators. Disjuncts comment on the style, form, or content of what was said; they are peripheral to the clause and do not allow syntactic focusing (1985:1070–71).

b. *At the turn of the century*, city governments often took aim at monopolistic private corporations and utilities. *Now*, the focus is more often on monopolistic government agencies.

c. Our French teacher, a crusty character named Bertram Bradstock, made it clear *that in studying French*, speaking it was an unnecessary luxury.

The first preposed adverb in (16a) is unrelated to the context; the second is linked to the first, since both express time intervals. The contrast from one preposed adverb to the other contributes to (16b). These adverbs set the scene for the situation expressed in the sentence.[8] In (16c), the metaphorical location of studying French is evoked by the prior phrase "our French teacher"; the example is from Lambrecht (1994).

The fragment in (17) has three preposed adjunct phrases:

(17)   1 The low price has been a mixed blessing . . . 2a *With little incentive for drillers to find and tap new oil*, supplies eventually dropped, b and *in the past year* the Organization of Petroleum Exporting Countries deliberately dropped its production as well. 3 *In response to the law of supply and demand*, prices have now risen.

In clause 2b the preposed phrase is temporally locative; the preposed phrases in 2a and 3 indicate more abstract relations wth nominal clauses. Nominals introduced by a preposition are temporally related to the main clause. None of these adjuncts is directly related to the prior context, by linking or a weaker relation.

There is a difference in the status of the information conveyed by locative and other adjuncts. Locationals are part of the assertion of a sentence, whereas non-locational PPs are presupposed. To demonstrate this I use the "lie test," due to Erteschik-Shir & Lappin (1979). These authors have shown that one can felicitously deny the truth of an assertion but that denial of presupposition is infelicitous. To test whether the information in a given clause is asserted or presupposed, then, one constructs a sentence that denies its truth. If the denial is felicitous the information is asserted. Example (18) uses this test with the locative preposing sentence from (16a):

---

8. There have been suggestions from time to time that scene-setting adverbials are topic phrases. Halliday's notion of theme essentially takes this view (1967). In some cases it is not implausible to claim that the adverbial is the topic referent, the locus for truth-conditional assessment and for storage of the information in the sentence. For (16a) one can say, "Speaking of the past fifteen years, biologists have made great progress," though the other topic paraphrases proposed in Chapter 7 are less felicitous. But in my judgment this analysis fails to account adequately for the main clause. Lambrecht calls adverbials like this "secondary topics." For him, scene-setting pertains to aboutness but does not have topic status.

(18)   In the past 15 years, they [biologists] have made great progress in unlocking
         the code that cells use for their internal communications.
         a. That's not true: they haven't made great progress.
         b. That's not true: it wasn't in the past 15 years.

Both denials are felicitous, which shows that the information of the locative is
asserted. In contrast, the information of non-locative PPs is presupposed rather
than asserted. Example (19) illustrates, using sentence 2 from the fragment
in (17):

(19)   With little incentive for drillers to find and tap new oil, supplies eventually
         dropped.
         a. That's not true – they didn't [drop].
         b. #That's not true – there wasn't [little incentive].

The denial of the main clause is felicitous but that of the adverbial is
not. The information in many adjunct clauses is also presupposed, as noted
below.

Semantically, preposed material is outside the scope of negation and other
operators in the main clause. For instance, the sentence "George doesn't eat
chocolate because he wants to be thin" is ambiguous. On one reading, the
because clause is within the scope of negation, on the other it is not. In preposed
position, however, the clause is outside the scope of negation: "Because he wants
to be thin, George doesn't eat chocolate." This difference holds for adverbials
generally (Davison 1984). One function of preposing, then, is to remove the
adjunct from the scope of semantic operators in the main clause.

Condensed clauses are sentences with participial or infinitival clause adjuncts. They are tightly bound to the main clause, as discussed in Chapter 6.
Condensed clauses usually have null subjects and lack a tense morpheme; (20)
illustrates.[9]

(20)   a. 1 it was the explosive growth of the steam-engine based textile industry
            that revived slavery. 2 *Considered to be practically dead by the Founders
            of the American Republic*, slavery roared back to life as the cotton gin –
            soon steam-driven – created a huge demand for low-cost labor and made
            breeding slaves America's most profitable industry for some decades.

---

9. English allows condensed clauses with overt subjects, but they are relatively rare in the modern
   language. I found one example only in the texts for this study:

   The moulds were made of a slightly greyish, compact stoneware clay with a concave
   recess on the underside, *the upper surface* being ornamented with a design of neatly
   carved intaglio.

> 3 *Punctuated by the most spectacular busts in economic history*, the boom
> continued in Europe for thirty years, until the late 1850s, by which time
> most of today's major railroads had been built.
>
> b. In "The Education of Henry Adams," *describing his college experience
> under a curriculum that had not changed in several decades*, Adams said
> he had received an 18th century education when the world was plunging
> into the 20th.

The subject of the condensed clause is coreferential with the main clause subject,
and reinforces its role as topic phrase. Condensed clauses are part of the assertion
of a sentence. The condensed clause in S2 of (20a) is related to the context by
the prior phrase "revived slavery." The other condensed clauses in (20) express
information that is new to the discourse. The condensed clause is temporally
dependent on the main clause; the situation it expresses precedes or overlaps
that of the main clause.

Temporal clauses with *after, as, before, when, while, unless*, etc., temporally
locate the situation of the main clause.[10] The clauses are complete but depend
temporally on the main clause, with a requirement of tense harmony.

(21) a. At his news conference here, even *before he took questions*, Schroeder
      implicitly challenged the official US explanation for the bombing of the
      Chinese embassy in Belgrade – that target analysts relied on a faulty street
      map – by renewing his demand for a formal NATO inquiry into the bombing.
      b. The 19-member alliance is at a critical crossroads: *as time runs out to
      prepare hundreds of thousands of ethnic Albanians to return to their homes
      before winter*, the allies are badly divided over the timing and conditions
      for the use of ground troops.
      c. Soon *after SH2 domains were identified*, investigators realized that these
      modules are present in well over 100 separate proteins.

The condensed clauses in these examples introduce new information to the discourse. The position of a temporal adverbial affects the interpretation of a sentence, as de Swart (1999) points out. In preposed position, temporal adverbials
provide Reference Time for the situation expressed in a sentence. Adverbials
in canonical right position may have other functions.

10. Temporal clauses are discussed in Partee (1984), Smith (1991), de Swart (1993), Kamp &
    Reyle (1993), Sandstrom (1993), among others. There are certain idiosyncrasies. For instance,
    the Event of a *before*-clause may not take place, due to the meaning of "before":

    Mary Jane brushed past the others and ran to the staircase, but before she reached it the
    singing stopped and the piano was closed abruptly.

    We infer that Mary Jane didn't get to the staircase after all.

Temporal clauses often convey presupposed information. On encountering *when, while, after* in a text, the receiver assumes the information and adds it to the ongoing discourse representation. The passage in (22) gives a striking example of a *when*-clause from the story *Un coeur simple* by Flaubert, the nineteenth-century French writer. *When*-clauses in French are presupposed as in English. The example is from Whitaker & Smith (1985).

(22)   The driver [of the mailcoach] . . . in a temper, raised his arm, and gave a full swing of his big whip, lashing her [Félicité] from the stomach to the nape of her neck, so that she fell to the ground on her back.
    The first thing she did, *when she regained consciousness*, was to open her basket.

In this fragment Félicité, the main character of the story, tries to stop a mailcoach. The *when*-clause informs us as an accepted event that Félicité came back to consciousness (and indirectly that she had lost consciousness); the receiver adds these Events to the ongoing discourse model. This is a compact way to convey information and gives it a certain authority since no source or justification is cited. *Unless, until,* and certain cases of *before* (see footnote 10) do not presuppose the situations they express.

Temporal clauses usually involve a consequential relation between situations as well as a temporal one. In some cases the temporal aspect is less important than the consequential, as the examples in (23) illustrate:

(23)   a. *When inflation is taken into account*, that 1999 price was the lowest in modern history, while oil has gone above today's seemingly high price several times.
    b. *When puberty meets education and learning in modern America*, the victory of puberty masquerading as popular culture and the tyranny of peer groups based on ludicrous values meets little resistance.

Indeed, a sentence asserting a purely temporal relation is odd unless a consequential relation also exists, as Moens & Steedman (1987) emphasize. For instance, the sentence "When my car broke down the sun set" is odd in isolation because there is no obvious relation between the events. But in certain contexts the sentence would be felicitous – for instance, if the reader knew that the narrator was in a difficult situation, far from help.

Discourse relations are sometimes necessary to understand the contribution of a clause with a temporal connective. For instance, *while*-clauses may be temporal or concessive, as Caenepeel (1997) observes. Example (24) illustrates *while*-clauses of both types:

(24)   a. Brunel's tunnel shield, a giant iron frame, was forced through soft soil by
          screw jacks *while miners dug through shuttered openings in the shield's*
          forward face.
        b. *While Darwin came in for severe criticism from other scientists and in*
          turn often expressed his disagreement with their views, he responded cour-
          teously, used scientific arguments, and completely avoided personalizing
          disputes.
        c. In the United States, we have lost over 500,000 jobs in the oil industry
          while we have grossly increased our dependency on foreign oil; we now
          import 55 percent of what we use.

In (24a) "while" is temporal; in (24b) it is concessive; in (24c) "while" has both
a temporal and a concessive meaning. Caenepeel argues that both sentence-
internal and discourse factors determine the interpretation of a *while*-clause as
temporal or concessive. The relevant factors that she mentions are whether a
clause expresses an Event or a State; the position of the clause; parallelism and
contrast in the context; and whether the context is narrative or discursive.

Adjunct clauses introduced by *because, although,* etc., also appear in preposed position. Like temporal clauses, many of them presuppose the information that they express. Also like temporal clauses, they may be linked to the
context, otherwise related to it, or unrelated to it. The connectives that appear
in combined clauses are a large class, including *as, despite, whereas, since,*
though, if (conditional), *even if*, etc. Many of them introduce nominals as well
as clauses; several require modals or subjunctives.

9.4   Multi-clause sentences

Sentences with more than one clause are non-canonical. They represent the
choice of the writer to organize information in sentential chunks.

The encoding of a sentence as full or reduced, dependent or independent, is
part of presentation. Sentences with more than one clause may have relative
clauses and adjunct clauses. Conjoined sentences, and sentences with more than
one independent clause, are also in this class. The first two groups have clauses
that are traditionally subordinate. It has been suggested that subordinate clauses
contain given information, especially since many are presupposed (Bever 1970,
Givón 1979). However, empirical studies show that this hypothesis cannot be
maintained. Relative clauses, for instance, often express information that is new
to a discourse (Prideaux 1993, S. Thompson 2001).

Relative clauses. Restrictive and appositive relatives are referentially dependent on a shared NP. Temporally, they may be dependent or independent of the

main clause. Relative clauses typically have the shared NP referent as topic: they are about their topics, as Kuno (1976) argues. However, relatives of locative phrases and locative inversion are exceptions to the generalization.[11]

The function of a restrictive relative clause is to modify the shared Noun-Phrase. More precisely, the relative contributes to a referring expression by narrowing down the set of possible referents. Example (25) illustrates restrictive relative clauses on subject and object NounPhrases:

(25)　Restrictive Relative Clauses
>　a. The political machines that men like White despised had been created to bridge the material and cultural distance separating the immigrants from native society. In cities *that offered newcomers few formal services*, the immigrant-driven city machines supplied housing, fuel, charity and – most importantly – jobs.
>　b. A female cuckoo, for instance, lays her egg in the nest of another species, such as a warbler, and leaves it for the host to rear. The brown-headed cowbird does the same. Each bird has evolved so that it produces eggs *that match those of its chosen babysitter*.

The material in a subject restrictive relative like (25a) is pragmatically presupposed, since the existence of the subject referent is presupposed. There are no familiarity status requirements for relative clauses: the information may be familiar, new, or inferrable from the preceding discourse. Non-subject relative clauses like (25b) are not pragmatically presupposed, and tend to present new information.

Appositive relatives give information about their head nouns; they may follow the head noun or appear elsewhere in the sentence, often as a parenthetical.

(26)　Appositive Relative Clauses
>　a. Dragons, *which are relatively uncommon in earlier examples*, are usually arranged almost heraldically round a conceptual center point, so that like the floral scrolls they appear to rotate.

---

11. For instance, the following sentence has three relative clauses on NPs after the colon, all preposed with prepositions, and all underlined.

> Between these rival ends ran parallel lines of side-dishes: two little minsters of jelly, red and yellow; a shallow dish full of blocks of blancmange and red jam, a large green leaf-shaped dish with a stalk-shaped handle, <u>on which</u> lay bunches of purple raisins and peeled almonds, a companion dish <u>on which</u> lay a solid rectangle of Smyrna figs, a dish of custard topped with grated nutmeg, a small bowl full of chocolates and sweets wrapped in gold and silver papers and a glass vase <u>in which</u> stood some tall celery stalks.

All three are inverted locatives: presentational clauses in which the postverbal NP is the new information.

    b. All the humpbacks in a given region sing the same song, *which is constantly evolving.*

Appositive relative clauses in rightmost position may advance narrative time, as in "She gave the letter to the clerk, who copied it" (Depraeterre 1996:699).

    When they appear with non-argument NPs, relative clauses do not contribute to the topic structure of a sentence. Example (27) illustrates relative clauses on both argument and non-argument NPs. The first sentence has a relative clause on the object NP, an argument; the second has a relative clause on the head noun of the adverbial.

(27)   1 As they [workers] moved on, they removed mud, blasted through rock, and bolted together the iron rings *that would form the lining of the tunnel.* 2 On a good day, they moved about 40 feet. 3 Near the New York shore, *where they ran into a thousand feet of solid rock*, progress slowed to less than a foot a day.

In the S1 relative the topic is "that," coreferential with "the iron rings." The S3 relative clause has "the New York shore" as topic; this is the noun of a locative PP, and does not contribute to the topic structure of the main clause.

    Adjuncts. Adverbials, PPs, and adjunct clauses of all types appear in rightmost position after the verb. In this position the information expressed is not presupposed. This presentation emphasizes the relations between clauses or PPs. The contribution of the different connectives is usually interpreted in terms of the discourse relations, as Matthiessen & Thompson (1988) argue.

    Conjunctions also emphasize the close relations between situations. Conjunction is the only other context besides the condensed clause that allows null subject pronouns in English, as in (28):

(28)   The Littleton killers felt trapped in the artificiality of the high school world and believed it to be real.

Discussion of the many types of conjunction is beyond the scope of this chapter.

    Complex sentences. In written texts one sometimes encounters complex sentences related by connectives, semicolons, colons, and/or dashes. The examples in (29) illustrate:

(29)   a. In the United States, we have lost over 500,000 jobs in the oil industry while we have grossly increased our dependency on foreign oil; we now import 55 percent of what we use.
       b. Mr Browne, whose face was once more wrinkling with mirth, poured out for himself a glass of whisky while Freddy Malins exploded, before he had well reached the climax of his story, in a kink of high-pitched bronchitic

> laughter and, setting down his untasted and overflowing glass, began to run the knuckles of his left fist backwards and forwards into his left eye, repeating words of his last phrase as well as his fit of laughter would allow him.

Such complex sentences are an artifact of the written mode and the subtle possibilities of punctuation.

9.5   Paragraphs

Paragraphs are text units, integral parts of modern written texts. Paragraphs organize the text into chunks, each set off with spaces and indentations. The beginnings and endings of paragraphs are salient positions in the text, as are very short paragraphs. Paragraphs vary in length and organization. They represent a writer's choices of chunking and highlighting information. The presentational aspects of a text thus include its paragraphs. The authors' paragraphs have been retained in the examples in this book.

One question is whether paragraphs coincide significantly with Discourse Modes; another is whether presentational patterns relate to paragraph units. More generally, we ask whether paragraphing is significant for understanding text structure.

Although some regularities can be found in paragraphs, they do not conform to any single pattern or convention. Linguistic, rhetorical, and psychological studies agree that paragraphs are flexible and can be used in more than one way. Some paragraphs are about a particular theme or topic, others are not. Some paragraphs are long; others are short, drawing attention to a particular point or direction in a text. There is no one convention but rather a set of possibilities.[12]

Linguists have discussed the nature of the paragraph as a semantic unit. According to Giora (1983), semantic unity revolves around a discourse topic, which tends to hold for a paragraph. She suggests that discourse topics are analogous to sentence topics and can be recognized with the intuitive notion of aboutness. Another approach to paragraph unity is taken by Longacre (1979) and Hinds (1979), who argue that cohesive and pragmatic relations between sentences unify the sentences of a paragraph. The relations they invoke are those currently known as discourse relations (see Chapter 11). Of course, discourse relations are not peculiar to paragraphs. They are relevant at all levels of a text: sentences, parts of paragraphs, paragraphs, and larger segments. This point is

---

12. Chafe (1994) suggests that paragraphs in written texts correspond to topic boundaries in speaking. They can appear at different levels, according to the writer's choice.

made with particular force by Mann & Thompson (1987, 1992), who use the same discourse relations to structure texts at successively higher levels. Fries (1983) argues for the thematic unity of paragraphs as structural units, using Halliday's notion of theme as the starting point of a sentence.

Coreference patterns often provide linguistic cues to paragraphs. Shifts from pronoun to full NPs tend to coincide with paragraph breaks in narrative and expository prose, according to Fox (1987a,b). The impetus for such shifts is usually a change of theme, or topic. Longacre (1979) suggests that coreferential expressions indicate thematic unity. Other cues are change of direction or discontinuity, "theme-marking" with non-canonical syntactic structures, and repetition of terms within a paragraph (Crothers 1979, Bond & Hayes 1984, Hoey 1991). In some languages there are linguistic forms that have the paragraph as their domain.[13]

Paragraph boundaries can be significant indicators of the linear organization of texts. In a study of discourse topic continuity and discontinuity, Goutsos (1997) found that paragraph breaks are powerful signals of a shift from one discourse topic to another.[14] However, there is another important pattern for the introduction of new discourse topics. In some texts, a new discourse topic is introduced in the final position of a paragraph and then developed in the paragraph immediately following (Giora 1983).

There is no single pattern for paragraphs and Discourse Modes. Discourse Modes are often maintained within a paragraph; but a Discourse Mode may shift in the middle of a paragraph. Examples given in Chapters 2 and 5 have a shift of Discourse Mode that coincides with the paragraph break; and shifts that do not so coincide. In other cases, passages of a Discourse Mode may continue for more than one paragraph. I conclude that there is no clear relation between Discourse Modes and paragraphs.

The history of texts shows that they were not always divided into paragraphs. With the development of printing and industrialization in sixteenth- and

---

13. Longacre (1979) points to markers for paragraph boundaries in Huichol (Mexico), Shipibo (Peru), Gurung (Nepal), Sanio-Hiowe (New Guinea). Paez and Ica (Colombia) have anaphoric devices with the paragraph as their domain. In Ica there is a special verbal suffix for referring to the most prominent participant in a paragraph (Tracy & Levinsohn 1977). This is reminiscent of the discourse uses of pronouns in proximal–obviative systems of American Indian languages discussed briefly in Chapter 6.

14. Goutsos found that paragraphs did not necessarily coincide with discourse topic continuity – more than one discourse topic may occur in a single paragraph. However, topics rarely continue across paragraphs. Goutsos worked with three corpora of English expository texts. The paragraphing for newspaper articles was slightly different than other genres, probably reflecting journalistic norms and requirements.

seventeenth-century Europe, paragraphs became quite common. Paragraphs as blocks of type were useful for the printer, and broke up the mass of text on a page. Conventions about paragraphing sought to balance the demands of rhetorical structure and logical relationships of a text (Parkes 1993:89). In the nineteenth century people began to consider the paragraph as a unit in its own right (McArthur 1992).

The modern rhetorical tradition of the paragraph began with Bain's (1877) rules for achieving unified and coherent paragraphs in expository writing. Bain recommended that the subject of a paragraph be prominently indicated, thus beginning the tradition of the "topic sentence" (Markels 1984:42). Rhetoricians, however, note that, although the topic sentence can be useful, the main desideratum of a paragraph is coherence; see Christiansen (1965), Winkler & McCuen (1988). A study of actual paragraphs carried out by Braddock (1974) found many types of organization.

The psychological reality of the paragraph has been studied experimentally. Koen *et al.* (1966) presented people with texts and asked people to put in paragraphs. Their subjects generally agreed with the original paragraphing of the texts, and with each other. Koen *et al.* concluded that paragraphing is a reliable phenomenon; another study by Stern (1976) found less agreement. Later studies, however, have also found good agreement between subjects' divisions and original texts. Stark (1988) asked subjects to paragraph texts. They were able to paragraph in agreement with the authors and with each other. Stark looked for the basis of her subjects' decisions. Neither length, nor changes in surface subject, were consistent cues for paragraph breaks in the three texts she studied. Quite good cues were non-canonical structures in which the subject was not the first element and discontinuities. Stark concludes that people have multiple conventions at their disposal: there is more than one way to segment a text into paragraphs.

9.6 *Presentational information in Discourse Representation Structure*

The structures of Discourse Representation Theory represent the conceptual meanings of a text. They arise from semantic and pragmatic information. I have argued that some presentational information should be represented in Discourse Representation Structure. However, I do not provide a formal account. Topic referents can't be identified by compositional rules, for the reasons given in Chapter 8. Focus information is complex and beyond the scope of this discussion. I assume that a full text representation includes information about sentence topic and focus. Such a representation would require a much more powerful set of construction rules than those used here. For another view see McNally (1988).

Whether other aspects of surface presentation should be included in a DRS is debatable. Syntactic structures have the potential for a certain rhetorical force, from general effects such as surprise, emphasis, and contrast, to specifics such as proposition concession and affirmation.[15] Such interpretations depend on details of the context as well as on a given structure: there is no single rhetorical function for syntactic structures. For instance, proposition affirmation is conveyed by certain inversions, Ward (1985) argues. In the cases he considers, an affirmed proposition is evoked but not entailed by the context, as in "It's odd that dogs eat cheese, but eat it they do." Concession/affirmation is a special rhetorical meaning of inversions, according to Horn (1991). The speaker concedes one proposition and affirms another; the second may follow from the first but contrasts with it rhetorically, as in "They barely made it, but make it they did."

Subtleties of presentation such as the difference between independent and relative clauses, or between full and condensed clauses, belong to the surface of the text. They contribute to rhetorical interpretation. Certain close connections between clauses are indirectly preserved in the DRS. For instance, since a condensed clause has no tense, no independent times for that clause appear in the DRS.

The rhetorical effects of inversion and other non-canonical constructions are part of text meaning, however. Levinson (2000) suggests that they are General Conversational Implicatures. They occupy a level of pragmatics between the general Gricean maxims and the particular implicatures conveyed by a given sentence in context. These rhetorical interpretations depend on pragmatic reasoning, and require access to surface structure. Such pragmatic interpretation may take place in parallel with the conceptual. The two are distinct in kind, perhaps belonging to different modules, Levinson suggests. I shall assume that rhetorical meanings are treated differently from the conceptual meanings adduced in this book.

There is reason to think that the surface structure of a sentence is not included in the discourse representations that people actually construct. Evidence from psycholinguistics shows that people do not remember the surface structures of sentences. For instance, Sachs (1967) found that people rapidly forget details of

---

15. The studies of construction grammar emphasize the pragmatic meanings of particular constructions (as in Lambrecht 1986, Goldberg 1995, etc.). They tend to focus on internal aspects of a structure rather than its role in a context.

sentence structure, after eighty syllables or more. Similarly, studies by Johnson-Laird and his colleagues (1970) showed that people remember the meaning but not the linguistic encoding of a sentence.[16] Further experimental studies have shown that the linguistic form of a sentence is standardly not remembered after a short time, though people can remember if asked to do so (Garnham 1985).

16. It was seen that after less than a minute people were not able to recall the linguistic forms of sentences they had seen. They remembered the meanings conveyed, however.

Example sources

(1a) and (9a) Jared Diamond, A tale of two reputations. *Natural History*, February 2001.

(1b), (24a), and (27) Jim Collins, How it works. *US Airways Magazine, Attaché*, May 2001.

(1c), (11), (23b), and (28) Leon Botstein, Let teenagers try adulthood. *New York Times*, May 1999.

(2), (3c), and (20a) Peter Drucker, The information revolution, *Atlantic Monthly*, October 1999.

(3a), (9b), and (25b) Howard Topoff, Slave-making queens. *Scientific American*, November 1999.

(3b) Tony Judt, Tyrannized by weaklings. *New York Times*, April 5, 1999.

(4), (8a), and (15b) Alan Ehrenhalt, Hijacking the rulebook. *New York Times*, December 20, 1998.

(5a), (8b), and (26b) Douglas H. Chadwick, Listening to humpbacks. *National Geographic*, July 1999.

(5b), (15a), (16b), and (25a) Peter Beinart, The pride of the cities. *New Republic*, June 1997.

(6a), (16a), and (21c) John D. Scott & Tony Pawson, Cell communication. *Scientific American*, June 2000.

(6b) After a victory, Ethiopia looks toward other fronts. *New York Times*, May 20, 2000.

(7) and (26a) Margaret Medley, *The Chinese Potter*, London: Phaidon, 1989, pp. 106, 112.

(10) and (24b) Jared Diamond, *Guns Germs and Steel*. New York: W. W. Norton, 1997, p. 40.

(12) and (13) Charles Dickens, *The Chimes*. Oxford: Oxford University Press, pp. 89, 93.

(14) and (29b) James, Joyce, "The Dead." In *Dubliners*, 1916: reprinted, London: Penguin Books, 1982, pp. 175, 185.

(17), (23a), (24c), and (29a) Robert Mosbacher, Cheap oil's tough bargains. *New York Times*, March 13, 2000.

(20b) Arthur Levine, The Soul of a New University. *New York Times*, March 13, 2000.

(21a) and (21b) Kosovo strategy splitting NATO. *New York Times*, May 20, 1999.

IV Discourse Modes and their context

10 *Information in text passages*

This chapter brings together the main points of Discourse Mode, subjectivity, and presentational progression; and analyzes passages of text with the tools developed above. Section 10.1 gives the basic points of each area of analysis, with a reprise of the criteria for determining Primary Referents and sentence topics.

Section 10.2 analyzes text passages of the five Discourse Modes, according to temporality and types of entities, I discuss temporal, spatial, and metaphorical progression. For each passage, I also consider subjectivity and presentational factors. Section 10.3 presents a temporal and an atemporal DRS, with information about Discourse Mode and subjectivity.

10.1 The Discourse Modes

To introduce the discussion I summarize the characteristics of the Discourse Modes. They fall into two classes, temporal and atemporal, according to the main types of situation introduced in each mode.

The temporal modes are Narrative, Report, and Description. They introduce situations that are located in the world. In Narrative, events and states are related to each other in time; the text progresses with bounded events interpreted in sequence, and/or time adverbials. In Reports, events, states, and General Statives are related to Speech Time: texts progress back and forth. The mode of Description has events and states, and time is static. The text progresses spatially through a scene. Text progression in Description depends on lexical information, unlike the two other temporal modes.

The Information and Argument modes are atemporal. General Statives predominate in the Information mode, while Argument has both General Statives and abstract entities. Text progression in these modes proceeds by metaphorical motion through the domain of the text. Motion, or lack of it, depends on the Primary Referent in a clause; it occurs when metaphorical location changes.

The Primary Referent is semantically central in the situation expressed by a clause. The Primary Referent of an Event is the entity which moves or changes;

in States, the Primary Referent is located, characterized, or emergent, as discussed in Chapter 6. The criteria for determining the Primary Referent of a clause are listed below.

(1)   Criteria for Primary Referent
       Events
       a. Undergoes a change of state
       b. Causally affected by another participant
       c. Doesn't exist independently of the event
       d. Moves or otherwise changes

       States
       e. Literally or metaphorically located
       f. Dependent on the situation for existence
       g. Figure relative to a Ground
       h. Has a property ascribed to it

These criteria determine the Primary Referents in Informative and Argument text passages. They are applied to text passages below.

10.1.1   Subjectivity

In texts of all modes there are forms that convey subjectivity, access to a mind. The major categories are communication, contents of mind, evidentiality/evaluation, and perception and perspective. To interpret the forms of subjectivity we identify the mind responsible – the Responsible Source – and its scope.

Verbs of communication introduce quoted speech, represented speech, and indirect speech. Indirect speech is systematically ambiguous: responsibility for the content may rest with the reporter or with the original speaker. In reports of belief and other contents of mind such as "Mary believed that John was sick" we ascribe the belief expressed in the complement clause to Mary. Perception and perspective follow the same principles as contents of mind. The speaker is responsible for modals, evidentials, and evaluative forms unless they are clearly associated with a text participant.

The scope of a subjective form may extend over several sentences, so long as subjective continuity is maintained. Subjective continuity is broken with a change of time or place, or introduction of a new candidate for Responsible Source.

10.1.2   Presentational progression

The surface structure of sentences determines presentation. The main factors are the initial phrase, the final phrase, grammatical relations, how information is organized; and how sentences are connected to each other in a text. Sentences may be linked by poset linking, in the technical sense presented in Chapter 9, or connected by weaker relations of familiarity.

Presentational progression depends on sentence topics: texts progress from one topic phrase to another. The subject phrase is canonically the topic of a sentence, since the subject is salient grammatically and positionally. In non-canonical structures other phrases may be topic. If there is no topic the entity introduced is the locus for progression.

The topic phrase refers to what a sentence is about. The main criteria for identifying the topic phrase are salience, familiarity, and continuity. The criteria are listed below, repeated from Chapter 8.

(2)   Criteria for Topic Phrase
        An NP may be the topic phrase of a sentence if it
        a. is the subject of a sentence;
        b. is a pronoun;
        c. realizes the agent or experiencer argument of the main verb;
        d. is coreferential with the topic phrase in the preceding sentence;
        e. is coreferential with a topic phrase in the context;
        f. is coreferential with a phrase in the context;
        g. is lexically related to other material in the context;
        h. is in a parallel grammatical position with an NP in the context.

NPs with sentence accent or other focus cues are not candidates for topic.

This approach allows for some variation in the position of topic phrases. However, there is a striking consistency in the text passages that I have examined. Topics almost always appear in the subject position of a sentence, whether the syntactic structure is canonical or not.

10.1.3 *Patterns of organization in texts*
Three patterns of presentational progression were identified in Daneš (1974); they are still useful. The topic phrases of sentences relate to each other, and to focus phrases, in different ways. As Daneš notes, various combinations of these patterns can appear in a text.

The first pattern, which I call Focus–Topic Chaining, is a simple linear pattern in which the focus phrase referent of one sentence appears as the topic of the next; the examples are from Daneš (1974):

(3)   Focus–Topic Chaining
        1 The first of the antibiotics was discovered by Sir Alexander Flemming in 1982. 2 He was busy at the time investigating a certain species of germ which is responsible for boils and other troubles.

"Sir Alexander Flemming" is the focused referent of S1 and the topic referent ("he") of S2. "A certain species of germ" is focus of S2, and topic of the relative clause at the end of S2. The chaining relation is allowed by the syntactic structures of the sentences. The passive S1 ends with a proper name, which is coreferential with the subject and topic phrase of S2.

The second type has a "continuous theme": the same topic referent recurs in a succession of sentences. I call this type Topic Chaining, following Givón (1983).

(4)   Topic Chaining
       The Rousseauist especially feels an inner kinship with Prometheus and other Titans. *He* is fascinated by any form of insurgency...*He* must show an elementary energy in his explosion against the established order and at the same time a boundless sympathy for the victims of it. Further, *the Rousseauist* is ever ready to discover beauty of soul in anyone who is under the reprobation of society.

All sentences in (4) have the same topic, *the Rousseauist*. Note the shift from pronoun subject back to full nominal in the last sentence. The shift suggests a change of direction, perhaps the end of a paragraph, as noted in Chapters 6 and 9.

In the third type, Unchained, each sentence has a different topic and a different focus referent, as in (5). The sentences of the passage are not unrelated, however: they all predicate something about New Jersey, as Daneš recognized:

(5)   Unchained
       New Jersey is flat along the coast and southern portion; the northwestern region is mountainous. The coastal climate is mild, but there is considerable cold in the mountain areas during the winter months. Summers are fairly hot. The leading industrial production includes chemicals,... food, coal, petroleum, metals, and electric equipment.

The topic pattern approach does not give a way to establish the connections we intuitively make between these sentences.

The connections can be established nicely by the poset linking of Chapter 9. Recall that poset linking relates a referent to a salient poset that can be inferred in the context. In (5) each subject phrase after the first sentence refers to a characteristic of New Jersey. The poset of such characteristics is evoked by the "New Jersey" in the first sentence. Thus the topic phrases of (5) are in effect chained at the level of poset linking.

The topic phrases in the examples are all surface structure subjects, although the syntactic position is not the concern of the topic pattern analysis. This is the position that recurs strikingly across the text passages examined for this study.

Topic phrases tend to appear at the beginning of a sentence, usually as subject and occasionally in an inverted or preposed phrase; and they tend to involve relatively familiar information. The pattern was noticed in work of the Prague School, in Halliday (1967), and has the status of a truism today. Nevertheless I know of few detailed studies of texts that demonstrate the pattern and how it comes about.[1] Note that the language and the notion of topic allows other positions for the topic phrase. In fact, I showed in Chapters 8 and 9 that topic phrases need not be in subject position. However, topic phrases in non-subject position are rare in the texts of this informal study.

10.2   *Multiple analyses of text passages*

This section presents analyzed examples of each mode, as in the first chapter; we are now in a position to discuss and more fully appreciate the analysis.

I begin with a passage in the Narrative mode, first presented in Chapter 1. There are two versions: the first shows the situation entities and text progression in tensed clauses, the second adds subjectivity and topic information.

(6)   Narrative a: Situations and Text Progression
$1_E \to$ A few days later I called on Dr P and his wife at home, with the score of the Dichterliebe in my briefcase and a variety of odd objects for the testing of perception. $2a_E \to$ Mrs. P showed me into a lofty apartment, b_S which recalled fin-de-siècle Berlin. $3a_S$ A magnificent old Bösendorfer stood in state in the centre of the room, b_S and all around it were music stands, instruments, scores. $4a_S$ There were books, b_S there were paintings, c_S but the music was central. $5a_E \to$ Dr. P came in, a little bowed, b_E and $\to \emptyset$ advanced with outstretched hand to the grandfather clock, c_E but, $\emptyset$ hearing my voice, $\to$ corrected himself, d_E and $\to \emptyset$ shook hands with me. $6a_E \to$ We exchanged greetings b_E and $\to \emptyset$ chatted a little of current concerts and performances. 7 Diffidently, $a_E \to$ I asked him b_S if he would sing.

The clauses with event verb constellations all have the perfective viewpoint, presenting bounded events. They are taken as sequential, advancing the narrative, on the continuity tense pattern. States are expressed in clauses 2b, 3a–b, 4a–c, and 7b; they are located at the preceding Reference Time on the limited anaphora tense pattern. Since states overlap or surround Reference Time the states are not limited to that time but are understood as continuing indefinitely before and after it. The state sentences constitute a small descriptive passage in themselves.

I now add information about subjectivity and topic phrases; forms of subjectivity appear in bold, and the topic phrases are italicized. Several clauses

1. This pattern was demonstrated for the essay The Elements of Ethics by Bertrand Russell in Smith (1971).

are presentational and do not have topics; for them, the phrases introducing referents are noted with single quotes.

(7)   Narrative b: Situations, text progression, **subjectivity**, *Topic*

$1_E \rightarrow$ A few days later *I* called on Dr P and his wife at home, with the score of the Dichterliebe in my briefcase and a variety of odd objects for the testing of perception. $2a_E \rightarrow$ Mrs. P showed *me* into a lofty apartment, b_S *which* **recalled** fin-de-siècle Berlin. $3a_S$ *A magnificent old Bösendorfer* stood in state in the centre of the room, b_S and all around it were 'music stands, instruments, scores.' $4a_S$ There were 'books,' b_S there were 'paintings,' c_S but *the music* was central. $5a_E \rightarrow$ *Dr. P* came in, a little bowed, b_E and $\rightarrow \phi$ advanced with outstretched hand to the grandfather clock, c_E but, ϕ hearing my voice, $\rightarrow$ corrected himself, d_E and $\rightarrow \phi$ shook hands with me. $6a_E \rightarrow$ *We* exchanged greetings b_E and $\rightarrow \phi$ chatted a little of current concerts and performances. 7 Diffidently, $a_E \rightarrow$ *I* asked him b_S if *he* would sing.

The topic phrases are subjects in all but one clause. Most have several topic properties. In 1, and 5–7 the topic phrases are agents. After S1 the dynamic topic phrases are coreferential with earlier phrases; the clauses in 5–6 have parallel syntactic structures.

The topic pattern follows the shift in mode from Narrative to Description and back. The first narrative chunk has two clauses, 1 and 2a; the sentences are related by Topic Chaining.[2] The second chunk, a description, consists of clause 2b, and 3 and 4. 2b is linked to 2a by Focus–Topic Chaining. The other clauses have no topic phrase. Sentences 4a–b are existential *there*-sentences; S3b is a predicate inversion structure. The inverted pronoun is linked to the context, since it is coreferential with the topic of the preceding clause. The inversion maximizes continuity. The third chunk, also narrative, has Topic Chaining. At S6 the focus phrase of 5c is picked up, and the topic shifts from "Dr. P" to "we"; then to "I."

The one subjective expression is the verb "recall" which implies an experiencer. Since the narration is in the first person, the Responsible Source is both author and participant.

The next example is a passage in the Descriptive mode. The mode is temporal and static: time does not change. Text progression is spatial through the scene. The phrases that indicate spatial location are underlined; phrases that introduce referents in presentational clauses are in single quotes.

---

2. The topic phrase of clause 2a is the direct object of a canonical S-V-O sentence. The subject and object phrases are both possible topics: they meet slightly different criteria. The subject "Mrs P" is coreferential with "his wife" in S1, and has the agent role. The object is coreferential with the topic of S1 and a pronoun. I identify the object pronoun as the topic phrase, by the criteria of local topic continuity.

(8)   Description a: Situations and <u>spatial progression</u>
        1$_S$ <u>The front part</u> of the shop was cluttered with goods for tourists. 2$_S$ There
        were 'locally knit sweaters' <u>on shelves</u> on the walls, '<u>tables</u> of pottery' –
        some of which Mara had made – and '<u>trays</u> of trinkets', such as key-rings
        bearing the Dales National Park emblem – the black face of a Swaledale
        sheep. 3$_S$ As if that weren't enough, <u>the rest of the space</u> was taken up by fancy
        notepaper, glass paperweights, fluffy animals and fridge-door magnets shaped
        like strawberries or Humpty Dumpty. 4$_S$ <u>In the back</u>, though, the setup was
        very different. 5a$_S$ <u>First</u>, there was a 'small <u>pottery workshop</u>,' complete with
        wheel and dishes of brown and black metallic oxide glaze, b and <u>beyond that</u>
        [there was] 'a drying room and a small electric kiln.' 6a$_S$ <u>The workshop</u>$_i$ was
        dusty and messy, crusted with bits of old clay, b and <u>it</u>$_i$ suited a part of Mara's$_j$
        personality. 7a$_S$ Mostly <u>she</u>$_j$ preferred cleanliness and tidiness, b$_S$ but there
        was 'something special,' c she found, about creating beautiful objects in a
        chaotic environment.

The verb constellations are all states, though of different types. The first clauses
are locational; 6b and 7 indicate personal experience. The passage begins with
a tour of the front of the shop, then moves to the back with its workshop and
drying room, and to Mara. The spatial progression is due to lexical information
and world knowledge.

This passage occurs in a novel, just after a dialogue between Mara and a
friend; context and the subjective forms indicate the perspectival standpoint of
Mara. The subjective elements are given in bold in (9).

(9)   Description b: Situations, <u>spatial progression</u>, **subjectivity**
        1$_S$ <u>The front part</u> of the shop was cluttered with goods for tourists. 2$_S$ There
        were 'locally knit sweaters' <u>on shelves</u> on the walls, '<u>tables</u> of pottery' – some
        of which Mara had made – and '<u>trays</u> of trinkets,' such as key-rings bearing the
        Dales National Park emblem – the black face of a Swaledale sheep. 3$_S$ **As if that**
        weren't enough, <u>the rest of the space</u> was taken up by fancy notepaper, glass
        paperweights, fluffy animals and fridge-door magnets shaped like strawberries
        or Humpty Dumpty. 4$_S$ <u>In the back</u>, **though**, the setup was very different.
        5a$_S$ <u>First</u>, there was a 'small <u>pottery workshop</u>,' complete with wheel and
        dishes of brown and black metallic oxide glaze, b$_i$ and <u>beyond that</u> [there
        was] 'a drying room and a small electric kiln.' 6a$_S$ <u>The workshop</u>$_i$ was dusty
        and messy, crusted with bits of old clay, b and <u>it</u>$_i$ suited a part of Mara's$_j$
        personality. 7a$_S$ **Mostly** <u>she</u>$_j$ preferred cleanliness and tidiness, b$_S$ but there
        was 'something special,' c **she found**, about creating beautiful objects in a
        chaotic environment.

The introductory phrase of S3 "As if that weren't enough" is a sentence adverb
or parenthetical; we take it as the voice of Mara, the Responsible Source for all
the subjective elements in the paragraph. The second clause of S7 gives Mara's
thought: the inversion is typical of represented thought and speech.

The third version of the passage adds topic information. The topic phrases are italicized; in sentences without topics, phrases in presentational constructions appear in single quotes.

(10)   Description c: Situations, <u>spatial progression</u>, **subjectivity**, *topic*

1$_S$ *The front part* of the shop was cluttered with goods for tourists. 2$_S$ There were 'locally knit sweaters' <u>on shelves</u> on the walls, 'tables of pottery' – some of which Mara had made – and '<u>trays</u> of trinkets,' such as key-rings bearing the Dales National Park emblem – the black face of a Swaledale sheep. 3$_S$ **As if that weren't enough,** *the rest of the space* was taken up by fancy notepaper, glass paperweights, fluffy animals and fridge-door magnets shaped like strawberries or Humpty Dumpty. 4$_S$ <u>In the back</u>, **though**, *the setup* was very different. 5a$_S$ <u>First</u>, there was 'a small <u>pottery workshop</u>,' complete with wheel and dishes of brown and black metallic oxide glaze, b and <u>beyond that</u> [there was] 'a drying room and a small electric kiln.' 6a$_S$ *The workshop*$_i$ was dusty and messy, crusted with bits of old clay, b and <u>it</u>$_i$ suited a part of Mara's$_j$ personality. 7a$_S$ **Mostly** <u>*she*</u>$_j$ preferred cleanliness and tidiness, b$_S$ but there was 'something special,' c **she found**, about creating beautiful objects in a chaotic environment.

When spatial location and topic phrase coincide, a phrase has both underlining and italics.

The subject and topic phrases in all but the last sentence are related by poset linking. The passive in S3 puts the locational phrase in subject position; the preposed phrase in S4 also highlights location. Both S2 and 5a–b are presentational *there*-sentences which do not have a topic phrase. The quotation inversion of S7b puts presentational "there" in subject position. Thus the paragraph has relatively few topic phrases. The effect is to highlight the spatial progression.

Now consider a passage in the Report mode, from Chapter 2; as usual only the tensed clauses are analyzed.

(11)   Report: Situations, temporal progression, **subjectivity**, *topic*

1a At his news conference **here**, a$_E$ even before *he* took questions, b$_E$ → *Schroeder* implicitly challenged the official US explanation for the bombing of the Chinese embassy in Belgrade – that c$_E$ target analysts relied on a faulty street map – by renewing his demand for a formal NATO inquiry into the bombing.

2a$_E$ → Diplomats **say** that *Schroeder*, b$_E$ who just returned from China, c$_S$ was angry that c$_E$ *a trip* d$_S$ he had long planned to herald his chairmanship of the European Union was transformed into an official apology for the embassy bombing.

The situation entities in this passage are all events and states. The passage is intricate in syntax and temporal relations. There are two events in S1, related to each other. The temporal clause has strong focus due to the operator "even."

The event of the appositive clause is not related to the others except by world knowledge. S2 returns to the present with a report about the past. The subjective elements have different sources. For the deictic "here" the author is Responsible Source. For the complement of the "say" the Responsible Source is the subject referent, "diplomats." Presentational progression proceeds by Topic Chaining until S2c, where a new topic appears.

An Informative passage is presented in (12). The entities are marked as subscripts on clauses – "Ge" for Generalizing sentence; the Primary Referent phrases are underlined.

(12)   Informative a: Situation entities, <u>Primary Referents</u>
         1a$_{Ge}$ <u>The Information Revolution</u> is now at the point b$_{Ge}$ at which <u>the Industrial Revolution</u> was in the early 1820s, about forty years c$_E$ after James Watt's improved steam engine (first installed in 1776) was first applied, in 1785, to <u>an industrial operation</u> – the spinning of cotton. 2a$_{Ge}$ And <u>the steam engine</u> was to the first Industrial Revolution what b$_{Ge}$ <u>the computer</u> has been to the Information Revolution – its trigger, but above all its symbol. 3a$_{Ge}$ Almost everybody today believes b$_{Ge}$ that <u>S</u> [nothing in economic history has ever moved as fast as, or had a greater impact than, <u>the Information Revolution</u>]. 4a$_{Ge}$ But <u>the Industrial Revolution</u> moved at least as fast in the same time span, b$_{Ge}$ and ϕ had probably <u>an equal impact</u> if not a greater one.

The choices of Primary Referent are justified below. The letters following each phrase refer to the relevant criterion for Primary Referent in (1).

(13)   Justification for Primary Referents of (12)
         1. a. "The Information Revolution": *e* metaphorical location
            b. "Industrial Revolution": *e* metaphorical location
            c. "an industrial operation": *b* causally affected
         2. a. "the steam engine": *e* metaphorical location
            b. "the computer": *e* metaphorical location
         3. a. S: *e* metaphorical location, object of belief
            b. "the Information Revolution": *d* entity that moves (metaphorically)
         4. a. "Industrial Revolution": *d* entity that moves (metaphorically)
            b. "an equal impact": *f* dependent on the situation

The Primary Referents are in parallel throughout the passage. The text progresses from the "Information Revolution" and "Industrial Revolution" to more detail with "steam engine" and "computer"; in the last two sentences the first parallel is resumed. There is little metaphorical motion in the passage.

Next consider the presentational aspects of the passage. The topic phrases are in italics, the Primary Referents are underlined, and the subjective forms are in bold. The syntax is relatively complex in the predicates of the clauses, but this does not affect the topic phrases: they are the subject NPs in every clause.

(14)   Informational b: *Topic*, <u>Primary Referent</u>, **subjectivity**
1a$_{Ge}$ *The Information Revolution* is **now** at the point b$_{Ge}$ at which <u>*the Industrial Revolution*</u> was in the early 1820s, about forty years c$_E$ after James Watt's improved *steam engine* (first installed in 1776) was first applied, in 1785, to <u>an industrial operation</u> – the spinning of cotton. 2a$_{Ge}$ And *the steam engine* was to the first Industrial Revolution b$_{Ge}$ what <u>*the computer*</u> has been to the Information Revolution – its trigger, but above all its symbol. 3a$_{Ges}$ Almost *everybody* **today** believes b$_{Ge}$ that nothing in economic history has ever moved as fast as, or had a greater impact than, the Information Revolution. 4a$_{Ge}$ But <u>*the Industrial Revolution*</u> moved at least as fast in the same time span, b$_{Ge}$ and ϕ had **probably** <u>an equal impact</u> if not a greater one.

Topic and Primary Referent are the same in S1a–b, S2a–b, and S4a. They differ in clauses expressing events with effects or changes: S3b and S4b. The topic referent tends to be the cause of a change or an effect in canonical sentences; the Primary Referent is usually the entity that changes.

Finally I present a short passage in the Argument mode. The first version indicates the situation entities and the Primary Referents:

(15)   Argument a: Situations, <u>Primary Referents</u>
1a$_S$ A pretty good argument can be made <u>that</u> b$_{Prop}$ <u>the defining moment</u> of American democracy didn't occur in 1776 or 1787, as commonly supposed, but in 1801 – on the day c$_E$ that <u>John Adams</u>, having been beaten at the polls, quietly packed his things and went home. 2a$_E$ Only then did we know for sure b that$_{Fact}$ <u>the system</u> worked as advertised.
3a$_{Ge}$ <u>The routine transfer of power</u> may not be the most dramatic feature of American democracy, b but <u>it</u> is the most important.

(16)   Justification for Primary Referents of (15)
1. a. "that S," clausal complement: *f* dependent on the situation
   b. "defining moment": *e* temporally located
   c. "John Adams": *d* moves
2. a. "that S," clausal complement: *e* metaphorically located (possessed mental State)
   b. "the system": *h* property ascribed
3. a. "The routine transfer of power": *h* property ascribed
   b. "it": *h* property ascribed

The first two sentences introduce abstract entities. The complement *that*-clause in S1b refers to a proposition. The corresponding *wh*-question form would be ungrammatical, so it meets the substitution criteria for a proposition, discussed in Chapter 4. The complement clause of 2b refers to a fact: it is a *that*-clause, and would allow substitution of the *wh*-question form. The entity introduced by S1a is technically a state because of the modal; S2a introduces an event because the verb "know" is used in an inchoative sense, meaning "come to know." S3 is a generalizing stative: it does not express a particular situation.

Metaphorical progression is from the specific to the general; "defining moment," "John Adams," and then "the system," "the routine transfer of power."

Now I add subjective information. The passage has several indications of subjectivity, all with the author as Responsible Source. The dense subjective forms partly explain the strong sense of authorial presence.

(17)   Argument b: Situations, <u>Primary Referents</u>, **subjectivity**
        1a$_S$ A pretty good argument **can** be made <u>that</u> b$_{Prop}$ <u>the defining moment</u> of American democracy didn't occur in 1776 or 1787, **as commonly supposed**, but in 1801 – on the day c$_E$ that <u>John Adams</u>, having been beaten at the polls, quietly packed his things and went home. 2a$_E$ Only **then** did **we** know for sure b that$_{Fact}$ the system worked as advertised.
        3a$_{Ge}$ <u>The routine transfer of power</u> **may** not be the most dramatic feature of American democracy, b but <u>it</u> is the most important.

Also contributing to the sense of subjectivity is the agentless passive, which in context suggests the author as maker of the argument, and the lexical item *for sure*, arguably an evidential.

The topic phrases are consistently subjects.

(18)   Argument c: Situations, <u>Primary Referents</u>, **subjectivity**, *topic*
        1a$_S$ *A pretty good argument* **can** be made <u>that</u> b$_{Prop}$ *<u>the defining moment</u>* of American democracy didn't occur in 1776 or 1787, **as commonly supposed**, but in 1801 – on the day c$_E$ that *<u>John Adams</u>*, having been beaten at the polls, quietly packed his things and went home. 2a$_E$ Only **then** did **we** know for sure b that <u>S</u>$_{Fact}$ *the system* worked as advertised.
        3a$_{Ge}$ *<u>The routine transfer of power</u>* **may** not be the most dramatic feature of American democracy, b but *<u>it</u>* is the most important.

The main clause of S1 is passive, putting the phrase "a pretty good argument" in subject position. S2 has a preposed adverbial phrase with subject–auxiliary inversion. The syntax highlights the temporal adverbial by putting it in initial position; demotes the subject phrase from its canonical position of prominence; and highlights the complement clause, now in final position. Thus non-canonical syntax enables the topic phrase pattern.

The topic phrases are not related by chaining, poset linking, or familiarity. Both presentational and text progression pick out the same phrases in four clauses, giving the text a strong forward sense. When topic and Primary Referent phrase are different, as in the other three clauses, the organization is more complex.

This explication sorts out some of the information conveyed and automatically processed by the reader in the text passage above.

10.3   Formalization in Discourse Representation Structures

The interpretation of text passages has been formalized in rules and representations of Discourse Representation Theory as much as possible. Where there is a close connection to the linguistic forms, construction rules can be written. Thus situation entities, temporal advancement, and subjectivity are recognized by formal rules and entered into a Discourse Representation Structure.

For atemporal progression, the Primary Referents of a clause can be identified according to thematic role information. However, the calculation of whether metaphorical location has changed cannot be treated in the same manner. Such calculation needs another kind of reasoning, and access to several sources of information. Similarly, spatial progression and topic progression are beyond the scope of this kind of discourse representation.

The structures developed here could serve as input to richer interpretation. As I suggest in Chapter 9, this kind of pragmatic interpretation may be parallel to the analysis given in the DRSs here.

This section presents a Discourse Representation Structure for one temporal and one atemporal text passage. For the temporal passage, the DRS gives information about situation type, temporal advancement, and subjectivity. The DRS for the atemporal passage has situation type, Primary Referent, and subjectivity. Temporal information is included but it does not key text progression for this passage.

Because of the complexity of a full DRS I give only short, simplified passages. The DRS below is based on the first two sentences of the narrative fragment in (6):

(19)   1 A few days later I called on Dr P and his wife at home. 2a Mrs. P showed me into a lofty apartment, 2b which recalled fin-de-siècle Berlin.

I give some explanatory comments on the DRS beforehand.

The times of the different clauses are listed with subscripts a, b, c. Speech Time is always the default for t_1, it is not entered as a condition in the DRS. Since this passage occurs in the middle of a narrative, the event of S1, e_1, is related to a previously established past time. I assume a prior Reference Time (RT), noted as t_{2a-1}; the RT of the first sentence, t_{2a}, follows that time, by the principle of narrative advancement. The event of S2a, e_2, also advances the narrative: t_{2b} follows t_{2a}. S2b introduces a state, which has the same RT as the prior Event, by the principle of limited anaphora.

The coreference judgments are assumed. Coreference is automatic for "I" and "me," and for "a lofty apartment" and "which"; but recognizing "Mrs. P" and "his wife" as coreferential is based on pragmatic knowledge.

The subjective form is the state verb "recall." The implicit Experiencer argument is included with the state condition, and its content given in a sub-DRS, indicated by dots. The Author is a discourse entity (A) at the top of the DRS, and is interpreted as Responsible Source, RS. Identifying the RS with the narrator is automatic for a first-person narrator since the passage has no other candidate for this role. The referents of the "recall" relation appear in the sub-DRS and also in the main DRS because their existence is not contingent on the sub-DRS.

(20)   1 A few days later I called on Dr P and his wife at home. 2a Mrs. P showed me into a lofty apartment, 2b which recalled fin-de-siècle Berlin.

t_{1a} t_{2a} t_{3a} x y z w e1 t_{1b} t_{2b} t_{3b} u v s e2 t_{1c} t_{2c} t_{3c} r q p o A

1. e_1: call on (x,y,z)
2. $t_{2a} < t_{1a}$
3. $t_{2a} > t_{2a-1}$
4. t_{2a} = a few days later t_{2a-1}
5. $t_{3a} = t_{2a}$
6. x = I
7. y = Dr P, z = his wife
8. w = later

9. e_2: show (u,v into s)
10. $t_{2b} < t_{1b}$
11. $t_{2b} > t_{2a}$
12. $t_{3b} = t_{2b}$
13. u = z
14. v = x
15. s = a lofty apartment

16. s: recall (r, ... to p)
17. $t_{2c} < t_{1c}$
18. $t_{2c} = t_{2b}$
19. $t_{3c} = t_{2c}$
20. r = s
21. o = fin-de-siècle Berlin
22. p = x
23. p = A
24. A = Author
25. A = RS ...

RS ...

q p

26. q = r
27. p = o

The next DRS interprets an atemporal text passage. I use a simplified fragment from a passage presented earlier. The DRS encodes information about Discourse Mode – situation entities and Primary Referents – and subjectivity.

(21)   Within the next fifty years fish farming may change us from hunters and gatherers into marine pastoralists. It is likely that other new technologies will appear.

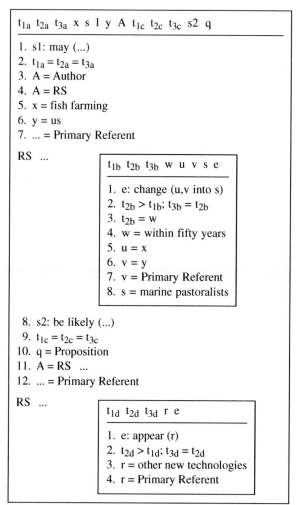

The situation entities of the fragment consist of states, a proposition, and events in the sub-DRSs. The complement clause of "likely" refers to a proposition, as we know from the class of predicate and the substitution possibilities ("that S" may appear but not a *wh*-complement).

Entities of situations, times, and individuals appear at the top of the DRS if they exist independently. In the first clause, for instance, "fish farming" and "us" are listed independently; but "marine pastoralists" depends for existence on the sub-DRS. In the second clause "other new technologies" depends on the sub-DRS.

The Primary Referents are identified by a condition on the entity. In each case the complement is Primary Referent for the clause. Within the first complement, "us" is Primary Referent, the entity that changes; within the second complement, "other new technologies" is primary, dependent on the situation for existence.

There are forms of subjectivity in both clauses; the Author is the Responsible Source.

Example sources in this chapter:

(6–7) Oliver Sacks, *The Man who Mistook His Wife for a Hat*, New York: Harper & Row, 1970, p. 11.

(8–10) Peter Robinson, *A Necessary End*, New York: Avon Books, 1989, p. 103.

(11) German chancellor vows to block use of ground forces in Yugoslavia. *New York Times*, May 20, 2000.

(12, 14) Peter Drucker, The information revolution. *Atlantic Monthly*, October 1999.

(15, 17) Alan Ehrenhalt, Hijacking the rulebook. *New York Times*, December 20, 1998.

11 *Discourse structure and Discourse Modes*

This inquiry into local text structure has stayed close to the linguistic ground, concentrating on linguistic forms and categories. In this final chapter I widen the range of discussion to consider some of the organizing principles of discourse. I begin with hierarchical structure and functional units, and then discuss discourse relations. Finally, I comment on how the Discourse Modes pertain to discourse relations and to lexical patterns, which distinguish units at different levels of text structure.

11.1 *Organizing principles of texts*

11.1.1 *Hierarchical structure*

Discourse is organized by its purpose, like many other human activities. To understand its structure we can turn to work in cognitive science on intentions and plans generally. Intentions have hierarchical structure, G. Miller, Galanter, & Pribram argue convincingly in an early study. They propose an abstract unit, the Test-Operate-Test-Exit or TOTE, to represent such structures. TOTE units can be used to model human intentional behavior: they represent a top level of control in planning and executing intentions. Intentions themselves are organized hierarchically into sub-goals, which in turn may have sub-goals, and so on. For instance, to hammer something once a person must plan and execute the two sub-goals of lifting and striking (1960:33):

(1)   HAMMER
            /   \
       Lifting   Striking

Repeated hammering consists of many such steps, each with the same hierarchically organized sub-goals. More complex activities have many sub-goals. Even a relatively simple activity such as going to work has a number of sub-goals: getting ready, leaving the house, deciding how to get there, choosing a route, etc.

If we assume that intentions are hierarchical, and that discourse is organized into functional units of goals and sub-goals, we both predict and explain its hierarchical nature. The recognition of hierarchical structure has led to studies of how plans are made, executed, and recognized, as in Allen & Perrault (1980), Litman (1985). Much of this work applies to written discourse as planned, intentional action. Intentional structure is proposed as a distinct level of discourse structure by Grosz & Sidner (1986).

The intuition that texts have hierarchical structure is shared by all who work with them. Hierarchical structure is often modeled in abstract tree structures.[1] The units posited may function as part of the global structure of the discourse; their parts may be topically related;[2] or they may realize discourse relations such as Causation, Evidence, etc., discussed below.

11.1.2 Functional units

Texts consist of functional units that are hierarchically structured, each contributing to the purpose of the whole. The units each realize a goal and may have smaller units with their own sub-goals.

The functional units and their sub-structure are evident in "scripted" discourse such as legal trials and task-oriented activities. Dialogues between experts and novices on dismantling a water-pump were studied in Grosz (1977). Grosz found that the dialogue structure mirrored the structure of the task. Other types of discourse are organized implicitly by the nature of the material. Asked to describe the layouts of their apartments, people consistently came up with clearly defined journeys through the apartments, treating each room as a separate unit (Linde & Labov 1975). Scientific reports are structured quite rigidly, according to recognized convention.

---

1. Linguists come to this conclusion from many traditions; they include Halliday (1967), Linde (1979), Grimes (1975), Longacre (1983/1996), Polanyi (1988), Martin (1992), and many others.

   The tree structures of linguistics are generated with phrase structure rules, which encode hierarchical relations. Thus the first rule of a simple sentence grammar might be: S → NP + VP which would be realized in a tree structure with a topmost node S, dominating the two nodes NP and VP:

2. Topically related means, roughly, "about the same thing." The parts of a topically related segment may or may not have an explicit shared topic; see Chapter 8 for discussion.

Narrative often has a relatively clear functional structure. Gerald Prince in his 1987 *Dictionary of Narratology* recognizes three main units: Beginning, Complicating Action, End.[3] Each of these units may have a relatively complex internal structure. For instance, the Complicating Action may have one or more episodes. An episode consists of a coherent set of situations that have "some kind of thematic unity – identical participants, time, location, global Event or action" (van Dijk 1982:199). There is experimental evidence from psycholinguistics that people use episodes for encoding story information in memory (Black & Bower 1980).

The functional units of a text can be determined by analyzing its intentional structure. For instance, Longacre discusses the structure of a fund-raising letter. He identifies a main goal of influencing and finds four parts, or "high-level moves," of the letter (1992:110): (i) establish authority; (ii) present problem and solution; (iii) issue command to contribute money; (iv) motivation, threats and promise. The parts are realized by different sections of the letter. The functional units for other types of text can be determined by understanding their intentional structure.

11.2   *Discourse relations*

This section begins by introducing discourse relations; 11.2.1 gives some background; 11.2.2 discusses current approaches; in 11.2.3 I suggest three main classes of discourse relations.

Texts are understood in terms of abstract units that realize discourse relations. They may consist of situations related by Cause or Result, or by rhetorical relations such as Elaboration, Evidence, Parallelism, etc. These units do not consist directly of clauses or sentences, but of the situations and propositions evoked by a text. They are hierarchical in structure, organized by the relationship that is realized. The units are also known as "coherence relations" and "discourse coherence relations."

People recognize or construct relations between the entities and propositions introduced in a discourse. They do this by inference if the relation is not explicitly given. In (2) is a natural example in which the situations expressed are related tacitly by causation:

---

3. In a study of spoken personal narratives, Labov & Waletsky (1966) posit similar functional units: Orientation, Action, and Evaluation, with an optional Preface. These studies owe much to the work of Propp (1958), which identified the basic units of stories and the ways in which they combine and vary.

(2)   (a) He was in a foul humor. (b) He hadn't slept well that night. (c) His electric blanket hadn't worked.

The event of (2b) is the cause of the state expressed in (2a), and (2c) gives the cause of the situation in (2b); the example is cited by Hobbs (1985:13). The urge to find relations is so powerful that we can make sense of almost anything even if many inferences are needed. Inventing texts which are incoherent is actually quite difficult; Knott gives this example (1996:3):

(3)   Sally decided to take the history course. The ducks on the lake were not eating the bread.

He comments that the text fragment can be understood if we imagine Sally to have unusual superstitions about the ducks on the lake.

Discourse relations notionally weave together into relational units clauses or larger parts of a text – more precisely, the entities, propositions, and concepts that they express. They segment texts into abstract units of increasing size: the larger units overlap or coincide with genre-based functional units. I will refer to the material related by a discourse relation as a "relational segment." The units that realize discourse relations are hierarchically structured and hold for spans of discourse of virtually any size. Within such a unit, or relational segment, more than one such relation may be realized.

After a brief discussion of background and types of discourse relations, I propose that three classes of relations be recognized.

11.2.1   Background of discourse relations

Discourse relations appear in different guises in most efforts to understand text structure. In the mid-1970s linguists discussed "coherence" and "deep structure" relations which need not be overtly marked on the surface of the text. Grimes (1975) proposes a set of "rhetorical predicates": they form abstract propositions that relate material in the text. The list includes Conditionality, Causation, Equivalence, Amplification, Summary, Identification, Example. Specifically, Grimes distinguished two types of predicates: "paratactic predicates" dominate all of their arguments in coordinate fashion; with "hypotactic predicates" one argument is the center and the other subordinate. The relation of Explanation is hypotactic, for instance: one argument is central and the subordinate argument different in kind (1975:216).

The basis for many of these ideas comes from linguists who translated the Bible into different languages. According to Grimes, Fuller's (1959) work on

Bible study was the first attempt to identify and work with discourse relations. Fuller recognized "increasingly large sections of text according to a small number of explicit organizing relations" (Grimes 1975:208). The approach is further developed in Beekman (1970). Along similar lines, Halliday & Hasan noted four types of "underlying semantic relations" which they saw as conjunctions that are optionally signaled on the surface: Additive, Adversative, Causal, and Temporal (1976). Again, Longacre (1983) discusses deep structure relations, "combinations of predications" into larger units; his list includes such notions as Conjunction, Contrast, Alternation, Comparison.

11.2.2   Current approaches

Understanding of how discourse works advanced quite dramatically in the 1980s with the impetus of Artificial Intelligence. Computational study of discourse structure led to Jerry Hobbs' (1985) theory of coherence relations. Hobbs was interested in the inferences that people make in understanding a text, and the kinds of knowledge that are implicit in such inferences. He theorized that understanding of a text proceeds as the receiver constructs "discourse coherence relations" between its parts. Hobbs posited four classes of relation: (1) Occasion relations, which concern events and states; (2) Evaluation relations, which relate "what has been said to a goal of the conversation"; (3) a class that relates segments of discourse to the listener's prior knowledge, e.g. Background and Explanation; and (4) Expansion relations such as Exemplification, Generalization, Contrast, Violated Expectation.

   Another approach is Rhetorical Structure Theory, which seeks relational propositions in a text (Mann & Thompson 1987, 1992). The theory describes "relational organization" according to the relations between "spans of text." Relations may be indicated by particular words, or be implicit in the text. Mann & Thompson build on Grimes' insight about types of relations. They distinguish symmetric and asymmetric relations, assigning the latter a Nucleus–Satellite structure. Most relations are asymmetric, including Evidence, Justify, Solution, Circumstance, Enablement, Elaboration. For instance, in an Elaboration segment one part is the primary nucleus and the elaborating part is the satellite. Symmetric relations include Contrast, List, and Sequence. The relations hold for successively larger spans of a discourse. Mann & Thompson give examples in which entire texts are analyzed into relational segments with hierarchical internal structure.

   One major insight about discourse relations is that they do not depend on the presence of words that explicitly signal such relations, words such as *because*, *and, but*, etc. Nevertheless there has been some useful study of such words. Schiffrin looked at the distribution and interpretation of certain "discourse markers" in conversation. She found that the scope of these words varies: for instance, in some contexts *because* has scope over multiple clauses (Schiffrin 1987:197).[4] Knott (1996) collected over 200 such "cue words" and used them in a substitution task to test for basic discourse relations that are psychologically real.

Relational words and concepts are not always one-to-one. For instance, the relation "cause" is signaled by several cue words, e.g. *so, therefore, consequently, thus, as a result*. Conversely, one word may indicate different relations, e.g. *but* can indicate "thesis–antithesis" and/or "concession" (Mann & Thompson 1987:71). Relational words do not necessarily translate directly from one language to another: the semantic space covered may differ (Fabricius-Hansen & Behrens 2000). In computational generation of texts, Hovy uses a large set of coherence relations. He distinguishes three classes, Semantic, Interpersonal, and Presentational (1993). Grosz & Sidner (1986) offer a computationally based theory of text structure that emphasizes attentional and intentional phenomena. They argue that it is futile to seek a fixed list of discourse purposes, instead recognizing two general "intentional structural relations," dominance and satisfaction–precedence.

Taking a semantic–pragmatic approach, Asher & Lascarides have developed formal accounts of certain discourse relations (Lascarides & Asher 1993). They propose a defeasible logic and theory of commonsense entailment to account for the patterns of inference that people use. Their aim is to "place knowledge in a logic where its implications can be precisely calculated" (1993:439). For simple narrative texts they offer a procedure for determining the relations of Elaboration, Explanation, Narration, and Background in short text segments (Asher & Lascarides 2000).

The abstract relational structures of discourse are represented in an extension of DR Theory, Segmented Discourse Representation Theory (SDRT). The theory, due to Asher (1993), constructs hierarchical structures of text segments that realize the relational segments of discourse relations. The output of the SDRT construction rules is not a single DRS but a complex propositional structure of DRSs. The complex representation is a recursive structure of clausal

---

4. Schiffrin (1987) posits the following components: exchange, action, and idea structures; information State; participation framework. She investigated the expressions *oh, well, and, but, or, so, because, now, then, I mean, y'know*. Some of these expressions signal relations in the sense under discussion here, others do not.

DRSs, linked together by relations such as Narration and Parallel. The construction procedure requires that new units be attached only to tree nodes which are "structurally accessible." The rightmost nodes of each sub-tree or constituent are taken to be accessible, following Polanyi (1988).

In the extended version of the theory, DRSs or SDRSs are organized to form discourse segments. The stated goal is to model as precisely as possible the insights of Hobbs, Mann & Thompson, and others about discourse relations. The theory infers discourse relations with a formal theory of pragmatics which draws on multiple information sources. The sources of information are primarily semantic content, including lexical semantics; domain and world knowledge; and Gricean principles of orderliness. The type of discourse relation that a segment realizes is notated in the SDRT representation.

11.2.3   Classes of discourse relations

People disagree as to whether there is a basic set of discourse relations. Culling different lists, I found that some relations appear often: Cause, Goal or Purpose, Evidence, Elaboration, Background, Contrast, Parallel. Others are more idiosyncratic. For instance, Solution appears on one list only. Mann & Thompson (1987) claim that their list of about twenty relations has been adequate to account for a wide number and range of texts. But it may be futile to attempt an exhaustive listing: another relation can always be found in principle.

The most useful approach may be to classify discourse relations by the kind of contribution they make to a text. I suggest that three such classes of discourse relations be recognized: Consequential, Organizing, and Rhetorical.

Consequential relations hold between the situations introduced in a text. The main consequential relations are Cause, Enablement, and Result. Example (2) above illustrates the Cause relation.

Organizing relations hold between the concepts and propositions of a text, taking proposition as the content that a sentence expresses. The relations in this class are abstract and cover a wide range. The class includes Concession, Contrast, Evaluation, Evidence, Explanation, Elaboration, Generalization, Purpose, Reason, Solution. Some pertain to building an argument or making a case of some kind (Evaluation, Evidence), others would also be appropriate in other contexts as well (Contrast, Elaboration, Purpose, Reason).

The third class of relations, the Rhetorical, reflects how the material of a text is presented. Relations of this class include Parallel, Restatement, and Summary. They relate propositions or stretches of text to each other. These relations do not reflect the way situations or propositions are related, but decisions about the text that presents them.

11.3 Discourse Modes and text structure

This book has taken perhaps as far as possible an analysis of text passages based on linguistic form. I have argued that the Discourse Mode passage is a significant unit of text structure. One natural direction for further study is to look at whether and how the Discourse Modes pertain to discourse relations; another direction is to look at how the modes relate lexical patterns in texts.

The level of discourse relations is more abstract than the passage. Discourse relations are sometimes indicated by particular forms in a text, but they are most often arrived at by pragmatic inference and world knowledge. Relational segments and Discourse Mode passages are units of different types.

There is no simple mapping between Discourse Modes and relational segments. However, the nature of discourse relations suggests certain predictions. One prediction concerns Consequential relations and types of entities. The class of Consequential relations – Cause, Enablement, etc. – relates situations to each other, so that we can predict that relational segments of this class will be realized by the Discourse Modes that introduce such entities.

The distinction between symmetric and asymmetric relations yields other predictions. The symmetric relations should involve entities of the same type. Therefore, we would expect them to be realized by passages of a single Discourse Mode. For instance, a relational segment realizing the Contrast, Alternative, or Parallel relations would probably involve passages of a single Discourse Mode.

Asymmetric relations would be expected to involve different Discourse Modes, following this line of thinking. For instance, the relations of Evidence, Explanation, and Elaboration tend to have parts that are different in kind: they often consist of a generalization and then specifics that illustrate (Grimes 1975:210). Thus, relational segments might have a passage corresponding to the nucleus of the Information or Argument mode; the passage corresponding to the satellite might be of the Narrative, Description, or Report mode. The prediction about the same or different Discourse Modes does not hold generally for the asymmetric discourse relations, however. For some relations, e.g. Circumstance and Antithesis, one would expect nucleus and satellite to involve the same type of discourse entity. We can expect to learn more about discourse relations by looking carefully at how they are expressed in terms of the Discourse Modes. The interaction of the Discourse Modes with discourse relations is another topic for investigation.

Turning to lexical patterns, the lexical items of a text fall into clusters that at once mirror and contribute to text organization. Patterns of lexical co-occurrence and distribution can be used to divide a discourse into units, as noted in Chapter 2, and the units developed on this basis correspond nicely to topic boundaries. A natural question is how Discourse Mode passages relate to units like this, which are established on a lexical basis. One might expect them to coincide. Indeed, it would be surprising if a shift from one Discourse Mode to another did not have ramifications, lexical and notional. Lexical ramifications would include changes in the lexical items expressed by passages of a given Discourse Mode. There might also be shifts at the boundaries of Discourse Mode passages in types of repetition and coreference. For the notional ramifications of Discourse Modes I turn to the level of discourse relations.

11.4   Conclusion

The classification of text passages into Discourse Modes is a fairly radical extension of aspectual and temporal notions, and it has been quite successful in bringing out important features of texts. The essential point is that the modes are notional units with linguistic correlates.

This book is devoted to English, but it is likely that Discourse Modes are a general phenomenon in language. There are bound to be differences in the linguistic correlates to the Discourse Modes. Some language-particular correlates are already known: for instance, in French the Descriptive mode is conventionally realized by the *imparfait*, a past tense with the imperfective viewpoint. The linguistic features of abstract entities may vary, since not all languages have the formal variety in their clausal complements of English. The expression of temporal progression in tenseless languages must rely on linguistic features other than tense. The features of the discourse modes provide a useful research tool for studying similarities and differences between languages.

Appendix A: The texts

Appendix A presents a selection of texts that are found frequently in the chapters. Short texts are given in their entirety; fragments are excerpted from the longer texts. Unless otherwise noted, the fragment begins at the beginning of the text. The original paragraphing is preserved. The texts are given in the order presented in this book.

The texts: (a) from *A Necessary End*, by Peter Robinson, New York: Avon Books, 1989, p. 182; (b) Barak fights on many fronts, *New York Times*, May 20, 2000; (c) Cheap oil's tough bargains by Robert Mosbacher, *New York Times*, March 13, 2000; (d) After a victory. Ethiopia looks toward other fronts, *New York Times*, May 20, 2000; (e) from Cell communication, by John Scott & Tony Pawson, *Scientific American*, June, 2000; (f) from Listening to humpbacks, by Douglas H. Chadwick, *National Geographic*, July 1999; (g) from Slave-making queens, by Howard Topoff, *Scientific American*, November 1999; (h) Hijacking the rulebook, by Alan Ehrenhalt, *New York Times*, December 20, 1998; (i) The Information Revolution, Peter Drucker, *Atlantic Monthly*, October 1999; (j) *The Chinese Potter*, by Margaret Medley, London: Phaidon, 1989; (k) from The pride of the cities, by Peter Beinart, *New Republic*, June 1997; (l) from How it works, by Jim Collins, *US Airways Magazine*, *Attaché*, May 2001; (m) from "The Dead" by James Joyce. In *Dubliners*, 1916; reprinted London: Penguin Books, 1982, pp. 177–79; (n) Let teenagers try adulthood, by Leon Botstein, *New York Times*, May 1999.

THE TEXTS

(a)   *Fragment from* A Necessary End, *by Peter Robinson; pages 81ff.*

Mara walked along the street, head down, thinking about her talk with Banks. Like all policemen, he asked nothing but bloody awkward questions. And Mara was sick of awkward questions. Why couldn't things just get back to normal so she could get on with her life?

"Hello, love," Elspeth greeted her as she walked into the shop.

"Hello. How's Dottie?"

"She won't eat. How she can expect to get better when she refuses to eat, I just don't know.

They both knew that Dottie wasn't going to get better, but nobody said so.

"What's wrong with you?" Elspeth asked "You've got a face as long as next week."

Mara told her about Paul.

"I don't want to say I told you so," Elspeth said, smoothing her dark tweed skirt, "but I thought that lad was trouble from the start. You're best rid of him, all of you."

"I suppose you're right." Mara didn't agree, but there was no point arguing Paul's case against Elspeth. She hadn't expected any sympathy.

"Go in the back and get the wheel spinning, love," Elspeth said. "It'll do you a power of good."

The front part of the shop was cluttered with goods for tourists. There were locally knit sweaters on shelves on the walls, tables of pottery – some of which Mara had made – and trays of trinkets, such as key-rings bearing the Dales National Park emblem – the black face of a Swaledale sheep. As if that weren't enough, the rest of the space was taken up by fancy notepaper, glass paperweights, fluffy animals and fridge-door magnets shaped like strawberries or Humpty Dumpty.

In the back, though, the setup was very different. First, there was a small pottery workshop, complete with wheel and dishes of brown and black metallic oxide glaze, and beyond that a drying room and a small electric kiln. The workshop was dusty and messy, crusted with bits of old clay, and it suited a part of Mara's personality. Mostly she preferred cleanliness and tidiness, but there was something special, she found, about creating beautiful objects in a chaotic environment.

She put on her apron, took a lump of clay from the bin and weighed off enough for a small vase. The clay was too wet, so she wedged it with a flat concrete tray, which absorbed the excess moisture. As she wedged – pushing hard with the heels of her hands, then pulling the clay forward with her fingers to get all the air out – she couldn't seem to lose herself in the task as usual, but kept thinking about her conversation with Banks.

Frowning, she cut the lump in half with a cheese wire to check for air bubbles, then slammed the pieces together much harder than usual. A fleck of clay spun off and hit her forehead, just above her right eye. She put the clay down and took a few deep breaths, trying to bring her mind to bear only on what she was doing.

No good. It was Banks's fault, of course. He had introduced her to speculation that caused nothing but distress. True, she didn't want Paul to be guilty, but if, as Banks had said, that meant someone else she knew had killed the policeman, that only made things worse.

Sighing, she started the wheel with the foot pedal and slammed the clay as close to the centre as she could. Then she drenched both it and her hands with water from a bowl by her side. As the wheel spun, clayey water flew off and splashed her apron.

She couldn't believe that any of her friends had stabbed Gill. Much better if Osmond or one of the students had done it for political reasons. Tim and Abha seemed nice enough, if a bit naive and gushing, but Mara had never trusted Osmond; he had always seemed somehow too oily and opinionated for her taste.

(b)   *A year after victory, Barak fights on many fronts.* New York Times, *May 20, 2000*

A week that began in violence ended violently here, with bloody clashes in the West Bank and Gaza and intensified fighting in Southern Lebanon. On the one-year anniversary of his election by a sweeping majority, Prime Minister Ehud Barak was trying to put out fires on many fronts at once. Because of trouble in the north, the south, and within his political coalition, he was weighing a cancellation of his scheduled departure this weekend to the United States to confer with President Clinton and meet with Jewish American leaders.

Despite the violence, back-channel talks continued in Sweden. Israelis, Palestinian and American officials have characterized them as a serious and constructive dialogue on the process itself and on the final status issues.

News accounts here say that Israel is offering as much as 90 percent of the West Bank to Palestinians, although it is difficult to assess what is really happening by the bargaining moves that are leaked.

Near a heavily fortified Jewish settlement in the Gaza Strip, an Israeli soldier and a Palestinian policeman were wounded as Palestinian protests for the release of 1,650 prisoners degenerated into confrontations. Israeli military officials say they are investigating the source of fire that wounded the soldier, but that there was no gun-battle between troops like the one that took place on Monday near Ramallah in the West Bank.

"The prime minister views the events severely and has ordered the Israeli Defense Forces to act accordingly to restore calm," Mr. Barak's office said in a statement tonight.

The protests today, which began as the Friday prayer services ended, were organized before Monday's demonstrations erupted into severe rioting that ended with three Palestinians dead. Palestinian authorities said they were trying to keep tensions low, although in Ramallah their effort did not appear to be of sustained high intensity. Many officers stepped to the side as a march, organized by the militant Islamic group Hamas, headed toward confrontation with the Israeli forces. In Qalqilya, in contrast, Palestinian police officers held back demonstrators with nightsticks.

At least 20 Palestinians were injured by rubber-coated bullets. Another "day of rage" was scheduled for Saturday. It was unclear whether the violence would delay the transfer of Abu Dis and two other villages near Jerusalem to the Palestinian Authority. Mr. Barak's advisers said he would turn over the towns within days, provided that Palestinian officials calmed the streets and cooperated with their investigation of how things got out of hand on Monday.

In the north, Israeli warplanes attacked suspected guerrilla positions in southern Lebanon today. This followed fighting Thursday, the heaviest in two weeks, in which 14 people were wounded, including 4 Lebanese civilians and a United Nations peacekeeper.

(c)   *Cheap oil's tough bargains, by Robert Mosbacher,* New York Times, *March 13, 2000*

The press has trumpeted the news that crude oil prices are three times higher than they were a year ago. But it was the $10 or $11 price of February 1999, not the one today, that really deserved the headlines.

When inflation is taken into account, that 1999 price was the lowest in modern history, while oil has gone above today's seemingly high price several times. And for the past 14 years, at $17.50, oil has been one of the real bargains of the modern age.

The low price has been a mixed blessing. In the United States, we have lost over 500,000 jobs in the oil industry while we have grossly increased our dependency on foreign oil; we now import 55 percent of what we use. With little incentive for drillers to find and tap new oil, supplies eventually dropped, and in the past year the Organization of Petroleum Exporting Countries deliberately dropped its production as well. In response to the law of supply and demand, prices have now risen.

A high oil price is not the inflationary threat it once was because with the shift toward the information and service economy, and away from manufacturing, the United States is less dependent on oil. But try to tell a consumer paying to heat his home, a trucker moving goods across the country or a commuter who goes by car that oil and gasoline are not major factors in the economy, and the answer is likely to be, "It feels like I'm being ripped off."

American consumers have been lulled into thinking cheap oil is their entitlement. Syndicated columnist Carl T. Rowan wrote recently: "We are truly a spoiled society! We insist on driving gas guzzlers and using a grossly disproportionate amount of the world's energy, and we believe we should forever be able to do so at bargain rates."

Sooner or later, oil prices are likely to drop. But prices at today's level have their advantages. With the incentive for more production back in place, there will be more drilling in new places, like the deep water off the coasts of many countries of the world, including the United States. Off our Gulf Coast, deep-water drilling, developing and producing are already going on.

Remarkable new technology now allows pipelines to bring oil from miles out to sea, where the water is as much as 8,000 feet deep. The ubiquitous deep waters of the world have great potential for additional oil and gas reserves, but drilling in 5,000 to 10,000 feet of water and then through many thousands of feet of sand, shale and other formations makes for huge costs. In many cases, this kind of oil production can only be justified by prices of at least $25 to $35 a barrel.

A high price also encourages development of other new technologies already on the horizon, including three-dimensional seismology for mapping and horizontal drilling. And $30 oil also brings attention back to development of synthetic fuel, solar energy, wind power, gasification of coal and other methods of producing energy.

Some members of Congress have been lobbying for taking oil from the Strategic Petroleum Reserve to help bring prices down, and President Clinton recently announced he is not ruling this out. But these reserves are set aside for use in an emergency, and tapping them is only justified if there is a genuine threat of a supply interruption, as there might be in a war or political crisis. The reserve holds about 570 million barrels, not much when we use about 19.4 million barrels of oil products daily. Even releasing all of it could be only a temporary solution to the price problem. Tapping it would also signal the main oil-producing countries that we were trying to control world energy prices, which is inconsistent with our normal free and fair trade policies.

Even if the control of oil prices were in American hands, which it is not (since we have no means of influencing it other than using our reserves or jawboning OPEC), we would still face a daunting decision. Would we be better off getting prices back under $20 a barrel to prevent any oil-influenced inflation today, or should we take the longer view and let today's price work to bring about more drilling and new interest in other sources of energy?

Simple realities argue for the latter course: In the long term, even if bent by cartels, the law of supply and demand will rule. And in the long term, we will need the new sources of energy that high prices can bring.

(d)   *After a victory, Ethiopia looks toward other fronts.* New York Times,
        May 20, 2000

It took three days for Ethiopian troops to battle their way into this town, and now that they have it, they are pressing deeper into Eritrea, denying with every step that they plan any long-term invasion of their neighbor and once-tight ally. "We have no intentions, no plans, no need to occupy Eritrea," an Ethiopian commander, Colonel Gabre Kidane, said tonight as he stood on the old Italian fortress in this hilly town 45 miles inside Eritrea. "The only intention we have is to weaken the forces that have occupied our country and to regain our sovereignty. That is all."

A week after Ethiopia started an offensive that it says is aimed at ending the two-year-old war, it is now clear that the whole of Eritrea could become a battlefield. With hundreds of civilians fleeing the region, Colonel Kidane said Ethiopian soldiers continue to skirmish with Eritrean soldiers on the run here in western Eritrea.

Tonight, Ethiopian officials said planes bombed the main Eritrean military training center at Sawa, an American-built base 100 miles west of Asmara, the capital. The officials also said they had taken a village, Maidema, 30 miles from Asmara, on the way from the western front to the central front along the disputed border. That is where the next round of fighting, already heavy, is generally expected.

For Eritrea, Ethiopia's rapid advance out of the border trenches into the countryside is not merely a military setback. For 30 years, when Eritrea was the northernmost province of Ethiopia, rebels fought two successive governments in Addis Ababa for their independence. Those rebels, the Eritrean People's Liberation Front, are now in power in Eritrea, and they say this advance is a frightening continuation of Ethiopia's attempts at domination.

An Eritrean government statement said today that a bombing on Thursday south of the port of Massawa killed a civilian. That death, the statement said, was "further evidence of Ethiopia's resurgent aim to annex this country and, in so doing, to make targets of Eritrea's civilian populations." Ethiopia said the target was a military installation.

The paradox is that the leaders of Ethiopia fought side by side with the Eritreans to oust the military government of Mengistu Haile Mariam in 1991. For the first two years, the two governments were close friends, so close that they never demarcated the border when Eritrea became independent in 1993. But tensions grew over personality clashes and economic rivalry, exploding in May 1998 when Eritrea claimed the Badme border region based on old colonial maps. Eritrea moved troops into the area. Ethiopia said it was invaded, and a war ignited that has defied long peace talks and claimed tens of thousands of lives on both sides.

Until Ethiopia began its offensive last Friday, the fighting had been confined to three fronts along the 620-mile border. But since then, Ethiopia has pressed 65 miles into Eritrea, displacing 340,000 people, the World Food Program said today.

Officials in neighboring Sudan said today that an additional 50,000 Eritreans had fled across their border. In both places, relief officials said, people lack food and shelter. Even without the war, the United Nations says 800,000 Eritreans face food shortages because of drought. Most civilians fled from around this town, the regional capital and a strategically important point because the area was a main supply route for Eritrea's westernmost front.

The battle has been intense. Starting on Monday, Colonel Kidane said, Ethiopian troops had pounded areas around the town with bombs, tanks and artillery and then engaged Eritrean troops along a mountain pass eight miles from town. Along the heavily mined road from the south, the route of Ethiopia's advance, huge numbers of empty mortar shells, captured Eritrean ammunition and destroyed trucks from both sides remain. At spots, the smell of rotting corpses was strong. Colonel Kidane would not give the number of casualties.

On Thursday morning, Ethiopian troops took the town, the biggest one that they have captured, and called it a major victory. The Eritreans said they had staged a tactical withdrawal.

This evening, Ethiopian troops milled around and ate their rations at the hilltop building that was once a fortress for Italian troops in the colonial period and that, until Thursday, according to the Ethiopians, was the command center for Eritrean troops in the region. The Ethiopians joked about marching to Asmara. "It's nice to take the place of the invading army," said an Ethiopian soldier, Seife Yechenju, 21, who has fought in the army since the war began. "There is no question that I am very happy."

(e)   Fragment from cell communication, by John D. Scott & Tony Pawson,
          Scientific American, *June 2000*

As anyone familiar with the party game "telephone" knows, when people try to get a message from one individual to another in a line, they usually garble the words beyond recognition. It might seem surprising, then, that mere molecules inside our cells constantly enact their own version of telephone without distorting the relayed information in the least.

Actually, no one could survive without such precise signalling in cells. The body functions properly only because cells communicate with one another constantly. Pancreatic cells, for instance, release insulin to tell muscle cells to take up sugar from the blood for energy. Cells of the immune system instruct their cousins to attack invaders, and cells of the nervous system rapidly fire messages to and from the brain. Those messages elicit the right responses only because they are transmitted accurately far into a recipient cell and to the exact molecules able to carry out the directives.

But how do circuits within cells achieve this high-fidelity transmission? For a long time, biologists had only rudimentary explanations. In the past 15 years, though, they have made great progress in unlocking the code that cells use for their internal communications. The ongoing advances are suggesting radically new strategies for attacking diseases that are caused or exacerbated by faulty signaling in cells – among them cancer, diabetes and disorders of the immune system.

The earliest insights into information transfer in cells emerged in the late 1950s, when Edwin G. Krebs and Edmond H. Fischer of the University of Washington and the late Earl W. Sutherland, Jr., of Vanderbilt University identified the first known signal-relaying molecules in the cytoplasm (the material between the nucleus and a cell's outer membrane). All three received Nobel Prizes for their discoveries.

By the early 1980s researchers had gathered many details of how signal transmission occurs. For instance, it usually begins after a messenger responsible for carrying information between cells (often with a hormone) docks temporarily, in lock-and-key fashion, with a specific receptor on a recipient cell. Such receptors, the functional equivalent of antennae, are able to relay a messenger's command into a cell because they are physically connected to the cytoplasm. The typical receptor is a protein, a folded chain of amino acids. It includes at least three domains: an external docking region for a hormone or other messenger, a component that spans the cell's outer membrane, and a "tail" that extends a distance into the cytoplasm. When a messenger binds to the external site, this linkage induces a change in the shape of the cytoplasmic tail, thereby facilitating the tail's interaction with one or more information-relaying molecules in the cytoplasm. These interactions in turn initiate cascades of further intracellular signalling.

Yet no one had a good explanation for how communiqués reached their destination without being diverted along the way. At that time, cells were viewed as balloonlike bags filled with a soupy cytoplasm containing floating proteins and organelles (membrane-bound compartments, such as the nucleus and mitochondria). It was hard to see how, in such an unstructured milieu, any given internal messenger molecule could consistently and quickly find exactly the right tag team needed to convey a directive to the laborers deep within the cell that could execute the order.

Today's fuller understanding grew in part from efforts to identify the first cytoplasmic proteins that are contacted by activated (messenger-bound) receptors in a large and important family: the receptor tyrosine kinases. These vital receptors transmit the commands of many hormones that regulate cellular replication, specialization or metabolism. They are so named because they are kinases – enzymes that add phosphate groups to ("phosphorylate") selected amino acids in a protein chain. And, as Tony R. Hunter of the Salk Institute for Biological Sciences in La Jolla, Calif., demonstrated, they specifically put phosphates onto the amino acid tyrosense.

In the 1980s work by Joseph Schlessinger of New York University and others indicated that the binding of hormones to receptor tyrosine kinases at the cell surface causes the individual receptor molecules to cluster into pairs and to attach phosphates to the tyrosines on each other's cytoplasmic tails. In trying to figure out what happens next, one of us (Pawson) and his colleagues found that the altered receptors interact directly with proteins that contain a molecule they called an SH2 domain. The term "domain" or "module" refers to a relatively short sequence of about 100 amino acids that adopts a defined three-dimensional structure within a protein.

At the time, prevailing wisdom held that messages were transmitted within cells primarily through enzymatic reactions, in which one molecule alters a second without tightly binding to it and without itself being altered. Surprisingly, though, the phosphorylated receptors did not necessarily alter the chemistry of the SH2-containing proteins. Instead many simply induced the SH2 domains to latch onto the phosphate-decorated tyrosines, as if the SH2 domains and tyrosenes were Lego blocks being snapped together.

(f)   *Fragment from Listening to humpbacks, by Douglas Chadwick,* National
      Geographic, *July 1999*

When a big whale dives, currents set in motion by the passage of so many tons of flesh come eddying back up in a column that smooths the restless surface of the sea. Naturalists call this lingering spool of glassy water the whale's footprint. Out between the Hawaiian islands of Maui and Lanai, Jim Darling nosed his small boat into a fresh swirl. The whale that had left it was visible 40 feet below, suspended head down in pure blueness with its 15-foot-long arms, or flippers, flared out to either side like wings.

"That's the posture humpbacks most often assume when they sing," Darling said. A hydrophone dangling under the boat picked up the animal's voice and fed it into a tape recorder. We could listen in with headphones but hardly needed them. The music was reverberating through the hull and rising from the waves. Bass rumbles that could have issued from the lowest octave of a cathedral pipe organ gave way to plaintive moans and then to glissandos like air squealing out of a balloon when you stretch the neck taut.

With the notes building into phrases and the phrases into repeated themes, the song may be the longest – up to 30 minutes – and the most complex in the animal kingdom. All the humpbacks in a given region sing the same song, which is constantly evolving. Experts have analyzed the frequencies, rhythms, and harmonics and the way themes change from year to year and vary from one population to the next. Yet no one really understands what these intricate arias are about.

We do know that humpbacks are found in every ocean. Together with blue, fin, sei, Bryde's, and mink whales, they belong to the rorqual family of baleen whales. Fully grown females, which are bulkier than the males, can weigh 40 tons and reach lengths of 50 feet.

Humpbacks tend to favor shallow areas, often quite close to shore, and they are among the most sociable of the great whales and the most active at the surface, all of which makes them among the easiest to observe. As a result, we know more about them than about any other large whale. But we still don't know a lot.

One thing the experts are certain of is that this species, depleted by whaling and not protected throughout its range until 1966, is showing signs of a comeback. Early population estimates are unreliable, and recent ones are hard to get, but numbers in the North Atlantic seem to have rebounded from a few thousand to between 10,000 and 12,000. The North Pacific population was thought to have tumbled from 15,000 to fewer than 2,000. That group stands at 5,000 to 8,000 today.

Knowing I was eager to absorb what biologists have been discovering about humpbacks and their ongoing recovery, Darling, director of the West Coast Whale Research Foundation in Vancouver, British Columbia, brought me along to Hawaii.

Since the singer beneath the boat didn't seem bothered by our company, Darling asked his longtime research partner, photographer Flip Nicklin, who often serves as Darling's eyes underwater, to slip overboard. I followed.

(g)   *Fragment from Slave-making queens, by Howard Topoff,* Scientific American, *November 1999*

In the animal world, both predators and parasites survive at the expense of other species. Nevertheless, they don't get the same press. I am besieged with mail containing pleas for money on behalf of wolves and killer whales, but I have yet to see a T-shirt with the slogan "Long Live the Hookworm." The problem is, of course, that humans associate a parasite lifestyle with disease. Our perception is of a furtive organism that insinuates itself inside us and, unlike a decent predator, intends to destroys us ever so slowly.

... But there exists a form of parasitism considerably less macabre. Social parasitism, as it is called, has evolved independently in such creatures as ants and birds. A female cuckoo, for instance, lays her egg in the nest of another species, such as a warbler, and leaves it for the host to rear. The brown-headed cowbird does the same. Each bird has evolved so that it produces eggs that match those of its chosen baby-sitter.

Even more varied than these avian parasites are the slave-making ants. The unusual behavior of the parasitic ant *Polyergus breviceps* – which I have been studying for 15 years in Arizona at the American Museum of Natural History's Southwestern Research Station – offers a perfect example. Like the other four species of *Polyergus* found throughout the world, these ants have completely lost the ability to care for themselves. The workers do not forage for food, feed the young or the queen, or even clean up their own nest. To survive, *Polyergus* ants must get workers from the related ant genus *Formica* to do their chores for them. Thus, *Polyergus* workers periodically undertake a slave raid in which about 1,500 of them travel up to 150 meters (492 feet), enter a *Formica* nest, expel the *Formica* queen and workers, and capture the pupae.

Back at the *Polyergus* nest, slaves rear the raided brood until the young emerge. The newly hatched *Formica* workers then assume all responsibility for maintaining the mixed-species nest. They forage for nectar and dead arthropods, regurgitate food to colony members, remove wastes and excavate new chambers. When the population becomes too large for the existing nest, it is the 3,000 or so *Formica* slaves that locate another site and physically transport the approximately 2,000 *Polyergus* workers, together with eggs, larvae, pupae and even the queen, to the new nest.

(h)   *Hijacking the rulebook, by Alan Ehrenhalt,* New York Times,
          December 20, 1998

A pretty good argument can be made that the defining moment of American democracy didn't occur in 1776 or 1787, as commonly supposed, but in 1801 – on the day that John Adams, having been beaten at the polls, quietly packed his things and went home. Only then did we know for sure that the system worked as advertised.

The routine transfer of power may not be the most dramatic feature of American democracy, but it is the most important. It separates us from the majority of countries in the world, which have still not achieved it. Conceding defeat and going home, or staying on in the minority and allowing the winner to govern – these are not just the elements of good manners and sportsmanship. They are the core of patriotism.

Those are rather windy thoughts, but I have had a hard time escaping them the last few weeks as I've tried to make some sense of the events surrounding President Clinton, Congress and impeachment. What will people say about all this 20 years from now? Will they quiz each other on the minutiae of the Starr report, as they do on the contents of the Warren report? Will the cigar and the stained dress become icons of American political history? Or will posterity simply conclude that one of the two political parties, having lost an election, saw an opportunity to nullify it and proved too weak to resist the temptation?

You may find that a difficult question. I don't. I feel reasonably certain of the final verdict on the current impeachment affair because I think history will see it as the climax of a six-year period marred by a troubling and deepening failure of the Republican party to play within the established constitutional rules.

It was on Election Night 1992, not very far into the evening, that the Senate minority leader, Bob Dole, hinted at the way his party planned to conduct itself in the months ahead: it would filibuster any significant legislation the new Democratic President proposed, forcing him to obtain 60 votes for Senate passage.

This was a form of scorched-earth partisan warfare unprecedented in modern political life. Congress is supposed to operate by majority vote. It is true that the filibuster has a long and disreputable Senate history and that, over the years, it has been used more by Democrats than by Republicans. But only after 1992 did it become the centerpiece of opposition conduct toward an elected President. What the Republicans did in the Senate in 1993 amounted to an unreported constitutional usurpation. It should have been denounced as such at the time, but it wasn't. The punditocracy chose not to notice.

In any case, it worked. Little that the President proposed became law in the two years that he operated with Democratic majorities. There was no health care reform, no economic stimulus package. On the merits, that is just as well. But the procedural consequences turned out to be grave: Congressional Republicans were tempted by success into even more dangerous constitutional mischief.

In the fall of 1995, emboldened by new majorities in both the House and the Senate, they forced the closure of the Federal Government. For all the millions of words that have been written about this event then and since, the reality of it has rarely been portrayed in succinct terms. This was not a political showdown – it was an attempted constitutional coup.

The Founding Fathers provided a mechanism for resolving disputes between Congress and the White House: Congress passes a bill, the President vetoes it, and if sufficient votes do not exist to override the veto, Congress lives with the decision. For the Republicans to act as they did in 1995 – attempting to make the President sign legislation against his will rather than trying to find the votes to override him – was an act of recklessness so blatant that even an inattentive public understood it. Newt Gingrich backed down, the Government reopened, and Mr. Clinton was re-elected.

But Republicans were already on the road to further adventure. In August of 1994, they had orchestrated the dismissal of Robert Fiske, the independent counsel investigating the Whitewater land deal, and replaced him with Kenneth Starr.

Reasonable people may differ on the quality of the evidence Mr. Starr has accumulated, on the tactics he has used, on the way he has presented himself to the public. But his appointment in the first place is impossible to defend.

Republicans selected as independent counsel a lawyer who was already involved in consultations with a plaintiff suing the President in a civil dispute. No one concerned with ultimate constitutional fairness could possibly have made such a choice; no legislative majority interested in the appearance of justice could ever have approved it.

Now it is four years later. Congress is consumed by impeachment, and the majority party seems genuinely puzzled by the absence of public support for the process. It shouldn't be. The American people aren't suspicious about impeachment because of their love for Bill Clinton. They are suspicious, in large part, because of the track record of those bringing the charges. It's not that there is no legitimate case to be made against the President. It's that Republicans, over a six-year career of consistent disrespect for constitutional rules, have forfeited any right to be taken seriously in making it.

The unpleasant truth is that Congressional Republicans, in the generation before 1994, spent too many years out of power – too many years on the sidelines, uninvolved in managing the governmental process and free to lob grenades at the institutions that make it work. Eventually, they became very effective at it: that is one reason they won the election of 1994.

Habits learned over decades do not fade easily. Having been lifted by the American electorate into a position of genuine power, they have continued to behave more like a party of insurgents, probing for cracks in the constitutional structure rather than taking its rules seriously and looking for ways to make them work.

If Republicans in Congress have a common self-image, it is an image of conservatism. No doubt every one of the Republicans in the current House would accept "conservative" as an ideological label. But being a conservative must, in the end, be about something more than tax cuts or family values. It must be about taking some responsibility for the fragile procedures and institutions that over 200 years have made an orderly public life possible.

There is nothing conservative about the way Republicans in Congress have conducted themselves, either in the current impeachment debate or in most of the important confrontations of the past six years. The American people seem to know that, and there is every sign that they are willing to judge accordingly.

(i)   *Fragment from The information revolution, by Peter Drucker,* Atlantic Monthly, *October 99*

The truly revolutionary impact of the Information Revolution is just beginning to be felt. But it is not "information" that fuels this impact. It is not "artificial intelligence." It is not the effect of computers and data processing on decision-making, policymaking, or strategy. It is something that practically no one foresaw or, indeed, even talked about ten or fifteen years ago: e-commerce – that is, the explosive emergence of the Internet as a major, perhaps eventually the major, worldwide distribution channel for goods, for services, and, surprisingly, for managerial and professional jobs. This is profoundly changing economies, markets, and industry structures; products and services and their flow; consumer segmentation, consumer values, and consumer behavior; jobs and labor markets. But the impact may be even greater on societies and politics and, above all, on the way we see the world and ourselves in it.

At the same time, new and unexpected industries will no doubt emerge, and fast. One is already here: biotechnology. And another: fish farming. Within the next fifty years fish farming may change us from hunters and gatherers on the seas into "marine pastoralists" – just as a similar innovation some 10,000 years ago changed our ancestors from hunters and gatherers on the land into agriculturists and pastoralists.

It is likely that other new technologies will appear suddenly, leading to major new industries. What they may be is impossible even to guess at. But it is highly probable – indeed, nearly certain – that they will emerge, and fairly soon. And it is nearly certain that few of them – and few industries based on them – will come out of computer and information technology. Like biotechnology and fish farming, each will emerge from its own unique and unexpected technology. Of course, these are only predictions. But they are made on the assumption that the Information Revolution will evolve as several earlier technology-based "revolutions" have evolved over the past 500 years, since Gutenberg's printing revolution, around 1455. In particular the assumption is that the Information Revolution will be like the Industrial Revolution of the late eighteenth and early nineteenth centuries. And that is indeed exactly how the Information Revolution has been during its first fifty years.

The Railroad

The Information Revolution is now at the point at which the Industrial Revolution was in the early 1820s, about forty years after James Watt's improved steam engine (first installed in 1776) was first applied, in 1785, to an industrial operation – the spinning of cotton. And the steam engine was to the first Industrial Revolution what the computer has been to the Information Revolution – its trigger, but above all its symbol. Almost everybody today believes that nothing in economic history has ever moved as fast as, or had a greater impact than, the Information Revolution. But the Industrial Revolution moved at least as fast in the same time span, and had probably an equal impact if not a greater one. In short order it mechanized the great majority of manufacturing processes, beginning with the production of the most important industrial commodity of the eighteenth and early nineteenth centuries: textiles. Moore's Law asserts that the price of the Information Revolution's basic element, the microchip, drops by 50 percent every eighteen months. The same was true of the products whose manufacture was mechanized by the first Industrial Revolution. The price of cotton textiles fell by 90 percent in the fifty years spanning the start of the eighteenth century. The production of cotton textiles increased at least 150-fold in Britain alone in the same period. And although textiles were the most visible product of its early years, the Industrial Revolution mechanized the production of practically all other major goods, such as paper, glass, leather, and bricks. Its impact was by no means confined to consumer goods. The production of iron and ironware – for example, wire – became mechanized and steam-driven as fast as did that of textiles, with the same effects on cost, price, and output. By the end of the Napoleonic Wars the making of guns was steam-driven throughout Europe; cannons were made ten to twenty times as fast as before, and their cost dropped by more than two thirds. By that time Eli Whitney had similarly mechanized the manufacture of muskets in America and had created the first mass-production industry.

(j)   Fragment from The Chinese Potter, *by Margaret Medley; p. 106*
The predominant output was the white ware with transparent ivory toned glaze which made the kilns famous. The other wares were a soft, dark brown or dense black glazed type, which is rare, a white ware painted in soft iron brown of rather light tone, again a rare type, and a group of uncertainly dated monochrome and polychrome lead glazed earthenwares about which there is at present relatively little information.

The kilns clearly specialized in the production of the porcellanous ware. It is characterized by the extreme whiteness and hardness of the body, which may be translucent, and the glassy, transparent, and warm ivory tone of the glaze. On some bowls this may show what the Chinese call "tear stains," slight thickenings where the glaze has run down the foot after dipping. That the kilns confined themselves very largely to the production of bowls, basins, dishes and plates, is evident from the immense waste heaps in the vicinity of the kilns, and from the predominance of these shapes in collections all over the world. There is by contrast a very small number of vases. It was good economic sense to limit production to the most popular and practical forms; for it made the achievement of high quality and large output easier; moreover it may well have contributed to the long survival of the kilns in this somewhat remote area.

During the late tenth and early eleventh centuries production was more varied than it became later. There are, for instance, vases and jars dating from this fairly early stage with rather heavily carved decoration in which lotus petals played a large part. By the second half of the eleventh century production was already concentrated, to the virtual exclusion of other shapes, on the manufacture of open and flat wares with carved and incised decoration of floral scrolls and sprays (especially lotus), of ducks and geese among reeds, dragons, and of fish. The carving and incising was a highly developed skill and must have been carried out by craftsmen specially trained in this work. Were this not the case it would be almost impossible to account for the consistency in design, the fluency of line and the almost unequalled high quality.

(k)   *Fragment from The pride of the cities, by Peter Beinart,* New Republic, *June 1997*

Michael White, the mayor of Cleveland, is a Democrat, an African American and the son of a union activist. And he is at war with his party. First, he backed an end to forced busing. Then, he supported Republican Governor George Voinovich's radical school choice law, which offers students vouchers at parochial as well as private schools. Then, he made city workers compete against private firms for garbage collection, road maintenance and other contracts, prompting union officials to walk out of a speech he gave at the Democratic National Convention. Now, he's allied with the governor again, backing a bill by two Republican State legislators to grant him control over Cleveland's destitute school system and the authority to get "rid of any people who aren't directly tied to the direct education of children." Arrayed against him: the teachers' union, the NAACP and just about every elected Democrat in the city of Cleveland.

For a big-city mayor to be so at odds with his party would seem peculiar. Except that it's happening everywhere. Mike White got the idea to take over the schools from Richard Daley, the Democratic mayor of Chicago, who battled the municipal unions and his own party's nominee for governor, and two years ago won the right to introduce radical reforms to the management of Chicago's public schools. And White learned about the introduction of competition into city services in part from a study trip he and his staff took to Indianapolis, where Republican Mayor Steven Goldsmith has reduced city bureaucracy so radically that he's angered both patronage-minded GOP officials and the traditional pro-Republican police unions. Goldsmith is also viewed as a "kindred spirit" by Mayor John Norquist of Milwaukee, a Democrat who, for the sin of supporting Republican Governor Tommy Thompson's welfare and school choice reforms, has made himself persona non grata with his city's public employee unions, the NAACP and the Democratic speaker of the House of Representatives.

It goes on. Los Angeles Mayor Richard Riordan, whose support for affirmative action, gay rights and Senator Dianne Feinstein has led GOP Californians to dub him a RNO (Republican in Name Only), journeyed to Indianapolis during his first week in office and cited Goldsmith in his inaugural address. And Rudolph Giuliani, the Mario Cuomo-endorsing, illegal-immigrant defending, New York Republican who recently admitted that ideologically he is a "moderate Democrat," has met with Goldsmith on four separate occasions. Giuliani and Riordan also received pre-inauguration seminars from Philadelphia Mayor Ed Rendell, a Democrat, who, like Mike White, forced city employees to compete for contracts with outside firms, outraging municipal unions and most of his party.

Something interesting is happening here. Over the past five years or so, a half dozen Democratic and Republican mayors have come together in what an aide to one calls "an informal network." They speak to each other regularly, they cite each other without prompting, they copy each other's initiatives. In almost every case, they represent a radical break with their predecessors in office, and that break is largely about managing city government efficiently in the public interest rather than using it as a mechanism for arbitrating competing group interests. The new mayors are hugely popular: Mike White, Richard Daley, Steven Goldsmith, John Norquist, Richard Riordan and Ed Rendell have all been re-elected by wide margins, and Rudy Giuliani will almost certainly follow suit this fall. But they are outsiders in their own parties, viewed with suspicion and even contempt by the parties' most powerful constituencies. To explain their success and their iconoclasm, the press often dubs them pragmatists. But that misses the point. They have an ideology: that cities can dramatically alleviate seemingly endemic urban afflictions without a massive redistribution of wealth, that the way to achieve this is by using competition to make city services radically more efficient, and that cities must tolerate diverse identities without celebrating them to the detriment of a shared sense of public interest. These ideas have a coherence and a history. They just don't have a party, yet.

The history is progressivism. At the turn of the last century, America's cities were a scandal. The squalor, pathology and cultural transformation to which mass immigration had given rise shocked and terrified the native-born middle class. And, as outraged as they were by the immigrants themselves, respectable people were even more hostile to the municipal regimes the immigrants spawned. As Andrew White, the president of Cornell, wrote in the journal *Forum* in 1890, "the city governments of the United States are the worse in Christendom."

The political machines that men like White despised had been created to bridge the material and cultural distance separating the immigrants from native society. In cities that offered newcomers few formal services, and in which the private sector often remained closed, the immigrant-driven city machines supplied housing, fuel, charity and – most importantly – jobs. Under machine leadership, America's cities built roads, sewers, streetlights and railcars at a furious pace, usually with little attention to the projects' cost-effectiveness, creating as many jobs as possible and distributing them to appease different constituencies. As Kenneth Fox notes in *Better City Government*, his history of that era, America's big cities in 1880 spent more than twice as much per capita as did the federal government. And the machines appealed to the immigrants symbolically as well as materially, installing ward leaders and aldermen who looked and talked like them, and defending their traditions against a disapproving native middle class that wanted to close down the immigrants' saloons and their dance halls – and bust their corrupt, powerful machines.

(l)   Fragment from How it Works, by Jim Collins, US Airways Magazine, Attaché, *May 2001*

The largest and most complex highway-engineering project in American history has been making headlines over the past several months. Boston's central artery project, known as the Big Dig, has become nightly news fare thanks to the massive cost overruns and steadily growing complaints of mismanagement and corruption. Overshadowed by scandal, the work itself – whose scale and ambition are truly mind-boggling – continues almost as matter of course.

The heart of the project is an eight-to-ten-lane highway. It is being built below ground to relieve the legendary traffic pressure caused by Boston's two major arteries, which converge downtown awkwardly near the harbor, skyscrapers, and historic buildings.

Threading 35 lane-miles of tunnel through Boston's 3-D maze of subway lines and building foundations, all without drastically disturbing the normal routines of surface life, is an engineering plan that borders on the fantastic. In some places the tunnels are 120 feet deep. In some particularly delicate places the road-work passes within just a few feet of skyscraper foundations or beneath construction projects. The first two frequently asked questions on the project's official Web site are "What are you building?" and "Are you nuts?"

Surprisingly, tunnels are among the most ancient engineering feats. The earliest were very likely extensions of prehistoric cave dwellings. The Babylonians, in the twenty-second century BC, built a masonry tunnel beneath the Euphrates River that connected the royal palace with a major temple. The Egyptians, using copper-bladed saws, excavated long passageways and intricate rooms inside soft-rock cliffs. The Romans built an elaborate network of above- and below-ground acqueducts to carry water. And they tunneled through solid rock by repeatedly heating it with fire and then cooling it with water, causing the rock face to fracture. The greatest of those acqueduct tunnels, which eventually drained Lake Fucino in central Italy, stretched more than three miles underground.

By the 1700s, tunnels were increasingly being constructed for use with canal systems. In the history of freight transportation, prior to the invention of the railroad, canals proved the most logical way to ship material over great distances. Sections of the canals often need to be buried beneath ground, and this was accomplished with long open trenches that were dug down from the surface, faced with masonry, then covered over. Canals of extraordinary length were built in this manner, including the longest in the United States, the 729-feet Union Canal Tunnel in Pennsylvania.

About the same time, an important hard-rock blasting technique was developed using explosives. Dynamite was something new, and it gave engineers their most powerful tool for tunneling through hillsides that couldn't be opened by digging from above.

One of the most famous – and costly – early examples of a corridor blasted with dynamite is the Hoosac Tunnel, in the Berkshire Mountains of Western Massachusetts. Started in 1851, the Hoosac was a desperate attempt to compete with the convenient Hudson River transportation corridor. It was hoped that direct east–west rail service would connect and help exploit the burgeoning centers that were springing up in the Midwest and around the Great Lakes. The planned route had just one major problem: a small mountain directly in its path, an obstacle that would require an unprecedented tunnel almost five miles long. The Hoosac was the first commercial project to make use of the powerful and extremely unstable explosive nitroglycerine. Its human toll would be immense, as science-and-technology writer Fred Hapgood vividly describes: "In those days hard-rock tunnels were dig by chiseling a hole, filling it with explosive, lighting a fuse, running back behind a shield, waiting for the blast, then returning to the heading to wedge reinforcing timers into place, shatter the "muck" with sledges, and shovel it into muckcars for excavation. This cycle could be interrupted at any point by falling rocks or machinery, collapsing timbers, unintended explosions, or a dozen other species of industrial accident, including fire and floods. In 1867 a wooden house built over a shaft caught fire and collapsed downward, killing all 13 in the shift working below. The explosives killed constantly, year after year . . . Nearly 200 were killed on the job.

The Hoosac Tunnel took 22 years and $21 million to complete. As with the Big Dig, critics railed against the project for overruns, poor planning, and delays in the construction schedule. But at 4.82 miles it was an engineering marvel and it remained the longest tunnel in America until 1916. It never came close, though, to approaching the economic expectations of its promoters.

The blasting technique used in the Hoosac's construction remains basically the same to this day. But during the final years of the Hoosac Tunnel's construction, blasting was enhanced by the safer technique of drilling, which British inventor George Law developed in 1865. A hammer tool operated by an air-driven piston was quickly being used to break up rock, which could then be excavated through horizontal shafts called drifts, or lifted through vertical shafts that also provided ventilation and exhaust.

By the time of the rock drill and the great railroad tunnels, a Frenchman named Marc Isambard Brunel had already solved another of tunneling's great challenges: how to excavate below water without mud and water seeping in and causing the opening to collapse. Borrowing an idea from nature, Brunel recreated the action of a tiny marine borer known as the shipworm, whose shell plates allow it to bore through timber and push sawdust out behind as it goes along. Brunel's tunnel shield, a giant iron frame, was forced through soft soil by screw jacks while miners dug through shuttered openings in the shield's forward face. Excavated earth was transported back through the frame as it slowly advanced. Brunel used his rectangular shield to complete the world's first true tunnel in 1843 in London, below the Thames River.

Within a few years such cutting shields would be made smaller, circular, and more powerful. Many of them even made use of compressed air to keep water out while the steel linings were being installed.

And it was these developments, taken together, that set the stage for one of the truly remarkable achievements of the twentieth century, the construction of New York and New Jersey's Holland Tunnel.

(m)   Fragment from "The Dead" by James Joyce; pp. 177–79
"Is it snowing again, Mr Conroy?" asked Lily.

She had preceded him into the pantry to help him off with his overcoat. Gabriel smiled at the three syllables she had given his surname and glanced at her. She was a slim, growing girl, pale in complexion and with hay-coloured hair. The gas in the pantry made her look still paler. Gabriel had known her when she was a child and used to sit on the lowest step nursing a rag doll.

"Yes, Lily," he answered, "and I think we're in for a night of it." He looked up at the pantry ceiling, which was shaking with the stamping and shuffling of feet on the floor above, listened for a moment to the piano and then glanced at the girl, who was folding his overcoat carefully at the end of a shelf.

"O, then," said Gabriel gaily, "I suppose we'll be going to your wedding one of these fine days with your young man, eh?" The girl glanced back at him over her shoulder and said with great bitterness:

"The men that is now is only all palaver and what they can get out of you."

Gabriel coloured, as if he felt he had made a mistake, and, without looking at her, kicked off his galoshes and flicked actively with his muffler at his patent-leather shoes.

He was a stout, tallish young man. The high colour of his cheeks pushed upwards even to his forehead, where it scattered itself in a few formless patches of pale red; and on his hairless face there scintillated restlessly the polished lenses and the bright gilt rims of the glasses which screened his delicate and restless eyes. His glossy black hair was parted in the middle and brushed in a long curve behind his ears where it curled slightly beneath the groove left by his hat. When he had flicked lustre into his shoes he stood up and pulled his waistcoat down more tightly on his plump body. Then he took a coin rapidly from his pocket.

"O Lily," he said, thrusting it into her hands, "it's Christmastime, isn't it? Just . . . here's a little . . ." He walked rapidly towards the door.

"O no, sir!" cried the girl, following him. "Really, sir, I wouldn't take it."

"Christmas-time! Christmas-time!" said Gabriel, almost trotting to the stairs and waving his hand to her in deprecation. The girl, seeing that he had gained the stairs, called out after him: "Well, thank you, sir."

He waited outside the drawing-room door until the waltz should finish, listening to the skirts that swept against it and to the shuffling of feet. He was still discomposed by the girl's bitter and sudden retort. It had cast a gloom over him which he tried to dispel by arranging his cuffs and the bows of his tie. He then took from his waistcoat pocket a little paper and glanced at the headings he had made for his speech. He was undecided about the lines from Robert Browning, for he feared they would be above the heads of his hearers. Some quotation that they would recognize from Shakespeare or from the Melodies would be better. The indelicate clacking of the men's heels and the shuffling of their soles reminded him that their grade of culture differed from his. He would only make himself ridiculous by quoting poetry to them which they could not understand. They would think that he was airing his superior education. He would fail with them just as he had failed with the girl in the pantry. He had taken up a wrong tone. His whole speech was a mistake from first to last, an utter failure.

(n)   *Let teenagers try adulthood, by Leon Botstein,* New York Times, *May 1999*
The national outpouring after the Littleton shootings has forced us to confront something we have suspected for a long time: the American high school is obsolete and should be abolished. In the last month, high school students present and past have come forward with stories about cliques and the artificial intensity of a world defined by insiders and outsiders, in which the insiders hold sway because of superficial definitions of good looks and attractiveness, popularity and sports prowess.

The team sports of high school dominate more than student culture. A community's loyalty to the high school system is often based on the extent to which varsity teams succeed. High school administrators and faculty members are often former coaches, and the coaches themselves are placed in a separate, untouchable category. The result is that the culture of the inside elite is not contested by the adults in the school. Individuality and dissent are discouraged.

But the rules of high school turn out not to be the rules of life. Often the high school outsider becomes the more successful and admired adult. The definitions of masculinity and femininity go through sufficient transformations to make the game of popularity in high school an embarrassment. No other group of adults young or old is confined to an age-segregated environment, much like a gang in which individuals of the same age group define each other's world. In no workplace, not even in colleges or universities, is there such a narrow segmentation by chronology.

Given the poor quality of recruitment and training for high school teachers, it is no wonder that the curriculum and the enterprise of learning hold so little sway over young people. When puberty meets education and learning in modern America, the victory of puberty masquerading as popular culture and the tyranny of peer groups based on ludicrous values meets little resistance.

By the time those who graduate from high school go on to college and realize what is really at stake in becoming an adult, too many opportunities have been lost and too much time has been wasted. Most thoughtful young people suffer the high school environment in silence and in their junior and senior years mark time waiting for college to begin. The Littleton killers, above and beyond the psychological demons that drove them to violence, felt trapped in the artificiality of the high school world and believed it to be real. They engineered their moment of undivided attention and importance in the absence of any confidence that life after high school could have a different meaning.

Adults should face the fact that they don't like adolescents and that they have used high school to isolate the pubescent and hormonally active adolescent away from both the picture-book idealized innocence of childhood and the more accountable world of adulthood. But the primary reason high school doesn't work anymore, if it ever did, is that young people mature substantially earlier in the late 20th century than they did when the high school was invented. For example, the age of menstruation has dropped at least two years since the beginning of this century and not surprisingly, the onset of sexual activity has dropped in proportion. An institution intended for children in transition now holds young adults back well beyond the developmental point for which high school was originally designed.

Furthermore, whatever constraints to the presumption of adulthood among young people may have existed decades ago have now fallen away. Information and images, as well as the real and virtual freedom of movement we associate with adulthood, are now accessible to every 15- and 16-year-old.

Secondary education must be re-thought. Elementary school should begin at age 4 or 5 and end with the sixth grade. We should entirely abandon the concept of the middle school and junior high school. Beginning with the seventh grade, there should be four years of secondary education that we may call high school. Young people should graduate at 16 rather than 18.

They could then enter the real world, the world of work or national service, in which they would take a place of responsibility along with older adults in mixed company. They could stay at home and attend junior college, or they could go away to college. For all the faults of college, at least the adults who dominate the world of colleges, the faculty, were selected precisely because they were exceptional and different, not because they were popular. Despite the often cavalier attitude toward teaching in college, at least physicists know their physics, mathematicians know and love their mathematics, and music is taught by musicians, not by graduates of education schools, where the disciplines are subordinated to the study of classroom management.

For those 16-year-olds who do not want to do any of the above, we might construct new kinds of institutions, each dedicated to one activity, from science to dance, to which adolescents could devote their energies while working together with professionals in those fields.

At 16, young Americans are prepared to be taken seriously and to develop the motivations and interests that will serve them well in adult life. They need to enter a world where they are not in a lunchroom only with their peers, estranged from other age groups and cut off from the game of life as it is really played. There is nothing utopian about this idea; it is immensely practical and efficient, and its implementation is long overdue. We need to face biological and cultural facts and not prolong the life of a flawed institution that is out of date.

Appendix B: Glossary

Abstract entity: The class of situations, and discourse entities, that consists of Facts and Propositions. They are licensed by clausal complements of certain predicates. For instance, the clausal complement of "I know that Mary refused the offer" refers to a Fact; the clausal complement of "Mary's refusing the offer was unlikely" refers to a Proposition.

Accommodation: A type of inference in which the receiver infers the existence of an entity if it is necessary to do so for coherence. For instance on encountering *the cat* if no cat has been introduced, one infers the existence of a cat.

Accomplishment: An event that is telic, durative, and dynamic, resulting in a change of state, e.g. "John ate an apple," "Mary walked to school."

Achievement: An event that is telic, instantaneous, and dynamic, resulting in a change of state, e.g. "Mary won the race," "John reached the top." Instantaneous events consist only of a single stage.

Activity: An event that is atelic, durative, and dynamic, e.g. "John strolled in the park," "Mary slept."

Anaphora: The interpretation of a pronoun or tense that depends on an antecedent for interpretation. For instance, in "John washed himself," "Mary said that she was ready," the anaphor *himself* and the pronoun *she* depend the antecedent proper names for interpretation.

Anaphoric Tense: The pattern of tense interpretation in which a time is identified with an earlier time in the discourse. It is typical of passages in the Description mode.

Aspectual viewpoint: Viewpoint makes visible for semantic interpretation all or part of a situation. It is indicated by the simple and progressive verb forms. The simple form conveys the perfective viewpoint, making visible a bounded event or state, as in "Mary talked to Bill." "Kim was here." The progressive makes visible part of an ongoing event, as in "Mary was talking to Bill."

Background: Sentences can be partitioned into background and focus. The background may consist of a topic phrase and other material,

286

not necessarily forming a syntactic constituent. Typically, background represents what is salient or inferrable in the discourse. "Background" also contrasts with "foreground" in that background presents supportive rather than essential information.

Bounded event: An event that is bounded in some way, conveyed in sentences by the perfective viewpoint. Telic and instantaneous events have intrinsic bounds, as in "The child drew an eggplant," "The bird flapped a wing." States and atelic events may have explicit bounds, as in "She slept from 3 to 4"; or implicit bounds, as in "She walked."

Bounded Event Constraint: A pragmatic constraint that bars the expression of bounded events in the present. By convention, communication occurs in a single moment, so that events can only be expressed as ongoing. The constraint leads to the understanding of perfective event sentences with present tense as generalizing statives, e.g. "John feeds the cat."

Canonical structure: The basic syntactic structure of English, Subject-Verb-Object-Adjunct; the subject argument is agent if there is an agent in the sentence, as in "Mary planted a rosebush yesterday." Canonical structures are defined for assertions: questions and imperatives are different in some way.

Cleft sentence: A non-canonical syntactic structure in which one phrase is extracted from a clause while the rest appears in a relative-like structure: "It was Mary who planted a rosebush," "What Mary planted was a rosebush." The information in the relative-like clause I (the "clefted" clause) is presupposed.

Closed system: A limited set of forms of a sub-system, as in tense, aspectual viewpoint, and type of referring expression. The choice of a form has contrastive force and can suggest additional discourse meanings beyond the lexical content. For instance, using a full NP or a pronoun to refer to a person (*Mary Jones* vs *she*) suggests that the person is identifiable or already familiar in the discourse.

Coercion: A shift of situation type from a basic type to another, derived situation type. Shifts are triggered by adverbials in the context – for instance, a state verb constellation shifts in the presence of a dynamic adverbial: compare "Mary knew the truth," a state, with "Suddenly Mary knew the truth," a dynamic event. Derived situation

	types include the basic verb constellation and the triggering adverbial.
Comment:	The part of a sentence that says something about the topic. Sentences may be partitioned into topic phrase and comment. The comment typically conveys new information, the topic is typically familiar information.
Composite:	A group of linguistic forms that together convey a particular meaning; they may come from different phrases in a sentence, or from different sentences. For instance, the temporal location of a sentence is conveyed by the verb tense and temporal adverbial, if any; aspectual situation types are conveyed by a composite of the main verb, its arguments, and adverbials, if any.
Continuity pattern:	Pattern of tense interpretation for narrative non-first clauses, in which bounded events are taken as sequential, advancing narrative time.
Deixis, deictic:	the term for linguistic expressions that are understood in relation to the speaker's time and place, the here and now. Tenses are anchored to Speech Time: we understand past tense to locate a time before Speech Time for instance. Other deictic forms are the pronouns *I* and *you*; *this* and *that*; the adverbs *here, there*.
Derived situation type:	A situation type that is derived by shifting from a simpler type.The shift is triggered by an adverbial or other information in the context. The derived verb constellation includes the adverbial as well as the verb and its arguments, e.g. "Mary read a book" is telic; "Mary read a book for an hour" is atelic, derived by coercion due to the durative adverbial "for an hour."
Discourse entity:	Symbols in a Discourse Representation Structure, that represent the people, objects, times, situations talked about in the discourse and introduced into the universe of discourse.
Discourse topic:	The subject of a large or small chunk of discourse. Discourse topics need not be explicitly stated: they are often inferred or constructed by the receiver.
Dynamism:	The semantic property that distinguishes events from states. Dynamic events occur at successive stages in time. The linguistic correlates of dynamism include the progressive viewpoint ("Laura was swimming"), the "do" of pseudo-cleft sentences ("What Laura did was swim"), forms implying agency or volition.
Event:	The class of situations with the property of dynamism. Events may be durative or instantaneous, telic or atelic. They are expressed by the composite of a verb and its arguments. Event clauses have linguistic properties

	associated with dynamism and other features; they accept the progressive or perfective aspectual viewpoint.
Evidential:	Linguistic expressions that convey evaluation, or different degrees of commitment to what is asserted. Evidentials include adverbials (*probably, possibly,* etc.), modals (*could, may*).
External override principle:	This principle applies to most cases of coercion, in which a verb constellation is shifted to a derived verb constellation. Adverbials often trigger the shift. When there is a clash between temporal features of the verb constellation and the adverbial, the value of the adverbial feature overrides. For instance, "John feeds the cat" is an event verb constellation; "John often feeds the cat" is a Generalizing Stative.
Extraposition:	A syntactic construction that is non-canonical, with a clause or phrase moved to the rightmost edge of the sentence. The most frequent type has a clausal subject moved to the right, with a non-referring *it* in subject position: "It was surprising that the plane left on time."
Familiarity status:	Classification of individual entities in discourse according to whether they are familiar in the discourse or to the receiver. The main classes of familiarity status are New, Evoked, or Inferrable. New entities may be brand-new, or Unused; Evoked entities are familiar, usually coreferential with an entity already introduced; Inferrable entities are triggered from background knowledge by information in the text.
Figure–Ground:	Information organized so that one referent, the Figure, is located in terms of the other, the Ground. In sentences the subject is Figure and the predicate is the Ground, as in "The bicycle is near the house." The Figure is salient, usually smaller and less permanent than the Ground.
Focus:	The focus phrase gives the main contribution of a sentence. Focused information is new to the discourse; or presented in a new way. The focus phrase is canonically rightmost in a sentence and receives the sentence accent. If in another position, it is highlighted by intonation and/or non-canonical syntactic structure. "Strong focus" is contrastive or emphatic; it is conveyed by heavy stress or underlining, or focus operators such as *only, even*. "Informational focus" occurs in all sentences.

General Stative:	The class of situations, and discourse entities, that consist of generalizations rather than particulars. The class consists of Generic sentences that refer to classes or abstract individuals, e.g. "Elephants are gentle beasts"; and Generalizing sentences that express a pattern of events or states, e.g. "Mary often walks to school."
Generalizing Stative:	Generalization over a pattern of events or states, with an implicit or explicit frequency adverbial. Sentences that express them are derived statives, often with an event verb constellation, present tense, and the perfective viewpoint, e.g. "John reads the newspaper in the evening."
Generic:	Sentence that predicates something of a class or abstract individual, rather than a particular referent. Such sentences often have subjects with a bare plural NP or the definite article: "Whales live in ocean waters"; "The whale lives in ocean waters."
Indirect speech and thought:	Linguistic presentation in which the contents of a person's speech or thought are in a complement clause, as in "Mary said that she was pleased." The names and deictics are systematically shifted: actual speech would have *I* and *am*.
Inversion:	A type of syntactic structure in which the canonical order is inverted, often so that a phrase canonically in the predicate appears at the beginning of the sentence. In locative inversion, a location phrase is first: "On the table I saw a small notebook." In other inversions a complement clause may appear first, as in "'Let's go,' he said"; or, subject and predicate may be reversed: "On the table was a small notebook"; etc.
Limited anaphora:	Pattern of tense interpretation, typical of narrative non-first clauses, in which states and ongoing events are located at the most recently established Reference Time.
Link:	An element in the partitioning of a sentence; the others are Focus and Tail. The Link phrase indicates a locus of update in the theory of Vallduví & Engdahl (1996).
Locally free reflexive (LFR):	A reflexive not locally bound by an antecedent. The antecedent may be relatively far away, not in a position to bind the reflexive by Binding Theory principles – "She pulled the blanket over herself." LFRs convey logophoric meaning; subjective meanings of empathy; contrast or emphasis.

Logophoric:	Pronouns that indicate coreference to an antecedent subject of consciousness, as in "Mary$_i$ thought that she$_i$ would win."
Metaphorical progression:	The type of text progression found in atemporal texts. They progress metaphorically through the information space of the text. A Primary Referent is identified for each clause; progression occurs when Primary Referents have different metaphorical locations.
Non-canonical structure:	Syntactic structures that depart from the canonical in some way. Phrases may not be in their original position, as in a passive: "The rosebush was planted by Mary"; there may be special emphasis or syntactic highlighting, as in the cleft sentence "It was a rosebush that Mary planted." Non-canonical structures may convey special meanings: cleft sentences presuppose the truth of the *that*-clause.
Perfect:	A tense–aspect form with auxiliary *have* and past participle form of the main verb. The perfect conveys that a situation occurred prior to Reference Time, for instance "Mary and John have left"; "She had solved the problem". Perfect sentences are stataive although the prior situation may be dynamic.
Perfective viewpoint:	The aspectual viewpoint indicated by the simple form of a verb, without an auxiliary. The perfective conveys bounded events, and states (in English; this viewpoint differs across languages), as in "Mary ate an apple," "Kim believes in ghosts."
Poset linking:	A type of connectedness between sentences in which a discourse entity is linked to the context. Entities are linked through a poset licensed by information in the context. If a salient poset can be inferred, there is a linking relation. The link entity is ranked with other entities in the poset according to formal relations such as part-of, attribute-of, prior-to, identity. Entities may be inferred through poset linking.
Presentational constructions:	Syntactic structures that introduce a referent, usually unfamiliar, to a discourse. For instance, "There was a unicorn in the garden," and certain inversions: "In the garden was a unicorn." These structures have a focus phrase ("the unicorn" in each example) but no topic phrase.
Presentational progression:	Text progression from one sentence topic to another. It is presentational because the sentence topic

depends in part on the syntactic surface structure of a sentence.

Presupposition:
In "semantic presupposition," particular linguistic expressions conventionally establish that information is shared knowledge: "Tom stopped running" entails that "Tom ran." In "pragmatic presupposition," the receiver infers that an entity or a proposition is an already-established, uncontroversial part of the common ground. The sequence "Mary had an accident driving home from work. The steering-wheel was defective." pragmatically presupposes the car that Mary was driving.

Primary Referent:
The semantically central entity in a situation expressed by a clause. In events, the Primary Referent moves or changes; in states, a property is ascribed to the Primary Referent. The Primary Referent corresponds to the Theme/Patient argument of a clause. The Primary Referent is the locus for metaphorical motion in atemporal text passages.

Progressive:
The aspectual viewpoint indicated by the progressive verb auxiliary *be+ing*. The progressive is a type of imperfective viewpoint. It conveys open, unbounded events, as in "Mary was eating an apple." The progressive does not occur neutrally with states.

Reference Time (RT):
One of three times introduced by a tense: the temporal standpoint time. In present tense, RT = Speech Time; in simple past tense, RT precedes Speech Time; in future, RT follows Speech Time. RT = t_2 in Discourse Representation Structure.

Responsible Source:
The mind to which responsibility for subjective interpretation is ascribed.

Semelfactive:
A type of event with the features dynamic, atelic, instantaneous, for instance "The bird flapped a wing," "Bill coughed." Instantaneous events consist only of a single stage.

Situation:
The term is used generally, for all types of aspectual entities; it also refers to the sub-type of particular events and states.

Situation time (SitT):
One of three times introduced by tense: the time at which a situation occurs. With the simple tenses, Situation Time is the same as Reference Time. With the perfect tenses, SitT precedes RT; with the future-in-past, SitT follows RT. SitT = t_3 in Discourse Representation Structure.

Situation type:
Situations classified according to their internal temporal properties, e.g. Events and States, Generalizing Statives, Facts and Propositions. The situation types are semantic concepts, idealizations of situations according to internal

	temporal properties. They have linguistic correlates of distribution and interpretation.
Telic–Atelic:	A feature of internal temporal structure that distinguishes types of events by whether they have a goal (a "telos") or natural final endpoint. Telic events have a natural final endpoint (*draw a circle*, *walk to school*); atelic events can stop at any time, and thus have arbitrary final endpoints (*walk in the park*, *sleep*).
Thetic sentence:	The term refers to a sentence that is understood as an unpartitioned whole rather than a predication about a particular referent, as "There are yellow flowers" or "It's raining." Thetic sentences can answer questions such as "What happened?" or "What is there?" that do not single out any referent. Thetic sentences have no topic phrase.
Topic of a sentence:	The referent that a sentence is about. Topic phrases are tracked in the presentational progression of a text. The topic phrase of a sentence is usually the subject, and the topic referent is often familiar in a text; but neither is a defining property.
Verb constellation:	The verb and its arguments. Verb constellations express the situation type of a sentence. In derived situation types adverbs are part of a derived verb constellation.

References

Abusch, Dorit, 1997. Sequence of tense & temporal de re. *Linguistics & Philosophy* 20: 1–50.

Acker, Liane, & Bruce Porter, 1994. Extracting viewpoints from knowledge bases. *Proceedings of the 12th National Conference on Artificial Intelligence. Menlo Park, Calif.*: 547–52.

Allen, James, 1983. Maintaining knowledge about temporal intervals. *Communications of the Association for Computing Machinery* 26 (11): 832–43.

Allen, James, & C. Raymond Perrault, 1980. Analyzing intentions in utterances. *Computational Linguistics*, 15: 143–78.

Ariel, Mira, 1989. Referring and accessibility. *Journal of Linguistics* 24: 65–87.

1990. *Accessing Noun Phrase Antecedents*. London: Routledge.

Arnold, Jennifer, Thomas Wasow, Anthony Losonoco, & Ryan Ginstrom, 2000. Heaviness vs newness: The effects of structural complexity and discourse status on constituent ordering. *Language* 76: 28–55.

Asher, Nicholas, 1993. *Reference to Abstract Objects in Discourse*. Dordrecht: Kluwer Academic Publishers.

Asher, Nicholas, & Alex Lascarides, 1993. Temporal interpretation, discourse relations and commonsense entailment. *Linguistics & Philosophy* 16: 437–94.

1998a. Bridging. *Journal of Semantics* 15: 83–113.

1998b. The semantics and pragmatics of Presupposition. *Journal of Semantics* 15: 239–99.

Bach, Emmon, 1981. On time, tense, and aspect: An essay in English metaphysics. In P. Cole (ed.), *Radical Pragmatics*. New York: Academic Press.

Bach, Kent, 1999. The semantics–pragmatics distinction: What it is and why it matters. In K. Turner (ed.), *The Semantics–Pragmatics Interface from Different Points of View*. Oxford: Elsevier, pp. 65–84.

Bain, Alexander, 1877. *English Composition and Rhetoric*. London: Longmans.

Baker, Carl Lee, 1995. Contrast, discourse prominence, and identification, with special reference to locally free reflexives in British English. *Language* 71: 63–101.

Baker, Mark, 1988. *Incorporation*. Chicago, Ill.: University of Chicago Press.

Bal, Mieke, 1991. *On Story-telling*. Sonoma, Calif.: Polebridge Press.

Banfield, Ann, 1982. *Unspeakable Sentences*. Boston: Routledge & Kegan Paul.

Barker, Chris, 2000. Definite possessives and discourse novelty. *Theoretical Linguistics* 26: 211–27.

Bartsch, R., 1976. Topik-Fokus-Struktur und Kategoriale Syntax. In V. Ehrich & P. Find (eds.), *Grammatik und Pragmatik*. Kronberg: Scriptor Verlag.

Bechtel, William, & Arthur Abrahamsen, 1991. *Connectionism and the Mind: An Introduction to Parallel Processing in Networks*. Cambridge, Mass.: Blackwell.

Beekman, John, 1970. Propositions and theory relations within a discourse. *Notes on Translation* 37: 6–23.

Benson, James, & William Greaves, 1992. Collocation and field of discourse. In W. Mann & S. Thompson (eds.), *Discourse Description: Diverse Linguistic Analyses of a Fund-raising Text*. Amsterdam: John Benjamins.

Bever, Thomas, 1970. The cognitive basis for linguistic structures. In J. R. Hayes (ed.), *Cognition and the Development of Language*. New York: John Wiley.

Biber, Douglas, 1988. *Variation across Speech and Writing*. Cambridge: Cambridge University Press.

1989. A typology of English texts. *Linguistics* 27: 3–43.

Biber, Douglas, & Edward Finegan, 1989. Drift and the evolution of English style: A history of three genres. *Language* 65: 487–517.

Birner, Betty, 1994. Information status and word order: An analysis of English inversion. *Language* 70: 233–59.

1996. *Form and Function in English By-phrase Passives. Proceedings of the Chicago 23rd Annual Meeting, Chicago Linguistic Society*. Chicago, Ill.: Chicago Linguistic Society.

Birner, Betty, & Gregory Ward, 1998. *Information Status and Non-Canonical Word Order in English*. Amsterdam: John Benjamins.

Black, J. B., & Gordon Bower, 1980. Story understanding as problem solving. *Poetics* 9: 224–350.

Blakemore, Diane, 1988. The organization of discourse. In F. Newmeyer (ed.), *Linguistics: The Cambridge Survey*, Vol. IV. Cambridge: Cambridge University Press.

1989. Denial and contrast: A relevance theoretic account of BUT. *Linguistics & Philosophy* 12: 15–38.

Blass, Regina, 1990. *Relevance Relations in Discourse*. Cambridge: Cambridge University Press.

Bolinger, Dwight, 1961. Contrastive accent and contrastive stress. *Language* 37: 83–96.

1972. Accent is predictable (if you're a mind-reader). *Language* 48: 639–44.

1977. *Meaning and Form*. London: Longman.

Bond, S. J., & John Hayes, 1984. Cues people use to paragraph text. *Research in the Teaching of English* 18: 147–67.

Bosch, P., & R. van der Sandt (eds.), *Focus: Linguistic, Cognitive, and Computational Perspectives*. Cambridge: Cambridge University Press.

Bower, G. H., J. B. Black, & T. J. Turner, 1979. Scripts in memory for text. *Cognitive Psychology*, 2: 177–220.

Braddock, Richard, 1974. The frequency and placement of topic sentences in expository prose. *Research in the Teaching of English* 8: 287–302.

Bransford, John, J. Richard Barclay, & Jeffery Franks, 1972. Sentence memory: A constructive vs interpretive approach. *Cognitive Psychology* 3: 193–209.

Brennan, Susan E., 1995. Centering attention in discourse. *Language & Cognitive Processes*, 10: 137–67.

Britton, James, Tony Burgess, Nancy Martin, Alex McLeod, & Harold Rosen, 1975. *The Development of Writing Abilities (11–18)*. London: Macmillan.

Brooks, Cleanth, & Robert Penn Warren, 1958. *Modern Rhetoric*. New York: Harcourt, Brace & Company.

Brown, Gillian, & George Yule, 1983. *Discourse Analysis*. Cambridge: Cambridge University Press.

Brown, Penelope, & Colin Fraser, 1982. Social markers in speech. In K. Scherer & H. Giles (eds.), *Advances in the Social Psychology of Language*. Cambridge: Cambridge University Press.

Bruder, Gail, & Janyce Wiebe, 1995. Recognizing subjectivity and identifying subjective characters in third-person fictional narrative. In J. Duchan, G. Bruder, & L. Hewitt (eds.), *Deixis in Narrative: A Cognitive Science Approach*. Hillsdale, N.J.: Lawrence Erlbaum Associates.

Büring, Daniel, 1999. Topic. In P. Bosch & R. van der Sandt (eds.), *Focus: Linguistic, Cognitive, and Computational Perspectives*. Cambridge: Cambridge University Press.

Caenepeel, Mimo, 1989. Aspect, temporal ordering and perspective in narrative fiction. Ph.D. thesis, University of Edinburgh.

   1995. Aspect and text structure. *Linguistics* 33: 213–53.

   1997. Putting *while* in context. Human Communication Research Centre, #RP-85. Edinburgh: University of Edinburgh.

Caenepeel, Mimo, & Mark Moens, 1994. Temporal structure and discourse structure. In C. Vet & C. Vetters (eds.), *Tense and Aspect in Discourse*. Berlin: Mouton de Gruyter.

Caenepeel, Mimo & Görel Sandström, 1992. A discourse-level approach to the past perfect in narrative. In M. Aurnague, A. Borillo, M. Borillo, and M. Bras (eds.), *Semantics of Time, Space, Movement and Spatio-temporal Reasoning*. Toulouse: Université Paul Sabatier.

Cairns, William B., 1902. *The Forms of Discourse*. Boston: Ginn & Co.

Cantrall, William, 1969. On the nature of the reflexive in English. Ph.D. dissertation, University of Illinois.

Carlson, Greg, 1977. Reference to kinds in English. Ph.D. dissertation, University of Massachusetts.

Carlson, Greg, & Geoffrey Pelletier, 1995. *The Generic Book*. Chicago: University of Chicago Press.

Chafe, Wallace, 1976. Given, contrastiveness, definiteness, subject, topics and point of view. In Charles Li (ed.), *Subject and Topic*. New York: Academic Press.

   1982. Integration and involvement in speaking, writing, and oral literature. In D. Tannen (ed.), *Spoken and Written Language: Exploring Orality and Literacy*. Norwood, N.J.: Ablex Publishing Company.

   1987. Cognitive constraints on information flow. In R. Tomlin (ed.), *Coherence and Grounding in Discourse*. Amsterdam: John Benjamins.

   1994. *Discourse, Consciousness, and Time*. Chicago: University of Chicago Press.

Chafe, Wallace, & Joanna Nichols (eds.), 1986. *Evidentiality: The Linguistic Coding of Epistemology.* Norwood, N.J.: Ablex Publishing Corporation.

Chierchia, Gennaro, 1992. Anaphora and dynamic binding. *Linguistics & Philosophy* 15: 111–83.

Chomsky, Noam, 1970. Remarks on nominalization. In R. Jacobs & P. Rosenbaum (eds.), *Readings in English Transformational Grammar.* Waltham, Mass.: Ginn & Co.

1971. Deep structure, surface structure and semantic interpretation. In D. Steinberg & L. Jakobovits (eds.), *Semantics: An Inter-Disciplinary Reader.* Cambridge: Cambridge University Press.

1981. *Lectures on Government and Binding.* Dordrecht: Foris.

Christiansen, Francis. 1965. A generative rhetoric of the paragraph. *College Composition and Communication* 15: 144–57.

Chu, Chauncy, 1983. *A Reference Grammar of Mandarin for English Speakers.* New York: Peter Lang.

Cinque, G. 1999. *Adverbs and Functional Heads: A Cross-linguistic Perspective.* Oxford: Oxford University Press.

Clancy, Patricia, 1980. Referential choice in English and Japanese narrative discourse. In W. Chafe (ed.), *The Pear Stories.* Norwood, N.J.: Ablex.

Clark, Andy, 1989. *Microcognition.* Cambridge, Mass.: MIT Press.

Clark, Herbert, 1973. Space, time, semantics, and the child. In T. Moore (ed.), *Cognitive Development and the Acquisition of Language.* New York: Academic Press.

1996. *Using Language.* Cambridge: Cambridge University Press.

Cohan, Jocelyn, 2001. Reconsidering identificational focus. In M. Kim & U. Strauss (eds.), *Proceedings of the New England Linguistic Society 31.* Amherst, Mass.: GLSA, University of Massachusetts.

Cohn, Dorritt, 1978. *Transparent Minds.* Princeton, N.J.: Princeton University Press.

Comrie, Bernard, 1976. *Aspect.* Cambridge: Cambridge University Press.

1983. Switch reference in Huichol: A typological study. In J. Haiman & P. Munro (eds.), *Switch Reference and Universal Grammar.* Amsterdam: John Benjamins.

1985. *Tense.* Cambridge: Cambridge University Press.

Connors, Robert J., 1997. *Composition–Rhetoric.* Pittsburgh, Pa.: University of Pittsburgh Press.

Corbett, Edward P., 1965. *Classical Rhetoric for the Modern Student.* New York: Oxford University Press.

Couper-Kuhlen, Elizabeth, 1989. Foregrounding and temporal relations in narrative discourse. In A. Schopf (ed.), *Essays on Tensing in English*, Vol. II. Tübingen: Niemeyer.

Creider, Chet, 1979. On the explanation of transformations. In T. Givón (ed.), *Discourse and Syntax*, Syntax & Semantics, 12. New York: Academic Press.

Croft, William, 1991. *Syntactic Categories and Grammatical Relations: The Cognitive Organization of Information.* Chicago: University of Chicago Press.

Crothers, Edward, 1979. *Paragraph Structure Inference.* Norwood, N.J.: Ablex.

Culicover, Peter, 1997. *Principles and Parameters: An Introduction to Syntactic Theory.* Oxford: Oxford University Press.

Dahl, Oesten, 1974. Topic and comment structure revisited. In O. Dahl (ed.), *Topic & Comment, Contextual Boundedness and Focus*, Papers in Text Linguistics, 6. Hamburg: Buske.

Danasio, Antonio, 2002. Remembering when. *Scientific American* 287: 66–73.

Daneš, Frederik, 1974. Functional sentence perspective and the organization of the text. In F. Daneš (ed.), *Papers on Functional Sentence Perspective*. Prague: Academia.

Davison, Alice, 1984. Syntactic markedness and the notion of sentence topic. *Language* 60: 797–846.

Davison, Alice, & Richard Lutz, 1985. Measuring syntactic complexity relative to discourse. In D. Dowty (ed.), *Natural Language Processing: Psycholinguistic, Computational and Theoretical Perspectives*. Cambridge: Cambridge University Press.

de Beaugrande, Robert-Alain, & Wolfgang Dressler, 1981. *Introduction to Text Linguistics*. London: Longman.

Delin, Judy, 1995. Presupposition and shared knowledge in It-clefts. *Language and Cognitive Processes* 10: 97–120.

Delin, Judy, & Jon Oberlander, 1995. Syntactic constraints on discourse structure: the case of It-clefts. *Linguistics* 33: 465–500.

Dendale, Patrick, & Liliane Tasmowski (eds.), 2001. Evidentiality and related notions: Special issue. *Journal of Pragmatics* 33: 339–48.

de Swart, Henriette, 1993. *Adverbs of Quantification: A Generalized Quantifier Approach*. New York: Garland Publications.

1998. *Introduction to Natural Language Semantics*. Stanford, Calif.: Center for the Study of Language and Information Publications.

1999. Position and meaning: Time adverbials in context. In P. Bosch & R. van der Sandt (eds.), *Focus: Linguistics, Cognitive, and Computational Perspectives*. Cambridge: Cambridge University Press.

van Dijk, Teun, 1972. *Some Aspects of Text Grammars*. The Hague: Mouton.

1977. *Text and Context*. London: Longman.

1982. Episodes as units of discourse analysis. In D. Tannen (ed.), *Georgetown University Roundtable on Languages & Linguistics*. Washington, D.C.: Georgetown University Press.

van Dijk, Teun, & Walter Kintsch, 1983. *Strategies of Discourse Comprehension*. New York: Academic Press.

Dowty, David, 1979. *Word Meaning and Montague Grammar*. Dordrecht: Kluwer.

1986. The effects of aspectual class on the temporal structure of discourse: Semantics or pragmatics? *Linguistics & Philosophy* 9: 37–62.

1991. Thematic proto-roles and argument selection. *Language* 67: 547–619.

Dowty, David, Robert Wall, & Stanley Peters, 1981. *Introduction to Montague Semantics*. Dordrecht: Reidel.

Duchan, Judith, Gail Bruder, & Lynne Hewitt (eds.), 1995. *Deixis in Narrative: A Cognitive Science Perspective*. Hillsdale, N.J.: Erlbaum.

Dundes, Alan, 1975. *Analytic Essays in Folklare*. The Hague: Mouton.

Eggins, Suzanne, 1994. *Introduction to Systemic Functional Linguistics*. London: Pinter Publishers.

Enç, Murvet, 1986. Towards a referential analysis of temporal expressions. *Linguistics & Philosophy* 9: 405–26.

1987. Anchoring conditions for tense. *Linguistic Inquiry* 18: 633–57.

1991. Tense and modality. In S. Lappin (ed.), *The Handbook of Contemporary Semantic Theory*. Oxford: Blackwell.

Erbaugh, Mary, 1986. Taking stock: The development of Chinese noun classifiers. In C. Craig (ed.), *Noun Classes and Categorization*. Philadelphia: Benjamins.

Erteschik-Shir, Nomi, 1979. Discourse constraints on dative movement. In T. Givón (ed.), *Discourse and Syntax*, Syntax and Semantics, 12. New York: Academic Press.

1997. *The Dynamics of Focus Structure*. Cambridge: Cambridge University Press.

Erteschik-Shir, Nomi, & Sheldon Lappin, 1979. Dominance and the functional explanation of island phenomena. *Theoretical Linguistics* 6: 41–85.

Erteschik-Shir, Nomi, & Tova Rapoport, in press. Bare aspect: A theory of syntactic projection. In J. Guéron and J. Lacarme (eds.), *The Syntax of Time*. Cambridge, Mass.: MIT Press.

Fabricius-Hansen, Cathrine, & Bergljot Behrens, 2000. Elaboration and related discourse relations viewed from an interlingual perspective. In *Proceedings of the Third Workshop on Text Structure*. Austin, Tex.: Department of Linguistics, University of Texas.

Faigley, Lester, & Paul Meyer, 1983. Rhetorical theory and readers' classification of text types. *Text* 3: 305–25.

Fauconnier, Gilles, 1985. *Mental Spaces: Aspects of Meaning Construction in Natural Language*. Cambridge, Mass.: MIT Press. Reprinted 1994, Cambridge: Cambridge University Press.

Fauconnier, Gilles, & Eve Sweetser (eds.), 1996. *Spaces, World, and Grammar*. Chicago, Ill.: University of Chicago Press.

Ferro, Lisa, 1993. On "self" as a focus marker. In Michael Bernstein (ed.), *Proceedings of the Ninth Eastern States Conference on Linguistics*. Ithaca, N.Y.: Cornell University Department of Modern Languages and Linguistics.

Fillmore, Charles, 1975. *Santa Cruz Lectures on Deixis*. Bloomington, Ind.: Indiana University Linguistics Club.

von Fintel, Kai, 1994. Restrictions on quantifier domains. Ph.D. dissertation, Massachusetts Institute of Technology.

Firbas, Jan, 1964. On defining the theme in functional sentence analysis. *Travaux de Circle Linguistique de Prague* 1: 267–80.

1974. Some aspects of the Czechoslovak approach to functional sentence perspective. In F. Daneš (ed.), *Papers on Functional Sentence Perspective*. Prague: Academia.

1992. *Functional Sentence Perspective in Written and Spoken Communication*. Cambridge: Cambridge University Press.

Flashner, Vanessa, 1987. The grammatical marking of theme in oral Polish narrative. In R. Tomlin (ed.), *Coherence and Grounding in Discourse*. Amsterdam: Benjamins.

Fleischman, Suzanne, 1991. Verb tense and point of view in narrative. In S. Fleischman & L. Waugh (eds.), *Discourse-Pragmatics and the Verb*. London: Routledge.

Forster, Kenneth, 1979. Levels of processing and the structure of the language processor. In W. E. Cooper & E. C. T. Walker (eds.), *Sentence Processing: Psycholinguistic Studies Presented to Merrill Garrett*. Hillsdale, N.J.: Lawrence Erlbaum.

Fox, Barbara, 1987a. Anaphora in popular English written narratives. In R. Tomlin (ed.), *Coherence and Grounding in Discourse*. Amsterdam: Benjamins.

1987b. *Discourse Structure and Anaphora in Written and Conversational English*. Cambridge: Cambridge University Press.

Frank, Anette, & Hans Kamp, 1997. On context dependence in modal constructions. In A. Lawson (ed.), *SALT VII*. Ithaca, N.Y.: Cornell University.

Frantz, Donald, 1966. Person indexing in Blackfoot. *International Journal of American Linguistics*, 32: 50–58.

Freksa, C., 1992. Using orientation information for qualitative spatial reasoning. In M. Aurnague *et al.* (eds.), *Semantics of Time, Space, Movement and Spatio-temporal Reasoning*. Toulouse: Université Paul Sabatier.

Friedman, William, 1993. *About Time*. Cambridge, Mass.: MIT Press.

Fries, Peter, 1983. On the status of theme in English: Arguments from discourse. In J. Petöfi & E. Sözer (eds.), *Micro and Macro Connexity in Texts*. Hamburg: Helmut Buske.

Fuller, Daniel, 1959. *The Inductive Method of Bible Study*, 3rd edition. Pasadena: Fuller Theological Seminary.

Galbraith, Mary, 1995. Deictic shift theory and the poetics of involvement in narrative. In J. Duchan, G. Bruder, & L. Hewitt (eds.), *Deixis in Narrative: A Cognitive Science Approach*. Hillsdale, N.J.: Lawrence Erlbaum Associates.

Garnham, Alan, 1983. What's wrong with story grammars? *Cognition* 15: 145–54.

1985. *Psycholinguistics*. London: Methuen.

1987. *Mental Models as Representation of Discourse and Text*. Chichester: Ellis Horwood.

Garnham, Alan, & Jane Oakhill, 1989. The everyday use of anaphoric expressions: Implications for the "mental models" theory of text comprehension. In N. E. Sharkey (ed.), *Modelling Cognition: An Annual Review of Cognitive Science*, Vol. I. Norwood, N.J.: Ablex.

Garrod, Simon, & Anthony Sanford, 1985. On the real-time character of interpretation during reading. *Language & Cognitive Processes* 1: 43–61.

1994. Resolving sentences in a discourse context. In M. A. Gernsbacher (ed.), *Handbook of Psycholinguistics*. New York: Academic Press.

Gazdar, Gerald, Ewan Klein, Geoffrey Pullum, & Ivan Sag, 1985. *Generalized Phrase Structure Grammar*. Oxford: Blackwell.

Gelman, Rachel, 1990. First principles organize attention to and learning about relevant data: Number and the animate/inanimate distinction. *Cognitive Science* 14: 79–106.

Genette, Gérard, 1980. *Narrative Discourse: An Essay in Method*. Ithaca, N.Y.: Cornell University Press.

Genung, John F., 1900. *The Working Principles of Rhetoric*. Boston: Ginn & Co.

Giora, Rachel, 1983. Functional sentence perspective. In J. Petöfi & E. Sözer (eds.), *Micro and Macro Connexity in Texts*. Hamburg: Helmut Buske.

Giorgi, Alessandra, & Fabio Pianesi, 1991. Towards a syntax of temporal representations. *Probus* 2: 187–213.

1997. *Tense and Aspect*. Oxford: Oxford University Press.

Givón, Talmy, 1979. From discourse to syntax: Grammar as a processing strategy. In T. Givón (ed.), *Discourse and Syntax*, Syntax and Semantics, 12. New York: Academic Press.

1983. Topic continuity in discourse: An introduction. In T. Givón (ed.), *Topic Continuity in Discourse: A Quantitative Cross-Language Study*. Amsterdam: Benjamins.

1993. The pragmatics of de-transitive voice: Functional and typological aspects of inversion. In T. Givón (ed.), *Voice and Inversion*. Amsterdam: Benjamins.

Glenberg, A. M., M. Mayer, & K. Linden, 1987. Mental models contribute to foregrounding during text interpretation. *Journal of Memory & Language* 26: 69–83.

Goddard, Ives, 1990. Aspects of the topic structure of Fox narratives: Proximate shifts and the use of overt and inflectional NPs. *International Journal of American Linguistics* 56: 317–40.

Goldberg, Adele, 1995. *Constructions*. Chicago, Ill.: University of Chicago Press.

Gordon, Peter, & Davina Chan, 1995. Pronouns, passives, and discourse coherence. *Journal of Memory & Language* 34: 216–31.

Gough, Philip, 1965. Grammatical transformations and speed of understanding. *Journal of Verbal Learning & Verbal Behavior* 5: 107–11.

Goutsos, Dionysis, 1997. *Modeling Discourse Topic: Sequential Relations and Strategies in Expository Texts*. Norwood, N.J.: Ablex.

Graesser, Arthur, 1981. *Prose Comprehension Beyond the Word*. New York: Springer.

Green, Georgia, 1974. *Semantics and Syntactic Regularity*. Bloomington, Ind.: Indiana University Press.

Grice, H. P., 1975. Logic and conversation. In P. Cole & J. Morgan (eds.), *Speech Acts*, Syntax and Semantics, 3. New York: Academic Press.

1989. *Studies in the Way of Words*. Cambridge, Mass.: Harvard University Press.

Grimes, Joseph, 1975. *The Thread of Discourse*. The Hague: Mouton.

Grimshaw, Jane, 1990. *Argument Structure*. Cambridge, Mass.: MIT Press.

Groenendijk, Jeroen, & Martin Stokhof, 1991. Dynamic predicate logic. *Linguistics & Philosophy* 14: 39–100.

Gropen, J., S. Pinker, S. Hollander, R. Goldberg, & R. Wilson, 1989. The learnability and acquisition of the dative alternation in English. *Language* 65: 203–55.

Grosz, Barbara, 1977. The representation and use of focus in dialogue understanding. Tech Note, 15. Menlo Park, Calif.: Artificial Intelligence Center, SRI International.

Grosz, Barbara, & Candace Sidner, 1986. Attention, intensions, and the structure of discourse. *Computational Linguistics* 12: 175–204.

Gruber, Jeffrey, 1965. *Studies in Lexical Relations*. Ph.D. dissertation, MIT. Reprinted Bloomington, Ind.: Indiana University Linguistics Club.

Gundel, Jeannette, 1974. The role of topic and comment in linguistic theory. Ph.D. dissertation, University of Texas. Reprinted 1977, Bloomington, Ind.: Indiana University Linguistics Club.

1998. Centering theory and a givenness hierarchy. In M. Walker, A. Joshi, & E. Prince (eds.), *Centering Theory in Discourse*. Oxford: Clarendon Press.

1999. On different kinds of focus. In P. Bosch & R. van der Sandt (eds.), *Focus: Linguistic, Cognitive, and Computational Perspectives*. Cambridge: Cambridge University Press.

Gundel, Jeannette, Nancy Hedberg, & Ron Zacharski, 1993. Cognitive status and the form of referring expressions in discourse. *Language* 69: 274–307.

Gussenhoven, Carlos, 1983. Focus, mode and the nucleus. *Journal of Linguistics* 19: 377–417.

Gutwinski, Waldemar, 1976. *Cohesion in Literary Texts*. The Hague: Mouton.

Hagège, Claude, 1974. Les pronoms logophoriques. *Bulletin de la Société de Linguistique de Paris* 69: 297–310.

Haiman, John, & Pamela Munro (eds.), *Switch Reference and Universal Grammar*. Amsterdam: John Benjamins.

Hajičová, Eva, 1971. Some remarks on presupposition. *Prague Bulletin of Mathematical Linguistics* 17: 11–23.

Hajičová, Eva, & Petr Sgall, 1987. The ordering principle. *Journal of Pragmatics* 11: 435–54.

Hajičová, Eva, M. Cervenka, O. Leška, & Petr Sgall (eds.), 1995. *Travaux du Cercle Linguistique de Prague, nouvelle série*, Vol. I. Amsterdam: John Benjamins.

Hajičová, Eva, Barbara Partee, & Petr Sgall, 1998. *Topic-Focus Articulation, Tripartite Structures, and Semantic Content*. Dordrecht: Kluwer Academic Publishers.

Hale, Kenneth, & Samuel Jay Keyser, 1993. On argument stucture and the lexical expression of syntactic relations. In K. Hale & S. J. Kayser (eds.), *The View from Building 20: Essays in Honor of Sylvan Bromberger*. Cambridge, Mass.: MIT Press.

Halliday, Michael A. K., 1967. Notes on transitivity and theme in English, Part II. *Journal of Linguistics* 3: 199–244.

1992. Some lexicogrammatical features of the Aero Population Growth Text. In W. Mann & S. Thompson (eds.), *Discourse Description: Diverse Linguistic Analyses of a Fund-raising Text*. Amsterdam: John Benjamins.

Halliday, Michael A. K., & Ruqaiya Hasan, 1976. *Cohesion in English*. London: Longman.

Hamburger, Käte, 1973. *The Logic of Literature*. Trans. Marilynn Rose. Bloomington, Ind.: Indiana University Press.

Hannay, Mike, 1991. Pragmatic function assignment and word order variation in a functional grammar of English. *Journal of Pragmatics* 16: 131–55.

Harris, Zellig, 1982. *A Grammar of English on Mathematical Principles*. New York: Methuen.

Haviland, Susan, & Herbert Clark, 1974. What's new? Acquiring new information as a process in comprehension. *Journal of Verbal Learning & Verbal Behavior* 13: 512–21.

Hawkins, John, 1994. *A Performance Theory of Order and Constituency*. Cambridge: Cambridge University Press.

Hearst, Marti, 1997. TextTiling: Segmenting text into multi-paragraph subtopic passages. *Computational Linguistics* 23: 33–64.

Hedberg, Nancy, 1990. Discourse pragmatics and cleft sentences in English. Ph.D. dissertation, University of Minnesota.

Heim, Irene, 1982. The semantics of definite and indefinite Nounphrases. Ph.D. dissertation, University of Massachusetts.

Herbst, Peter, 1956. The nature of facts. In A. Flew (ed.), *Essays in Conceptual Analysis*. New York: MacMillan.

Heycock, Caroline, & Anthony Kroch. 1999. Pseudo-cleft connectedness: Implications for the LF interface level. *Linguistic Inquiry* 30: 365–98.

Heyrich, Wolfgang, Fritz Neubauer, Janos Petöfi, & Erich Sözer (eds.), 1989. *Connexity and Coherence*. Berlin: De Gruyter.

Hinds, John, 1977. Paragraph structure and pronominalization. *Papers in Linguistics* 10: 77–99.

1979. Organizational patterns in discourse. In T. Givón (ed.), *Discourse and Syntax*, Syntax & Semantics, 12. New York: Academic Press.

Hinrichs, Erhard, 1986. Temporal anaphora in discourses of English. *Linguistics & Philosophy* 9: 63–82.

Hirose, Yukio, 2000. Public and private self as two aspects of the speaker: A contrastive study of Japanese and English. *Journal of Pragmatics* 32: 1623–56.

Hirschberg, Julia, 1991. *A Theory of Scalar Implicature*. New York: Garland Press.

Hobbs, Jerry, 1985. *On the Coherence and Structure of Discourse*. Report No. CSLI-85–37. Stanford, Calif.: Center for the Study of Language and Information.

Hockett, Charles, 1958. *A Course in Modern Linguistics*. New York: Macmillan.

Hoey, Michael, 1991. *Patterns of Lexis in Text*. Oxford: Oxford University Press.

Hopper, Paul, 1979. Aspect and foregrounding in discourse. In T. Givón (ed.), *Discourse and Syntax*, Syntax & Semantics, 12. New York: Academic Press.

Horn, Laurence, 1988. Pragmatic theory. In F. Newmeyer (ed.), *Linguistic Theory: Foundations*. Cambridge: Cambridge University Press.

1991. Given as new: When redundant information isn't. *Journal of Pragmatics* 15: 305–28.

Hornstein, Norbert, 1990. *As Time Goes By*. Cambridge, Mass.: MIT Press.

Hovy, Eduard, 1993. Automated discourse generation using discourse structure relations. *Artificial Intelligence* 63: 341–85.

Hunston, S., & G. Thompson (eds.), 2000. *Evaluation in Text*. Oxford: Oxford University Press.

Jackendoff, Ray, 1972. *Semantic Interpretation in Generative Grammar*. Cambridge, Mass.: MIT Press.

1987. The status of thematic relations in linguistic theory. *Linguistic Inquiry* 18: 369–411.

1990. *Semantic Structures*. Cambridge, Mass. MIT Press.

Jacobsen, William, 1967. Switch-reference in Hokan-Coahuiltecan. In D. Hymes & W. Biddle (eds.), *Studies in Southwestern Ethnolinguistics*. The Hague: Mouton.

Jakobson, Roman, 1957. Shifters, verbal categories, and the Russian verb. In L. Waugh & M. Halle (eds.), *Russian and Slavic Grammar: Studies 1931–1981*. Berlin: Mouton, 1984.

Jesperson, Otto, 1940. *A Modern English Grammar on Historical Principles*. London: George Allen & Unwin.

1924/1965. *The Philosophy of Grammar*. New York: W. W. Norton.

Johnson-Laird, Philip, 1983. *Mental Models: Toward a Cognitive Science of Language, Inference, and Consciousness*. Cambridge: Cambridge University Press.

1988. *The Computer and the Mind*. Cambridge, Mass.: Harvard University Press.

1989. Mental models. In M. Posner (ed.), *Foundations of Cognitive Science*. Cambridge, Mass.: MIT Press.

Johnson-Laird, Philip, & Rosemary Stevenson, 1970. Memory for syntax. *Nature* 227: 412.

Joshi, Aravind, & Scott Weinstein, 1981. Control of inference: Role of some aspects of discourse structure – centering. *Proceedings of the International Joint Conference on Artificial Intelligence, Vancouver*.

Kameyama, Megumi, 1985. Zero anaphora: The case of Japanese. Ph.D. dissertation, Stanford University.

1998. Intrasentential centering: A case study. In M. Walker, A. Joshi, & E. Prince (eds.), *Centering Theory in Discourse*. Oxford: Oxford University Press.

Kamio, Aki, 1994. The theory of territory of information: The case of Japanese. *Journal of Pragmatics* 27: 67–100.

Kamp, Hans, 1981. A theory of truth and semantic interpretation. In J. Groenendijk, T. Janssen, & M. Stockhof (eds.), *Formal Methods in the Study of Language*. Amsterdam: Mathematisch Centrum Tracts. Also in J. Groenendijk *et al.* (eds.), *Truth, Interpretation, and Information*. Dordrecht: Foris.

1985. Context, thought and communication. *Proceedings of the Aristotelian Society* 85: 239–61.

Kamp, Hans, & Uwe Reyle, 1993. *From Discourse to Logic*. Dordrecht: Kluwer Academic Publishers.

Kamp, Hans, & Christian Rohrer, 1983. Tense in texts. In R. Bauerle, R. Schwarze, & A. von Stechow (eds.), *Meaning, Use and Interpretation of Language*. Berlin: de Gruyter.

Karttunen, Lauri, 1976. Discourse referents. In J. McCawley (ed.), *Notes from the Linguistic Underground*, Syntax and Semantics, 7. New York: Academic Press.

Keenan, Elinor, & Bambi Schieffelin, 1976. Topic as a discourse notion. In Charles Li (ed.), *Subject and Topic*. New York: Academic Press.

Kennedy, George, 1991. *Aristotle on Rhetoric. Translation and Introduction*. Oxford: Oxford University Press.

Kinneavy, James, 1971. *A Theory of Discourse*. Englewood Cliffs, N.J.: Prentice-Hall.

Kintsch, Walter, 1988. The role of knowledge in discourse comprehension: A construction–integration model. *Psychological Review* 95: 163–82.

Kiss, Katalin, 1986. The order and scope of operators in the Hungarian sentence. In W. Abraham & S. de Meij (eds.), *Topic, Focus and Configurationality*. Amsterdam: John Benjamins.

1998. Identificational focus versus information focus. *Language* 74: 245–73.

Klaiman, M. H., 1991. *Grammatical Voice*. Cambridge: Cambridge University Press.

Knott, Alistair, 1996. A data-driven methodology for motivating a set of coherence relations. Ph.D. dissertation, University of Edinburgh.

Koen, Frank, Alton Becker, & Richard Young, 1966. The psychological reality of the paragraph. In E. Zale (ed.), *Proceedings of the Conference on Language and Language Behavior*. New York: Appleton.

Kratzer, Angelika, 1981. The notional category of modality. In H. Eikmeyer & H. Rieser (eds.), *Words, Worlds, and Contexts*. Berlin: De Gruyter.

Kratzer, Angelika, 1995. Stage-level and individual-level predicates. In G. Carlson & F. J. Pelletier (eds.), *The Generic Book*. Chicago, Ill.: University of Chicago Press.

Krifka, Manfred, 1989. Nominal reference, temporal constitution and quantification in event semantics. In R. Bartsch *et al.* (eds.), *Semantics and Contextual Expressions*. Dordrecht: Foris.

1991. A compositional semantics for multiple Focus constructions. In *Proceedings from Semantics and Linguistic Theory* 1, Working Papers in Linguistics, 10. Ithaca, N.Y.: Cornell University Press.

Krifka, Manfred, Francis J. Pelletier, Gregory Carlson, Alice ter Meulen, Gennaro Chierchia, & Godehard Link, 1995. Genericity: An introduction. In G. Carlson & F. J. Pelletier (eds.), *The Generic Book*. Chicago, Ill.: University of Chicago Press.

Kuno, Susumo, 1972. Functional sentence perspective. *Linguistic Inquiry* 3: 161–95.

1976. Subject, theme, and speaker's empathy: A re-examination of relativization phenomena. In C. Li (ed.), *Subject and Topic*. New York: Academic Press.

Kuno, Susumo, 1987. *Functional Syntax: Anaphora, Discourse, and Empathy*. Chicago, Ill.: University of Chicago Press.

van Kuppevelt, Jan, 1995. Disourse structure, topicality, and questioning. *Journal of Linguistics* 31: 109–47.

1996. Directionality in discourse: Prominence difference in subordination relations. *Journal of Semantics* 13: 363–95.

Kuroda, Yuki, 1973. Where epistemology, grammar and style meet: A case study from Japanese. In S. Anderson & P. Kiparsky (eds.), *A Festschrift for Morris Halle*. New York: Holt, Rinehart Winston.

Labov, William, & Joshua Waletzky, 1966. Narrative analysis: Oral versions of personal experience. In *Essays on the Verbal and Visual Arts: Proceedings of the 1996 Annual Meeting, American Ethnological Society*. Seattle: University of Washington Press.

Lambrecht, Knud, 1986. Pragmatically motivated syntax: Presentational cleft constructions in spoken French. In *Proceedings of the 13th Annual Meeting, Chicago Linguistic Society*. Chicago, Ill.: Chicago Linguistic Society.

1994. *Information Structure and Sentence Form*. Cambridge: Cambridge University Press.

Larson, Richard, 1984. Classifying discourse. In R. J. Connors, L. S. Ede, & A. Lunsford (eds.), *Essays on Classical Rhetoric and Modern Discourse*. Carbondale: Southern Illinois Press.

Lascarides, Alex, & Nicholas Asher, 1993. Temporal interpretation, discourse relations, and commonsense entailment. *Linguistics & Philosophy* 16: 437–93.

Lee, Gregory, 1971. *Subjects and Agents II*. Working Papers in Linguistics, 7. Columbus, Ohio: Department of Linguistics, Ohio State University.

Leška, Oldrich, 1995. Prague school teaching of the classical period and beyond. In E. Hajičová, M. Cervenka, O. Leška, & P. Sgall (eds.), *Travaux du Cercle Linguistique de Prague, nouvelle série*, Vol. I. Amsterdam: Benjamins.

Leslie, A. M., 1994. ToMM, ToBy, and Agency: Core architecture and domain speci-ficity. In L. Hirschfield & S. Gelman (eds.), *Mapping the Mind: Domain Specificity in Cognition and Culture*. Cambridge: Cambridge University Press.

Levin, Beth, 1993. *English Verb Classes and Alternations*. Chicago, Ill.: University of Chicago Press.

Levinson, Stephen, 1979/1992: Activity types in language. *Linguistics* 17: 356–99.

2000. *Presumptive Meanings*. Cambridge, Mass.: MIT Press.

Lewis, David, 1979. Scorekeeping in a language game. In R. Bauerle, U. Egli, & A. von Stchow (eds.), *Semantics from Different Points of View*. Berlin: De Gruyter.

Li, Charles, & Sandra Thompson, 1976. Subject and topic: A new typology of language. In C. Li (ed.), *Subject and Topic*. New York: Academic Press.

Linde, Charlotte, 1979. Focus of attention and choice of pronouns in discourse. In T. Givón (ed.), *Discourse and Syntax*, Syntax & Semantics, 12. New York: Academic Press.

1993. *Life Stories: The Creation of Coherence*. Oxford: Oxford University Press.

Litman, David, 1985. Plan recognition and discourse analysis: An integrated approach for understanding dialogues. Ph.D. dissertation, University of Rochester.

Longacre, Robert, 1968. *Discourse, Paragraph, and Sentence Structure in Selected Philippine Languages*. Santa Ana, Calif.: Summer Institute of Linguistics.

1979. The paragraph as a grammatical unit. In. T. Givón (ed.), *Discourse and Syntax*, Syntax and Semantics, 12. New York: Academic Press.

1983/1996. *The Grammar of Discourse*. New York: Plenum Press.

1992. The discourse strategy of an appeals letter. In W. Mann & S. Thompson (eds.), *Discourse Description: Diverse Linguistic Analyses of a Fund-raising Text*. Amsterdam: John Benjamins.

Loriot, James, & B. Hollenbach, 1970. Shipibo paragraph structure. *Foundations of Language* 6: 43–66.

Lunsford, Andrea, & Lisa Ede, 1984. On distinctions between classical and modern rhetoric. In R. J. Connors, L. Ede, & A. Lunsford (eds.), *Essays on Classical Rhetoric and Modern Discourse*. Carbondale: Southern Illinois University Press.

Lyons, John, 1977. *Semantics*. Cambridge: Cambridge University Press.

1982. Deixis and subjectivity: Loquor, ergo sum? In R. J. Jarvella & W. Klein (eds.), *Speech, Place, and Action*. New York: John Wiley & Sons.

Mann, William, & Sandra Thompson, 1987. *Rhetorical Structure Theory: A Theory of Text Organization*. ISI Reprint Series, ISI /RS-87–90. Marina Del Rey, Calif.: Information Sciences Institute.

1992. Rhetorical Structure theory and text analysis. In W. Mann & S. Thompson (eds.), *Discourse Description: Diverse Linguistic Analyses of a Fund-raising Text*. Amsterdam: John Benjamins.

2000. *Two Views of Rhetorical Structure Theory*. Lyon, France: Society for Text and Discourse.

Markels, Robin Bell, 1984. *A New Perspective on Cohesion in Expository Paragraphs*. Carbondale: Southern Illinois University Press.

Marr, David, 1982. *Vision*. San Francisco, Calif.: Freeman.

Marslen-Wilson, William, E. Levy, & Lorraine Tyler, 1982. Producing interpretable discourse: The establishment and maintenance of reference. In R. J. Jarvella & W. Klein (eds.), *Speech, Place and Action*. Chichester: Wiley.

Martin, J. R., 1992. *English Text: System and Structure*. Amsterdam: Benjamins.

Mathesius, Vilém, 1928/1964. On linguistic characterology with illustrations from modern English. Reprinted in J. Vachek (ed.), *A Prague School Reader in Linguistics*. Bloomington, Ind.: Indiana University Press.

Matthiessen, Christian, & Sandra Thompson, 1988. The structure of discourse and "subordination." In J. Haiman & S. Thompson (eds.), *Clause Combining in Grammar and Discourse*. Amsterdam: John Benjamins.

McArthur, Tom (ed.), 1992. *The Oxford Companion to the English Language*. Oxford: Oxford University Press.

McClelland, James, & David Rumelhart, 1986. *PDP: Explorations in the Microstructure of Cognition*, Vol. II. Cambridge, Mass.: MIT Press.

McNally, Louise, 1998. On recent formal analyses of topic. In J. Ginzburg, Z. Khasidashvili, C. Vogel, J. Lévy, & E. Vallduví (eds.), *The Tbilisi Symposium on Logic, Language, and Computation: Selected Papers*. Stanford, Calif.: Center for the Study of Language and Information.

Michaelis, Laura, 1994. The ambiguity of the English present perfect. *Journal of Linguistics* 30: 111–57.

Miller, George, Eugene Galanter, & Karl Pribram, 1960. *Plans and the Structure of Behavior*. New York: Holt, Rinehart & Winston.

Miller, Philip, 2001. Discourse constraints on (non)-extraposition from subject in English. *Linguistics* 39: 683–701.

Milner, Jean-Claude, 1973. *De la syntaxe à l'interprétation: Quantités, Insultes, Exclamations*. Paris: Seuil.

Milsark, Gary, 1977. Toward an explanation of certain peculiarities of the existential construction in English. *Linguistic Analysis* 3: 1–30.

Mitchell, Jonathan, 1986. The formal semantics of point of view. Ph.D. dissertation, The University of Massachusetts.

Moens, Mark, 1987. Tense, aspect, and temporal reference. Ph.D. thesis, Centre for Cognitive Science, University of Edinburgh.

Moens, Mark, & Mark Steedman. 1987. Temporal ontology in natural language. *Proceedings of the 25th Annual Conference of the Association for Computational Linguistics, Stanford, California*.

Morgan, Jerry L., 1975. Some remarks on the nature of sentences. In *Papers from the Parasession on Functionalism, Chicago Linguistic Society*. Chicago, Ill.: Chicago Linguistic Society.

Morris, Jane, & Graeme Hirst, 1991. Lexical cohesion computed by thesaural relations as an indicator of the structure of text. *Computational Linguistics* 17: 21–48.

Moyne, John, 1971. Reflexive and Emphatic. *Language* 47: 141–62.

Neisser, Ulric, 1967. *Cognitive Psychology*. New York: Appleton Century Croft.

Nuyts, Jan, 1993. Modality and the layered representation of conceptual and linguistic structures. *Linguistics* 31: 933–69.

Oakhill, Jane, Alan Garnham, & Willem Vonk, 1989. The online construction of discourse models. *Language & Cognitive Processes* 4: SI 263–86.

Ogihara, Toshiyuki, 1996. *Tense, Attitude, and Scope*. Dordrecht: Kluwer.

Olman, Lynda, 1998. Evidence for iconicity: The instance relation in informational exposition. MA thesis, University of Texas at Austin.

Palacas, Arthur, 1993. Attribution semantics: Linguistic worlds and point of view. *Discourse Processes* 16: 239–77.

Palmer, Frank, 1983. Semantic explanations for the syntax of English modals. In F. Heny & B. Richards (eds.), *Linguistic Categories: Auxiliaries and Related Puzzles*, Vol. II. Dordrecht: Reidel.

   1986. *Mood and Modality*. Cambridge: Cambridge University Press.

Parkes, M. B., 1993. *Pause and Effect*. Berkeley, Calif.: University of California Press.

Parsons, Terence, 1990. *Events in the Semantics of English*. Cambridge, Mass.: MIT Press.

Partee, Barbara, 1973. The syntax and semantics of quotation. In S. Anderson & P. Kiparsky (eds.), *A Festschrift for Morris Halle*. New York: Holt, Rinehart & Winston.

   1984. Nominal and temporal anaphora. *Linguistics & Philosophy* 7: 243–86.

   1987. Nounphrase interpretation and type-shifting principles. In J. Groenenjik, D. de Jongh, & M. Stockhof (eds.), *Studies in Discourse Representation theory and the Theory of Generalized Quantifiers*. Dordrecht: Foris.

   1991. Topic, focus, and quantification. In S. Moore & A. Wyner (eds.), *Proceedings of SALT I*. Ithaca, N.Y.: Department of Linguistics, Cornell University.

Penhallurick, John, 1984. Full-verb inversion in English. *Australian Journal of Linguistics* 4: 33–56.

Peterson, Philip, 1997. *Fact, Proposition, Event*. Dordrecht: Kluwer Academic Publishers.

Petöfi, J. S., 1978. A few comments on the methodology of text theoretical research. *Journal of Pragmatics* 2: 365–72.

Pierrehumbert, Janet, 1980. The phonology and phonetics of English intonation. Ph.D. dissertation, MIT.

Polanyi, Livia, 1988. A formal model of the structure of discourse structure and discourse. *Journal of Pragmatics* 12: 601–38.

Polinsky, Maria, 1996. Situation perspective: on the relations of thematic roles, discourse categories, and grammatical relations to figure and ground. In A. Goldberg (ed.), *Conceptual Structure, Discourse, and Language*. Stanford, Calif.: Center for the Study of Language and Information Publications.

Porter, Bruce, *et al.*, 1988. *AI Research in the Context of a Multifunctional Knowledge Base*. AI Laboratory Report, 88–88. Austin, Tex.: University of Texas.

Portner, Paul, & Katsuhiko Yabushita, 1998. The semantics and pragmatics of topic phrases. *Linguistics & Philosophy* 21: 117–57.

Prideaux, Gary, 1993. Subordination and information distribution in oral and written narratives. *Pragmatics & Cognition* 1: 51–69.

Prince, Ellen, 1978a. Comparison of Wh-clefts and It-clefts in discourse. *Language* 54: 883–906.

1981. Toward a taxonomy of given–new information. In Peter Cole (ed.), *Radical Pragmatics*. New York: Academic Press.

1986. On the syntactic marking of presupposed open-propositions. In *Papers from the Parasession on Pragmatics and Grammatical Theory, Chicago Linguistic Society*. Chicago, Ill.: Chicago Linguistic Society.

1992. The ZPG Letter: Subjects, definiteness, and information status. In W. Mann & S. Thompson (eds.), *Discourse Description: Diverse Linguistic Analyses of a Fund-Raising Text*. Amsterdam: John Benjamins.

1997. On the functions of Left-dislocation in English discourse. In A. Kamio (ed.), *Directions in Functional Linguistics*. Amsterdam: John Benjamins.

Prince, Gerald, 1987. *A Dictionary of Narratology*. Lincoln, Nebr.: University of Nebraska Press.

Propp, Vladimir, 1958. *Morphology of the Folktale*. Bloomington, Ind.:Indiana University Press.

Quirk, Randolph, Sidney Greenbaum, Geoffrey Leech, & Jan Svartvik, 1985. *A Comprehensive Grammar of the English Language*. London: Longman.

Reichenbach, Hans, 1947. *Elements of Symbolic Logic*. London: Macmillan.

Reinhart, Tanya, 1980. Conditions for text coherence. *Poetics Today* 1: 161–80.

1982. *Pragmatics and Linguistics: An Analysis of Sentence Topics*. Indiana University Linguistics Club.

Reinhart, Tanya, & Eric Reuland, 1991. Anaphors and logophors: An argument structure perspective. In J. Koster & E. Reuland (eds.), *Long Distance Anaphora*. Cambridge: Cambridge University Press.

Reinhart, T., & E. Reuland, 1993. Reflexivity. *Linguistic Inquiry* 24: 657–720.

Rieser, Hannes, 1978. On the development of text grammar. In W. Dressler (ed.), *Current Trends in Textlinguistics*. Berlin: De Gruyter.

Rizzi, Luigi, 1997. The fine structure of the left periphery. In L. Haegeman (ed.), *Elements of Grammar*. Dordrecht: Kluwer.

Roberts, John, 1988. Arnele switch-reference and the theory of grammar. *Linguistic Inquiry* 19: 45–63.

Rochemont, Michael, 1986. *Focus in Generative Grammar*. Amsterdam: John Benjamins.

Rooth, M., 1992. A theory of focus interpretation. *Natural Language Semantics* 1: 75–116.

Ross, John, 1970. On declarative sentences. In R. Jacobs and P. Rosenbaum (eds.), *Readings in English Transformational Grammar*. Waltham, Mass.: Ginn & Co.

1972. Act. In D. Davison and G. Harmon (eds.), *Semantics of Natural Languages*. Dordrecht, Holland: Reidel.

Rumelhart, David, 1975. Notes on a schema for stories. In D. G. Bobrow & A. M. Collins (eds.), *Representation and Understanding: Studies in Cognitive Science*. New York: Academic Press.

Sachs, Jacqueline, 1967. Recognition memory for syntactic and semantic aspects of connected discourse. *Perception and Psychophysics* 2: 437–42.

Sanders, José, & Gisela Redecker, 1996. Perspective and representation of speech in narrative discourse. In G. Fauconnier & E. Sweetser (eds.), *Spaces, World, and Grammar*. Chicago, Ill.: University of Chicago Press.

Sandstrom, Görel, 1993. *When-clauses and the Temporal Interpretation of Narrative Discourse*. Umea, Sweden: University of Umea.

Sanford, A. J., & Simon Garrod, 1981. *Understanding Written Language*. Chicester: Wiley.

Sanford, Anthony, & Linda Moxey, 1995. Aspects of coherence in written language: A psychological perspective. In M. Gernsbacher & T. Givón (eds.), *Coherence in Spontanteous Text*. Amsterdam: John Benjamins.

Sasse, Hans-Jürgen, 1987. The thetic–categorical distinction revisited. *Linguistics* 25: 511–80.

Schank, Roger, & R. P. Abelson, 1977. *Scripts, Plans, Goal, and Understanding: An Inquiry into Human Knowledge Structures*. Hillsdale, N.J.: Erlbaum.

Schiffrin, Deborah, 1987. *Discourse Markers*. Cambridge: Cambridge University Press.

Schlenker, Phillipe, 1999. Propositional attitudes and indexicality: A cross-categorial approach. Ph.D. dissertation, MIT.

Sells, Peter, 1987. Aspects of logophoricity. *Linguistic Inquiry* 18: 445–79.

Sgall, Petr, 1995. Formal and computational linguistics in Prague. In E. Hajičová, M. Cervenka, O. Leška, & P. Sgall (eds.), *Travaux du Cercle Linguistique de Prague, Nouvelle Série*, Vol. I. Amsterdam: John Benjamins.

Sgall, Petr, Eva Hajičová, & E. Burànová, 1986. *The Meaning of the Sentence in its Semantic and Pragmatic Aspects*. Prague: Academia.

Smith, Carlota S., 1971. Sentences in discourse: An analysis of a discourse by Bertrand Russell. *Journal of Linguistics* 7: 213–35.

  1980. Temporal structures in discourse. In N. Rohrer (ed.), *Time, Tense and Quantifiers*. Tübingen: Niemeyer.

  1991. A valediction for sentence topic. In C. Georgopoulos & R. Ishihara (eds.), *Interdisciplinary Approaches to Language*. Dordrecht: Kluwer.

  1995a. The range of aspectual situation types: Shifts and a bounding paradox. In P. Bertinetto *et al.* (eds.), *Temporal Reference: Aspect and Actionality*. Turin: Rosenberg & Sellier.

  1995b. The relation between aspectual viewpoint and situation type. Address, Linguistic Society of America. Published electronically, Eric database.

  1995c. Aspect and temporal location in Discourse Representation Theory. Unpublished ms., University of Texas.

  1997. *The Parameter of Aspect*, 2nd edition. Dordrecht: Kluwer.

  1999a. Closed systems in texts. *In Proceedings of the Second Workshop on Text Structure*. Austin, Tex.: Department of Linguistics, University of Texas.

  1999b. Activities: States or Events? *Linguistics and Philosophy* 22: 479–508.

Smith, Carlota S., & Mary Erbaugh, 2001. Temporal information in sentences of Mandarin. In X. Liejiong and S. Jingmin (eds.), *New Views in Chinese Syntactic Research: International Symposium on Chinese Grammar for the New Millennium*. Hangzhou: Zhejiang Jiaoya Chuban she.

Speas, Margaret, 1990. *Phrase Structure in Natural Language*. Dordrecht: Kluwer.

Speas, Margaret, & Carol Tenny, in press. Configurational properties of point of view roles. In A. di Scuillo (ed.), *Proceedings of UQAM Asymmetry Workshop*. Montreal: University of Québec at Montreal.

Sperber, Dan, & Deirdre Wilson, 1986. *Relevance: Communication and Cognition.* Oxford: Blackwell.

Stalnaker, Richard, 1978. Assertion. In P. Cole (ed.), *Pragmatics*, Syntax and Semantics, 9. New York: Academic Press.

Stark, Heather, 1988. What do paragraph markings do? *Discourse Processes* 11: 275–303.

Steedman, Mark, 2000. *The Syntactic Process.* Cambridge, Mass.: MIT Press.

Stern, Arthur, 1976. When is a paragraph? *College Composition and Communication* 36: 253–57.

Stirling, Leslie, 1993. *Switch-Reference and Discourse Representation.* Cambridge: Cambridge University Press.

Stoddard, Sally, 1991. *Text and Texture: Patterns of Cohesion.* Norwood, N.J.: Ablex.

Stowell, Tim, 1996. The phrase structure of tense. In J. Rooryck & L. Zaring (eds.), *Phrase Structure and the Lexicon.* Dordrecht: Kluwer.

Strawson, Peter, 1964. Identifying reference and truth value. *Theoreia* 30: 96–118. Reprinted in D. Steinberg & L. Jakobovits (eds.), 1971. *Semantics.* Cambridge: Cambridge University Press.

Svarthvik, Jan, 1966. *On Voice in the English Verb.* The Hague: Mouton.

Swales, John, 1990. *Genre Analysis: English in Academic and Research Settings.* Cambridge: Cambridge University Press.

Talmy, Leonard, 1978. Figure and ground in complex sentences. In J. Greenberg, C. Ferguson, & E. Moravcsik (eds.), *Universals of Human Language: Syntax.* Stanford, Calif.: Stanford University Press.

1985. Lexicalization patterns: Semantic structure in lexical forms. In T. Shopen (ed.), *Language Typology and Syntactic Description*, Vol. III: *Grammatical Categories and the Lexicon.* Cambridge: Cambridge University Press.

2000. *Towards a Cognitive Semantics.* Cambridge, Mass.: MIT Press.

Tannen, Deborah, 1989. *Talking Voices.* Cambridge: Cambridge University Press.

Tardieu, Hubert, Marie-France Ehrlich & Valérie Gyselinkck, 1992. Levels of representation and domain-specific knowledge in comprehension of scientific texts. *Language & Cognitive Processes* 7: 335–51.

Taylor, Barry, 1977. Tense and continuity. *Linguistics & Philosophy* 1: 199–220.

Thomason, Lucy, 1994. The assignment of proximate and obviative in informal Fox narrative. Ms., The University of Texas at Austin.

Thompson, Ellen, 1999. The temporal structure of discourse: The syntax and semantics of temporal *then. Natural Language & Linguistic Theory* 17: 123–60.

Thompson, Geoff, & Susan Hunston, 2000. Evaluation: An introduction. In S. Hunston & G. Thompson (eds.), *Evaluation in Text: Authorial Stance and the Construction of Discourse.* Oxford: Oxford University Press.

Thompson, Sandra, 1987. The passive in English: A discourse perspective. In R. Chaman & L. Shockey (eds.), *In Honor of Ilse Lehiste.* Dordrecht: Foris.

2001. "Object complements" and conversation: Towards a realistic account. To appear in *Studies in Language.*

Thorndyke, P. W., 1977. Cognitive structures in comprehension and memory of narrative discourse. *Cognitive Psychology* 9: 77–110.

Tomlin, Russell (ed.), 1987. *Coherence and Grounding in Discourse*. Amsterdam: John Benjamins.

Tracy, H. P., & S. H. Levinsohn, 1977. Participant reference in Ica expository discourse. In R. Longacre (ed.), *Discourse Grammar*, Part III. Dallas, Tex.: Summer Institute of Linguistics.

Turner, Elizabeth, & Ragnar Rommetveit, 1968. Focus of attention in recall of active and passive sentences. *Journal of Verbal Learning and Verbal Behavior* 7: 543–48.

Vallduví, Enric, 1992. *The Informational Component*. New York: Garland Press.

Vallduví, Enric, & Elisabet Engdahl, 1996. The linguistic realization of information packaging. *Linguistics* 34: 459–519.

Vallduví, Enric, & Maria Vilkuna, 1998. On rheme and kontrast. In P. Culicover & L. McNally (eds.), *The Limits of Syntax*, Syntax and Semantics, 26. New York: Academic Press.

Vendler, Zeno, 1957. Verbs and times. *Philosophical Review* 66: 143–60. Reprinted in Vendler, 1967. *Linguistics in Philosophy*. Ithaca, N.Y.: Cornell University Press.

1967. *Linguistics in Philosophy*. Ithaca, N.Y.: Cornell University Press.

1972. *Res Cogitans: An Essay in Rational Psychology*. Ithaca, N.Y.: Cornell University Press.

Venneman, Theodor, 1975. Topic, sentence accent, ellipsis: A proposal for their formal treatment. In E. Keenan (ed.), *Formal Semantics of Natural Language*. Cambridge: Cambridge University Press.

Verkuyl, Henk, 1972. *On the Compositional Nature of the Aspects. Foundations of Language Supplementary Series*, Vol. XV. Dordrecht: Reidel.

Verstraete, Jean-Christophe, 2001. Subjective and objective modality: Interpersonal and ideational functions in the English modal auxiliary system. *Journal of Pragmatics* 33: 1505–28.

Vlach, Frank, 1981. The semantics of the progressive. In P. Tedeschi & A. Zaenen (eds.), *Tense and Aspect*, Syntax and Semantics, 14. Academic Press, New York.

Voegelin, C. F., & F. M. Voegelin, 1975. Hopi (-qa). *International Journal of American Linguistics* 41: 381–98.

Vonk, Wietske, Lettica Hustinx, & Wim Simons, 1992. The use of referential expressions in structuring discourse. *Language & Cognitive Processes* 7: 302–33.

Walker, Marilyn, Aravind Joshi, & Ellen Prince (eds.), 1998. *Centering Theory in Discourse*. Oxford: Clarendon Press.

Ward, Gregory, & Ellen Prince, 1991. On the topicalization of indefinite NPs. *Journal of Pragmatics* 16: 167–77.

Whately, Richard, 1828/1963. *Elements of Rhetoric*. Carbondale, Ill.: Southern Illinois Press.

Whorf, Benjamin L., 1956. *Language, Thought and Reality: Selected Writings of Benjamin Lee Whorf*. New York: Wiley and Son.

Whitaker, Jeanne, & Carlota S. Smith, 1985. Some significant omissions: Ellipsis in Flaubert's "Un Coeur Simple." *Language, and Style* 14: 251–92.

Wiebe, Janyce, 1991. Tracking point of view in narrative. *Computational Linguistics* 20: 233–87.

Willett, Thomas, 1988. A crosslinguistic survey of the grammaticalization of evidentiality. *Studies in Language* 12: 51–97.

Winkler, Anthony, & Jo Ray McCuen, 1988. *Rhetoric Made Plain*. New York: Harcourt Brace Jovanovich.

Wittgenstein, Ludwig, 1958. *The Blue and Brown Books*. Oxford: Basil Blackwell.

Woodbury, Anthony, 1987. *Native American Discourse: Poetics and Rhetoric.* Cambridge: Cambridge University Press.

Wright, Karen, 2002. Times of our lives. *Scientific American* 287: 58–65.

Zagona, Karen, 1990. Times as temporal argument structure. Unpublished ms., University of Washington, Seattle.

Zribi-Hertz, Ann, 1989. Anaphor binding and narrative point of view: English reflexive pronouns. *Language* 65: 695–727.

Zwicky, Arnold, 1971. In a manner of speaking. *Linguistic Inquiry* 11: 222–33.

General index

Responsible Source 13, 156, 158
rhetoric
classical 38
modern 39, 238
rhetorical modes 40–42
Rhetorical Structure Theory 262
role 121

salience 146, 198–208
sentence Topic 13, 15, 19, 58, 187, 192, 197,
    207, 212, 216, 221, 225, 229, 234, 246,
    252, 253, 260
aboutness 189, 190
and grammatical voice 193
identifying cues 198
paraphrase tests 190
sentences without topic 195
terminology 195–96
topic–comment partition 185, 188, 209
unclear cases 200
shifts, discourse mode 22, 34, 35, 38
situation entities 12, 24, 67, 82
Situation Time 100, 102, 106
situation type 68, 69, 82, 83, 86
derived 71, 85
shifts, *see* coercion
situations – classified 23–25, 69
space, spatial 26, 58, 115
spatial progression 26–28, 29
specific situations 22, 32, 37
Speech Time 30, 99, 106, 121
State 71
static, *see* dynamism, dynamic/static
sub-interval property 71
subjectivity 13, 58, 156, 162, 167, 244
construction, compositional rules 176,
    178
in fiction 157, 158–80
lexical choice 156
linguistic forms 175

modeled with subordination 156, 176
objective sentences 157, 158
scope 162, 168
syntax, syntactic 11, 53–59, 96, 239

telic/atelic 76, 118
temporality 12
tense 26, 30, 92, 95, 99, 102, 105, 160
anaphora 97, 112
continuity 28, 94–95, 108–10
deictic pattern 95, 106, 113, 114
present 76
text
linguistics 45
units 9, 45
well- and ill-formed 44
text progression 12
atemporal 132
presentational 19
temporal, *see* advancement
text type 43–44
thematic role 31, 128
Experiencer 15
Theme/Patient 17, 58, 128, 130
Theme 189, 196
thetic sentences 195, 202
time, temporality 12, 99
Topic, *see* sentence topic, discourse topic
topicalization 225

unbounded situations 27, 71, 102–3, 125–29

variety in texts 8, 40
verb constellation 23, 68, 72–73, 83
viewpoint
aspectual 68–69, 70, 82
in DRS 90
visible information 68, 71, 82, 124

will auxiliary 30, 100, 121

Index of names